The Making of the Modern Scottish Highlands, 1939–1965

ULSTER AND SCOTLAND

General editors
Professor John Wilson and Dr William Kelly

A series published by Four Courts Press
in association with the
Institute of Ulster Scots Studies
University of Ulster

1. William Kelly & John R. Young (eds), *Ulster and Scotland, 1600–2000: history, language and identity*
2. Brad Patterson (ed.), *Ulster–New Zealand migration and cultural transfers*
3. John McGurk, *Sir Henry Docwra, 1564–1631: Derry's second founder*
4. David A. Wilson and Mark G. Spencer (eds), *Ulster Presbyterians in the Atlantic world: religion, politics and identity*
5. Andrew James, *The Nabob: a tale of ninety-eight*, with notes and afterword by John Wilson Foster
6. David A. Wilson (ed.), *The Orange Order in Canada*
7. Frank Ferguson (ed.), *Ulster-Scots writing: an anthology*
8. W.P. Kelly and John R. Young, *Scotland and the Ulster plantations: explorations in the British settlement of Stuart Ireland*
9. Frank Ferguson & Andrew R. Holmes (eds), *Revising Robert Burns and Ulster: literature, religion and politics, c.1770–1920*
10. Robert Gavin, William Kelly & Dolores O'Reilly, *Atlantic gateway: the port and city of Londonderry since 1700*
11. John A. Burnett, *The making of the Scottish Highlands, 1939–1965: withstanding the 'colossus of advancing materialism'*

The Making of the Modern Scottish Highlands, 1939–1965

*Withstanding the
'colossus of advancing materialism'*

John A. Burnett

FOUR COURTS PRESS

Set in 10.5 on 12.5 point Ehrhardt for
FOUR COURTS PRESS LTD
7 Malpas Street, Dublin 8, Ireland
e-mail: info@fourcourtspress.ie
www.fourcourtspress.ie
and in North America for
FOUR COURTS PRESS
c/o ISBS, 920 N.E. 58th Street, Suite 300, Portland, OR 97213.

© John A. Burnett and Four Courts Press 2011

A catalogue record for this title
is available from the British Library.

ISBN 978-1-84682-241-4

All rights reserved. No part of this publication may be reproduced, stored in or introduced into a retrieval system, or transmitted, in any form or by any means (electronic, mechanical, photocopying, recording or otherwise), without the prior written permission of both the copyright owner and the publisher of this book.

Printed in England
by Antony Rowe, Chippenham, Wilts.

For my mother and father

'Life can only be understood backwards; but it must be lived forwards'
Kierkegaard

Lionar bearn mòr le clachan beaga
'Great gaps may be filled with small stones'

Contents

	ACKNOWLEDGMENTS	9
	ABBREVIATIONS	11
1	Introduction	13

PART I: IMAGE AND REALITY: THE HIGHLANDS AND ISLANDS OF SCOTLAND, 1745–1939

2	Economic and social perspectives on the Highlands and Islands, 1745–1939	29
3	The idea of Highland culture, 1745–1939	57

PART II: GOVERNING THE HIGHLANDS, 1939–1965

4	Reconstruction, regeneration and regional development: government approaches to the 'Highland problem', 1939–1965	95
5	Government agencies and the 'Highland problem', 1939–1965	135

PART III: VOICES 'WITHIN', LAMENTS FROM 'BELOW': THE HIGHLANDERS THEMSELVES, 1939–1965

6	'The English way and the wrong way': social philosophy, political policy and the 'view from within'	183
7	'*Cùm a' Ghaidhlig beò*': the Gaels' response to the 'colossus of advancing materialism'	218
8	Conclusion	268
	BIBLIOGRAPHY	283
	INDEX	299

Acknowledgments

The writing of this book has been a long-term project and numerous people have helped me, in a variety of ways, during the preparation of this work. I am obliged to the staff of a number of libraries and archives, including the National Library of Scotland, particularly those in the north reading room; the National Archives of Scotland; Edinburgh central library; Inverness public library; the Mitchell library; and the libraries at the universities of Edinburgh Napier, Aberdeen and Sunderland. I am grateful to Robert Shaw, Sarah Beattie-Smith and Bill Jack for providing technical assistance.

A number of friends and colleagues have given encouragement and backing throughout. I would particularly like to thank Jo Fowler, Henry and Sandra Cowper, Howard Wollman, John Bryden, Danny Mackinnon, Jon Shaw, Mark Shucksmith, the late Ronald Morrison, Maureen Harris, Claire Horrax, Kevin Mogey, Peter Waldron and Dave Walker. Gratitude also to the lecturers in the history and politics departments at Strathclyde University for enjoyable and stimulating classes; most notably Tom Devine and Arthur McIvor for their support and encouragement. Colleagues and students at the universities of Sunderland and Edinburgh Napier have provided a wonderful atmosphere to work in. Thanks also to Billy Kelly, the late Michael Adams, Martin Fanning and Michael Potterton at Four Courts Press for their support and patience.

The late Tony Hepburn and Don MacRaild showed remarkable serenity and understanding during my doctoral supervision and their suggestions undoubtedly helped improve the thesis. Colin Holmes and Chris Harvie also gave generously of their time with informative thoughts on how to take the thesis forward. Don, Lisa and the family have shown tremendous warmth, generosity and kindness over many years. Don's ancestral links to Glendale in Skye, coupled with his deep understanding of history, made for hugely enjoyable and stimulating discussions. His enthusiasm for my research, willingness to comment on my draft workings, and solid counsel on every aspect of my career has been enormously beneficial to me – *mòran taing a Dhòmhnaill*!

Special thanks go to different members of my family for assisting my research in various ways – Elizabeth, Robert and Anne, Kathryn and Keith, Allan and Linda, and Deirdre.

A final debt of gratitude is owed to my mother and father. The benefits of being brought up in Kintail and then Benbecula have helped enormously to inform my views on the Highlands and Islands. Spending my formative years there, in addition to being immersed in the piping tradition from an early age, has provided a rich environment to draw on. Numerous friends and acquaintances spanning the generations in the Hebrides, the Highlands and among the urban diaspora have instilled in me a deep appreciation for the history and culture of the region and the *Gàidhealtachd*. Finally, I owe an enormous intellectual debt to my father. His passionate interest in and knowledge of the Highlands, Scotland and beyond have inspired me from an early age. He has also provided insightful comments on parts of this book with his customary thoroughness. Needless to say, any errors in the book are entirely down to me. This book is dedicated to my parents with love and affection.

Abbreviations

ACG	An Comunn Gàidhealach
AG	*An Gaidheal*
CC	Crofters Commission
DAFS	Department of Agriculture and Fisheries
EHR	*Economic History Review*
FE	Further Education
FIS	Folklore Institute of Scotland
FUEN	Federal Union of European Nationalities
GH	*Glasgow Herald*
GRO	General Registry Office
HDA	Highland Development Association
HIDB	Highlands and Islands Development Board
HLLRA	Highland Land Law Reform Association
HMI	His/Her Majesty's Inspectorate
HTB	Highland Transport Board
JSHS	*Journal of Scottish Historical Studies*
MP	Member of Parliament
NAS	National Archives of Scotland
NLS	National Library of Scotland
NM	Naomi Mitchison
NMG	Neil Miller Gunn
NSHEB	North of Scotland Hydro-Electric Board
PEP	Political and Economic Planning
SBI	Scottish Board for Industry
SED	Scottish Education Department
SESH	*Scottish Economic and Social History*
SGM	*Scottish Geographical Magazine*
SGS	*Scottish Gaelic Studies*
SHR	*Scottish Historical Review*
SLP	Scottish Labour Party
SNP	Scottish National Party
TGSI	*Transactions of the Gaelic Society of Inverness*
VHF	Very high frequency

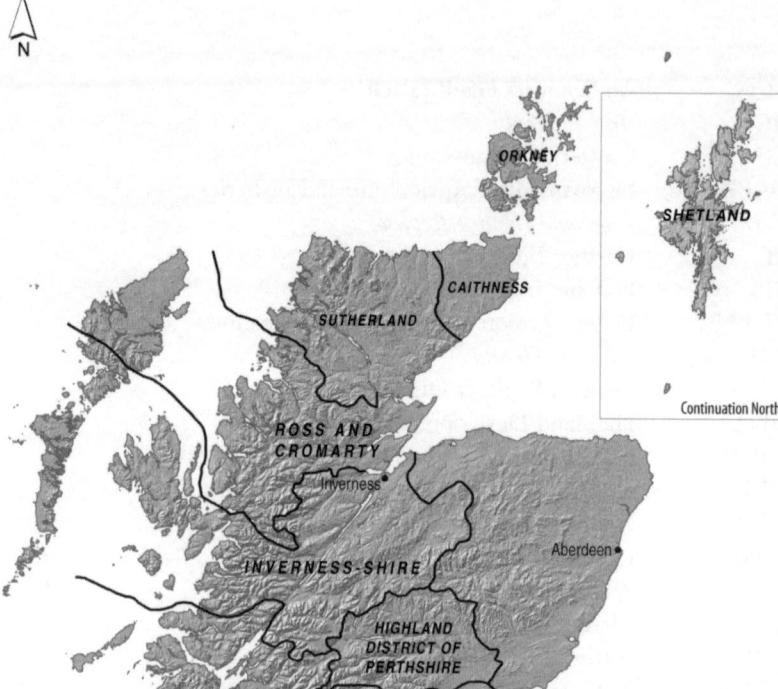

The Highlands and Islands of Scotland, *c*.1890–1974

Introduction

> The simplicity of the Isles life particularly close to the mainland is disappearing and modern conditions with their resultant haste are gradually taking its place. The single wire of a crude aerial is to-day a not uncommon sight beside the cottage on the windswept moorlands. The lone cottager today looks through his wireless window into the whirling vortex of modernity.
>
> I.F. Anderson, To introduce the Hebrides (1933).

Chan fhaic mi fàth mo shaothrach	I do not see the sense of my toil
bhith cur smaointean an cainnt bhàsmhoir,	putting thoughts in a dying tongue
a nis is siùrsachd na Roinn-Eòrpa	now when the whoredom of Europe
'na murt stòite 's 'na cràdhlot;	Is murder erect and agony;
ach thugadh dhuinn am muillion bliadhna	but we have been given the million years,
'na mhir an roinn chianail fhàsmhoir,	a fragment of a sad, growing portion,
gaisge 's foighidinn nan ciadan	the heroism and patience of hundreds
agus miorbhail aodainn àlainn.	and the miracle of a beautiful face.
Chan fhaic mi ...	I do not see ...
Somhairle MacGhill-eain, 1943.	Sorley Maclean, 1943.

1939–65: THE FINAL CONFLICT

In 1933, a perceptive visitor saw the 'single wire of a crude aerial' on the skyline of Skye as the modern communication inroad through which the Highlands and Islands would be irresistibly drawn into 'the whirling vortex of modernity'. It was the means whereby 'the Boat Race, the Grand National, the Changing of the Guard, and the hundred other topical events broadcast to-day', became 'the talk of the Isles tomorrow'.[1] As the 1930s unfolded, a young and prescient Gaelic poet saw the engulfing currents as rather more than the society calendar of metropolitan and Home Counties England. Fascist tyranny, the '*siùrsachd na Roinn-Eòrpa*', the 'whoredom of Europe', was about to unleash the maelstrom of total war on Scotland, Europe and the world. When it was over, the pace and pattern of change, the irreversible shift in attitudes, values and relationships that it unleashed, local, national and international, would accelerate and quicken over two brief post-war decades in a manner that would change the nature of the

---

1 Anderson, *To introduce the Hebrides* (1933), pp 116–17.

Highlands and Islands of Scotland forever.[2] These far-reaching tides of change from 1939 to 1965, the responses they evoked both for and against, from within and without the *Gàidhealtachd* are the subject of this book.

The reflective view of the Skye visitor as his ferry departs from Uig and the insightful imagery of the poet whose thoughts on the agonies of Europe are refracted through a profound sense of place and belonging deriving from his home island of Raasay are representative of two very different 'ways of seeing' the Highlands. Invariably they are conveniently seen as two mutually exclusive camps: the external and the internal; the 'outsider' and the 'native'. The expediency of this superficial polarization, however, masks the actuality: thoughts on the merits and demerits of the changes facing the Highlands over this period were as diverse and different within as they were between each of these ascribed categories. Tracing the at times confused, occasionally conflicting and sometimes convergent 'ways of seeing' the dangers, challenges and opportunities faced by the region over this era by a wide spread of residents, observers, policy makers and players forms the basis of the way in which the story of this pivotal moment in Highland history is told. The two languages, in three registers, English, Gaelic and the poet's own translation into English for those who do not share MacLean's 'dying tongue', embodies the particular and specific dimension through which this study approaches its subject. For in the critical mid-twentieth century era it is through the specific prism of notions of culture and identity that the concerns and fears, the hopes and aspirations associated with the process of modernity were primarily expressed and evoked.

In comparison with earlier historical periods, the experience of Gaels and Highlanders in the twentieth century has been the subject of several interesting sociological and anthropological studies but has received comparatively little attention from historians.[3] One consequence of privileging the land question as the dominant narrative of Highland history is that the main corpus of Highland historiography does not extend beyond the early decades of the twentieth century when the issue of land reform had largely been settled.[4] The impression is thereby given, whether intentional or otherwise, that the pivotal moment, as it were, in which the old Highlands became the new is to be found somewhere in the years immediately before or after the First World War. While there are undoubtedly several factors – political, economic and structural – that might appear to support such an interpretation, one of the central arguments in this

---

2 Maclean, *Dain do Eimhir* (2002 ed.), pp 110–11 for Gaelic poem and English translation. See also pp 263–4 for discussion on this including MacLean's letter to Douglas Young on the weakness of the Gaelic language. 3 For sociological, anthropological, ethnographic and heritage studies of particular relevance to the issues address here, see MacDonald, *Reimagining culture* (1997); Burnett, 'Local heroics' (1998); MacDonald, 'Colloquium' (2005); Basu, *Highland homecomings* (2007). 4 Among the exceptions are Cameron, 'Highlands as special policy area' (1997); Hunter, *Claim of crofting* (1991); Robertson, 'Governing the Highlands' (1997); Burnett, 'Highland land raids' (1985).

study is to suggest that from a more specifically cultural historical perspective, the location of this pivotal moment between what was seen to be the old and the new came significantly later. On the surface, land settlement, reformed local government, an enhanced provision of social services and improved integration into the communications and public administration infrastructure at national level may have given the impression that the era of the old 'Highland problem' was at an end but within the social and cultural fabric of the region the stresses of unresolved issues were palpable. As this study seeks to demonstrate, it was not until the years 1939–65 that the tension between the old and the new reached the moment of its final conflict. This was the critical juncture over which the residents of the region witnessed and engaged with the final onslaught on that much favoured but elusive phenomena, the 'traditional way of life' of the Highlands and Islands.

'WAYS OF SEEING': MODERNIZATION

Delineating 'modernization', the process that was perceived to be threatening to destroy the precious and unique characteristics of the Highlands in the post-war era, is more usefully addressed by some introductory clarification. Within the sociology of development, modernization theory as it relates to the complex political, social and economic forces involved in underdeveloped and traditional societies has been a contentious area. The debate and its relevance to the Highlands of Scotland were touched on in the 1970s but without further evident follow up.[5] More recently, the discourse of development as it relates to advanced Western societies and specifically as it applies to the outlying, peripheral and marginal regions, has acquired its own peculiar ambiguities, in particular a distinctive engagement with issues of identity and belonging. From a background and perspective based in cultural theory, these particular dimensions of the phenomenon have been analyzed in some detail in Ireland. Yet, while the echoes of relevance are readily apparent, rural Scotland, not least the Highlands and islands, at the time of writing awaits a similarly vigorous examination.[6]

In the period with which this study is concerned, the discourse of development and modernization was most often presented in economic terms. Yet, these

5 See in particular Carter, 'The Highlands of Scotland' (1974). See also Hunter, *The other side of sorrow* (1995) for a perspective focusing on environmental issues.   6 For Ireland see, among others, Brown, *Ireland: a social and cultural history, 1922–79* (1981); Gibbons, *Transformations in Irish culture* (1996); Kiberd, *Inventing Ireland* (1996); Graham and Kirkland (eds), *Ireland and cultural theory* (1999); Devereux, 'Saving rural Ireland' (1991), pp 23–30. For preliminary forays into how the discourse of development might be explored from a cultural historical perspective within the Highlands and Islands, see Lorimer, 'Ways of seeing the Scottish Highlands' (1999); Burnett, 'The cheviot, the stag and the last munro' (1999).

terms in themselves carried their own cultural and ideological undertones through which the notion of modernization assumed such ambiguity. Since the late eighteenth century, modernization has been a central term in the lexicon of progress associated with the development of industry and commerce, improvement in agriculture, advances in communications and social mobility.[7] Simultaneously, it carried both positive and negative connotations as a social and cultural process dependant on the perspective, values and beliefs of the observer. On the contested terrain of the Highlands and Islands, however, the tenets of 'modernization' acquired a deeply unfavourable resonance through its negative associations with the destruction of the old order, cultural loss and eclipse. In the Highlands it assumed a particular significance in relation to Gaelic culture, language and identity. At the same time, it was a process that involved improved communications, enhanced services and utilities, economic diversification, less isolation, all of these being aspects of modernization that were taken up and welcomed across the region.

Paradoxically, the place that the Highlands and Islands assumed in the wider context of the reshaping and manufacturing of Scottish history and identity through the nineteenth and early twentieth century led to such an overlay of specific imagery and symbolism that the Highlands were held in such a permanent time-warp, as a timeless moment of the past recycled to meet the needs of an external present, that the actual consequences of a long process of exposure to the process of modernization on the internal social and cultural fabric of the region was not initially apparent. Consequently, when the process acquired a new, accelerating momentum, and a far more transformative and visible impact on even the most domestic, familial and individual aspects of everyday life throughout the region, it would have a deep and enduring imprint on the collective *psyche* of the Highlands. In even the most isolated townships in the Highlands and Islands over the years 1939–65, the ascribed notion of what 'the Highlands' constituted and what it meant to be a 'Highlander' were challenged. In this final moment of modernization, the belief was widespread that it was precisely through a loss of difference and distinctiveness, whether through the magnitude of the material transformation associated with the war, a raft of postwar government legislation and secondary commercial initiatives, or closer integration with the rest of Scotland and the UK, that the Highlands finally had entered the modern era. In social terms, this was generally felt to be most evident in the major shifts in the region's traditional economy away from the primary industries of fishing and agriculture. In cultural terms, such penetrating exposure to this most invasive wave of modernizing forces was perceived to be threatening the whole basis of the Highland 'way of life', the very survival of a distinct culture, language and identity itself.

7 Williams, *Keywords* (1976), pp 174–5.

'WAYS OF SEEING': IDENTITY

As will have already become apparent, it is for this reason that this book is not about the Highlands and Islands as a geographical area or an administrative region, but about the Highlands in a more specifically cultural sense of 'the Highlands' as the *Gàidhealtachd* – with the latter term understood, as it generally was in the period in question, as the 'land of the Gael' as opposed to the 'Gaelic-speaking area'. Working out the differences between the administrative concept of the 'Highlands and Islands' and the cultural notion of the region, not to mention separating out the 'Highland problem' from the 'Gaelic problem', were key elements in the story of the period under scrutiny.[8] One factor contributing to this blurring of boundaries was the increasing divergence between the territory where Gaelic was the predominant everyday language of the community, an area that was steadily and inexorably retreating to the islands and western seaboard, and the spatial spread of the Gaelic speech community which increasingly was weighted towards Glasgow and the non-Highland urban centres as the drift of Gaelic speakers from the Highlands to the cities of Scotland intensified. Despite connections with the traditional homeland of the Highlands and Islands remaining strong, the significance of this dichotomy at a time of overall linguistic decline became ever more obvious, particularly as Glasgow and Edinburgh increasingly began to play a key role as vibrant centres of Gaelic cultural activity.[9] In the post-war Highlands, it was becoming all too apparent that a policy for the linguistic or cultural promotion of Gaelic and the revival and development of the Highlands were no longer necessarily the same thing.

Notwithstanding the evident changes that had reshaped and were continuing to reshape the cultural composition of the region and intensify the tensions within Gaeldom, the legacy of the past, the inherited equation whereby all matters 'Highland' equalled all things 'Gaelic' persisted. It was an assumption that had caused not a little understandable irritation to those with a cultural orientation to the Nordic, or indeed Pictish, elements in the hybrid heritage of the small croft and fishing communities of Scotland's northern uplands and northern isles in the pre-war era when the modern construction of the

---

8 For an insight into how the boundaries between 'Highland', 'Lowland' and 'Gaelic Scotland' originated, developed and altered see Withers, 'Scottish Highlands outlined' (1982). As a resurgence of interest in cultural, language and heritage issues has grown rapidly in Scotland in recent years the difficulties of relating them to the increasingly variegated forms that being Highland, a resident of the Highlands, or a Gael might take in the twenty-first century can only intensify. These comments relate to the prevailing tendency to equate the Highlands with the *Gàidhealtachd* where the situation is already increasingly complicated. When Orkney and Shetland are taken into consideration – as they necessarily ought to be – then the situation assumes a further daunting complexity.   9 For two very different perspectives on these cities and Gaels see MacInnes, *Eriskay* (1997); MacIver, *Pilgrim souls* (1990).

Highlands and Islands as an administrative region had first taken shape.[10] Now, in the post-war era it assumed a further complicating dimension with the expansion of the *breac-Gàidhealtachd*, the 'speckled Gaeldom' that now constituted the vast majority of the terrain of the Highlands, the wide spread of parishes and communities where a sense of an undeniable Gaelic past and identity lingered but the number of actual Gaelic-speaking residents had dwindled to a few speckles on a map of Gaelic's linguistic retreat as the natural speech community of everyday life.[11] The difficulty that emerged was that all too often the notion of the essential 'Highland' values, attitudes and habits deemed worthy of protection from the pace and inroads of modern developments, a collective structure of feeling generally encapsulated by the phrase 'the traditional Highland way of life', were also taken to be the cultural attributes of the Gael, in the sense of Gaelic-speaking, even in the vast majority of Highland communities where the latter were in an ever-decreasing minority. It was an association and an equation that is readily discernible in a significant proportion of the primary sources of the period containing the thoughts and observations of many of the region's first hand observers, policy informers and players.[12]

Despite this tendency to elide the Highlands with the *Gàidhealtachd*, many of these commentators had great difficulty in dealing with the disconnections faced in addressing the cultural and identity issues of the period. As these are the particular concerns that this study of the post-war 'Highland problem' examines, they also provide the prism through which the Highlands can be conveniently defined. For the purposes of this study, the 'Highlands', therefore, are neither the seven former 'crofting counties' of the administrative Highlands and Islands from Argyll to Orkney and Shetland, nor are they the *Gàidhealtachd* in the sense of solely comprising those localities that were predominantly Gaelic-speaking at that period but excluding the *breac-Gàidhealtachd*. As the latter were as much part of the area with which the key observers and policy-makers were concerned with as the former, the Highlands on which the attention of this study is focused are the former counties perceived by both themselves and by those outwith the region, as carrying a deep cultural imprint of Gaelic culture and identity, notwithstanding the prevailing strength and extent of the Gaelic language. For the period 1939–65 this comprised Highland Perthshire, Argyll, Inverness-shire, Ross & Cromarty, Sutherland and Caithness.[13]

---

10 For a description of the 'battle' being waged in print during the inter-war period between those who sought to place primacy on the Norse origins of the Highlands and Islands against those that prioritised the influence and legacy of the Gael, see D'Arcy, *Scottish skalds and sagamen* (1996), pp 37–52.   11 The term *breac-Gàidhealtachd* roughly translates as 'speckled Gaelic-speaking area' and refers to those areas where Gaelic had a presence, but a fairly marginal one. To get an impression of where these two cultural 'zones' were, see Campbell, *Gaelic in Scottish education and life* (1945), pp 18–19.   12 For example, see Collier, *Crofting problem* (1953), Darling, *West Highland Survey* (1955) and the relevant County editions of *The third statistical account of Scotland*.   13 It is worth noting the ambiguity of Caithness, or indeed of Cromarty

Table 1.1 Percentage of Gaelic-speaking population by county, 1881–1971 (figures taken from Withers, *Gaelic in Scotland* (1984), p. 213).

	1881	1891	1901	1911	1921	1931	1951	1961	1971
Argyll	65.25	60.88	54.35	47.06	34.56	33.17	21.69	17.20	13.72
Caithness	9.48	11.96	9.16	5.62	3.76	2.59	1.25	0.90	1.55
Inverness	75.99	73.24	64.85	59.07	50.91	43.97	30.57	25.91	22.02
Orkney	0.12	0.31	0.26	0.31	0.27	0.27	0.21	0.25	0.55
Ross	76.57	76.92	71.76	64.01	60.20	57.29	46.05	41.31	35.12
Shetland	0.04	0.25	0.21	0.17	0.44	0.15	0.11	0.10	0.42
Sutherland	80.40	77.10	71.75	61.75	52.25	44.05	25.26	18.83	14.51
Scotland	*6.76*	*6.84*	*5.57*	*4.56*	*3.47*	*2.97*	*1.98*	*1.64*	*1.78*

'WAYS OF SEEING': THE SOURCES

The retreat of the Gaelic speech community, the shift in the demographic profile of the language, the declining number of monoglot speakers, allied to the dispersal of increasing numbers of Gaelic speakers to urban centres outwith the Highland area, all raised an important question both at the time and for any subsequent historical research. Given these changes and the increasing mismatch between the Gaelic-speaking community and the actual residential community, the question in the Highlands was: where was the voice of the Gael to be heard and to what extent was the latter the same as the voice of the Highlander? Was there a Gaelic 'way of seeing' the Highlands specific only to those with a fluency in the language and that could only be expressed in Gaelic? Or was it possible to have a Gaelic 'way of seeing', through rooted and historic familial connections to a specific place within the *Gàidhealtachd*, for example, without necessarily having a personal ability in the language? By 1939–65 the Highland region, as defined above, had become and was increasingly a highly variegated mixture of communities, all bilingual, some trilingual and only an ever decreasing minority predominantly Gaelic-speaking in composition. In short, there were several 'Highlands' in the Highlands, a range of 'Gaeldoms' in the *Gàidhealtachd* and the 'voice of the Gael' was expressed in several registers. For the written expression of an argument, an opinion, a policy, the articulation of a point of view on the social, economic and cultural aspects of modernization and development issues, a document in Gaelic was the least likely option.

Even in the eventful years of the nineteenth and early twentieth centuries there is scant evidence of the publication in the medium of Gaelic of comments on the traumatic social, economic and political matters relating to development and modernization issues. As the author of the definitive survey of published

and Easter Ross and the exclusion of the Gaelic eastern Highlands in Moray, Banff and Aberdeenshire in this definition. See Table 1.1 for changes in the Gaelic-speaking population, and p. 12 above for map of some of the areas mentioned here.

Gaelic prose over that period has noted, even during the resurgence of the 1880s, the stated aim of the leading land and language campaigner, John Murdoch, to put 'Gaelic in the forefront' in all things was not reflected in the pages of his own newspaper, *The Highlander*. Having examined the Gaelic content of the latter, Donald John MacLeod concluded that

> serious discussion of current affairs is confined to the English section of the paper and the Gaelic section consists mainly of poems, traditional stories and anecdotes, reflecting a view on the relative roles of the two languages which is current in some quarters to the present day [1976].[14]

With rare exception, the principal 'voice of the Gael', as expressed through the medium of Gaelic, on contemporary socio-economic issues was that of the Gaelic poet and songster. A desire to ensure that this voice would be not just heard but also critically assessed from a Gaelic perspective was evident as early as the 1930s, most notably in the critical commentary of Sorley MacLean. Thereafter the interest ebbed in the initial post-war era, that is, in the very 1939–65 era when the fresh wave of modernity was at its most penetrating, but from the 1970s onwards there has been a renewed interest in reclaiming the Gaelic voice of the bards through some notable and important scholarly editions and anthologies. In this study where occasion requires reference back to the Gaelic voice through the poets of the preceding era, it is these recent works by contemporary Gaelic scholars that are used. Their understanding of the subtlety and nuance of the Gaelic language – incorporating the dialect, context and background of the poets cited – is an invaluable tool for the student of the several nuanced aspects of Highland history.

By 1939–65, this issue of the role and the use of Gaelic as the principal medium to articulate the 'voice of the Gael' had reached a critical juncture. While the 1880s to the 1920s may have lacked written expression on policy matters in the medium of Gaelic, at least the poets were heard and their views expressed orally in the still sizeable areas of the Highlands that were predominantly Gaelic-speaking. In the post-war era this was most emphatically no longer the case. The problems for Gaelic in the Highlands were now of a deeper, more profound nature. Not only was there little realistic possibility of discussion, debate and advocacy of a specifically Gaelic point of view in written form, it was now becoming increasingly less likely as oral community expression at township level. The nature of the problem is most graphically outlined, from within as it were, through the observations of a series of leading Gaelic promoters and writers from the period.

14 MacLeod, 'Gaelic prose' (1974–6), p. 203.

Thus, by 1939 the Revd Tom Murchison, editor of *An Gaidheal*, was regretting that they had now reached the stage where 'the Gaelic language has declined in use as the daily vernacular of the Highland people'.[15] This situation would worsen as the impact of war ushered in further changes, the social, cultural and linguistic consequences of which were felt across the area, even beyond the mainland out in the island redoubt of South Uist, widely regarded as one of the one of most resilient and enduring strongholds of Gaelic language, culture and identity. In 1945, when the local island bard Donald Allan MacDonald, returned home to the Uists from war service, although still at the prime of his artistic talents he no longer felt able to resume his poetic outpourings, such was the degree of alienation he now felt towards the people for whom he had composed so many songs.[16] He later spoke of this dramatic shift in his perception of his native island Gaelic community and the traditional role of the township bard within it to his fellow South Uist islander, Fr John A. MacDonald. Introducing a published collection of the hitherto largely unpublished verse of Dhòmhnaill Ailean Dhòmnaill na Bainich to a new generation of islanders, the latter summarized the significance of the transformation of traditional island life the local bard had experienced on his return home in 1945:

> With the Second World War, a sea-change came over the community for which he had created his poetry and these social structures and occasions which had sustained his compositions now went into rapid decline. As the audience for his compositions went into ever decreasing decline, our bard ceased to practice his art.[17]

Nor was a gloomy assessment of the post-war situation confined to South Uist. The view from within the urban Gaelic context where publication in the language was largely based was equally despondent. 'Gaelic publishing generally was severely affected by the Second War', by the late 1950s the annual average of new titles in Gaelic had dropped to around four or five, and though there was a 'gradual improvement' from the early 1960s onwards, difficulties were to remain.[18] It was in an attempt to counteract this trend that *Gairm*, the Gaelic quarterly journal was established in 1952. As a new publication in a consciously adopted modern style, *Gairm* was an 'important development' that deliberately

15 Murchison, 'Highland life' (1937–41), p. 218. 16 This perceived sense of a change in the depth and the purity of the Gaelic language among the local community was also evident in the reception to another contemporary Uist bard, Donald John MacDonald. See his edited collection *Chì mi* (1998), p. xxii. 17 MacDonald, 'Poetry of Donald Allan MacDonald' (1992–4), p. 40; MacDonald (ed.), *Orain Dhòmhnaill Ailean* (1999), pp 51–2. See also Black, *An Tuil* (1999) for further poets and critical commentary. 18 MacLeod, 'Gaelic prose', p. 216. Footnote 45 (pp 229–230), provides a comprehensive list of twentieth-century serial publications that contain regular contributions in Gaelic. As MacLeod's survey demonstrates, the number of such publications during the period 1939–65 was very small.

sought to encourage the evolution and emergence of new Gaelic terms and registers to enable the language to be a valid and relevant medium through which to engage with the issues of the modern world. The pace of decline in the language, however, further ensured that *Gairm* would plough a fairly lonely furrow. When the 1961 census was published it confirmed the fears and predictions of many. Over the 1950s there had been a further sharp decline in the number of speakers, including the now virtual disappearance of Gaelic monoglots. Despite the apparently healthy percentages of Gaelic speakers in the Outer Hebrides, 'the true heartland of the language', as Gaelic entered the 1960s critical questions were being raised over the depth and quality of Gaelic language usage within a bilingual world.[19] Faced with the difficulties imposed by 'the cult of anglicization', one informed observer feared that 'the language we finally bury will not be the Gaelic we know, but a patois whose loss we need hardly mourn'.[20]

By 1965, Derick Thomson, the founder and one of the editors of *Gairm*, who had left his native Lewis for an academic career in Glasgow, was similarly apprehensive about the future of the language, particularly with regard to the 'mixed and unsatisfactory' Gaelic literacy levels:

> A large percentage of the population has been educated through the medium of English, and has come to believe that their native culture is depressed and second-rate. A majority of Gaelic speakers cannot read or write Gaelic with any ease, whereas they can read and write English with ease, and they are therefore attracted to English publications and have no real need for Gaelic to be used in public notices or administration, and indeed tend to regard the use of Gaelic for any purposes other than everyday conversation or religious services as affected, or eccentric, or pertaining to a new and old class, that of the language revivers. It is clear that a process of denationalization has been carried out with considerable success, and that the natural relationship between the spoken language and the written language, in a specific area has been upset.

As Thomson saw it, not only did the majority of Gaelic speakers see 'no real need' to express their views in Gaelic on public affairs such as the economic and social impact of modernization and development, they were actually incapable of doing so. Within the Gaelic-speaking remnants of the Highlands, such were the terminal consequences of the linguistic and cultural decline he was witnessing that the community itself was too weakened and contaminated to respond far less resist as, 'the social organism which exists in that area of this minority

---

19 MacDonald, 'Gaelic language' (1968), pp 177–80.   20 MacDonald, 'Last days of Gaelic' (1958).

culture, in the Scottish Gaelic area, is diseased, or that parts of it are living and parts dead'.²¹

An earlier, more sensitive and arguably more perceptive commentary had also been made by another Lewis exile, the noted Gaelic poet and novelist Iain Crichton Smith. The implications of the 'change taking place in the Highlands of a fundamental character' had already been exercising his mind when he addressed the Gaelic Society of Inverness in 1961. Speaking primarily as a writer, Smith acknowledged the dearth of Gaelic prose on 'serious human themes artistically treated' and he appealed to his fellow Gaels to use the clash caused by 'images of the present [...] breaking against' the 'images of the past' to create a 'vigorous literature'.²² Despite this plea, however, Smith was fearful for the future. It was not simply a matter of language. It was also a question of the intellect and the mind:

> our problem is that we speak English a great part of our lives. I am talking in particular of the class of people from whom writers of the kind I have been discussing will be presumed to emerge. When these writers do not discuss aesthetics and general theory in their own language (and how painfully little good criticism we have in Gaelic!), they will tend to form habits of thought which are in fact English.²³

These austere and despairing comments from the period reflect not just the paucity of Gaelic language commentary on any aspect of public affairs but the reasons why such comment in Gaelic was so unlikely in a published or documented form. They are also of direct relevance to the issue of the use, or rather the perceived lack of use, of Gaelic sources for Highland historical research. There is a school of thought within the Gaelic community that, without the necessary linguistic skills to draw on and utilize primary sources in the Gaelic language, any study of the Highlands, including the latter's recent past, must necessarily and a priori be deficient. Without full fluency and command of Gaelic sources it is not possible to locate the 'voice of the Gael', to take into account the mindset of the Gael or to recognize and assess the Gaelic 'way of seeing'. Furthermore, it is also not possible to comprehend the 'way of seeing' of the 'Highlander', for from this viewpoint only the fluent Gaelic speaker is a Gael and only a Gael is a Highlander.²⁴ It is a point of view that raises many questions but with specific regard to the recent historical past of the Highlands, not least the particular post-war period under examination, it

---

21 Thomson, 'Role of the writer in a minority culture' (1964–6), pp 263–4. 22 Smith, 'Future of Gaelic literature' (1960–3), p. 173. 23 Ibid., p. 179. 24 This viewpoint was most explicitly stated a few years ago in a vigorous online debate on the qualifications deemed necessary to engage in historical, cultural and related scholarship in and about the Highlands. The discussion was on http://www.jiscmail.ac.uk/lists/highlands.html, accessed November 2000.

demonstrates a surprising unawareness of the actual paucity of Gaelic sources and the circumstances of language decline and fragility that contributed to this being the case. Apart from the obvious fact that in the overwhelming majority of communities and districts the number of Gaelic-speaking residents was an ever decreasing minority, even in the marginal areas where Gaelic remained the first language of the majority, there were the problems so graphically identified as above to contend with. More ominously, it also reflects an apparent lack of knowledge or understanding as to what the full implications of this decline had meant for the post-war Highlands, repercussions that were only too discernible to the several noted Gaelic writers and scholars cited above whose own concern for their Gaelic language and culture was self-evident. Given the candid assessments of the latter as to the consequences of such a fundamental shift in the linguistic situation throughout the Highlands, including the primarily Gaelic-speaking periphery, it is difficult to sustain the argument that the Gaelic thought process, or 'way of seeing' as expressed in print, whether in Gaelic or not, differed greatly from that of a mindset overwhelmingly shaped by the English language. It is in this sense that the views expressed by Gaels writing in English that occur throughout this book, particularly in chapter seven, are acknowledged to be representative of a body of opinion reflective of the 'voice of the Gael' and a particular 'way of seeing' from within both the Gaelic-speaking and the wider Highland community.

THE PARADOXES OF GAELDOM

In teasing out the various strands that have a bearing on how the post-eighteenth-century 'Highland question' was perceived and discussed, two other specifically Gaelic aspects of the inherited set of deeply embedded values, beliefs and perceptions that contextualized much of the debate on 'the future of the Highlands' or 'the Highland problem' in the post-war era need to be assessed. Each is reflective of the innate ambiguities, ambivalences and contradictions within Gaelic culture and Highland historiography. They underpin the paradoxical inconsistencies of attitudes that make the latter such an absorbing framework in which matters of social, cultural and normative reaction, adaptation and change are debated and assessed.

Firstly there is the paradox behind the valorization of the simple, uncomplicated, close to the earth 'way of life' of the humble Highland crofter set against Gaeldom's innate sense of cultural sophistication and superiority, past prowess and present worth.[25] The outward inferiorized public presentation of the Gael

---

25 This sense of superiority goes back a long way in Gaelic culture and is discernible even in the early mediaeval era among the *peregrini Scotti* of Scotland and Ireland. It was also, of course, even more prevalent in Ireland.

Introduction 25

and the Highlander as the declining remnant of a poor, marginalized and 'historyless' people was the antithesis of the internalized but largely private sense of inherited significance that permeated much of the Gaelic community's deep self-belief in the historic importance of the Gael, the Gaelic language and culture as being the essential heart of Scottish identity and of Scotland itself.[26] Alongside an awareness of their historic role in 'cradling' the embryonic nation of Scotland, Gaeldom was also imbued with a sense of cultural worth and accomplishment, a belief in the Gaels as the custodians of a culture on a par with all the other high cultures of Europe, not least through their advanced state of learning and sophisticated artistic achievement in the medieval period.[27] This Gaelic 'golden age', symbolized by the Lordship of the Isles, had centred on a sense of kinship and of belonging. It had manifested itself in the clan system, a distinctive social formation that had nurtured the Gaels' strong sense of ethnic identity and generated feelings of confidence and self-assurance.[28] It was precisely these sentiments, resonating within the *Gàidhealtachd* for centuries, that had made the post-1745 transformation and subsequent traumatic upheavals all the more difficult for Gaels to bear. Yet notwithstanding the deep social and psychological dislocations of that era, this innate perception of Gaelic superiority survived tenaciously into the twentieth century. To most of Gaeldom's advocates and activists, it was the forebears of the Gaels who had provided the essential elements that had made Scotland – *Alba* – a distinctive nation.[29] As summarized by a contemporary Scottish Gaelic scholar,

> Long ago [...] Scotland was ruled by a Gaelic leadership: Gaelic culture was the ascendant culture, the Gaelic language was the major language through which meaning in all prestigious domains [...] was mediated. The very name 'Scotland' denoted Gaeldom.[30]

A second contradiction relates to the widely held belief that the Gael and the Highlander was the unwilling victim of early modernizing forces that foisted outside values on the region and its people, marginalized Gaelic culture and introduced the notion that the Highlands were a 'problem' to be controlled and managed.[31] However, both Gael and Highlander were actively involved in the

---

26 This sense of importance to Scotland and of cultural achievement was not without some considerable justification. 27 See Thomson, 'Gaelic literature' (1993). For this and other aspects of Gaelic society in this era, consult the entries and bibliography in Thomson (ed.), *Companion to Gaelic Scotland* (1994) as a starting point for further examination. 28 Bannerman, 'Lordship of the Isles' (1977), pp 209–40; Dodgshon, *From chiefs to landlords* (1998). 29 See Broun, 'Scotland before 1100' (2006), pp 2–3 for analysis of the provenance and meaning of the word '*Alba*'. 30 MacAulay, 'Canons, myths and cannon fodder' (1994), 35. 31 These are obviously broad and complex subjects but for an insight into how they impacted on Highland society, and vice-versa, consult: MacInnes, *Clanship* (1996); Whyte, *Scotland before the industrial revolution* (1995), pp 235–9, 251–70; Withers, *Gaelic in Scotland, 1698–1981* (1984), chs 2–4;

very agencies that advanced these projects and the ideas that underpinned them – from the House of Argyll to the Scottish Society for the Propagation of Christian Knowledge. Furthermore, Gaeldom was complicit in the very value system and reconstruction of a manufactured 'Highlands' and 'Highlander' that was seen to be the debilitating cultural consequence of the external forces of modernity. This active involvement in making the Highlands a political 'problem', coupled with widespread participation in the commodification of the Highlands, as exemplified by 'Balmorality', are complex and contentious issues that merit further research. It is hoped that this book will further that process. Certainly, traditional interpretations of Highland and Gaelic history that either overlook or downplay the involvement of Gaels in events and forces deemed injurious to the culture needs to be challenged. However, this paradox that it was the Highlander and Gael who helped introduce modernity into the Highlands does not fit with the dominant narrative through which Highland history and Gaelic society are viewed.

Developing an understanding and some degree of insight into what was meant by this frequently cited but seldom defined notion of a traditional and distinctive 'way of life' peculiar to the Highlands is in no small part what this book is about. Gaining purchase on such a deeply felt yet intangible 'structure of feeling' is an incremental process most appropriately spread over several chapters.[32] Each historical epoch draws on the past to shape attitudes to contemporary society. Just as this happened between 1939 and 1965, so too with the earlier period from 1745 to 1939. The dichotomy between an external view that characterized the region and its people as lawless, problematic and disloyal and an internal perspective that placed a strong emphasis on certain values and strengths unique to the Gaelic people is central to the opening chapters of this study.

Durkacz, *Celtic languages* (1983), pp 50–2.   32 For a discussion of the concept of 'structure of feeling', see Eldridge, *Raymond Williams* (1994), pp 79–80.

PART I

Image and reality: the Highlands and Islands of Scotland, 1745–1939

2

Economic and social perspectives on the Highlands and Islands, 1745–1939

> The Highland Clearances constitute one of the saddest tragedies that has ever come on a people, and one of the most astounding of all the successes of landlord capitalism in Western Europe, such a triumph over workers and peasants of a country as has rarely been achieved with such ease, cruelty and cynicism.
>
> Sorley MacLean, 'The poetry of the Clearances' (1939)[1]

LAND AND CULTURE: *THEMES AND MOTIFS*

When the Gaelic poet and scholar Sorley MacLean looked back on the post-1745 history of the Highlands in his powerful review of 'The poetry of the Clearances', he saw cataclysm of a profound nature. This was the insider's view, the perception of the Highlands from within the *Gàidhealtachd*.[2] MacLean's seminal paper drew widely on the poetry and song of the Gael that were transmitted by oral tradition and disseminated in popular published collections. The members of the Gaelic Society of Inverness may not have shared MacLean's contextualizing of the history of the Highlands by reference to a thinly veiled *marxisant* socialist valorization of the 'workers-peasants struggle' but they would have been familiar with the bardic and other oral sources which he held up to be equally as valid as the published text. The contemporary accounts of the traumatic events of the nineteenth century were published by a series of campaigning pamphleteers, notably Donald MacLeod, Thomas Mulock, Donald Ross, and Hugh Miller. These had all been collected together and kept in publication in Alexander MacKenzie's massively influential *A history of the Highland Clearances*, significantly subtitled *containing a reprint of Donald*

---

1 MacLean, 'Poetry of the Clearances' (1937–41), p. 294. MacLean initially delivered his paper to the Gaelic Society of Inverness on 10 February, 1939. 2 Sorley MacLean was the pre-eminent Gaelic poet of the twentieth century, and his work is regarded as of seminal importance in stimulating the 'Gaelic Renaissance' of the 1940s onwards. Addressing the mixed audience of Gaels and non-Gaels at the Gaelic Society of Inverness was a young, energetic Gaelic scholar and activist. For an appreciation of his work, consult the critical writings section at http://www.sorleymaclean.org/english/index.htm, accessed August 2010.

MacLeod's 'Gloomy memories of the Highlands'; Isle of Skye in 1882; and a verbatim report of the trial of the Braes crofters. And throughout the period, most notably in the 1880s and 1890s, the detailed evidence on social and economic conditions that had been given to a series of government boards, select committees and royal commissions was reported in detail by a vigorous and widely read Highland network of local newspapers, journals and magazines.

The purpose of this chapter is not to trace the varied nuances of Highland history but to address the over-arching themes within the historiography, from which a series of motifs, notions and concepts can be identified. These, it will be argued, have a significant bearing on the discursive context and framework within which the Highlands were considered in the core period of this study, 1939–65. Therefore, the summary of formative processes and events that created the post-1745 Highlands is necessarily selective. The economic and social themes are 'clearance', 'emigration' and 'resistance & resurgence'. In the development of the Highlands, these themes were, in practice, closely combined in a complex process of societal and cultural change, but for the purpose of identifying the underlying formative motifs, the economic and social themes considered here are essentially perceptions from within Gaelic Scotland. The third chapter examines the cultural dimension to the Highlands. Here, themes are examined which are primarily to do with perceptions from outwith Gaelic Scotland, although the external contribution to economic and social images and the internal contribution of the Gaels themselves to cultural reconstructions were also of critical importance.[3]

Over the last two to three decades there has been a major reassessment of all aspects of post-1745 Highland history – economic, social, cultural, linguistic and political.[4] There has always been an awareness of the ways in which Highland culture and history had been reconstructed; yet serious scholarly analysis of this process has been of recent origin.[5] Prior to this reappraisal, Highland historiography mostly comprised political, genealogical or popular works that, by simply reformulating earlier writings, were largely emotive in tone and polemical in purpose.[6] The tendency towards polemic was emphatically captured by Smout's memorable assessment of Ian Grimble's *The trial of Patrick Sellar* as being 'thick with passion but thin on research'. John Prebble's books on aspects of Highland history have also been subjected to strong criticism – guilty in Smout's view of being 'heavily charged with emotion'.[7]

---

[3] One thing that must be considered is the extent to which the Gael was a willing and active participant. This aspect has not been addressed by Scottish Gaels, but it forms a vital part of colonial discourse. [4] Devine, *Clanship to crofters' war* (1994); Richards, *Highland Clearances* (1982 & 1985); Withers, *Gaelic Scotland* (1988). [5] Chapman, *Gaelic vision* (1978); Clyde, *Rebel to hero* (1995); Stafford, *Sublime savage* (1988); Withers, 'Historical creation of the Scottish Highlands' (1992); Womack, *Improvement and romance* (1989). [6] Prebble, *Highland Clearances* (1963). [7] Smout, *History of the Scottish people* (1969), p. 541; Smout's review of *The Darien disaster* (1970), 112–13. See also Smout's 'An ideological struggle' (1972).

A key charge from academics that underpinned much of their criticism of popular historians such as Prebble was a 'lack of attention to modern work' and the difficulty 'in separating circumstantial conjecture from documented fact', which in the case of Prebble left him open to 'some doubts about his methods and therefore lingering unease [...] about the scholarly nature of his conclusions'. These weaknesses were deemed all the more problematic because Prebble's undoubted skills as 'a splendid storyteller', allied to the power of the material, made (and makes) books like *The Highland Clearances* (1963) so marketable and influential.[8] It was this type of uncritical, emotive and polemical popular history that largely informed public discourse and provided the historiographical 'grounding' on the Highlands, both within the *Gàidhealtachd* and outside it, in the decades immediately prior to the core period of this study. For this reason, the dominant themes and motifs are elucidated from the texts and the oral traditions that were part of the essential felt experience of Gaelic Scotland in the inter-war years.[9] Recent scholarship and reassessment is presented throughout the chapter as a 'double dialogue' within this outline of key themes.

CLEARANCE

Thàinig oirnn do dh'Albainn crois,	There has come on us in Scotland a cross,
Tha daoine bochda nochdte ris,	poor people are naked before it;
Gun bhiadh, gun aodach, gun chluain,	without food, without clothing, without solace,
Tha 'n àird a tuath air a sgrios.	the Land of the North is utterly destroyed.
'Oran nan Ciobairean Gallda',	'Song of the Lowland Shepherd'
Ailean Dall, *c.*1800[10]	Allan MacDougall, *c.*1800

The overarching moment in Highland history was the initial removal of the Gaels from their land. The legacy of the Highland Clearances continues to the present day.[11] The phrase itself has a powerful emotive quality, casting a long shadow over all other aspects of Highland history. By analyzing this issue in an

---

8 Ibid. and see also Mitchison's review of Prebble's *The lion in the north* (1972).   9 For a fuller illustration of some of the key texts see Burnett, 'Ethnic culture in transtion' (2000).   10 The difficulties of translation are evident with this poem. In 1938, Sorley MacLean translates 'gun chluain' as 'without pasture' ('Poetry of the Clearances') but in *Calgacus* (vol. 2), he translates it as 'without solace'. He felt the word had both the physical sense of pasture but also the spiritual sense of pasture meaning solace. In a later article he explains that the word 'sgrios', which he translates as 'utterly destroyed', conforms with the Gaelic translation of the Bible for such holocausts as visited on Sodom and Gomorrah. It is also the word regularly used for eternal damnation. See MacLean, 'Vale of tears' (1986), p. 14.   11 For a standard interpretation which regards the Highland Clearances as an inevitable consequence of rising population and economic circumstance, see Gray, *Highland economy* (1957), pp 57–66 and Smout, *History of the Scottish people*, pp 351–60. A strong challenge to this view came with Hunter's *Making of the crofting community* (1976), pp 15–33. The complexity of the phenomenon is highlighted by Lynch, *Scotland* (1991), pp 368–9. Cameron's 'Introduction' to his *Land for the people* (1996) summarizes the positions of recent scholarly contributions.

episodic manner, focusing on key moments in the history of the region, certain motifs become apparent. These motifs or concepts are of critical relevance to the understanding of the core period of 1939 to 1965. The greatest sense from the collective consciousness of the Gaels was loss – a loss of a bygone era when the traditional values of the Gael regulated the Highlands. A second theme that emerges is the Gael as the victim of an anglicizing transformation of the old order; the victim of the intrusion of Lowland shepherds and sheep-farmers, and the victim of the preference for deer rather than people. Thirdly, there is an identifiable grievance at the process of pauperization. Through crofterization, Gaels witnessed the destruction of a natural economy and the reorganization of the pattern of settlement and of the relations of production. This led to the diminution of the Gael, and Gaeldom itself, to a redundant and impoverished peasantry. Fourthly, we can detect a feeling of fatalism, which mirrors the growing influence of evangelical Presbyterianism. Fifthly, there is the deep sense of injustice at the extirpation of a people from their homeland, a dispossession of place. Finally, there is a tension over the preference for deer over the human population of the region. This conflict reflects the different views on the Highlands as a resource area. Although there are other subjects one could consider, as with the key concepts that arise from the cultural and political cluster of themes, these are the principal ones to identify and tease out for their relevance to the context in which affairs and issues between 1939 and 1965 were discussed and contextualized.

Loss

In the decades following the defeat of the '45 Rising, the dynamic of economic and social change already evident within Gaeldom underwent a distinct acceleration as the range and scale of penetration by capitalism dramatically intensified. A political determination to eliminate Highland distinctiveness, followed by new ideas of agricultural 'improvement' (how to manage and utilize the diverse resources of the area), and the relentless, aggressive market demand for raw materials ensured the transformation and ultimate eclipse of the 'traditional' Gaelic social formation.[12] Most striking of all, the chief became a landlord and his kinship became a tenantry. Traditional reciprocal relationships of *dùthchas*, of mutual obligation, were replaced by the cash nexus, and extended familial bonds of cadet lineage were shattered on the rocks of differential rent.[13]

---

12 Political historians focus on the annexation, cultural agencies, road building and state agencies to pacify and assimilate the Highlands. Economic and social historians use the dual economy model of traditional and modern. The language is of 'penetration', of 'irresistible economic forces'. See Youngson, *After the Forty-Five* (1973); Gray, *Highland economy*; Hunter, *Crofting community*; Smout, *History of the Scottish people*. 13 The changing attitude to land is discussed in Mitchison, 'Highland Clearances' (1981); Smout, *Century of the Scottish people* (1986), pp 66–8.

The first to feel the traumatic consequences of the eclipse of the old order were the *daoine uasal*, the gentlemen of the clan, the tacksman class, through whom Gaeldom had once managed its physical and human resources. As the chiefs metamorphosed into frequently absentee landlords and reorientated their lives on Edinburgh and London, Gaelic society experienced a profound sense of loss, a disorientation that carried a deep sense of betrayal. The North Uist bard, John MacCodrum, witnessing the imposition of a new order, bitterly attacked those who had 'lost their sight' of Gaeldom's essential values:

Seallaibh mun cuairt duibh	Look around you
Is faicibh na h-uaislean	and see the nobility
Gun iochd annt' ri truaghain,	without pity for poor folk,
Gun suairceas ri dàimhich	Without kindness to friends;
'S ann tha iad am barail	They are of the opinion
Nach buin sibh do'n talamh,	that you do not belong to the land,
'S ged dh'fhàg iad sibh falamh	and though they have left you destitute
Chan fhaic iad mar chall e;	they do not see it as a loss.
Chaill iad an sealladh	They have lost sight
Air gach reachd agus gealladh	of every law and promise
Bha eadar na fearaibh	that was observed by the men
Thug am fearan-s' o 'n nàmhaid [...].	who took this land from the foe [...].
'Oran do na Fogarraich',	'Song to the Fugitives',
Iain Mhic Fhearchair.[14]	John MacCodrum.

MacCodrum's contempt for those who 'did not see it as a loss' was echoed elsewhere. The Sutherland bard, *Rob Donn*, poured scorn on those whose new yardstick for a gentleman tenant was the highest market price.[15] His songs reflected this deep respect for those who were constant to the values of traditional Gaeldom, an essential sense of kinship and mutual obligation, and a profound contempt for those who had betrayed these cardinal virtues for the impersonal commercialism of the new 'improving' order:

Thionail airgiod is fearann,	Who have gathered money and lands
Bhitheas buidheann eile 'g sgaoileadh,	That others will scatter,
Bhitheas féin air an gearradh	Men who will be cut off
Gun ghuth caraid 'g an caoineadh,	Without a friend to mourn them,
Air nach ruig dad do mholadh,	Whom no praise will reach
Ach 'Seall sibh fearann a shaor iad'.	Save: 'Look at the land they redeemed'.
'Cumha Iain Mac Eachainn',	'Elegy for John MacEachan',
Rob Donn.[16]	Rob Donn MacKay.

As the realization dawned that what the Highlands were experiencing was the death of a culture, the eclipse of a way of life, a profound sense of cataclysmic loss entered the popular culture and the collective consciousness of the *Gàidhealtachd*.

14 Matheson, *John MacCodrum* (1938), pp 202–3. 15 Grimble, *Rob Donn* (1979).
16 Morrison, *Rob Donn* (1899), p. 32.

Victim

When the improving agriculturists found a new breed of sheep that could survive the climate of the north and provide a highly profitable commercial return, the pattern of living in the *Gàidhealtachd*, indeed the very landscape itself, changed irreversibly.[17] Although sheep farming was introduced as early as 1762, the portent of a sweeping change in land-use, tenurial relationships and settlement patterns came in 1792, known as *bliadhna nan caorach*, 'the year of the sheep'. The traumatic removal of whole townships to the coast, or to poorer, marginal land as sheep farming established itself, occurred in every area of the Highlands from Perthshire to the Hebrides.[18] But it was the Sutherland evictions that came to epitomize what entered Scotland's history as 'the Highland Clearances'.[19] The Sutherland Clearances occurred early, and were on a large scale; thus they prompted much contemporary newspaper and pamphlet publicity:

> Every imaginable means short of the sword or the musket was put in requisition to drive the natives away, to force them to exchange their farms and comfortable habitations, erected by themselves or their forefathers, for inhospitable rocks on the sea-shore, and to depend on subsistence on the watery element in its wildest mood [...]. The country was darkened by the smoke of the burnings, and the descendants [...] were ruined, trampled upon, dispersed and compelled to seek asylum across the sea.[20]

The sense of victimization generated vitriolic attack against the new 'tenants' – the sheep:

Chunnaic mise 's mi 'nam chadal	I saw while I was sleeping
Aisling dhen do ghabh mi ioghnadh,	a dream that caused me to marvel,
Na Fenians a' tighinn a–nall	the Fenians coming over the sea
A thoirt nan ceann bho na caoraich;	to take the heads off the sheep;
Cha bhi claigeann dhiubh ri colainn,	not one skull will be left attached to a body,
Thèid an sgaradh bho gach aon dhiubh,	they will be lopped from each one of them;
Thèid an sgrios bho thràigh gu monadh;	they will be exterminated from shore to hill;
An sin thig sonas air an t-saoghal.	then peace will come to the world.
'Air Choinnich Gheasto'.	'Satire on Kenneth of Gesto'.
Anon., c.1860s[21]	

17 Caird, 'Creation of crofts' (1987). 18 Allan MacInnes identifies the events in Sutherland of the 1790s–1820s as constituting the 'first phase of Clearance'. See his 'Scottish Gaeldom' (1988). Eric Richard's *The leviathan of wealth* concentrates on the events in Sutherland during this key phase of clearance. For another perceptive commentary on the social and economic transformation on a specific locality, consult Cregeen, 'House of Argyll' (1970). 19 For a discussion on how the Clearances affected the Gaelic language in Sutherland, see Dorian, *Language death*, pp 29–37. For more detailed discussion of the folklore of this early but seminal phase of Clearance focused in Sutherland, see MacInnes, 'Gaelic song' (1964). 20 MacLeod, *Gloomy memories* (1857), pp xiv, 1.

Another area affected early was Glengarry, whose most famous bard, Ailean Dall, best captured the sense of destruction of the land of the Gael. For him, the perpetrator was the 'other', the *Gall*, the *Cìobairean Gallda*, the 'Lowland Shepherd', the subject of Ailean Dall's song. As the continuation of the opening stanza makes clear:

> Chan fhaicear ach caoraich is uain,   only sheep and lambs are visible,
> Goill mun cuairt daibh air gach slios;   Lowlanders surrounding them on every slope;
> Tha gach fearann air dol fàs,   all the lands have gone to waste,
> Na Gàidheil 's an ceann fo fhliodh.   chickweed has grown over Highlanders' heads.
> '*Oran do na Cìobairidh Gallda*'   'Song to the Lowland Shepherds'
> Ailean Dall, c.1800.[22]   Allan MacDougall.

It was Lowland dress, Lowland physical appearance, Lowland manners and, above all, the incongruity of Lowland speech, that Ailean Dall lambasted. Once there were the deer and the hunter, but now, the 'Lowlanders' screeching has banished the deer' and:

> An èirig gach cùis a bh' ann   as compensation for all the sounds that ever existed,
> Feadaireachd nan Gall 's gach glaic.   the whistling of Lowlanders sounds in every hollow.

The ethnic dimension, then, remains the pre-eminent *leit-motif* in virtually all Gaelic poetry and song on the Clearances. We are left with the impression of the Gael as the victim of *mìorun mòr nan Gall*, 'the great ill-will of the Lowlander'.[23] It is both the strength and the weakness of William Livingstone's '*Fios thun a' bhaird*'/'A message for the poet' (c.1863). This is a land of desolation, a land where, 'injustice, Foreigners and taxes have triumphed':

> Chuir gamhlas Ghall air fuadach   the bad feeling of the Foreigner has banished
> Na tha bhiainn 's nach till gu bràth;   those who have left us and will never return;
> Mar a fhuair 's a chunnaic mise,   just as I found and as I saw,
> Thoir am fios seo chun a' Bhàird.[24]   take this message to the Poet.

The most common focus for discontent was the incoming Lowland shepherd, or the 'Foreigner', but the bitterest satires were reserved for the man of power, the factor. One example, Patrick Sellar of Sutherland, came to symbolize the ruthlessness of Clearance.[25] His name became synonymous with cruelty because of his involvement in the clearances of Kildonan in 1813 and of Strathnaver the following year, as an anonymous composition makes clear:

---

21 The original was not published but remained in the folklore of the Gael. Collected and translated in Meek, *Tuath is tighearna* (1995), pp 64–5, 196.   22 MacKenzie, *Sar-obair* (1865), pp 302–3. Translation for this extract from Meek (ed.), *Tuath is tighearna* (1995), p. 186.   23 The phrase '*Mìorun mòr nan Gall*' comes from a poem of that title by Alasdair MacMhaighstir Alasdair.   24 MacDhunleibhe, *Duain agus orain* (1882), p. 151; translated in Meek, *Tuath is tighearna*, p. 201.   25 For further information on the intricacies of his trial, see Grimble, *Patrick Sellar* (1963) and Richards, *History of the Highland Clearances* (1985), ii, pp 220–3.

> Nam faighinn – s' air raon thu
> Is daoine 'ga do cheangal,
> Bheirinn le mo dhòrnaibh
> Trì òirlich a mach de d'sgamhan.
>   Anon., c.1809.[26]

> If I had you on the open field
> with men tying you up,
> with my fists I would take out
> three inches of your lungs.

Outwith the *Gàidhealtachd*, the imprint of the Sutherland Clearances on the popular consciousness was largely the result of Donald MacLeod. On leaving Sutherland in 1831, he set out to record the story for internal consumption. Less literary than others, but with an insider's knowledge and sense of the wrongdoing being afflicted on his fellow Highlanders, he helped galvanize resistance to the policy of clearance. He witnessed many of the events first hand, and although his impartiality has been questioned by later scholars, nonetheless his outpourings were crucial in shaping public perceptions of what had taken place in these northern counties during the early decades of the nineteenth century. His determination to bring to the attention of the public the excesses of the Sutherland Clearances mirrored the sense of ethnic oppression existing among Gaelic bards:

> had I possessed a less independent mind and a more crouching disposition, I might perhaps have remained. But stung with the oppression and injustice prevailing around me, and seeing the contrast my country exhibited to the state of the Lowlands, I could not always hold my peace.[27]

MacLeod wrote on a number of subjects, but he kept a special place for Patrick Sellar and his exploits during 1814, '*bliadhna an losgaidh*' or 'the year of the burnings'.[28] In the publications that followed, MacLeod gave harrowing tales of the pathetic scenes that accompanied the clearances in Sutherland. Of the 1814 Strathnaver evictions, he wrote:

> Many deaths ensued from alarm, fatigue and cold; the people being instantly deprived of shelter, and left to the mercy of the elements. Some old men took to the woods and precipices, wandering about in a state approaching to, or of, absolute insanity, and several of them, in this situation, lived on a few days. Pregnant women were taken with premature labour, and several children did not long survive their sufferings.[29]

In such a way, the Gael as helpless victim of clearance was documented.

---

[26] Translated in MacLean, 'Poetry of the Clearances', pp 55–6. [27] MacLeod, *Gloomy memories*, p. 46. [28] Prebble, *Highland Clearances*, p. 71. [29] MacLeod, *Gloomy memories*, p. 9.

Pauperization

Integral to the landlords' policy of clearance was the creation of croft-holdings. The crofting system was devised to maximize income for the landlord by leasing out previously inhabited land to sheep farmers and planting the former communities elsewhere, usually on the coast or in barren areas. Donald MacLeod rubbished the idea that the reorganization of the Sutherland estate improved the conditions for the peasants:

> those who spoke the Gaelic tongue were a proscribed race, and everything was done to get rid of them, by driving them into the forlorn hope of deriving subsistence from the sea, while squatting on their miserable allotments, where, in their wretched hovels, they lingered out an almost hopeless existence [...].[30]

For many Gaels, this policy of 'crofterization' meant learning new skills. But the transition to this new life was harshly felt, and much suffering ensued:

> The whole inhabitants of Kildonan parish, with the exception of three families, nearly 2,000 souls, were utterly rooted and burned out. Many, especially the young and robust, left the country, but the aged, the females and children, were obliged to stay and accept the wretched allotments allowed them on the seashore and endeavouring to learn fishing.[31]

In the Hebrides, most of the crofters were put to work gathering kelp. The inflated prices of the Napoleonic war enabled landlords to further subdivide holdings and maximize their income.

The sense of being herded into inadequate holdings is supported by the findings of economic and social historians on the demography of the Highlands and Islands during the early nineteenth century. Nonetheless, although population growth was apparent, the people themselves believed that overcrowding was a direct consequence of them being cleared off the fertile land and forced into the smaller crofting communities.

> The parish of Kildonan, numbering one thousand five hundred and seventy-four souls, were ejected from their holdings and their homes burnt to the ground [...]. The entire population were then compressed into a space of three thousand acres of the most barren in the parish; and the remaining one hundred and thirty thousand acres

---

30 Ibid., p. 27. 31 Ibid., p. 20; Sage, *Memorabilia domestica* (1889), p. 42.

were divided among six sheep farmers – who held an acreage upwards of twenty thousand acres each.³²

After the Napoleonic war, depression hit the Highlands. The creation of crofting communities had restricted the activities of the Gael, and left them even more exposed to the vagaries of the market and the spectre of impoverishment and famine.

Fatalism

The impoverishment and destitution of the people occasioned by loss of former grazings, resettlement on poor land, high rents, low incomes and the lack of ancillary employment opportunities was intensified by periodic famine. By the 1840s, as the population numbers continued to increase, despite significant out-migration, the potato became the staple diet of the people. In 1846, when the potato crop failed through blight, the west Highlands and Islands, the epicentre of over-crowding, penury and crop failure, faced disaster. These were the years of 'the great hunger', the Highland Famine.³³ The emergent crofting communities of the west became synonymous with ever-present destitution:

> I have seen the people reduced to such poverty that they were obliged to feed themselves upon dulse from the shore [...]. I see them now reduced to such hard condition that I can compare them to nothing but the lepers at the gates of Samaria – death before them and death behind them.³⁴

The traumatic impact of the Great Highland Famine led many to accept reluctantly the bitter alternative of emigration. Those who remained accepted their position with a debilitating combination of fatalism and despair. In the early part of the nineteenth century, a wave of Calvinist evangelicalism swept the Protestant Highlands.³⁵ Submission to the Divine Will required an acceptance of suffering, including eviction, destitution, hunger and penury. As the missionary zealots of the Gaelic Schools Society of Edinburgh at the height of the potato famine ordained:

> For He hath said I will never leave thee nor forsake thee. It is this word that your teachers are, day and night, occupied in dispensing to the starving families of the Highlands and Islands.³⁶

---

32 Napier Commission evidence, cited in MacLean & Carrell (eds), *As an fhearann* (1986), p. 11.
33 For a detailed analysis of the Highland famine, see Devine, *Great Highland Famine* (1988).
34 Donald Martin, Tolsta, Lewis, Napier Commission evidence, cited in MacLean & Carrell, *As an fhearann*, p. 17.   35 For more detail on religion and the Highlands during the eighteenth and nineteenth centuries, consult Devine, *Clanship to crofters' war*, ch. 7. For an alternative perspective, see MacColl, *Land, faith and the crofting community* (2006).   36 Quoted in Durkacz, *Decline*

The most poignant testimony to this fatalistic acceptance of suffering as the result of personal wickedness remains at the church of Croick, Easter Ross, where, in the graveyard, the people of Glencalvie sought shelter after their eviction in 1845. On the windows they scratched their submission:

> Glencalvie people was in the church here May 24, 1845 ...
> Glencalvie people the wicked generation ...
> Glencalvie is a wilderness blow ship them to the colony ...[37]

The famine occurred just after the Disruption of 1843, in which most of the Highlands followed the evangelicals into the Free Church of Scotland. Favourable comparisons to Catholic and inherently 'disloyal' Ireland, sympathetic press reports, increased accessibility, the wish of the new urban middle classes to find a suitable cause for their philanthropic zeal, all combined with the energetic relief activities of the Free Church urban Lowland network to ensure that the orthodoxies of free market political economy were overcome and that government intervention followed.[38] Although reluctant and at arm's length, it was a significant acceptance of government liability in what was soon to become known as the 'Highland problem'.[39]

Disinclination to intervene did not rest on principles of *laissez faire* economics alone. Among the governmental and landlord elite who managed Highland relief in the destitution years there were ingrained Malthusian notions about poverty and personal responsibility, allied to firm views on the hazards and limits of 'Christian charity' and pronounced convictions on the racial inferiority of the Gael. The Gael, as Sir Charles Trevelyan warned, had to be uplifted from his own backwardness and fecklessness:

> Next to allowing the people to die of hunger, the greatest evil that could happen would be their being habituated to depend upon public charity. The object to be arrived at, therefore, is to prevent the assistance given from being productive in idleness and, if possible, to make it conducive to increased exertion.[40]

---

of the Celtic languages, p. 129. **37** Cited in Prebble, *Highland Clearances*, p. 239. The etched markings of the Glencalvie people are still discernible to this day. **38** For a wider appraisal of some of the issues and personalities involved, see Devine, *Clanship to crofters' war*, ch. 11; Fenyo, *Contempt, sympathy and romance* (2000). **39** Ewen Cameron discusses the 'lineage' of government intervention and the pedigree of the 'Highland problem' in his 'special policy area' (1997). **40** Cited in Devine, *Clanship to crofters' war*, p. 164. Trevelyan's actions brought terse comment from the Irish journalist Thomas Mulock: 'Sir Charles was invited to try his hand in starving the poor Highlanders according to the most approved doctrines of political economy ... the Highlanders upon grounds of Catholic affinity, were to be starved after the Irish fashion'. See Mulock, *Western Highlands and Islands*, pp 81–2.

Relief became tied to a 'destitution test' and the system of relief dispersal in the distressed areas of the west Highlands and Islands was bitterly resented as a further step away from traditional notions of mutual support and 'moral economy'. It resulted in the ultimate demeaning, degradation and pauperization of the people, particularly for the growing landless cottar class, forced to squat on crofter land with no security or income:

Tha bochdan na rìoghachd	The paupers of the kingdom
Fo bhinn a tha cruaidh [...]	are under a hard sentence [...]
'S gun nì ach taigh nam bochd,	there is no alternative to the poorhouse –
'S b' fheàrr bhith crocht' na ann.	and better be hanged than there.
Tha Gàidhealtachd na h–Alba	The Highlands of Scotland
Gu dearbh 'na h-adhbhar bròin [...]	are a truly pitiful place [...].
'Bochdan na rìoghachd'	'The paupers of the kingdom'
Calum Caimbeul MacPhail, 1872.[41]	Calum Campbell MacPhail

Loss of place

Following the misery and distress of the 1840s, many landlords were determined to remove the residual population struggling to hold onto their existence. But the weaknesses of the Highland economy, and the cost of providing relief during the worst years of famine, had brought financial ruin to a number of landlords. The new owners had few, if any, ties with the Highlands and its people. They felt no compulsion to provide for their tenants.[42] Consequently, the 1850s witnessed 'mass clearance' with whole areas, particularly of the western seaboard, being emptied of people. Destined to seek their fortunes 'in the land of strangers', the consequences of the comprehensive and ruthless evictions were bitterly felt in the Gaelic communities for many years after.[43]

Biting testimony of the mass evictions taking place during this period and the sense of wilful removal of an indigenous people was relayed outside the Highlands by campaigning journalists such as Donald Ross, Hugh Miller and Thomas Mulock. Ross was particularly important as he conveyed the ruthless nature of clearance in Ross-shire. His account of the 'Battle of Greenyards' of 1854 still resonates:

> The police struck with all their force [...] not only when knocking down, but after the females were on the ground. They beat and kicked them while lying weltering in their blood. Such was the brutality with

---

[41] Meek, 'Poets of the land agitation', pp 370–1. [42] See Devine, 'New elite' (1989). [43] The phrase 'land of strangers' comes from 'Mary of Unnimore' describing the mass clearances in her part of Morvern to the Revd Norman MacLeod in his *Reminiscences of a Highland parish* (1863), pp 294–5, 303. The exodus of people from Coll and Tiree was still fresh in the memories of those who contributed to the Revd Hector Cameron's book, *Handbook to the islands of Coll and Tiree* (1937). It lives on, as demonstrated by David Craig in his *On the crofters' trail* (1990).

which this tragedy was carried through, that more than twenty females were carried off the field in blankets and litters, and the appearance they presented, with their heads cut and bruised, their limbs mangled and their clothes clotted with blood, was such as would horrify any savage.[44]

Alexander Mackenzie collated these accounts together in his 1883 publication and presented the information to emphasize the wholesale and systematic removal of entire communities from the Highlands.[45]

In Gaelic folklore, this 'unnatural' process meant not just the death of traditional Gaeldom, but the death of the land itself. This was emphatically proclaimed by an anonymous bard in a savage satire:

Am fearann 's iad féin	The land and themselves,
Gum bàsaich le chéil	they will die together,
O na dh'fhàs iad 'nam béistean doirbh,	since they have become hard monsters,
Rag-mhuinealach, cruaidh,	stiff-necked, mean,
Gun iochd no ath-thruas,	with no mercy or pity;
Iad puinnseanta, fuar	poisonous, cold
Ri 'n ìochdairean 's ri 'n tuath,	to their subjects and tenants,
'Gan casgairt le uallach dhoirbh.	killing them with hard burdens.
'Oran eadar Dòmhnall agus Dùghall'	'A song between Donald and Dougal',
Anon.[46]	Anon.

This sense of a landscape being cleansed of all its human resonance is evident in William Livingstone's poem '*Fios thun a Bhaird*', where he laments that 'Islay has lost her people, the sheep have emptied homes'.[47] Dr John MacLachlan's '*Dìreadh a-mach ri Beinn Shianta*'/'Climbing up towards Ben Shiant' is a poignant example of the desolation caused by landlord activity:

Dìreadh a-mach ri Beinn Shianta,	As I climb up towards Ben Shiant,
Gur cianail tha mo smuaintean,	my thoughts are filled with sadness;
A' faicinn na beinne 'na fàsach	Seeing the mountain as a wilderness,
'S i gun àiteach air a h-uachdar.	with no cultivation on its surface.
Seallltainn a-sìos thar a'bhealaich,	As I look down over the pass,
'S ann agamsa tha 'n sealladh fuaraidh.	what a chilling view I have!
'S lìonmhor bothan bochd gun àird air	So many poor cottages in disarray,
Air gach taobh 'nan làraich uaine,	in green ruins on each side,

---

44 Ross, *Russians of Ross-shire* (1854), p. 101. **45** See MacKenzie, *History of the Highland Clearances*. It is important to note that even when people remained in areas witnessing evictions, such as Suishnish in Skye, the impression given is of wholesale clearance. **46** Sorley MacLean described this poem as 'the most clear-headed and uncompromising comment on the situation in the Highlands that survives from the Gaelic poetry of the 18th century'. MacLean, *Ris a' bhruthaich* (1985), pp 54–5. **47** Translation in Thomson's *Gaelic poetry* (1974), pp 236–7. In much of the Clearance poetry the identity of the incoming 'stranger' oscillates between the 'English' and the 'Lowlander'. Whatever the target for attack, the sentiment remains that these 'foreign' people were introducing 'alien' ideas and values into the indigenous community.

Agus fàrdach tha gun mhullach	and houses without a roof,
Is 'na thulaich aig an fhuaran.	in heaps by the water-spring!
Far an robh 'n teine 's na pàisdean,	Where the fire and the children once were,
'S ann as àirde dh'fhàs an luachair.	that's where the rushes have grown tallest.
Far an cruinnicheadh na h-àrmainn,	Where the heroes used to gather,
Feuch a' chaora bhàn le h-uan ann.	behold the white sheep and her lamb there!
An Lighiche Iain MacLachlainn, c.1830.[48]	Dr John MacLachlan

MacLachlan's poem reflects the religious changes mentioned earlier, and closes with a grim reminder to the landlord that ignoring the Gaelic people's close association with the land will result in severe consequences on judgment day.

People or deer

Despite lacking the emotion of the first phase of sheep farms, the creation of deer estates for sporting purposes did generate passionate commentary from the mid-nineteenth century through to the period 1939–65. Although this phenomenon is understudied, it is no less important in terms of land-use, as the creation of the deer forests left an indelible mark on the Highlands.[49] The massive displacement of people between the 1840s and 1860s coincided with a new breed of landowner coming into the Highlands. These beneficiaries of industrialized Britain were eager to maximize their investment, and regarded the Highlands as an ideal setting for sporting estates. They did not have any vestiges of obligation or a sense of paternalism which some of the old landlords displayed during the worst excesses of the famine years.

To the Gael, the displacement of people for the purposes of sport was not only selfish but also indulgent. John Smith of Lewis provided his people with a bitter riposte to the 'snipes' in his popular poem '*Spiorad a' charthannais*'/'The spirit of kindliness':

Gun chuair iad fo na naosgaichean	They handed over to the snipe
An tìr a b' aoidheil sluagh;	the land of happy folk
Gun bhuin iad cho neo-dhaondachail	they dealt without humanity
Ri daoine bha cho suairc.	with people who were kind.
A chionn nach faodte 'm bàthadh,	Because they might not drown them
Chaidh an sgànradh thar a' chuain;	they dispersed them overseas;
Bu mhiosa na bruid Bhàbiloin	a thraldom worse than Babylon's
An càradh sin a fhuair.	was the plight they were in.
Iain Mac a' Ghobhainn, c.1874.[50]	John Smith.

Smith composed this poem shortly after the 'Bernera Riot' of 1874, which stemmed from grievances at the loss of grazing land to sporting estates in the Isle

---

48 Meek, *Tuath is tighearna*, pp 57–8, 192–3.   49 Hunter, 'Sheep and deer' (1973). For more detailed discussion of the politics of deer farming, see Orr, *Deer forests* (1982).   50 Translation in Thomson's, *Gaelic poetry*, pp 243–4.

of Lewis. The magnitude of the transformation in the Highlands was the cause of much concern and anger: 'these monstrous deer-forests have arisen out of the sheep-walks, into which large tracts of the mountain country [...] some three or four generations ago, have been violently converted; the transformation of sheep into deer, in preference to a human tenantry, having been effected' by economics or the 'antisocial principles of the commercial system' that the landlords having no compunction to ignore as they 'greedily seized on the large rent which the English or American deer-stalker was ready to pay for the free and unhindered range of the Bens'.[51] Once again, the perception among Highlanders was of the wanton misuse of Highland resources. It was especially hard to bear given the acceleration in the numbers of migrants.

The influx of 'sporting gentlemen' to the Highlands further highlighted the widening gap between people of different socio-economic backgrounds. John Stuart Blackie picked up on this point in the late nineteenth century. Moreover, he was unwilling to accept that the improvements to the infrastructure of the Highlands were for benign purposes given the continued penury which existed in certain areas:

> The occupation of these residenters, though only for a few months in the summer, no doubt may act beneficially in some cases to supply the want of the resident tacksmen, or small proprietors under the old kindly system; but it is not the Highlander proper that is benefited by these rusticating settlements so much as the rusticators themselves, who not unfrequently [sic] bring even their provisions with them from the large towns; and beyond paying rent for a month or two, contribute little to the prosperity of the district where they reside [...]. As for rusticating settlements in more remote quarters, the presence of a stranger with a gun and a game-bag is more likely to tend to the exclusion of the natives than to their preservation. All sorts of sportsmen, when they do not find, are very apt to create a solitude.[52]

Blackie was not only critical of the 'troops of Saxon tourists who spread themselves annually into the glens and over the Bens of old Caledonia', but also Highlanders who 'had begun to live like the Swiss, by making a show of their mountains and hanging on the skirts of the rich English Nimrods'. For him, and others, the end results for the 'real lifeblood of the people' was that their culture was regarded as 'destined to a hasty extinction' or 'painted all over with such a thick coat of Saxon whitewash that its distinctive features could no longer be recognized'.[53]

51 Blackie, *Scottish Highlands and the land laws*, p. 86. 52 Ibid., pp 228–9, 104. 53 Blackie,

By the 1880s, attitudes towards the 'sportsmen' and their indulgent practices were hardening. The insensitive activities of the American tycoon William Louis Winans, particularly his use of the courts to expand his sphere of influence and his lack of sporting etiquette, symbolized this new wealth in the Highlands.[54] Winans' harassment of a crofter who had allowed his pet lamb to stray off an unfenced road into his estate at Kintail helped to confirm his title as 'the most notorious lessee' in the Highlands.[55] Undoubtedly, the naked greed displayed in the pursuit of pleasure by the landed elite facilitated the spirit of resistance. The 1887 'Deer Park Raid' on Lady Matheson's Lewis estate had all the necessary elements for a heroic tale – deer being slaughtered, troops being deployed and the reading of the Riot Act. Three years earlier, the Napier commissioners were forewarned of impending trouble: 'Oh the deer! Oh the deer! Very backward regulations when deer would be the ruler and the sons of men starving without land to cultivate'.[56]

EMIGRATION

In reviewing the poetry of the Clearances for his 1938 paper, Sorley MacLean noted that 'in the Highlands of the 19th century, emigration of one kind or another was the phenomenon of phenomena'.[57] The trauma of emigration and a bewilderment at the powerful forces that lay behind the related process of clearance and removal meant that most nineteenth-century Gaelic poetry had a hopeless and depressing tone: 'Nostalgia is the most common sentiment in 19th-century Gaelic poetry, and there is a huge body of verse that says nothing explicitly about the Clearances, but that an emigrant's sadness pervades'.[58]

In his own later review of the songs of the resurgence, Donald Meek has also commented on the extent to which the recurring motif of nostalgia, inherent in what he terms the 'ceilidh-culture', overwhelmed and swamped almost everything else.[59] Within this 'ceilidh-culture' of the late nineteenth and twentieth centuries, the pre-eminent songs of Gaeldom were emigrant songs and through them a pervasive nostalgic representation of an idyll, a 'golden age' of a lost happiness, was an associated, endlessly recurring notion in the popular culture of the Gael. A second contrasting motif of suffering heightened the theme with its memory of the misery that mass emigration had entailed – the enforced boardings, the harrowing voyages, the harsh struggle for survival in a strange and

Language and literature of the Scottish Highlands (1876), pp 4–5. **54** For further information on the practices of deer estate owners in the Highlands, consult Orr's *Deer forests*, passim and pp 6–9 for a list and a map of deer forests in Scotland in 1884. **55** MacCombie Smith, *Men or deer in the Scottish glens* (1893), p. 16. **56** John and Farquar MacRae, Bundaloch, Napier Commission evidence, cited in Orr, *Deer forests*, p. ii. **57** MacLean, 'Poetry of the Clearances', p. 12. **58** Ibid., p. 64. **59** Meek, *Tuatha is tighearna*, p. 14.

hostile land. North America and Australia became the lands of 'Gaels beyond the sea' and this third motif of exile assumed a powerful association with the Scottish Highlands and Islands, not just in the *Gàidhealtachd*, but throughout Scotland and Victorian Britain. Finally, the diaspora of the Gaels was not only a product of overseas emigration. There was also a massive internal migration to the major cities of Scotland, particularly Glasgow.[60] This produced its own significant motif, the alienation of the Gael from the urban environment, the Gaels as an inherently peasant stock, whose only true and 'natural' home was in the repopulated islands and glens of the Highlands.

Nostalgia and idyll

John McCodrum's 'song to the fugitives' and the songs of Rob Donn came from the first wave of emigration when the tacksmen class, sensing their obsolescence, chose or felt compelled to seek a new life overseas.[61] It was this 'fever for emigration' which Boswell and Johnson so memorably described in their 1773 tour of the Hebrides, most notably and graphically on the Skye lands of Lord MacDonald: 'when the ship sailed from Portree for America, the people on shore were almost distracted when they saw their relations go off; they lay down on the ground and tumbled, and tore the grass with their teeth'.[62]

What has been described as 'undoubtedly the greatest of all emigrant songs', the popular '*A' choille ghraumach*', 'The gloomy forest', dates from this first phase of emigration, being composed by John MacLean, *Bàrd Thighearna Chola*, an emigrant from Tiree, in Pictou, Upper Canada, *c*.1820.[63] Perhaps the most powerful expression of 'the gnawing nostalgia' of the emigrant, however, occurs in the songs of *Iain MacMhurchaidh*, John MacRae, who emigrated from Kintail to North Carolina, *c*.1774.[64] In his song, *Gur muladach a tha mi*, 'Lonely am I', he looks back longingly to his happy days in Kintail:

Gur muladach a tha mi,	Lonely am I
'S mi 'n diugh gun aobhar gàire;	today without cause for laughter;
Cha b'ionnan 's mar a bha mi	It was not so
'S an àite bho thall ...[65]	in the land beyond [the sea] ...

---

60 The Gaelic settlements established overseas were important in facilitating later waves of emigration, especially after the 1820s when the fragility of the Highland economy was exposed and the mass movement of people began. For the reasons behind migration and the varied experience within the Highlands, consult Devine, *Clanship to crofter's war*; Bumsted, *People's clearance* (1982); Harper, *Adventurers & exiles* (2003). 61 MacCodrum's poem set out to commemorate the departure of the tacksmen class from North Uist in the 1770s. See MacLean, 'Poetry of the Clearances', pp 51–2. 62 Account given by a native of Skye, Mrs MacKinnon, to James Boswell of the migration of people in 1772. See Boswell, *Tour of the Hebrides* (1936), pp 242–3. Their account has become, in itself, the classic representation of this era of emigration. 63 MacDonnell, *Emigrant experience*, p. 17 and pp 68–79 for details of MacLean's career and other compositions. 64 The phrase is Margaret MacDonnell's. For details of Macrae's career and compositions, see ibid., pp 26–55. His songs and career were well known in his native land. 65 MacDonnell, *Emigrant experience*, pp 46–51.

It is even more poignant in his moving and popular song, *'S mi air fògradh bho fhoghair*, 'I have been a fugitive since autumn':

'S mi air fògradh bho fhoghair	I have been a fugitive since autumn,
Deanamh thaighean gun cheò unnta;	building huts with no smoke rising from them.
Tha mi sgìth dhe'n fhògar seo,	I am weary of this exile; ...
Thoir mo shoraidh le dùrachd	Bear my sincere greeting to the land
Gu'n dùthaich 's am bu chòir dhomh bhi	where I ought to be.
Thoir mo shoraidh Chinn t-Saìile	Bear my greeting to Kintail
Far am bi mànran 'us òranan;	where there is music and song.
A'n tric a bha mi mu'n bhuidheal	Often was I by the keg
Mar ri cuideachda shòlasaich	with pleasant company about me.
Cha b'e n' dram bha mi 'g iarraidh,	It was not the dram I sought
Ach na b' fhiach an cuid stòraidhean.	but their excellent stories.
Ceud soraidh le dùrachd	A hundred fond greetings
Gu Sguir-ùrain, 's math m' eòlas innt'.	to Sguir-ùrain, well do I know it.
'S tric a bha mi mu'n cuairt dhi	Often did I scout around it
Ag éisdeachd udlaich a' crònanaich.	listening to the stag bellowing,
A' bheinn ghorm tha ma coinneamh	and the blue mountain opposite it –
Leam bu shoillear an neòinean innt'.[66]	brilliant to me were its flowers.

Comparable songs and experiences from a wide range of areas all contributed to this overwhelming motif of nostalgia and its commensurate idyllic memory of the past. In comparison to subsequent forced emigrations, this was a 'voluntary' movement, albeit a reluctant one, in which emigration was seen as the lesser of two evils. It is this sense of the emigrant as a reluctant 'fugitive' that added an intensity to the enduring nostalgia.

The suffering of emigration

For a brief period in the early nineteenth century, although the people had been removed wholesale from the fertile lands now deemed to be more profitable if given over to sheep-farming, there was a reluctance on the part of landlords and government to encourage overseas emigration. The landowners of the west Highlands and Islands needed a tenantry available to work the highly profitable kelp industry. The government saw the Highlands as a valuable source of compliant military manpower. But when the kelp industry collapsed, the crops periodically failed and impoverishment and destitution prevailed, then the people of the Highlands became an essentially 'redundant population'.[67] It was also a population that was growing dramatically. Through the 1840s and 1850s, landlords found the solution in forced, mass emigration. As the owner of the Isle of Lewis, Sir James Matheson, put it: 'Redundancy of the population is notoriously the evil and emigration is the only effectual remedy'.[68]

Between 1851 and 1853, Matheson removed *c.*3,200 people from Lewis to Canada. Similar mass removals and forced emigrations occurred throughout the

---

66 Ibid., pp 50–5. 67 Devine, *Great Highland Famine*, passim. 68 Sir James Matheson in memorial to Lord John Russell, cited in MacLean & Carrell, *As an fhearann*, p. 13.

Highlands. Donald Ross, reporting on the evictions of Lord Macdonald's estates on Boreraig and Suishnish in Skye, captured the 'heart-rending' scenes with striking clarity. After noting how the evictions were planned for the daytime when the most of the men were away, Ross described how the 'women and children went about tearing their hair, and rending the very heavens with their cries. Mothers, with tender infants at the breast, could do nothing but look on, while their effects and their aged and infirm relations were cast out, and the doors locked in their faces!' The injustice of the actual clearance was compounded by the plight of the evictees:

> But alas! [T]he expulsion of the Highlanders is not carried on now by open or by honourable means. They are not expelled at sword-point, or slain on the spot for a refusal; but they are *quietly* elbowed out, or *starved* out. They *must* become emigrants, that a few *gentlemen* may live at home at ease; and if they do not choose to emigrate, they must die of want at home! A fearful alternative this! [Y]et it is realized to the very letter; and I fear that the chapters on *clearances* and *treatment of the poor* in the Highlands, will present an appalling record of injustice, inhumanity, and of shameful cruelty. The fact is, the extirpation of honest, peaceable and loyal subjects and the subsequent treatment of them, as was witnessed in Skye and Knoydart in the autumn of last year [1853], would form a blot on the pages of savage records.[69]

Moreover, emigration was inextricably linked with the suffering of those who were forced on board the emigrant ships, often chained and handcuffed, scenes which led to graphic and telling comparisons in the vivid accounts of witnesses:

> One morning, during the transporting season, we were suddenly awakened by the screams of a young female who had been recaptured in an adjoining house, she having escaped after her first capture. We all rushed to the door, and saw the broken-hearted creature, with dishevelled hair and swollen face, dragged away by two constables and a ground officer. Were you to see the racing and chasing of policemen, constables and ground officers, pursuing the outlawed natives, you would think, only for their colour, that you had been, by some miracle, transported to the banks of the Gambia, on the slave coast of Africa.[70]

Subsequent accounts of the appalling conditions endured on the voyage and the bitter reports back from disillusioned emigrants added to this intertwining of nostalgia for the past and the pain of the present.[71] A late nineteenth-century

---

69 Ross, *Real Scottish grievances* (1854), pp 6, 30. 70 Ibid. 71 Cameron, *Old and new Highlands and Hebrides* (1912), p. 22.

South Uist emigrant's song, *O mo dhùthaich, 's tu th'air m'aire*, 'O my country, I think of thee', still widely popular in the islands, perfectly captures this fusion of mixed emotions:

Tìr a' mhurain, tìr an eòrna,	Land of bent grass, land of barley,
Tìr 's am pailt a h-uile seòrsa,	Land where everything is plentiful,
Far am bi na gillean òga,	where young men
Gabhail òran 's 'g òl an leanna.	sing songs and drink ale.
Thig iad ugainn, carach, seòlta,	They come to us, deceitful and cunning,
Gus ar meallaidh far ar n-eòlais;	in order to entice us from our homes;
Molaidh iad dhuinn Manitòba,	they praise Manitoba to us,
Dùthaich fhuar gun ghual, gun mhòine [...].	a cold country without coal or peat [...].
Nam biodh agam fhìn do stòras,	If I had as much as two suits of clothes,
Dà dheis aodaich, paidhir bhrògan,	a pair of shoes
Agus m'fharadh bhith 'nam phòca,	and my fare in my pocket,
'S ann air Uibhist dheanainn seòladh.[72]	I would sail for Uist.

Emigration as exile

The eyewitness accounts, the campaigning journalists, and the pamphleteers ensured that this notion of exile became synonymous with the image of the Highlands and the Highlanders:

> The Collen [Cuillin] mountains were in sight for several hours of our passage; but when we rounded Ardnamurchan Point, the emigrants saw the sun for the last time glitter upon their splintered peaks, and one prolonged and dismal wail rose from all parts of the vessel; the fathers and mothers held up their infant children to take a last view of the mountains of their Fatherland which in a few minutes faded from their view forever.[73]

The same anguished sentiment entered the visual arts as in Tom Faed's famous painting *The last of the clan*. And while the scene depicted does not capture the squalor of passage, the despair of exile is apparent and is underlined in the poignancy of the text which accompanied the 1865 presentation:

> When the steamer had slowly backed out and John MacAlpine had thrown off the hauser, we began to feel that our once powerful clan was now represented by a feeble old man and his granddaughter who, together with some outlying kith and kin, myself among the number, owned not a single blade of grass in the glen that was once all our own.[74]

---

72 Shaw, *Folk songs & folklore of South Uist* (1977), pp 78–9. 73 Donald Ross' description from 13 November 1852, when 830 of the 'dispossessed' were put on board the *Hercules* bound for Adelaide, Australia. See Ross, *Real Scottish grievances*, p. 54. 74 Displayed in the Royal Academy in 1865. The sorrowful scenes were also present in the work of Alexander Fraser,

Gaelic song and oral tradition ensured that this notion of exile, dispersal and diaspora became firmly rooted in the popular consciousness of the Gael and the *Gàidhealtachd*.[75] The equation of the Highland experience with emigration and exile, however, also spread beyond Scotland and beyond Britain to touch all corners of the empire. Each of these exiled Gaelic settlers could give testimony to the power of the emotions of nostalgia, exile and loss evoked in the extraordinarily popular 'Canadian boat song':

> When the bold kindred, in time long vanished,
> Conquered the soil and fortified the keep,
> No seer foretold the children might be banished
> That a degenerate lord might boast his sheep.
> [...]
> And we in dreams behold the Hebrides.[76]

Alienation

Through the songs of emigration, the notion of *dhùthaich*, the 'homeland', became the dominant theme in nineteenth-century poetry. It was the 'homeland' as refracted through the eyes of the exile, but not all exiles were overseas. From the late eighteenth century onwards there was a growing migration of Gaels to the towns and cities of Scotland, particularly Glasgow. As will be discussed later, this internal diaspora to the cities of Scotland was of major significance in the development of a political resistance within the *Gàidhealtachd* in the late nineteenth and early twentieth centuries. The city Gaels also contributed to the notion that their enforced urbanization was 'unnatural' for the Gael and that the loss of the Highlanders from the Highlands was 'bleeding Scotland dry'.[77] Throughout the nineteenth century, the dispersal of the Gaels had been presented as a loss to the empire of its 'loyal' residual stock of 'sturdy Highlanders'. This portrayal of emigration as the loss of an essential human resource intensified in the turn of the century decades of high imperial military involvement. In the early twentieth century, as depopulation and internal out-migration to the cities increased, the contribution of the Highland regiments to the 1914–18 war fuelled further the debate on the future of the Highlands. Implicit in all the discussion, whether in government circles, the organs of Gaeldom, or Scotland's popular press, was the notion that Highland emigration

William Dyce and J.W. Nicol's 1883 canvas, *Lochaber no more*. See Moffat, 'Beyond the Highland landscape' (1986), pp 65–71, 8, 12. 75 It was evident in much of the testimony to the Napier Commission, see MacLean & Carrell, *As an fhearann*, p. 8; see also Craig, *Crofter's trail*. 76 Cited in MacDonnell, *Emigrant experience*, p. 50. This poem is sometimes attributed to John Galt, a Scottish emigrant to Canada in the late eighteenth century. Although Galt was not a Gael, the sentiments expressed in the song are typical of some of the more sentimental pieces from Scotland's Gaels and her diaspora. See Mackie, *Scottish verse* (1967). 77 For a discussion of Highland migration to the urban areas, see Withers' study, *Urban Highlanders* (1999).

and out-migration meant the loss of a valuable resource, a dependable 'peasant stock' from its 'natural' homeland of the Highlands.

RESISTANCE AND RESURGENCE

Within the collective memory of Gaeldom, the spirited response of the crofters in the 1880s is accorded great significance. The language itself – the 'Crofters' War', the 'Battle of the Braes', the 'Deer Park Raid' – reflects this and the period has entered popular Gaelic folklore as a symbol of resistance. To generations of future Gaels, the crofters' successes in the 1880s and 1890s would be the benchmark of future campaigns. This was certainly apparent in the core period between 1939 and 1965, when many hoped that the Highlands and their people would regain the importance and power which was so apparent earlier.

By partial and selective use of the past, images of the Highlander were projected to accord with the changing sense of collective identity. The period prior to the 1880s, though not erased from memory, is treated differently. The dominant view is that Highlanders were resigned to their situation and offered no determined and coordinated resistance against the socio-economic changes that enveloped them. To a degree, this view is justified. Earlier resistance was sporadic and lacked coordination and effective leadership. This lack of political focus was highlighted when the Highlands were compared to Ireland, as by Hugh Miller in 1846:

> They [the Irish] are buying guns and will be, by the bye, shooting magistrates and clegymen by the score: and parliament will in consequence do a great deal for them. But the poor Highlander will shoot no one [...] and so they will be left to perish unregarded in their hovels.[78]

Others also drew comparisons with Ireland, though not for divisive purposes. John Murdoch, culling from his own experiences there, urged Scotland's Gaels to recognize their common cause and work collectively to effect change. More than anyone, Murdoch helped to shake Highlanders from their torpor; to recognize that active resistance was more effective than passive acceptance. In realizing the maxim 'unity is strength', Murdoch argued that the Highlander should be the agent for change. It was also recognized, through the pan-Celticism of the 1870s, that political and social resistance needed to be accompanied by a rekindling of cultural pride. Murdoch was the pioneer, but others like John Stuart Blackie were key players in this resurgent Gaelic

---

78 Quoted in MacKenzie, *Hugh Miller* (1905), pp 190–1.

revivalism. The popular slogan *tir is teanga*/'land and language' emphasized the politicization of the language and the desire to recapture a sense of dignity and self-esteem. This fusion of Highlander and Gael reached its logical conclusion with the crofters' struggle of the 1880s. By championing events in the crofting communities of Skye and Lewis, and developing an effective Highland press and crofters' lobby, representatives from the Highlands were able to pressurize the Gladstone government into passing the Crofters' (Scotland) Act of 1886. Regarded as a symbolic victory for some and a milestone by others, this piece of legislation would come to dictate the dominant element within the Highlands – the land.

Resistance of the Highlander
From the 1870s onwards the spirit of resistance abroad in the Highlands was portrayed in a distinctive fashion. For internal and external audiences, the impression given was that the true Highlander was a Gael and a crofter.[79] This correlation can be detected in various sources of the time, and endured into the post-Second World War era. It was popularized by the land campaigner, socialist and Celtic nationalist, John Murdoch. By emphasizing the importance of unity, the concerns of the crofter are associated with the problems of the Highlands. In the first edition of *The Highlander*, 16 May 1873, Murdoch's editorial stated his case:

> We this day place in the hands of Highlanders a journal which they can call their own. This they do with the distinct view of stimulating them to develop their own industrial resources and of encouraging them to assert their nationality and maintain that position in the country to which their numbers, their traditions and their character entitle them.

Focusing on the root cause of the malaise in the Highlands – 'the vicious land system' – Murdoch sought to remove the disconsolate atmosphere which had hung over the region.[80] His early sojourn to Ireland confirmed his opinion that only radical reform of the land laws would resolve the plight of the Gael; both in Ireland and his native Highlands. His role as the 'messenger' for the Highlands resulted in an arduous campaign trail for Murdoch; in Scotland, Ireland and further afield.[81] In these forums, Murdoch listed the heinous crimes committed against the Highlander, and he never swayed from his conviction that the Gael should reclaim the land that was rightfully theirs: 'We lay it down as a

---

79 Moisley, 'Highlands and Islands: a crofting region?' (1962). 80 *The Highlander*, 24 May 1873; 12 July 1873. 81 See Hunter, 'Politics of Highland land reform' (1974) for further information on Murdoch's travels. See also Newby, *Ireland, radicalism and the Scottish Highlands* (2007) for wider considerations on the land question.

canon that if our people are to be prosperous, comfortable and independent, they must respect themselves, and they must set full value on what belongs to them'.[82] Murdoch was determined that the Highlanders should reclaim their identity, hence his involvement in setting up the Gaelic Society of Inverness in 1871. Restored to the capital of the Highlands, Murdoch argued that the society's interests should not just be confined to cultural matters.[83] Restricting its remit would render the organization useless in resisting the attacks on Gaeldom:

> the language and lore of the Highlanders being treated with despite has tended to crush their self-respect, and repress that self-reliance without which no people can advance. When a man was convinced that his language was a barbarism, his lore as filthy rags, and that the only good thing about him – his land – was, because of his general worthlessness, to go to a man of another race and tongue, what remained [...] that he should fight for?[84]

Murdoch's role in shaping external and internal perceptions of the changing nature of the 'Highland problem' is readily apparent in the output of the Highland Land Law Reform Association (HLLRA). Despite having a tortuous and brief history, the HLLRA was founded in 1883 to: 'unite Highlanders and their friends at home and abroad in endeavouring by constitutional means to obtain for the Highland people the right to live on their native soil under equitable conditions'.[85] The key inference of Murdoch's writing is clear: Highlanders shared a common identity. By collective action, focused on the land, Highlanders could make a conscious and active intervention in their destiny.

Tir is teanga: land and language

By drawing connections between the land and the language of the Gael, activists such as Murdoch revitalized the *Gàidhealtachd*. By politicizing the language, the endeavours of the land and language factions are seen to coalesce, and the membership of what has been coined 'the Gaelic movement' augmented.[86] The growing power of this lobby group is evident in the successful campaign to establish a chair of Celtic at Edinburgh University in 1872.[87] Central to this crusade was the 'professor of Greek and passionate Celticist', John Stuart Blackie.[88] Blackie lent authority to the Gaelic revival, a language he believed to

---

82 *The Highlander*, 6 June 1879. 83 In its first volume the role played by Murdoch is documented. He pleaded that 'the material interests of the Highlands' and the 'vindication of the rights and character of the Gaelic people' be uppermost in the minds of the society's members. See *TGSI*, 1 (1872), pp v, 1–3, 126–7. 84 This was Murdoch's submission to the Napier Commission. Cited in Hunter, 'The Gaelic connection' (1975), p. 183. 85 Cited in MacLean & Carrell, *As an fhearann*, p. 25. 86 Dewey, 'Celtic agrarian legislation and the Celtic revival' (1974). 87 For a more detailed discussion of the background, see Gillies, 'Century of Gaelic scholarship' (1989). 88 Hunter, *Crofting community*, p. 136. Hanham regards Blackie as the

be 'one of the oldest and least mongrel types of the great Aryan family of speech'.[89] His main contribution to this defining moment in Highland history was to convince the members of the existing Highland and Gaelic societies that ignoring the political dimension to events in the Highlands was misguided, even counter-productive. He chided them for taking a romanticized view of the Highland and its people. He told them to stop 'vapourizing about Ossian whom they have never read, and eulogizing Duncan Ban whom they did not sing [... and] buckle themselves to serious action in the practical world'.[90]

In calling on these Gaelic groups to embrace the struggle for land that was taking root in the north, Blackie had to capture the moral high ground and convince the vacillators that the resistance taking place in the Highlands was just. Thus, in his capacity as vice-president of the HLLRA, he sought to absolve the crofters from the accusation of lawlessness. Drawing on comparisons with the situation in Ireland, he argued that 'the highly stimulant recalcitration of a Kenmare or Killarney squatter' often compelled the government into taking remedial action. Accordingly, he believed that 'the lawbreakers in the Highlands were less to blame for recent disturbances than the lawmakers'.[91]

His address to the Perth Gaelic society in 1880 was typically forthright. He called on all Gaelic societies to have clear and consistent aims and a well-defined programme of action. This included compiling an annotated 'Book of the Clearances' in order to arrest 'the artificial extension of deer forests' and convince the British public of the need for an overhaul of the existing land laws. Blackie called for greater use of Gaelic in schools and urged Highland communities to fund their young scholars through university. By emphasizing the correlation between the vitality of the language and the Gaelic communities in the Highlands, Blackie's ultimate vision for the Highlands was a region with a 'resident middle class' and the 'maintenance of a race of genuine Highlanders in the Highlands'.[92]

The rejuvenation of Gaelic culture undoubtedly gave some self-respect back to the Gael. Again, the poetry reflects this:

Ach ma sinn bochd, gun d'fhuaireas	Although we are poor, we were found
Sinn na b' uaisle na iad fhein ...	to be noble compared with them ...
'Croitearan Leodhais'	'The Lewis Crofters'
Murchadh MacLeoid, Bru, Barbhas.[93]	Murdo MacLeod, Bru, Barvas.

main figure uniting the disparate elements of the 'Gaelic movement'. See Hanham, 'Highland discontent' (1969), p. 38.   **89** Blackie, *Language and literature*, p. 23.   **90** Blackie, *Gaelic societies* (1880), p. 4. Despite these comments, Blackie himself was often charged with being a 'romantic' when it came to matters pertaining to the Highlands.   **91** Blackie, *Scottish Highlanders and the land laws*, pp 192–202.   **92** Blackie, *Gaelic Societies*, pp 15, 16–19. Blackie was also concerned that the rich repository of Gaelic folklore should be preserved and he called on the Gaelic societies to appoint collectors to record the material before it was lost forever.   **93** This poem was composed during the General Election of 1885, and then published in two sections, the first appeared on 17 April 1886 in the *Oban Times*, the second appeared in the same paper on 24

Gaels always had a profound sense of their own history, but the politicization of the language imbued in them a feeling that the 1880s was a key moment in defining their future:

'S i mo shoraidh le dùrachd a dhùthaich nam beann	It is my sincere desire for the land of the mountains
Gun soirbhich gach cùis leo bhon dhùisgeadh a clann;	that its children may succeed now that they have been roused;
Tha eachdraidh toirt cunntais, cha mhùchar a cainnt,	history, whose evidence speaks for itself, indicates
Gur gaisgeil gu'n cùl iad an àm rùsgadh nan lann.	that they are heroes to the core when they unsheath their swords.
'Oran mu Chor nan Croitearan' Domhnall MacFhionghain, Glaschu.[94]	'Song on the Crofters' Plight' Donald MacKinnon, Glasgow.

The politicization of the Gaelic language was certainly apparent to the 'establishment' in the Highlands. To derisive heckling from the floor at a meeting of the Gaelic Society of Inverness in January 1884, the Earl of Dunmore gave his own thoughts on the [mis]use of Gaelic:

> The Gaelic language has never been put to a more unworthy and unpatriotic or wicked use than when it was employed, not as a means of tranquilizing the poor people by reasoning with them in a spirit of pacification and conciliation in their own tongue, but on the contrary, in urging them to rebellion and crime.[95]

This plea for a return to the days when Gaelic was used to instruct the people on Godliness, 'improvement' and progress was, in view of the events of the time, heavily discordant.

The crofters' struggle

Bratach nan croitearan tapaidh,	The banner of the brave crofters,
nach robh gealtach ga cur suas,	who were not afraid to raise it aloft,
Slàn don làimh a dheilbh sa bheairt i –	health to the hand that wove it in the loom –
'S gur tiugh, gasda chaidh a luadh.	it was waulked into a fine, thick cloth.
'S e suaicheantas 'Ceist an Fhearainn' –	Its motto is 'The Land Question' –
Thigibh 's leanaibh i gu cruaidh [...].	come and follow it with firm resolve [...].
'Bratach nan Croitearan' Domhnall MacDhomhnaill, Grianaig. 1885.[96]	'The Crofters' Banner' Donald MacDonald, Greenock.

April 1886. For the translation, see Meek, *Tuath is tighearna*, pp 244–7. **94** Original published in the *Oban Times*, 31 Jan. 1885. Translation in Meek, *Tuath is tighearna*, pp 241–2. **95** The words of the earl of Dunmore addressing the Gaelic Society of Inverness in 1884. Needless to say, his talk was greeted with derision and shouts of 'Rubbish!' See MacLean & Carrell, *As an fhearran*, p. 25. **96** Published in the *Oban Times*, 10 Oct. 1885, translated in Meek, *Tuath is tighearna*, p. 243.

The 'Crofters' Banner' was a powerful symbol during the turbulent events of the 'Crofters' War' of 1882–6.[97] It indicated the way in which the Highlands were being mobilized around the image of the crofter. The 'Battle of the Braes' on Skye in April 1882 entered into Gaelic folklore as the essence of the crofters' struggle. External interpretations of this encounter were largely shaped by newspaper coverage; it emphasized the sense of conflict over the question of land. Alexander Gow's eyewitness account reads like a military despatch:

> The crofters seemed to have become more infuriated by the loss of their position, and rushing along the shoulder of the hill prepared to attack once more. This was the final struggle. In other attacks the police used truncheons freely. But at this point they retaliated with both truncheons and stones. The consequences were very serious indeed.[98]

The escalation in the fight for land was indicative that collective action would bring results. The setting up of the Napier Commission in 1884 to inquire into the conditions of the crofters was a sign that the government would listen to a concerted voice. There was a sense of optimism in the Highlands, a sense that '[T]he landlords are on their knees'.[99] This resurgent attitude was bolstered by a belief that, with the successful election of four crofter MPs in 1885, remedial action would be imminent: 'The enemy have left the spoils and fled before the conquering hosts of land law reform. From the Mull of Kintyre to the Butt of Lewis the land is before us'.[1]

The successful passage of the Crofters' Act of 1886 was a vindication for those who had campaigned for collective action to effect change.[2] By bringing in the political dimension, the crofting lobby was now a factor in Scottish political culture.[3] For outsiders, Highland politics became synonymous with crofting politics. Within the region, the bards continued to act as the medium of expression and interpretation. *Màiri Mhòr nan Oran* (Mary MacPherson), the voice of the crofters' struggle, captured the sense of regeneration in her popular song, *Eilean a' Cheo*':

Cuimhnichibh ur cruadal,	Remember your hardihood,
Is cumaibh suas ur sròl;	And keep your flag flying;
Gun téid an roth mun cuairt duibh,	The wheel will turn for you
Le neart is cruas nan dòrn [...].[4]	by the strength and hardness of your fists [...].

97 MacPhail, *Crofters' war* (1989). **98** Gow's despatch was subsequently reprinted in Alexander MacKenzie's *The history of the Highland Clearances* (1883 ed.), pp 427–33. **99** *Oban Times*, 24 Jan. 1885. For information on how the landlords viewed these changes in the Highlands, see Cameron, 'Political influence of Highland landowners' (1994). **1** *Oban Times*, 12 Dec. 1885. **2** MacPhail, *Crofters' war*; Cameron, *Land for the people*. **3** Grigor, *Mightier than a Lord* (1979). For a discussion of the links between the Highlands, Glasgow and the early labour movement, see Kellas, 'Highland migration to Glasgow' (1966). **4** The poem continues:

Despite the concession of the Crofters' Act, there was a feeling in the Highlands that more needed to be done in order to resolve the 'land question'. In December 1887, the Lewis correspondent of the *Oban Times* wrote that

> The crofters' agitation has come to an end. It is the cottars' turn now [...]. The cottars not only demand the restoration of park [...] but all the other lands under sheep and deer, with compensation for the loss suffered by themselves and their fathers through the conduct of the evictors who ruined them and left them landless in pauperism.[5]

As in Ireland, the government responded by establishing the Congested Districts Board to address the problem of land hunger in the Highlands, particularly the western seaboard.[6] These partial successes demonstrated that the nature of the 'Highland problem' was more complex than land reform.[7] By 1914, there was a realization in certain quarters that crofting alone would not answer the economic and social problems; nor would it maintain the culture of the Gael. Members of the 'Gaelic movement' now appreciated that securing the land did not necessarily mean securing the culture.

'your cows will be on the fields,/every farmer a man of means,/and the English banished/ from the green Isle of the Mist'. Translated in Meek, 'Poets of land agitation', p. 365.   5 *Oban Times*, 17 Dec. 1887.   6 Mather, 'Congested Districts Board' (1986); Mather, 'Government agencies and land development' (1988).   7 Cameron, *Land for the people*; Leneman, *Land fit for heroes* (1989).

3

The idea of Highland culture, 1745–1939

> Every one who numbers a real Highlander among his friends knows that he inherits a number of qualities which mark him off from ordinary men. He is quick to take offence and he is a fighter. He is as punctilious in matters of honour as an Italian nobleman. Personal loyalty is a tradition with him. So is whisky. He loves to arrange, often on the flimsiest pretext, occasions for convivial celebration, a relic perhaps of old times when men, separated by mountain and flood, would meet together and pledge themselves in strong drink. He is supposed to be dour and mean. As a matter of fact contact with the world softens him and often induces the generosity, or the manners of an extremist.
>
> H.V. Morton, *In search of Scotland* (1929)

> One can well ask, does the romantic idea, understood in its true definition, have anything to do with glorification of Ossian and the acceptance of Balmoralism, with its panoply of Highland games, Highland meetings and grand shooting expeditions and processions? Is the temporary enthusiasm for Scottish nationalism more real than the faked Celtic imagery of the early romantics or the musings of Fiona MacLeod? Are the Songs of the Hebrides closer in content and in expression to the Highland spirit than the vivid imagery of Hugh MacDiarmid?
>
> Hugh Quigley, *The Highlands of Scotland* (1936)

The Highlands and Islands of Scotland is a place both 'real' and 'unreal'.[1] It is 'real' in the sense that it delineates the geographical space of the last remnants of an ancient or traditional pastoral way of life. Yet it is 'unreal' because the vitality and importance of this culture are so often lost in an idealized or romantic perception of the scenery, the customs and the music which bears little relation to daily life, as is evident in the extract from Morton's book. The roots of this mythical portrayal of the Highlands and its people lie in the defeat of the

---

[1] Womack argues: '[W]e know that the Highlands of Scotland are romantic. Bens and glens, the lone shieling in the misty island, purple heather, kilted clansmen, battles long ago, an ancient and beautiful language, claymores and bagpipes and Bonny Prince Charlie – we all know that, and we also know that it's not real'. See Womack, *Improvement and romance* (1989), p. 1.

Jacobites at Culloden in 1746 and the proscriptive legislation which followed. But the reality of these events has subsequently become hidden in the invention of a mythic tradition.

The English author Hugh Quigley referred to painters, poets, novelists and travel writers who had created the external image of the Highlands. From his external perspective, he referenced sources familiar to his audience. The pan-British readership of Quigley's popular contribution to Highland literature may not have fully shared his familiarity with the Scottish painters whose work he cited, but they would have been familiar with the reference to MacPherson's Ossian, Sir Walter Scott, Fiona MacLeod and the 'Celtic twilight', Hugh MacDiarmid, Scottish nationalism and the Scottish Renaissance. When he introduced *The Highlands of Scotland* in the new Batsford 'Faces of Britain' series, Quigley presented the Highlands through a cultural prism. This was the outsider's view – the external, and externalized, perception; the Highlands as an idea as much as a place. The social and economic forces outlined in the previous chapter paralleled the reconstructing of the modern Highlands as a cultural creation.

The idea of the Highlands has been long in the making, with particular moments proving to be momentous. The Romantics of the late eighteenth and early nineteenth centuries presented a sanitized version of events which, particularly in the case of the Gael, fascinated the educated classes of Europe. The European interest in the *Gàidhealtachd* and the process of 'Invention' originated from Macpherson's 'discovery' of the legendary warrior Ossian, despite the scepticism as to the text's veracity among some intellectuals.[2] This partial and selective appropriation of 'things Highlands' of course owed an enormous debt to Sir Walter Scott and other romantics. As industrialization made it increasingly difficult to distinguish between the Lowlands and industrial and urban areas elsewhere, so the symbols and imagery of the Highlands came to be appropriated to maintain a distinct Scottish identity.[3] Even though the *Gàidhealtachd* became a 'theme park' for curious intellectuals, with its own recognizable tourist trail taking in Loch Lomond, Ben Nevis and Fingal's Cave, this unprecedented degree of interest did little to stem the tide of 'noble savages' out of the region. That the Highlander could now be glorified proved in a very telling way that the 'pacification' of the Highlands and Islands following the Battle of Culloden was now complete. Indeed, when the Gaels became further appropriated by the British state through the establishment of Highland regiments, the fighting prowess of the Highlander and their quaint costumes and music became a cause

2 Ossian was the son of Fionn MacChumail, the legendary Celtic warrior. Tales, poems and songs were dedicated to the Ossianic saga among the Gaelic peoples of Ireland and Scotland. James MacPherson claimed to have found fragments of this ancient Ossianic poetry. See Stafford, *Sublime savage*. 3 See Chapman, *Gaelic vision* (1978); McCrone, *Understanding Scotland* (2000); Harvie, *Scotland and nationalism* (2004).

for British pride. Thus, the external perceptions of the Highlands underwent subtle but important changes during the nineteenth century.

It is the emergence of this 'invented' tradition that forms the basis of this chapter. A startling transformation in external attitudes towards the *Gàidhealtachd* was at the centre of the invention or reinvention of the region in question. So it is that the concept of 'invention' is taken as a recurrent theme throughout this chapter. Shifting notions of the Highlands and Islands of Scotland are considered in this historical dimension. The concepts of 'Balmorality and Empire' and 'Celtic twilightism' are analyzed in particular detail.[4] It is important to remember that sentimental, extraneous images continue to have enormous implications for the region and its inhabitants. This was consistently highlighted in the decades after the Second World War when cinematic portrayals of mythical Highland villages, valiant imperial warriors, noble savages, and canny islanders would continue the false and external representations of Highland and Gaelic culture. This mixture of romantic imagery and literary representation coloured perceptions of the Highlands, both in negative and positive terms. In the first half of the twentieth century, a more sober socio-economic perspective was encouraged by the growth of state intervention and the recognition that no amount of the sentimental yearning could hide the fact that the future of the region lay outside the traditional way of life. This later appreciation of the Highlands and Islands is considered towards the end of this chapter, under the heading 'demoralization and decline'.

INVENTING THE HIGHLANDS

> The Duke of Cumberland's brutalities founded our modern attitude to the Highlands as surely as Nero's extermination of the Christians created the saints. After nearly half a century of suppression the Highlander was seen through a revulsion of feeling as a high-minded martyr; and it was only necessary for the wizard of Abbotsford to fling a sentimental plaid over his wronged person for the whole country to flock north in belated sympathy.
>
> H.V. Morton, *In search of Scotland* (1929)

Central to the 'invention' of the Highlands and its people were James MacPherson's (1736–96) 'discovery' of the legendary saga of Ossian in the 1760s and Sir Walter Scott's historical novels where issues relating to the Highlands and Gaelic culture featured strongly.[5] But, before the combined efforts of

---

4 The extent to which the Gael was a willing and active participant in the discrete yet interlinked phases of 'Balmorality', 'Empire' and 'Celtic twilightism' has received limited academic attention. These issues were discussed by Burnett, 'Colonialism, complicity and the Gael' (2000).

MacPherson and Scott to 'rehabilitate' the Gael took root in the minds of ordinary people beyond the region, the dominant perception of the Highlands was of a lawless, ungodly and uncivilized region. As Morton demonstrated, the creative process produced, in time, a re-presentation of the Highlands in which the people and their resources became eulogized and exploited by a largely external audience. But before that the process of invention could develop, the Highlands had to be 'pacified'.

The threat posed by the Jacobite Rising of 1745, added to the manner in which it was portrayed, only confirmed southern prejudice.[6] After Culloden, it was recognized that in order to manage the Highlands, the region had to be defined. Once again the Highlands were considered a 'problem' as the resultant proscriptive legislation, the Annexing Act (1752),[7] demonstrated with its stated objectives of

> civilizing the inhabitants ... [and] ... the promoting amongst them [of] the Protestant religion, good government, industry and manufactures and the principles of duty and loyalty to his majesty, his heirs and successors and to no other use and purpose whatsoever.[8]

But, the heavy-handed treatment of the Gaels also demonstrated the lack of knowledge of the region and its people; recognized by Samuel Johnson in his 1773 tour. This acknowledgment that the Highlands were, by and large, an unknown entity would continue to be made right through to the twentieth century. Johnson, and the growing band of other visitors, was drawn to the region after the 'discovery' of fragments of ancient Ossianic poetry by James MacPherson.[9] The significance and legacy of the 'Ossian phenomenon' would demonstrate that, more often than not, the image of the Highlander was as important as the reality.

It is difficult to convey the enormity of the Ossian phenomenon. The 'cult of Ossian' pervaded all externally conceived aspects of Highland culture.[10] It seemed to confirm the existence of the noble savage, and the region offered a

---

5 However, Withers argues that the adverse commentary surrounding the 1745 Rebellion was only a confirmation of prejudice which already existed; thus, the earlier period was of seminal importance in 'creating' the Highlands. He believes that the background to the modern fascination with the Highlands derives from the cultural retreat of the Gaels to a region roughly coterminous with the highland zone. See Withers, *Gaelic in Scotland* (1984), pp 16–27. 6 For others, the 1745–6 Rising was 'central to the modernizing narrative of Anglo-British history'. See Kidd, *Subverting Scotland's past* (1993), pp 20–1; Pittock, *Myth of the Jacobite clans* (1995), pp 1–18; Clyde, *Rebel to hero* (1995), pp 181, 3–8. 7 Clyde, *Rebel to hero*, pp 11–17, 49–97; MacInnes, *Clanship*, pp 188–247. 8 Cited in Womack, *Improvement and romance*, p. 23. 9 For the external and sceptical perspective, see Trevor-Roper's 'The invention of tradition' (1983). For a corrective, consult Thomson, *Gaelic sources of MacPherson's Ossian* (1952). For a review of the literature, see Gaskill (ed.), *Ossian revisited* (1991). 10 The extent to which the Ossianic debacle shaped internal perceptions of Gaelic culture is a moot point.

plentiful source for inspiration, and a root cause of the Highlands' reimagining. Scotland's leading position in the Enlightenment, and its prominence among European Romanticism, encouraged a fascination with the Highlands. Scottish philosophers, convinced that Britain stood at the dawn of a new capitalist era, looked to the Highlands, 'the Scottish past on the doorstep', for instructive reasons for the progress of humanity.[11] The Highlands were a useful human laboratory for intellectuals reflecting on the new political economy and the process of social development. Therefore, the Highlands became 'the Other'; an instrument in a broader theoretical and ideological experiment; proof of the superiority of other parts of Scotland and Britain. The implications of this divisive conceptualization go to the core of the 'Highland problem'.[12]

As a result of this attitude of mind, policy-makers adopted a 'top-down' approach, importing into the region various elements which had allowed for the transformation of the rest of Britain. By associating the Gaels with an ancient mode of existence, one with barbarous intentions, it became necessary to instil a different value system, more in keeping with the emergent political philosophy:

> That spirit of industry which begins to take place among them, together with a more free and liberal education, will soon, it is to be hoped, polish their manners, take of the rust of barbarity, sloth and ignorance, and convert the uncouth savage into an industrious and useful member of society.[13]

Central to the whole process of 'improvement' was the determination to impart Godly virtues through religious instruction and education in the English language.[14] Despite the 'civilizing' of the Gael, the stereotype of the indolent Highlander would prove difficult to eradicate:

> He [the Highlander] is, like all Celts, a preordained exile, and exile is necessary for him unless he is to stagnate. There is something in the environment of the Highlands and also Ireland which saps the initiative and fosters the natural laziness of the Celt, so that if you want to see the Highlander and the Irishman at their best you must seek them in London or New York.[15]

---

11 See Withers, 'Historical creation', p. 147; Chapman, *Gaelic vision*, p. 19.   12 Womack (*Improvement and romance*, pp 166–7) argues that the oppositional relationship which the Highlands had with the rest of Britain reflected the needs of emergent capitalism. It provided an example of '*intrastate* peripheralization – a domestic "underdeveloped country"' in a subordinate relationship with the core.   13 *Monthly Review*, 11 (1754), 343; cited in ibid., p. 4.   14 To see how this affected the Gaelic language, see Durkacz, *Decline of the Celtic languages* (1983).   15 Morton, *In search of Scotland*, p. 122.

This notion that the physical environment of the Highlands debilitated its inhabitants would be subject to alteration in the future, but the association between the Highlander and the environment was a result of the interest in the landscape of the region generated by the controversy surrounding the Ossianic poetry.

Ossian had given the Highlanders a romantic edge, a spiritualism which would be drawn upon many times in the future. It was testament to the power of the cult of Ossian that it could be used by those imbued with the rational philosophy of the Enlightenment to impart 'improvement' rhetoric, while simultaneously inspiring those who disagreed with the strictures of the period. Whatever the rationale behind outsiders' interventions in the Highlands, those who accepted the myths of the Highlands and disseminated their own romanticized versions of the *Gàidhealtachd* presented serious problems for inhabitants of the region. This drastic and damaging mismatch in the perceptions of visitors and the underlying reality as experienced by the population of the Highlands and Islands was readily apparent in the growth of tourism. Again, the influence of Ossian is evident:

> the characteristic Ossianic vagueness, the mist on the mountains, the wild landscape under the uncertain moon, the undefined longings of the slackly characterized heroes of Fingal ... had certainly contributed much to the mental habit of the generation ... And from that day to this they have formed a great part of the meaning which readers and critics who did not know the Celtic languages have attached to the word 'Celtic'.[16]

The legacy of Ossian helped to focus peoples' attention on the Highlands as a tourist destination. Through this process of invention, the Highlands became adorned with concepts of the sublime and the picturesque, replacing the previous view that the Highlands were barren and displeasing.[17] Although disputing the authenticity of MacPherson's poetry, Hugh Blair nevertheless argued that its melodramatic passages were attuned to the rugged landscape of the Scottish Highlands. People now visited the region in pursuit of a landscape associated with Ossian, but they also went indiscriminately to find habitat and features which would inspire and terrify them.

It was the physical landscape, more than the people themselves which provided inspiration, and MacPherson's Ossian had fired the imagination. When the people were referred to it was usually in a contemptuous manner.

---

[16] R. Flower, 'Byron and Ossian', University College, Nottingham (1928), p. 6, cited in Chapman, *Gaelic vision*, p. 44. [17] See Smout, 'Tours in the Scottish Highlands' (1983), p. 102 and passim for examples of some of the key texts.

Dorothy Wordsworth remembered a Gael, 'half-articulate', 'hooting from the field close to us':

> His appearance was in the highest degree moving to the imagination: mists were on the hillsides, darkness shutting in upon the huge avenue of mountains, torrents roaring, no house in sight to which the child might belong; his dress, cry and appearance all different from anything we had been accustomed to. It was a text, as William has since observed to me, containing in itself the whole history of the Highlander's life – his melancholy, his simplicity, his poverty, his superstition, and above all, that visionariness which results from a communion with the unworldliness of nature.[18]

These early visitors emphasized, albeit indirectly, the importance of interpreting the scenery. The composition of the landscape needed to be of a certain type; viewed in a particular way, and carrying past associations with it. This combination, especially the historical dimension, would retain a powerful hold on Victorian travellers.

One of the more benign consequences of the interest in Highland and Gaelic culture emanating from the Ossianic controversy was the establishment of organizations among the elite of the Gaelic diaspora. The Highland Society of London was formed in 1778, initially for an entirely Gaelic-speaking membership, but the harsh realities of anglicization ensured that this noble aim was soon altered to allow for the inclusion of English-speaking Highland descendants. As with their counterpart in Edinburgh, formed in 1784, they investigated the authenticity of MacPherson's Ossian, which led to a more general interest in preserving key Gaelic documents, most notably the *Book of the Dean of Lismore*. Their patronage and sponsoring of 'ancient' Highland pursuits such as piping and Highland games remains to this day. There was a deep irony in such unedifying involvement, for many of these patrician figures were instrumental in dismantling Gaelic culture by other means.

The 'Great improvers' saw themselves as the new leaders of the Highland community. They were convinced that *their* actions were the most sensible and beneficial for the region and its inhabitants; indeed they felt morally obliged to usher in these changes. Their perceptions of the transforming Highlands were shaped, not by the Gaelic commentaries contained in poetry and song, but by the fall-out from Ossian and the literature of Scott and his followers. Given their prominent position in the Highlands and their close association with government-sponsored agencies, their role was crucial. But their perception of the inhabitants of the Highlands was not always a positive one, as indicated by these comments from Sir George MacKenzie of Coul:

18 Wordsworth, *Recollections of a tour* (1874), p. 116.

They live in the midst of smoke and filth; that is their choice. Whenever farms have been laid out on a proper scale, and are occupied by substantial and well-educated men, we find the farmhouses and offices handsome and commodious [...]. The present race of Highland tenants will yet find themselves happier and more comfortable in the capacity of servants to substantial tenants than in their present situation.[19]

These sentiments, written in 1813 by a noted Highland gentleman, were backed up by a growing number of visitors to the region. These 'tourists' came to the Highlands to enjoy its finest attribute – the physical landscape. Their itineraries, and expectations, were based largely on the writings of Sir Walter Scott, the 'wizard of the north'.

Scott's role in furthering the acceptance of the Gael cannot be overstated; and indeed his influence in projecting a particular image of Scotland stretched far beyond the shores of Britain. Along with his historical novels, which were written for mass consumption, Scott founded a number of historical clubs, some of which did produce genuine research which remain standard primary texts of pre-1707 Scotland. Scott was also actively involved in fostering interest in Highland culture, society and landscape through his association with the various Highland societies. Indeed, he acted as an unofficial patron to the Highland clubs and organizations that were being established on the back of an increasing interest in Highland culture, including the less authentic or genuine elements. But Scott's most obvious legacy was to indirectly promote the growth of tourism to the Highlands, as recognized by the Edinburgh publisher Robert Caddell.[20]

Some of the 'strangers', attracted to the region by Scott's literary genius, wrote telling commentaries on various aspects of life in the Highlands and Islands. Some of these early visitors were not fully conditioned into what elements of the host culture were meant to give pleasure. Hearing that 'a celebrated *Piper*' was in the village, and not having heard 'the instrument in its native country, that is to say, the mountains', the guide accompanying Necker was sent to 'invite this Orpheus of the North to entertain us with the harmonious sounds of his *bag-pipe*'. On the signal of the visitors,

> there issued sounds capable of deafening the most intrepid amateur of this wild instrument [...]. The bagpipe made such a noise that it was impossible, not only to hear each other, but even to hear an unfortunate drunkard who burst open the door in order, notwithstanding all we could do, to join the party. This animated dance, the singular steps

[19] MacKenzie, *Ross and Cromarty* (1810), pp 73–4. [20] Lockhart, *Life of Sir Walter Scott* (1898), p. 256. For further details on Scott's importance to the development of tourism in the Highlands, see Smout, 'Tours in the Scottish Highlands'.

of our guide, the lengthened mien of the Piper seated gravely in a corner of the room, formed a grotesque picture.[21]

Many of these early travellers tended to be of a scientific, artistic or literary type, and, accordingly, they visited the Highlands and Islands with a specific purpose in mind. However, there was also an increasing number of people who came to the region more out of curiosity than anything else. A flowering of guide books in the early nineteenth century attests to the expansion of tourism. Many were inspired by Scott's portrayal of the Highlands as a place, but the development of a mass tourist market had to wait until the railways made the region more accessible.

As well as fulfilling the role of publicist for the Highlands, Scott's most significant contribution to the 'invention' of the Highlander came when he and David Stewart of Garth orchestrated the splendid spectacle of George IV's visit to Edinburgh in 1822. This event marked the 'institutionalization' of the mythical Gael, unleashing forces which still have power today.[22] For Scott, the visit was an opportunity for a double act of reconciliation: on the one hand, between Highlanders and Lowlanders; and, on the other, between Scots and the monarchy. This theme of reconciling differences in fact runs through many of Scott's best literary works, not least *Waverley* (1814), which focused on the tensions generated by the Jacobite Rising of 1745-6. The royal visit was a huge spectacle, with the Highlanders, who were bedecked in 'their' respective tartans, recreating the Jacobites' famous entry into Edinburgh in 1745.[23] This time, however, by participating in a pageant that was loyal to a monarch – who was in any case present as a guest of honour – the Highlanders confirmed their fealty to the king. The whole escapade was eagerly supported by Highland chiefs and Lowland gentry. The former were keen to impress their southern nationals, while the latter were desperate to maintain a *Scottish* national image, an identity which was being sucked into a wider British identity. Nevertheless, a vital act of rehabilitation had been undertaken in breathtaking fashion.

This association between Scottish national identity, and later Scottish nationalism, with the Highlands and Gaelic culture burdens both elements because of its partial, enforced and often mythical status. Certainly eighteenth-century Scotland had a confused national identity, havering between the Scots' acceptance of their role as North Britons in the newly formed state, or as Caledonians, proud of their ancient, if troubled past.[24] This reflects the tensions inherent in modernization and nation-building, further complicated by the Union with

21 Necker, *Travels in Scotland* (1821), p. 69.   22 See Clyde, *Rebel to hero*, pp 185–6. The visit of George IV, along with Scott's historical novels geared for the mass market, have been charged with unleashing 'the excesses of a new ersatz, tartan version of Scottishness'. See Lynch, 'Scottish culture' (1993), p. 20.   23 Donald MacLeod (*Gloomy memories*, p. 22) commented on the bedraggled state of the Sutherland representatives to this pageant.   24 For a discussion of

England. For example, critics of Scotland and its politicians frequently caricatured the Scots as kilted savages, uncouth in manners.[25] This stimulated some Lowlanders to spurn and denigrate the Highlands and its people.[26] However, such was the complexity of the situation that others took to championing the cause of their fellow Scots, as with the response to attacks on the authenticity of Ossian.[27] But the role of the Highlands in the projection of Scotland is somewhat ironic given that the growing importance of that northern region was in inverse proportion to its diminishing relative socio-economic value to Scottish life: in other words, as more people moved to the industrial and urban Central Belt, the *Gàidhealtachd* became symbolically more important to Scottish identity.

Scott's desire to heal fissures within Scottish society led to his revision of perceptions of the Jacobite Rebellion of 1745 within Britain. Following Charles Edward Stuart's death in 1788, the cult of 'Bonnie Prince Charlie' took root, with popular songs being revived and reworked, and new additions being composed. The impression gained from narratives of this event was that the defeat of the Jacobites at Culloden heralded the passing of the old Gaelic way of life. Scott joined with those who felt compelled to absolve the Gaels of the main blame, reserving their displeasure for the Clan system, the Gaelic language and culture, the Catholic religion and the Clan Chiefs.[28] In order to conform to the developing Anglo-British form of nationalism, the Rising was portrayed as a futile gesture by a dissident Highland faction. Thus, both the nationalist aspect and the extent of middle class support for the Jacobites were deliberately downplayed. In presenting the '45 in these terms, Whig polemicists argued that the Gaels' misguided loyalty could be used to the advantage of the British Empire. These sentiments echoed down the years, with W. Blaikie Murdoch's *The spirit of Jacobite loyalty* (1907) notably subtitled, *an essay towards a better understanding of 'the Forty-five'*. The author argued that 'it is not sufficient merely to show that the clansmen rose as a matter of duty; it is necessary to show why loyalty was part of their creed'.[29] Along with this rewriting of Jacobitism and against the backdrop of the Ossianic fascination, Highlanders were now burdened with the tartan mania which followed George IV's visit to Edinburgh. It made for sardonic commentary on the Gael. The words of Sir John Carr (1809) are typical of the genre:

> Feminine delicacy has been sufficiently accustomed [...] even in the south, to contemplate the kilt, or short petticoat, of the Highlander without a shock, and I am therefore heartily glad that he is restored to

the competing identities of this period, see Finlay, 'Caledonia or North Britain' (1998). 25 Colley, *Britons* (1992), pp 105–17; Womack, *Improvement and romance*, pp 4–22. 26 Clyde (*Rebel to hero*, pp 1–20) illustrates the enthusiasm with which Lowland Scots participated in attacking Highlanders. 27 Lynch, 'Scottish culture', p. 20. 28 Clyde, *Rebel to hero*, pp 3–8. 29 Murdoch, *Spirit of Jacobite loyalty* (1907), p. 31.

his semi-nakedness, by which he is able to spring over his mountains with perfect ease and is no longer restrained within the rigid bounds of southern breeches.[30]

This connection between the Highlands and aspects of Scottish national identity would become stronger as the nineteenth century progressed. It made the Highlands a politically loaded place.

In the 1830s and 1840s, despite the foreboding sounds from certain quarters, many books appeared to satisfy the demand for information on tartan.[31] By the 1840s, the cult of Bonnie Prince Charlie was in full flow, and the different elements of the Highland, Gaelic and Scottish past were fused together by the colourful siblings, the 'Sobieski Stuarts'. Even with the growing scepticism about the authenticity of the tartans, their historical veracity was soon overtaken by events. The enthusiasm for the Highlands and the forced elements of its culture unleashed by MacPherson's Ossian and Scott's literary outpourings would prove hard to arrest:

> It was Sir Walter Scott who introduced him [the Highlander] to polite society. Before that time the courteous Highland gentleman, filled to overflowing with the sturdy virtues of the Golden Age, was by his contemporaries regarded as a low-down cattle lifter and assassin. All Lowlanders regard all mountaineers as thieves and bandits. But when Walter Scott turned the light of romance upon him all the meanness left him and he stood before the world in the grandeur of his rugged virtue. Here, it was discovered, stood nature's last perfect gentleman. Even the death of the clan system against the bayonets at Culloden became a noble and heroic thing. The clans were dead. Long live the clans! The tartan, driven from the hills by cruel acts of parliament, began to return again, not to the hills, but to the drawing-rooms. And then a shape rears itself in the mists of Deeside. Balmoral is ready to be born.[32]

---

30 Cited in Morton, *In search of Scotland*, p. 122. For a more accurate assessment of the origins and development of the kilt, see Cheape, *Tartan* (1995). 31 One of the best examples was James Logan's *The Scottish Gael* (1831). In this book, dedicated to William IV, Logan indicated which exact tartans belonged to whom. His collaboration with R.R. MacIan in 1845 led to the publication of *The clans of the Scottish Highlands*. Logan's text was embroidered by MacIan's colour plates of some authentic styles of Highland dress dating back to the Middle Ages and some spurious comments on the antiquity of some clan tartans. 32 Morton, *In search of Scotland*, p. 122.

'BALMORALITY AND EMPIRE'

> The number of foreign, but chiefly English travellers is extraordinary. They fill every conveyance and every inn, attracted by scenery, curiosity, superfluous time and wealth, and the fascination of Scott, while, attracted by grouse, the mansion-houses of half of our poor devils of Highland lairds are occupied by rich and titled Southrons. Even the students of Oxford and Cambridge come to the remote villages of Scotland in autumn to *study*!
>
> Lord Cockburn, *Circuit journeys* (1842)

> In the garb of old Gaul, wi' the fire of old Rome,
> From the heath-cover'd mountains of Scotia we come,
> Where the Romans endeavour'd our country to gain,
> But our ancestors fought, and they fought not in vain.
> 'Garb of Old Gaul', adopted as the regimental tune of the 42nd Regiment in 1767.[33]

The year 1822 holds a special significance for the Highlands. The tartan spectacle that greeted George IV's visit to Edinburgh in that year, confirmed the acceptance of the Highlander into the mainstream of Scottish culture. Aside from the royal visit, 1822 was also the year in which Colonel David Stewart of Garth published his *Sketches of the character, manners and present state of the Highlanders of Scotland*. In detailing the sacrifices of Highland Regiments for the benefit of the British Empire, Stewart furthered the rehabilitation of the Gael and enshrined the romanticized perceptions held by outsiders. The song, 'The Garb of Old Gaul' is indicative of the potent mixture of symbols and values deemed specifically Highland that were now being wedded to the constitutionalism of a victorious Hanoverian establishment.

Nearly three decades later in 1848 – a year of revolutions in Europe, a rising in Ireland and of the Great Charter in England – Scotland's history reached a somewhat more prosaic watershed. In that year, the royal couple, Victoria and Prince Albert, acquired the Balmoral estate and so cemented their love affair with Caledonia. This marked a new phase in the image of the Highlander held by those to the south of the Highland line. Queen Victoria's association with the Highlands could not help but contribute to a more inclusive British identity – but not necessarily to the detriment of a distinctive Scottish national identity.

---

33 Lord Cockburn, *Circuit journeys* (1842), pp 83–4, 25–6. This song was written during the Seven Years War (1756–63), where Highlanders of the 42nd Regiment distinguished themselves in battle. The words to the song were first published in 1765 and underwent many reprints. Cited in Womack, *Improvement and romance*, p. 32.

The queen's affection for the people of the north of Scotland, and the prince consort's prowess at the sporting activities, gave the impression that the landscape was a commodity to be exploited.

Traditions were thus being 'invented' to reflect the demands and needs of a British people that hungered for timeless rural images in an age of otherwise rapid change. Not only were the Highlands becoming a playground for the wealthier sections of western society, but as tourism developed around the expanding sporting estates, the 'natives' were perceived as a service class.[34] Other visitors flocked to the region as communications improved and the sentimental portrayal of the Highlands and its people filtered through to a wider audience. Their views, detailed in firsthand accounts, reinforced the various stereotypes of the Highlander: feckless, indolent, barbaric and truculent.

There was a certain irony in the fact that while the more privileged sections of British society trouped to the region for blood sports, an increasing number of Highlanders were shedding blood for the empire. Their sacrifices for the crown added substance to the fascination of the Highlander as a warrior race. What emerged from this focus was the expectation that the Highlander could be a dutiful and honourable servant. When the reality of living in the nineteenth-century Highlands was made apparent, visitors either condemned the population or treated them with contempt, ignoring the daily hardship of the lives of ordinary Gaelic people in favour of remembering a romanticized image that aligned with their preconceived ideas. This potent mixture of myth and reality would filter through to the next generation of 'privileged' observers – those, in fact, who would shape policy on the future of the Highlands and Islands during the period between 1939 and 1965.

Queen Victoria and Prince Albert had begun to visit the Highlands in 1842, attracted by the romantic images presented by Scott and the prospect of hunting challenges. On their first tour to the Highlands they were received by Lord Breadalbane, a laird who relished his role as a Highland chieftain:

> The house is a kind of castle, built of granite. The *coup d'oeil* was indescribable. There were a number of Lord Breadalbane's Highlanders, all in Campbell tartan, drawn up in front of the house, with Lord Breadalbane himself in a Highland dress at their head, and a few of Sir Neil Menzies' men (in the Menzies red and white tartan), a number of pipers playing, and a company of the 92nd Highlanders, also in kilts. The firing of the guns, the cheering of the great crowd, the picturesqueness of the dresses, the beauty of the surrounding country, with its rich background of wooded hills, altogether formed

---

34 For an analysis of the cultural politics associated with this 'sporting past-time', see Lorimer, 'Guns, game and the grandee' (2000). See also McNeil, *Writing the Highlands* (2007).

one of the finest scenes imaginable. It seemed as if a great chieftain in old feudal times was receiving his sovereign.[35]

The itineraries for the queen's Scottish holidays were carefully chosen to conform with the image of the Highlands as prepared by Scott and others. The royal party found a suitable place to de-camp and once Balmoral was acquired in 1848, Queen Victoria rebuilt it in the Scottish baronial form. Inside the mock-gothic castle, she created her own style with the carpets, curtains and upholstery bedecked in tartan, with both the dress and royal versions of the Stewart tartan predominant.[36] With the royals' encouragement of tartan and their approval of the mock-gothic architectural presentation, Britain's premier couple were starting a fashion that became a rage.

The royal party toured extensively in the Highlands, taking great delight in acknowledging the respect and devotion of her 'loyal Highland subjects'. The queen, anxious to demonstrate her Scottish, and Highland credentials, also embraced the fascination for Jacobitism, now that it was safely consigned to history. After following part of Bonnie Prince Charlie's trail, made when he was a fugitive, she recorded:

> I feel a sort of reverence in going over these scenes in this most beautiful country, which I am proud to call my own, where there was such devoted loyalty to the family of my ancestors – for Stuart blood is in my veins, and I am *now* their representative and the people are as devoted and loyal to me as they were to that unhappy race.[37]

The royals helped to broaden the acceptance of the 'invented' Highlander and all manner of cultural trappings that were now deemed appropriate. Suddenly, for example, Highland country dancing was now being performed at court balls, even in England. Victoria and Albert also acted as patron to the Braemar Highland games, another aspect of Highland culture that was refashioned to accord with the tastes and expectations of a largely external audience. Their preferences for certain accepted displays of 'Highlandness' were broadcast to an increasingly interested audience. Whatever means was adopted, the end result was to feed the tartan Hydra created by Scott.

While the most important insights into the monarch's affection and admiration for the Highlands and its inhabitants were made known through her own journals, the images which captured the imagination were produced by the

---

35 Queen Victoria, *Leaves from the journal* (1868), pp 23–24. As Jack Brand says: 'Victoria's diary is a remarkable revelation of a monarch's ignorance about her kingdom, in spite of having travelled through it'. See Brand, *National movement in Scotland* (1978), p. 93.   36 This style was, rather disapprovingly, labelled 'Balmorality'.   37 Queen Victoria, *More leaves from the journal* (1884), p. 173.

painter, Sir Edwin Landseer.[38] His first painting of the royal family abroad in the Highlands was *Queen Victoria sketching at Loch Laggan* (1847). The queen was so impressed that she commissioned Landseer to paint another two Highland scenes as Christmas presents for Albert.[39] Landseer's best known work – aside from *Monarch of the Glen* – is *Queen Victoria meeting the Prince Consort on his return from deer-stalking in the year 1850*, which provides a classic example of invention meeting reality. Exhibited in 1854 at the Royal Academy, it depicts Queen Victoria being led over a tartan gangplank by a kilted Prince Albert after a boat trip on Loch Muich. The painting also contains the faithful gillies, kneeling in the monarch's presence and the scene is set off by the dead stags in the foreground. In a sense it is the imagery provided by Landseer which underpins Balmorality and it was the romantic and gothic portrayals of the region which intrigued the aristocracy, and in turn, encouraged Victoria to embrace selected aspects of Highland life.

The royal family's undoubted affection for the Highlands was hugely influential in encouraging others to visit the north of Scotland. The acquisition of Balmoral and the purchasing of a sizeable estate made it fashionable for others to imitate and aspire to the lifestyle of the landed gentleman. Soon, the region was being developed by wealthy entrepreneurs, keen to take advantage of the sports available in the Highlands. The improvements in communications during the nineteenth century certainly made travel easier and the increase in literature on the Highlands and Islands and its inhabitants reflected this. In surveying this material, one can quickly identify certain themes that endured into the twentieth century. A mixture of romanticized literature and some fairly forceful and derogatory remarks made by travellers to the region shaped external perceptions of the Highlands.[40]

Some of the literature generated by the visits to the Highlands and Islands was relatively obscure, while other books had an enormous impact. Sometimes reporters would travel north, filing copy either for the main newspapers or the more specialist magazines and journals that were being published for target audiences. These publications, however insignificant their sales figures, nevertheless together represented a widespread attitude. This can be seen here in an anonymous account of a fair in the mythical location of 'Storport':

> On a smooth bit of green above the inn a ragged bagpiper and a blind fiddler are playing different tunes, and shepherds, herd-girls, farm-

---

38 For more information on Landseer, see Pringle, 'Landseer, Victoria and the Highland myth' (1988). 39 These were *Highlander and Eagle* and *Highland Lassie Crossing a Stream*, both finished in 1849. 40 Smout ('Tours in the Scottish Highlands', p. 105) claims: 'This outlook develops in the nineteenth century into an attitude of palpable contempt for contemporary Highlanders along with an attitude of reverence for the imagined "romance" of the Jacobite and clannish past. It is hard to imagine anything more divorced from reality'.

> women and drovers are dancing like mad people, with the usual shrieks that accompany the Highland reel. Here a couple of men are fighting, not in the knock-down English fashion but rearing, screaming and clinging to each other's throats like wild cats. The dirty inn is crammed, and the sound of roaring and singing comes from the rickety door. Half-naked Highlandmen in kilts are rushing about everywhere with bottles of whiskey [sic] in their hands, beseeching their friends to drink. When light comes [...] almost all the bacchanalians have disappeared from the hills and knolls, and the inn has subsided into its chronic state of dirt, darkness, languor and general misery.[41]

As this extract illustrates, the majority of visitors to the Highlands came with preconceived ideas. They were interested in the scenery; the 'natives' were largely incidental. Many seemed blind to the hardship imposed on Highlanders by the Clearances, indeed most did not want their make-believe image of the Highlands disturbed.

What shocked visitors was the extent of poverty in the Highlands and Islands. This contrasted with their idealized image and informed many of their moral judgments. Those responsible for distributing funding during the famines of the mid-1830s were certain that the 'wretched' houses had 'a tendency to degrade and brutalize the inhabitants'.[42] Some commentators expressed sympathy with the immiserated creatures they encountered. Joseph and Elizabeth Robins Pennell had departed for the Hebrides in the 1880s convinced that the newspaper reports of the abject poverty of the isles were false. Their voyage rudely awakened them. In the preface to their 1890 publication *Our journey to the Hebrides*, they remarked: 'We were not blind to the beauty, the sternness, the wildness of the country, but the sadness and sorrows of its people impressed us even more than the wonder and beauty of their land'.[43] The inequalities in wealth were also readily apparent in Tarbert, Harris:

> They starve on tiny crofts, their only homes; their landlord holds broad acres as playground for a few short weeks. The hovels were as cheerless within as without. I do not know why it is that one takes liberties with the poor which one would not dare take with the rich. It is no small evil of poverty that it is everybody's privilege to stare at it.[44]

---

41 *St Paul's Magazine* (1872), cited in Cooper, *Road to the Isles*, pp 137–8. Cooper identifies the mythical location as Lochmaddy, North Uist.   42 Fullerton and Baird, *Remarks on the evils* (1838), pp 14–15, 22.   43 Pennell, *Journey to the Hebrides* (1890), p. xv. It is worthwhile pointing out that the Pennells' first published their thoughts in *Harper's Magazine*.   44 Ibid., p. 134.

Most visitors were, however, contemptuous of the plight of the Highlanders. James Wilson writing in the 1840s attacked the 'natives' for their 'indolence and inactivity' and their prejudicial attitudes towards measures designed to improve their situation. Others shared Wilson's view that their squalid living conditions were a matter of 'free choice rather than nature's doom'.[45] Even exiled Gaels such as Malcolm Ferguson echoed a common perception held by 'outsiders' that the Highlanders could improve their situation if they had the will to do it:

> As a rule, they appear to be fairly well fed and clad, and I fancy that their greatest drawback and discomfort is the wretchedly miserable hovels of houses they live in, which, however, with a small amount of labour and taste, could be greatly improved and made more comfortable.[46]

Encouraged by reports of indolence and poverty, few could contain their disdain for the 'natives', referred to as the 'old aborigines' in some publications.

The growing number of cruises up the western seaboard contained a range of well-travelled people, many of whom had made their fortunes through the empire. They were often struck by the similar conditions they had witnessed in Africa:

> We passed a kraal of wretched looking huts, some of them so small and sad, so resembling decayed portions of mother earth upheaved by accident, that we did not at first regard them as human dwellings, till we observed a single pane of glass, in one instance sticking in the thatch [...]. The interiors were very miserable.[47]

A similar reaction came from the wealthy Highlander Osgood Hanbury MacKenzie. Although sympathetic to the plight of the people, he was stunned by their lifestyle. He was particularly struck by an incident he witnessed on a visit to Harris 'such as one could hardly have witnessed elsewhere than in a Kaffir kraal or an Eskimo tent or Red Indian tepe [sic]'.[48] During these visits to the townships, most experienced the expected hospitality, though they were aware of resentment at the intrusion as well.[49]

This insensitivity towards the cultural mores of the Gael and ignorance of their difficulties was evident during the land agitation of the 1880s. Heavily

---

45 Wilson, *Voyage round Scotland* (1842), pp 432-3, 436.   **46** Ferguson, *Rambles in Skye* (1885), p. 37.   **47** Wilson, *Voyage*, p. 365. Similar sentiments were voiced by John Inglis, who wrote under the pen-name 'The Governor'. Visiting a house in Isle Ornsay in Skye, he concluded that 'There was no pig to be seen, although the hovel was everything a pig could desire'. Inglis, *Cruising in the west Highlands* (1879), p. 130.   **48** MacKenzie, *Hundred years in the Highlands* (1921), p. 97.   **49** See Pennell, *Journey to the Hebrides*, pp 134-7.

influenced by the views of the landed gentry, visitors criticized disturbances involving crofters as injurious to the more respectable and law-abiding members of the community:

> I believe that owing to the crofters' ill-advised squabbles with their landlords, parties in the south did not care to venture amongst them; and I have been repeatedly informed by hotel-keepers that the crofters' doings have been the direct cause of preventing many tourists visiting Skye this year – probably the dullest season experienced for years by hotel-keepers. I know from personal knowledge that not a few parties in London and the south had written to friends asking them if they thought it would be safe to visit Skye this summer.[50]

Implicit in these comments was the desire for the Highlanders to behave in the manner to which outsiders were accustomed. Their conditioning from literary and other sources created expectations in the minds of visitors. The dominant attitude of those who took advantage of the improvements in communications to the Highlands were primarily there for sport. Deer, grouse, salmon, sea-trout and geese were the usual prey, but most types of wildlife were deemed fair game – even whales. As Revd George Hely Hutchinson demonstrated,

> There was nothing to be done now but to join in the chase. We could not succeed in turning or making any hand of the band, and they made good their retreat to the sea again. A good many shots were fired, and apparently a good many whales received rifle bullets, which drew blood; but they sank, and I do not think that eventually more than three or four carcasses were recovered.[51]

That particular hunt was disturbed by a group of local women, much to the disgust and anger of the sporting gentlemen. Other accounts of hunting in the Highlands also criticized the locals for interrupting the visitors as they attempted to bag the prey:

> Much of the pleasure of shooting in the Outer Hebrides is spoilt by the conduct of the crofters. It is not conducive to sport to be followed by a gang of men and ordered out of the country, nor is it pleasant to be cursed in Gaelic by a crowd of irate old women, even if you do not understand every word they say. They accused us of shooting their horses and sheep, filled in the pits which we dug in the sandhills for

50 Ferguson, *Rambles in Skye*, p. 36. 51 Hutchison, *Wild sport in the Hebrides* (1873), p. 17.

geese we were stalking, cut up the canvas and broke the seats of our folding-boat, and tried in every possible way to spoil our sport. They were especially insolent and troublesome in Benbecula and Barra. Taking them as a whole, the crofters are an ignorant lot of creatures and the less said about them the better.[52]

In view of the tensions aroused by the gross inequalities in wealth and lifestyles of the visitors and their 'hosts', some sportsmen took to warning others about the difficulties they might expect if they joined others who had bought shooting estates in the Highlands: 'The question of the irrepressible crofter is a more serious element; nor is it possible to avoid glancing at it in passing'. The estates in the north-west coast were singled out as the worst because they were 'more or less swamped in squatters'.[53] Thus, in their quest for sporting trophies, these sporting gentlemen were treating the Highlands and Islands as just another colonial outpost. They expected their hosts to show the loyalty and respect which Highlanders had displayed in the imperial context, by their conduct in the Highland regiments of the British Army.

The image of the loyal Highlander, faithful to the crown, and epitomized by John Brown, was a thread running through Balmorality. Parallel to this notion of the loyal Highlander and faithful servant was the raising of Highland regiments. A key element in the 'rehabilitation' of the Gael was their participation in the regiments of the British armed forces defending and expanding the British Empire.[54] As a result of the continuing policy of clearance, however, and the treatment of the region as a 'playground' by outsiders, this process of recruitment did produce tensions. Some Gaelic commentators bemoaned the lack of respect and honour from the government, arguing that young Highland men were being treated as cannon fodder, an accusation that could be levelled at the recruitment of any portion of the working class. That said, other Highlanders, particularly the more privileged sections, but even some lesser lineages, benefited from the opportunities presented by an expanding empire, and the pressure for a constant flow of young men for the officer class.[55] The disproportionate numbers of Highlanders in service to the crown led to the development of a culture in which the Highlands were seen as a source of human stock, a necessary reservoir to service and civilize the four corners of the globe.[56]

Given the mainly negative outside perceptions of the Highland people, the rewriting of Highland history, especially the Jacobite Rising of 1745–6, was

52 Peel, *Wild sport in the Outer Hebrides* (1901), p. xiii.   53 Shand, *Letters from the Highlands* (1884), pp 141–2.   54 For a useful corrective on the nature of Highlanders and the British army in this period, consult Mackillop, *Army, empire and the Scottish Highlands* (2000); for comparative figures on the number of recruits, see Hanham, 'Mid-Victorian army' (1973), pp 163–7.   55 See Fry, *Scottish empire* (2001); Devine, *Scotland's empire* (2003).   56 Colley, *Britons*, pp 117–32; Womack, *Improvement and romance*, p. 29.

hugely significant in allowing for the valorization of the Highlander. After repeated examples of heroism in the Seven Years War (1756–63), Pitt the Younger in 1766 offered a powerful eulogy in the House of Commons to the fighting prowess and loyalty of the Highland regiments:

> I sought for merit wherever it was to be found. It is my boast that I was the first minister who looked for it; and found it in the mountains of the north. I called it forth and drew it into your service, a hardy and intrepid race of men; men who, when left by your jealousy, became a prey to the artifices of your enemies, and had gone nigh to have overturned the state in the war before the last. These men, in the last war, were brought to combat on your side: they served with fidelity as they fought with valour, and conquered for you in every part of the world: detested be the national reflections against them![57]

Pitt was forced to make this statement because of continued slandering of the Highlander by some of his parliamentary colleagues. However, the climate of opinion was moving in the prime minister's favour, and earlier statements of support were being bolstered by the romanticized images emanating from the pens of travellers to the Highlands.

Highlanders were praised for having particular attributes that could be channelled to a useful purpose for the British state. It was said that Highland soldiers

> are caught in the mountains when young; and still run with a surprising degree of swiftness. As they are strangers to fear, they make very good soldiers when disciplined [...]. They discover an extraordinary submission to and affection for their officers, who are all young and handsome.[58]

Despite the growing commendations being made on behalf of the 'fiery warriors' from the north, Highlanders themselves pointed out that the key elements which went into 'making' the Highland soldier were being undermined by the Clearances. However, external commentators, and those with a vested interest in the removal of Highlanders from the more fertile areas of the north, were keen to downplay the potential harm to the recruiting offices of the British Army:

> At present, that barbarous ferocity, which was the offspring of feudal institutions, is completely extinguished; while their native valour, and

57 Cited in Womack, *Improvement and romance*, p. 31.   58 Description of Highland soldiers in the *Scots Magazine*, 24 (1762). Cited in Clyde, *Rebel to hero*, p. 88.

military character, remain unimpaired. They are intelligent, hospitable, religious, inoffensive in their manners, submissive to superiors, temperate, frugal, grateful, obliging, honest and faithful.[59]

Indeed, the Clearances were portrayed as being a positive element in 'civilizing' the Gael, while harnessing some of his more unsavoury characteristics for the benefit of the state. This concern to maintain a rich source of bodies for the empire was a recurrent theme throughout the period up until the Second World War. Satisfied that the 'improvement' of the Highlands would continue, social commentators were keen to identify the reasons for the doughtiness of the Highlander.

Once again, the physical landscape of the Highlands was the point of reference in explaining the unique Highland character. This time, however, indolence was not the end product, but personal courage:

> Mountaineers are warlike because by their feuds and competitions they consider themselves as surrounded by enemies, and are always prepared to repel incursions, or to make them [...]. Among a warlike people, the quality of highest esteem is personal courage, and with the ostentatious display of courage are closely connected promptitude of offence and quickness of resentment.[60]

This view that the fiery temperament of the Highlander was a product of geography would be reinforced by other commentators during the nineteenth and early twentieth centuries. Colonel David Stewart of Garth was a key figure in reconciling the Highlander with a southern audience. He emerged as a public relations officer for the Highland soldier, becoming the 'voice' of the Highland regiments. In his *Sketches of the character, manners and present state of the Highlanders of Scotland*, published in 1822, he retold many of Johnson and Boswell's stories of the fighting capabilities of the Highlander. Now safely consigned to history, these stories of earlier clan feuds, exceptional in themselves, fitted the popular perception. The best example of this selective use of history to conform to the image of the violent Highlander was the collection of stories in *The history of the feuds and conflicts among the clans*.[61] Published anonymously in 1764, and with numerous reprints, this form of literature would continue in the future. But with the growing number of heroic tales from imperial campaigns, writers were presented with a plentiful supply of material to relocate the sterling qualities of the Highlander.[62]

---

59 Knox, *View of the British Empire* (1785), i, p. 133. Thomas Pennant made a similar observation about the changes taking place in the Highlands during the late eighteenth century, but he speculated that 'the spirit of industry' taking root in the region could socialize the Highlander out of his military predilections. See his *Tour in Scotland* (1772), p. 174. 60 Johnson, *Journey*, pp 39–40. 61 Cited in Womack, *Improvement and romance*, pp 35–6, fn. 26. 62 A classic

The selective appropriation of Gaelic culture for an ostensibly threatened Scottish national identity also included the martial qualities of the Highlander. During the nineteenth century, militarism in Scotland borrowed certain elements from the Highland regiments, who themselves were taking certain features of their culture and adapting them for the modern era.[63] From 1854 onwards, Highland regiments had pipers officially attached to the regiments, now formed into pipe bands, playing and composing regimental marches. This development in a key element of the music of the Highlands did bring benefits for bagpipes, including the publication of collections of pipe music, although the regimented style differed from the earlier compositions.[64]

The previous chapter has demonstrated the problems endured by Highland emigrants, but there were also examples of enterprise among those who left their native land. The pioneering efforts of people like Alexander MacKenzie from Stornoway were seized on by those anxious to prove that Highlanders were not by nature feckless and lazy.[65] Within the Gaelic community, and among those sympathetic to the plight of the Highlander, these individual success stories provided nostalgic reminders of the drive and vision of earlier Gaels. However, as the bitter realities of the global depression of the inter-war period hit home, the dream of succeeding in a foreign land, as some of their forebears had done, seemed a distant prospect.

'CELTIC TWILIGHTISM'

Fair these broad meads – these hoary woods are grand;
But we are exiles from our father's land.
...
From the lone shieling of the misty island
Mountains divide us, and the waste of seas –
Yet still the blood is strong,
The heart is Highland,
And we in dreams behold the Hebrides.
　　　　　　　　　'Canadian boat song', Anon. (*c.*1800)[66]

---

example of this glorification of the Highland soldier was Keltie's (ed.), *History of the Scottish Highlands* (1875). **63** Clyde, *Rebel to hero*, pp 150–81. **64** For an excellent analysis of the development of the piping tradition in Scotland, incorporating the martial associations of the instrument, the patronage of the landed gentry and Highland Societies, Celtic revivalism and the importance of urban based Gaels for the promotion of bagpipe music see Donaldson, *Highland pipe and Scottish society* (2000). **65** Alexander Mackenzie travelled from Stornoway in 1793 to the Hudson Bay Company via New York and Montreal. He retold his story in his *Voyages from Montreal* (1801). For a discussion of the empire and its impact on Scottish literature, see MacGillivray, 'Exile and empire' (1988). **66** Cited in MacDonnell, *Emigrant experience*, p. 50.

> Whether the story of Oisin [sic], the Gaelic Orpheus, be a wanderer from archaic mythology, or arose clanless among the Gaelic hills ... matters little. The tale, at least, has a beauty that is certainly its own. Oisin, also, was the son of one who loved a woman of the deathless folk; for as the Thracian king Oegrus loved Calliope, of the divine race, so Fionn, the Agamemnon of the Gael, loved one of the Hidden People ...
>
> 'Fiona MacLeod' (William Sharp), 'Orpheus and Oisin' (1904)[67]

'Celtic twilightism' developed out of the romanticism inspired by the cult of Ossian and in reaction to the racial stereotyping of Celts by writers championing the Teutonic and Anglo-Saxon aspects of the British past.[68] One of the underlying themes of empire, despite the valorization of certain aspects of the Celt, was the racial and cultural superiority of the Anglo-Saxon. As this attitude developed, Celticism sprang up as the obverse of it. Matthew Arnold, Ernst Renan, George Russell and William Sharp were all skilled exponents of the 'Celtic twilight' school. Primarily a literary movement, it was part of a more general reaction against modernity. This fascination with primitivism and mysticism is represented in James George Frazer's classic work, *The golden bough: a study in magic and religion*.[69] But there was a deep interest in all aspects of folklore in the late nineteenth century.

Work produced by 'Celtic twilightists' was of a particular style – vague and mysterious. Because of its escapist tendencies, it sought inspiration in the myth and folklore of the Celtic peoples. The Gaels of Ireland and the west Highlands and Islands were regarded as particularly rich sources for the writers. These literary figures were keen to re-present the Highlands and Gaelic culture to the outside. As a result of their combined efforts, there was a subtle alteration to the external perceptions of the Highlands. Celtic gloom, mystical and mythical images were found in various literary works, and in turn, percolated through to a southern audience. But there was also an influence back into Gaeldom, evident in poems and songs such as the 'Canadian boat song', especially from those 'exiles' who harked back to the 'golden age' of Gaelic Scotland. Therefore, the twilightists offered another prism through which to view the Highlands, but again, the picture presented did not reflect the reality.

Nationalism is never static and the projected national identity is often fiercely contested. Because it reflects deeper political struggles within the polity, national identity can revolve around competing myths. In the eighteenth century, the Scots and the Celts in general were given centre-stage in the literature and historiography of Britain.[70] But as the political landscape of Britain altered, and

---

67 MacLeod, *Winged destiny* (1904), pp 79–80. 68 See Kidd, 'Race' (2003) for further discussion. 69 For a discussion of Frazer's work and its impact on Scotland, see Brown, 'Folk tradition' (1988).

'race' became the basis for distinguishing nations, there was a strong anti-Celtic backlash. The championing of an Anglo-Saxon identity during the Victorian period depended on the Celt as the 'anti-type'.[71] This resulted in the displacement of Celtic symbolism as new motifs came to represent Britain.

Within Scotland, a cultural nationalist movement took root that, although wedded to the cultural renaissance of the Gael, partially developed in reaction to these developments. Inspired by events in Ireland, and drawing on the spirit of resistance within the Highlands, the cultural movement evoked Gaelic imagery and symbolism for an external audience. Once more, attention was focused on the Highlands, and Scottish nationalists such as Ruaraidh Erskine of Marr tried to claim Scotland was a Celtic nation, and all the better for it.[72] Erskine, speaking on behalf of 'the progressive and militant forces of the Gaelic movement' aimed to convince Scots that their salvation lay in embracing their Celtic inheritance: 'We aim at "Scotland a Nation" [...]. The old cry of "Alba! Alba!" and the more recent one of "Sinn Fein a mhain!" are our cries'.[73] Erskine launched *Comunn nan Albannach* (Scots National League) in 1911 in order to promote his Celtic programme, but membership was low. Although the number of activists in Scotland was numerically small, their impact in intellectual circles was significant, offering a powerful rejoinder to the sense of inferiority produced by Scotland's cultural attachment to tartanry. This matches the pattern of other cultural nationalist movements in Europe at the time; the Irish experience being especially relevant for comparative reflection.[74] Against this background of cultural nationalism, the 'Celtic twilight' movement invoked Scotland's Gaels and selected aspects of their culture to inspire them and inform their writing.

One of the most influential of the 'Celtic twilight' writers was William Sharp. Born in Paisley in 1854, Sharp wrote a number of novels under a nom de plume, 'Fiona MacLeod'. Dismissing his work as 'sheer pastiche', critics and sceptics regarded Sharp as a writer in 'the most exaggerated manner of the "Celtic twilight" school'.[75] He defined the Celtic writer as someone 'whose mind is more ancient, more primitive, and in a sense more natural than that of his compatriot in whom the Teutonic spirit prevails'.[76] Sharp tried to present a pagan mysticism, with strong overtones of Ossianic influence in his writing style, especially in its rhythm and descriptive features.[77] Although he was capable of perceptive

---

70 Melman, 'Claiming the nation's past' (1992). 71 Ibid., 235–6, 238. 72 Erskine, 'Celt, Slav, Hun and Teuton' (1914). 73 See *Guth na bliadhna*, 6 (1909), 166. The journal's translated title was 'The voice of the year', running from 1904 to 1925. 74 John Hutchinson has demonstrated the potency of cultural nationalism in Ireland and how the 'Ireland for the Irish' movement acted as a crucial counter to the pressures of anglicisation. See Hutchinson, *Dynamics of cultural nationalism* (1987). 75 See King, 'Fiona MacLeod'. For more detail on Sharp's contribution to the 'Celtic twilight' school see Alaya, *William Sharp* (1970). 76 MacLeod, 'Celtic writers', *Fortnightly review* (1899), 36. 77 Wittig, *Scottish tradition in literature* (1972), pp 269–70.

impressions of the Gaelic world that were genuinely from the heart, ultimately he was drawn back to the lyricism of the 'Celtic twilight'.[78]

There was a degree of ambivalence between, and even opposition among, those who wrote in the 'twilight' genre and those who supported the principles of Celtic nationalism. Sharp was roundly condemned for his argument that '[I]n the world of literature there is no geography save that of the mind'.[79] Sharp believed that the best strategy for preserving the Celtic race was to foster its spiritual and artistic qualities, in which its talents for mythology would flourish. Hence, he felt that although the Gaels were a 'passing race', their spirit would endure irrespective of political boundaries.[80] Sharp was required to defend his stance in the wake of criticism from supporters of Celtic nationalism, but his position remained largely unchanged. Ultimately, Sharp believed that, irrespective of political associations, the Celt was a prized asset that should be supported because: 'as the Celt comes of a people who grew in spiritual outlook as they began what has been revealed to us by history as a ceaseless losing battle, so the Teuton comes of a people who have lost in the spiritual life what they have gained in the moral and the practical'.[81] But this valorization of the Gael rendered him politically impotent, and obfuscated the real and tangible concerns felt by those in the Highlands and Islands.

For Sharp, the island of Iona, the 'mecca of the Gael', held a special importance, as indicated in this dedication to his collection of essays, *The winged destiny: studies in the spiritual history of the Gael*:

> The south is beautiful, but has not the secrets of the north. Do you, too, not hold Iona, motherhood of all my dreams, as something rare and apart, one who has her own lovely solitude and her own solitary loveliness that is like no other loveliness? In your heart, as in mine, it lies an island of revelation and of peace. For you, too, is the enduring spell of those haunted lands where the last dreams of the Gaels are gathered, dwelling in sunset beauty.[82]

Sharp sought beauty, that 'spiritual energy', in the west Highlands and Islands.[83] But given his condemnation of Calvinism as a 'blight' on the people, he went to those areas where Catholicism was dominant.[84]

---

78 The noted Gaelic scholar John Lorne Campbell also attacked the pseudo-archaic styles of translation from the 'Celtic twilightists'. He argued that the Gaelic originals are characterized by 'an extreme concreteness of language, an 'epigrammatic concision of speech, the pleasure in sharp, bright colour' which is the antithesis of the mistiness of the Celtic twilight'. See Campbell, *Stories from South Uist* (1961), p. xiii.   79 Sharp, *Lyra Celtica* (1896), p. 427.   80 Ibid., p. 5.   81 MacLeod, 'Celtic writers' (1899), p. 36.   82 MacLeod, *Winged destiny* (1904).   83 Ibid., pp x–xi. However, as Flavia Alaya points out in her book (*William Sharp*, p. 170): 'But that "spirit" had little of the actual about it. Iona served as a geographical means of dramatizing nearly every aspect of transcendent Celticism until then perceived by Fiona MacLeod's fiction and criticism'.
84 MacLeod, *Winged destiny*, pp 207–46, 235 for quotation.

Academic writers also travelled to the Catholic Highlands and Islands for material. J.F. Campbell's *Popular tales of the west Highlands orally collected* (1862) was the first significant contribution to folklore studies in Scotland.[85] The best-known collection of the period was Alexander Carmichael's *Carmina Gadelica: hymns and incantations [...] collected in the Highlands and Islands of Scotland.*[86] The first two volumes of this detailed collection were published in 1900 and almost immediately drew criticism for tampering with the originals to make the material more accessible to an English-speaking audience. However, given the circumstances of the time, and the powerful influences of Ossianic sentimentality and 'Celtic twilightism', Carmichael showed considerable restraint in altering the Gaelic sources.[87]

Those who fell under the spell of 'mystical qualities' in the Highlands and Islands were a fairly diverse group. Most did not understand Gaelic, and many did not even live in Scotland. There was a definitive overlap between some of the writers. Amy Murray's book, *Father Allan's island*, was an appreciation of the work done by the Catholic priest, Fr Allan MacDonald in preserving the folklore of the Gael on his native island of Eriskay in the Outer Hebrides. But Murray's book was overbearingly sentimental, a fact evident from some of the chapter titles: 'True edge of the great world', 'Celtic gloom' and 'Cow of curses'. Readers would form the impression that islanders were a mystical bunch who believe in fairies and 'the other world' and practise spiritualism. Discussing her 'foregathering' with Fr Allan, she described the way he took her round the island 'after the old Highland way of one who has *The sight*, when he would show his vision to another'.[88] Ada Goodrich Freer was less gracious in acknowledging her debt to Fr Allan for the plentiful examples of the second sight she 'borrowed' from his notebooks.[89]

Eriskay, *Eilean na h-oige*, was also an important port of call for the musician Marjory Kennedy-Fraser. Her three-volume *Songs of the Hebrides* was hugely influential in popularizing some of the classics of Gaelic song, even though her interpretations met with criticism from different quarters. Despite her transgressions, such was the richness and power of the originals that her own material was taken up by Gaels themselves, especially in their urban settlements.

Kennedy-Fraser sought the help of Kenneth MacLeod, who was regarded as 'much more than an editor'. A scholar at Glasgow University, MacLeod had already demonstrated his enthusiasm for the Ossianic presentation of the Highlands.[90] In his Gaelic editor's foreword, MacLeod demonstrated his attitude to the work undertaken:

---

85 See Campbell's *Popular tales of the west Highlands* (1862). 86 See Carmichael's *Carmina Gadelica* (1900) with subsequent reissues by various editors since. 87 See Stiùbhart (ed.), *Alexander Carmichael* (2008) for recent discussion. 88 Murray, *Father Allan's island* (1936), p. 17. In the foreword (p. ix), Padraic Colum argues that the book has 'an inner rhythm with powerful memories behind it'. 89 Freer, *Outer Isles* (1902). 90 Murchison, 'Introduction'

> Eigg was in those days [c. 1800], and until recently, a nest of antique Celticism. Every inch of it was alive with legends and other-world beings. Mysterious tales made the caves and the kirkyard a terror by night; the sealwoman crooned on the reefs; the mermaid bathed in the cracks; the fairies sang and piped in the knolls; the water-sprite washed in a certain burn the shrouds of the dying; the kelpie hatched plots in the tarns against beautiful maidens; the spirits of murdered baby-heirs sobbed in gloomy nooks [...]. Such was the Eigg night under the stars.[91]

Therefore MacLeod, a Gael from Argyll, showed that even those of Highland extraction were caught up in the maelstrom. The early works of Paul Seton Gordon, such as *The charm of the hills* (1912), *The immortal isles* (1926) and *The charm of Skye* (1929), conformed to the genre, as did the work of another Highlander, Alasdair Alpin MacGregor.[92] In Compton MacKenzie, the magical and mystical elements were popularized in fiction and then recycled in cinematic productions such as *Whisky galore* and *Rockets galore*, released in 1949 and 1958 respectively. Consequently, the genre would last throughout the twentieth century.

One of the characteristics of those who sought inspiration in 'Celtic' lands was their opposition to modernity. The more explicit 'Celtic twilightists' acknowledged that they visited these cultural well-springs to find values that could stand against those of the modern industrial and urban world. William Sharp was typical of the genre. His perception of the Scottish Highlands was of a land untainted by the insidious effects of modernization – it was 'alien in all ways from the life of the cities'.[93] Such writers hoped to preserve the region in aspic; to keep it pure and uncontaminated by urbanization and industrialization. It was felt that any association with the modern world would harm the Gael. Contrasting a crowd of '"Glasgow fair" excursionists' in eastern Argyll, 'degraded in aspect, in mien, in language' with the 'islanders [...] so dignified in speech, so simple, so courteous', Sharp concluded that 'in the maelstrom of the cities, the old race perishes, drowns'.[94] Aside from the slight on working class Glaswegians, these sentiments betray an ignorance of the vibrant Gaelic communities established in the urban and industrial areas of Scotland.

During the period of land agitation, the sense of a changing landscape encouraged some poets to indulge in nostalgic reminiscences. This was especially true of the exiled Gael, but it can be detected in poets resident in the

---

(1988), pp xxxiv, xvi. **91** MacLeod, 'Gaelic editor's foreword' (1909), pp xxxvii–xxxviii. **92** Seton Gordon went on to produce work of much better quality and these books are essential reading for discerning hill walkers and nature enthusiasts. MacGregor's most famous contributions included *Behold the Hebrides* (1925) and *The haunted isles* (1933). **93** 'Fiona MacLeod', *Pharais* (1894), p. vii. **94** 'Fiona MacLeod', *Iona*, pp 166–7.

Highlands as well as the Gaelic settlements in Lowland Scotland. Neil MacLeod was the best example of this sentimental poetry:[95]

> An end will come to oppression;
> food and possessions,
> peace and joy also
> will abound in the land;
> the youth will sing sweetly
> their tunes and their ditties,
> and lovely young maidens
> tend the calves at the fold.
> 'The Skye Crofters'.[96]

Even more acclaimed poets such as Mary MacPherson indulged in sentimentality by romanticizing the pre-Clearance era as an idyllic existence.[97] She also pleaded with her fellow Gaels not to abandon their language because without it their whole ethos and value system would be overcome.[98] Her optimism about the future was based on a wholly unrealistic belief that somehow the past could be brought back.[99]

Therefore, by using language and opinions that echoed the sentiments of 'Celticists', one can detect traces of twilightist attitudes in the work of Gaelic folklorists.[1] It reflects the multifaceted nature of 'Celtic twilightism' and the fact that this literary school had many exponents. Consequently, in attacking the Clearances, some poets and songsters were themselves guilty of presenting a false picture of the Highlands and Islands.

[95] Sorley MacLean (*Ris a' bhruthaich*, p. 46) attacked Neil MacLeod's poetry as being 'symptomatic of the rapid decline in the backbone of Gaelic poetry. It is sentimental, pretty-pretty, weak and thin'. Donald Meek (*Tuath is tighearna*, p. 40) argues that 'Some [Gaelic poets] were unable to disentangle the issues as clearly as we might wish; several (notably Neil MacLeod) sought refuge in romanticism, and a number exhibited a marked tendency to retrospection, offering the past as an antidote to the present'. [96] Derick Thomson charges MacLeod with 'the defect of simulated emotion issuing in sentimentality'. See Thomson, *Gaelic poetry*, pp 223–9 for comments on MacLeod and the translated excerpt. [97] See her *Soraidh leis an Nollaig uir* (Farewell to the new Christmas), which contains verses that bemoan the displacement of a happy, welcoming and native community by alien sounds and sense. In her reminiscences of the past there is a sense of loss and injustice at the changes brought by modernization. Original in Nic-a-Phearsain, *Dain agus orain Ghaidhlig* (1891), p. 15; translation in Thomson's *Gaelic poetry*, pp 246–7. Similar sentiments are expressed in her song *Nuair bha mi og* (When I was young). [98] MacLean, *Ris a' bhruthaich*, pp 252–3. [99] Ibid., p. 256. [1] This older society was being portrayed as like the Garden of Eden before the Serpent. A classic example of this type of poetry was her composition 'Eilean a' cheo' where even the material items of pre-clearance society were romanticized. Although Sorley Maclean denies that Mary Macpherson was guilty of twilightism, nonetheless there were different aspects to twilightism, one of which was nostalgia and a denial of reality. Original in Nic-a-Phearsain, *Dain agus orain Ghaidhlig*, p. 28; translation in Thomson's *Gaelic poetry*, p. 247.

Given the power of the material, the cultural reservoir of the Gael, it was perhaps inevitable that the sentiments, even the style, of the 'Celtic twilightists' would also influence the Gael. One dominant and enduring message that emerged was the antipathy towards aspects of modernization. On one level, this reflected the greater accessibility of the Highlands as the railways and steamships linked the main centres of the Highlands – for example, Inverness and Kyle – to the industrialized south.[2] With this opening up of the Highlands in the latter part of the nineteenth century came improvements in standards of living. Therefore, the era of 'Celtic twilight' also witnessed some of the most significant advances in the lives of those living in the Highlands and Islands.

With the opening up of the Highlands and the growth in tourism, the various cultural elements of invention, Balmorality, empire and 'Celtic twilightism' converged and congealed into a false and damaging portrayal of this troubled region, evident in this tourist guidebook from 1905:

> Everything in Skye is so ancient, so romantic, that it will surprise nobody to learn that this island, or, as some say, Holm island to the north of Portree, was the famed *Tir na n'Og*, the Celtic land of youth and faery, *where falls not hail, not rain, nor any snow*. The days passed for the dwellers on this happy isle like a beautiful dream; thither Oisin was sent for a time to prevent the tongue of slander from wagging too freely, for his mother had been transformed into a deer by fairy enchantments.[3]

However, this notion that the Celts were to be cherished for their spiritual strength and sense of honour was doubled-edged, as W.B. Yeats recognized.[4] As the Highlands moved into the inter-war period, Scotland's Gaels would also react against the parodies of themselves which were being propounded by writers of the 'Celtic twilight' school.

DEPRESSION, DECLINE AND DEMORALIZATION

After the sense of resistance which permeated much of the late nineteenth and early twentieth centuries, the inter-war period was scarred by 'a spirit of

---

2 For instance, 'black houses' were being modernized in some parts. Employment opportunities also increased with the greater activity now occurring in the region. Highlanders who were engaged in temporary employment in the Central Belt also witnessed improvements in their journey times and the ease with which they picked up jobs. Therefore, as Hanham ('problems of Highland discontent', p. 43) puts it: 'the Gaelic-speaking crofter who lived on his croft in isolation was becoming something of an anomaly'.   3 MacCulloch, *Misty Isle of Skye*, p. 32.   4 Welch, *Yeats* (1993), pp xxii–xxiii.

restlessness and discontent, a spirit of interrogation and distrust [that] spread through the nation'.[5] Until the 1930s, the land question dominated government approaches to the 'Highland problem', but during the inter-war years, there was a shift in the government's policy. In the years leading up to the Second World War, politicians and civil servants came to recognize that the Highland problem was not necessarily just the crofting problem and that a more comprehensive and rounded approach was needed to stem the worrying levels of out-migration.

The 1920s and 1930s witnessed a resurgence in Scottish nationalism; the movement also came to acquire a distinctive Gaelic face. Campaigners like Ruaraidh Erskine of Marr and Hugh MacDiarmid believed that language revival was the raison d'être of political nationalism. It was deemed to be the external, visible element that demonstrated the nation's credentials. Cultural nationalism was a broad church that enjoyed something of a renaissance in the inter-war period, with positive benefits for the profile of the Gaelic language and culture.[6]

Consequently, the Highlands, and Gaelic culture, featured prominently in the rhetoric of nationalism. Problems that afflicted the Highlands were subsumed into a generally anglophobic attitude. As was the case in the late nineteenth century, nationalists propounded the view that Scotland was a Celtic nation. This provided the basis for repeated attacks against the dominance of England:

> The importance of the fact that we are a Gaelic people, that Scottish anti-Irishness is a profound mistake, that we ought to be anti-English, and that we ought to play our part in a three-to-one policy of Scotland, Ireland and Wales against England to reduce that 'predominant partner' to its proper subordinate role in our internal and imperial and our international relationships are among the important practical considerations which would follow from the acceptance of *Blutsgefuhl* in Scotland.[7]

However, others within the nationalist movement attacked this negative attitude, evoking the Highlands and Gaelic culture in more inclusivist, non-threatening language.[8]

The First World War was a catalyst in the changing attitudes of the Labour Party towards nationalism. The 1918 election witnessed an alliance between the party and the Highland Land League, itself now fulfilling a much smaller role, befitting its diminishing impact in the region. Nonetheless, the pact formed between these two organizations signified a common position between those on the left of the Labour Party and Highlanders still campaigning for land reform.

---

5 MacEwen, *Thistle and the rose* (1932), p. 1. 6 For more detail, see Hanham, *Scottish nationalism*, pp 27–8. 7 Hugh MacDiarmid quoted in MacEwen, *Thistle and the rose*, p. 9. 8 Ibid., p. 10.

A handbill issued in 1920 by the Highland Land League crystallizes this sentiment:

> SCOTLAND FOR EVER!
> HOW IS SHE BECOME TRIBUTARY!
> She that was Great among the Nations!
>
> COMUNN AN FHEARAINN
> (The Highland Land League)
> (Air son Dachaidh agus Dùthcha).⁹

However, within the ranks of the Labour Party, there was a deliberate retreat from any overtly Scottish nationalist aspirations. Clear evidence for this shift in the party's stance lies in the low priority given to the Government of Scotland Bill by the 1924 Labour government.¹⁰

Within Gaeldom itself there were signs of a more subtle interpretation of the merits of Gaelic culture for a modern Scotland in a post-war Europe.¹¹ This reflected fears among Gaels that they were being perceived as Gaelic separatists due to their association with some of the more colourful and eccentric members of the Scottish nationalist movement. Alexander MacEwen claimed that

> Gaelic has many virtues, but one of its most valuable and hitherto most neglected attributes is that by giving its people the gift of bilingualism it can lay the foundation of acquiring other languages – a facility which the Englishman has always lacked.¹²

This sober assessment of the merits of the Gaelic language for a future Scotland reflected a deeper sense of exasperation at the external images of the Highlands and Gaelic culture being promulgated by Romantics and adherents of the 'Celtic twilight' school. Reactions to the fantasy world being presented by these writers were swift. Many Gaels, such as those in the Gaelic Society of Glasgow (1887) were keen to dispel the erroneous images being promulgated by non-Gaels.¹³ Some felt it necessary to issue correctives to the sentimental versions of their homeland produced by the 'twilightists'. Contributors to the published papers of the Gaelic Society of Glasgow were applauded precisely because they did not

> insistently return to the field of Celtic myth, so peculiarly fascinating to men of letters who at all care for Celtic literature, but receded irrecoverably from the interest of Gaeldom, and yet so prominent in

---

9 Cited in Hanham, *Scottish nationalism*, p. 141.   10 Lynch, *Scotland*, p. 433.   11 MacEwen, *Thistle and the rose*, pp 10–12.   12 Ibid., p. 12.   13 This society published collections of papers presented at its meetings in three volumes – 1891, 1894 and 1908.

many recent Celtic writings as to intensify the English illusion that we are all children of mist and fantasy, cut off by temperament from ordinary humanity that finds poetry, romance, and a national spirit in the common interests of the day.[14]

To distinguish their scholarly work and general interest in the Highlands, the point was made that 'the proper study of the Gael is the Gaelic race', a route that was regarded as both the most direct and the safest in order to avoid a warped and artificial sense of the Highlands and its people.[15]

In the early part of the twentieth century, there emerged fictional works which were more representative of the Gaelic world than the treatment meted out by 'Celtic twilightists'. Neil Munro, an Argyll man, was typical of the new approach, producing works of serious historical fiction, such as *The new road* (1914) and the popular humorous tales of *Para Handy*, written under the pseudonym of 'Hugh Foulis'. J. MacDougall Hay, another Gael from Argyll, dedicated his novel *Gillespie* (1914) to Munro. Hay was trying to examine contemporary issues relevant to the inhabitants of the west central Highlands. Therefore, some literary figures were keen to move beyond further sentimental accounts of the Gael. Their critical attitudes towards the 'Celtic twilight' school were shared by those living and working in the Highlands and Islands.

Given the central importance of land reform to the development of the Highlands and Islands in the late nineteenth and early twentieth centuries, it took some time before other aspects pertaining to the vitality of the region were addressed. The Depression of the 1930s crystallized the Highland problem. For politicians and social commentators, it was readily apparent that crofting reform alone would not resolve the deep-seated difficulties affecting the Highlands.[16] Consequently, concerns about the quality of life were being raised along with a recognition that migration, even if only temporary, was not a viable option for sustaining the communities.

The Highlands and Islands were far from quiescent during these changes, though the resistance shown did not mirror that of the earlier Crofters' War (1882–8). The main feature indicating the Highlanders' displeasure at the failure to resolve their problems were the numerous land-raids occurring with varying degrees of intensity throughout 1906–20. By the 1920s, the dominant perception of crofting within government circles was negative. Crofting was charged with failing to bring economic security or parity of living standards with the rest of Britain.[17] For the Highlands, these difficulties were compounded by the fact that government treatment of the region's economic and social needs was based on the 1886 Act.[18] For the crofters of the Highlands and Islands, the 1886 act had

14 Munro (ed.), *The old Highlands* (1908), p. xi. 15 MacBean, 'Gael as seen in his language' (1908), p. 227. 16 Cameron, 'Objective one'. 17 Cameron, 'Special policy area', p. 201

been greeted with victorious acclaim. The intervention of the state to reallocate land at the expense of the landlords was hailed as nothing short of revolutionary.[19] However, some of the more astute policy informers felt that the divergent needs of the Highland economy were overlooked because the legislation of the late nineteenth century treated the Highlands as a monolithic entity.[20] It was felt that there had been an over emphasis on 'controversial issues to the virtual exclusion of either quantitative or comprehensive thinking'.[21]

But, in the 1880s, all interested parties generally felt that the peculiar circumstances of the Highlands merited a distinctive policy approach. Legislation was drawn up to reflect the exigencies of the Highlands. The creation of the Congested Districts Board (CDB) is an example of this approach. The CDB was initially set up to relieve the problems of overcrowding, while simultaneously trying to place crofting on a more secure economic footing. But the demand for new holdings to appease the landless cottars was addressed at the expense of existing crofters who wanted to extend their land and make crofting a viable and autonomous form of employment.[22] Unable to bring crofting into the modern era, and riven with ideological disputes, the Highlands were on the verge of terminal decline.

The post-war slump posed specific problems for the Highlands because of the reliance on the ancillary sector.[23] Difficulties and tension remained with the perceived misuse of land. Despite moves to improve the situation, with most of the available land now being settled, there had been a failure to induce any form of economic growth.[24] Consequently, the large scale Scottish emigration of the 1920s particularly affected the Highlands.[25] The parishes of the north-west Highlands and Islands were particularly affected, and the reappearance of emigrant ships brought a sober reminder of previous misfortune to the inhabitants of the region.

Against this backdrop of worsening economic and social conditions, the development of hydro-electric schemes was regarded in some quarters as a panacea for the troubled region. In 1929, the West Highland Water Power Bill was presented to parliament. The feelings generated by this proposal were in fact

---

18 The sense of malaise within the post-war Highlands contrasted markedly with the almost universal euphoria that greeted the passing of the Crofters' Act in 1886. But before the ink on the statute book was dry, some commentators were expressing reservations. Those who have taken a critical stance in relation to crofters reform include: Caird & Moisley, 'Leadership and innovation' (1961); Gillanders, 'Gaelic Scotland today' (1968); MacInnes, 'The Crofters' Holdings Act' (1987). For a radically different point of view, see Hunter, *Crofting community*.
19 Hunter, *Crofting community*, pp 161–2.   20 Congested Districts Board (CDB), *Annual report* (1897), p. ix.   21 Collier, *Crofting problem* (1955), p. 2.   22 Cameron, 'objective one', pp 155–6; Hunter, *Crofting community*, pp 184–5, 192.   23 The decline in stock prices and the decline of the fishing industry posed particular difficulties. See Hunter, *Crofting community*, p. 205.
24 For an example of the continued anger at deer forests, see MacDiarmid, *Deer forests* (1926).
25 Cameron, 'Objective one', p. 157.

a microcosm of the larger debate on economic and social development in the region, and the issue went to the core of the Highland problem. In the representations made to parliament, it became apparent that not everyone shared the enthusiasm of the developers. Objections were raised from various interested parties, including local politicians, fishery groups, coal producers and landowners. They argued that the proposed schemes would destroy the scenic beauty of the region, put intense pressure on the fragile infrastructure of the Highlands and cause untold damage to the tourist, fishing and sporting industries.[26] The opponents were successful in delaying the hydro scheme, but when it was reconsidered in 1936, the problems afflicting the region had become even more acute. Unemployment in the region had continued to rise and this stark reality, along with the work of the Highland Development League in assuaging peoples' concerns, helped to shift public opinion in the Highlands towards an acceptance of hydro-electric schemes.[27]

Alexander MacEwen, in a speech delivered to the Gaelic Society of Inverness on 19 March 1937, rounded on those who expressed antipathy to industrialization in the Highlands:

> I do not wish to refer to the merits or demerits of a controversy about which most of us are very tired, but I must say something about the objection which was brought very prominently forward viz., that it is wrong to industrialize the Highlands, which must be allowed to pursue their 'natural development'. Good heavens! What is the natural development of the Highlands? Is it the dole and the continual outcry for grants and subsidies?[28]

Reminiscent of a deeper attack on cultural perceptions of the Highlands and Islands held by romanticists and adherents of the 'Celtic twilight' school, he continued:

> I sometimes think that the loveliness of our country blinds us to the real human problem – the problem of men and women and young people eating out their hearts in boredom and despair. I am sick of all this talk of the charm of the 'misty island' and the 'Blue waves of Barra', and the eloquent orations on 'Tir nam Beann nan Gleann is

---

26 For specifics on this, see Payne, *The hydro* (1988), pp 29–30; Harvie, *No gods*, pp 46–7. 27 Cameron, 'Objective one', p. 157. The Highland Development league was established by volunteers in 1936. One of its members, Dr Lachlan Grant, published *A new deal for the Highlands* (1935). Based in Glasgow, the organization had links with the Sea League, national and local government and the Hilleary Committee of 1938. 28 See 'Annual dinner', *TGSI*, 38 (1937–41), 160–1.

nan Gaisgeach'. We still have the bens and the glens, but where are the heroes?

To the echoes of applause, he concluded by arguing that people in the Highlands must even contemplate locating factories in the region in order to address the very real problems that were causing so much distress: 'I don't like factories and machinery, but remember that the modern electrically driven factory is a very different thing from the old steam factory. Stone walls do not a prison make!'[29] It was a powerful attack on those 'Highland gentlemen' who were living in an idealized past.

But, despite the fiery comments from MacEwen and others like him, there was still a residual antipathy towards industrialism. This was evident in the resistance to the proposal to include the Highlands under the Special Areas Act. It was felt in some quarters that there would be negative connotations in being associated with declining industrial and urban regions of Scotland. Support for the more realistic and informed realities of the Highlands and Islands in the late 1930s were found in a government-sponsored initiative, the Hilleary Committee (1936–8). Inspired and informed by visionary projects such as the Tennessee Valley Authority (TVA) in America and the Dneiper Dam in the USSR, the Hilleary Report of 1938 pleaded for policy decisions to be based on a more informed and precise understanding of the current situation in the Highlands and Islands, and less on emotive perceptions of the region and its people. The members of the Hilleary Committee supported the view that the extension of the number of croft holdings had been achieved at the expense of improving existing holdings and therefore recommended methods which were 'of assured practical value'.[30] It called on the government to make the Highlands and Islands an area of 'special favours' in order to address the problems of depopulation and unemployment.[31] Because of the war, their recommendations were not acted upon, but the general thrust of their argument was taken up by activists in the region and informed much of government thinking in the following decades. The tensions surrounding these conflicting views on the future of the Highlands and Islands form the basis for the remainder of this book.

---

29 Ibid., 159–63. Even factories were preferred, 'rather than starving both their souls and bodies on dole-supported crofts'.   30 Scottish Economic Committee, *Highlands and Islands* (1938), p. 27.   31 Ibid., p. 15.

PART II

Governing the Highlands, 1939–1965

4

Reconstruction, regeneration and regional development: government approaches to the 'Highland problem', 1939–1965

They built a house with stones.
They put windows in the house, and doors.
They filled the room with furniture and the beards of thistles.
They looked out of the house on a Highland world, the flowers, the glens, distant Glasgow on fire.
They built a barometer of history.
Inch after inch, they suffered the stings of suffering.
Strangers entered the house, and they left.
But now, who is looking out with an altered gaze? What does he see? What has he got in his hand? A string of words.
He who loses his language loses his world. The Highlander who loses his language loses his world. . . .
       'Shall Gaelic die?', Iain Crichton Smith (1969)[1]

The 'lone shieling on the misty island' is always certain to bring a lump to the throat of the exile, but the probability is that had the shieling not been so lonely; had it possessed electric light, radio and a garage; had it been within reasonable reach of a cinema or good dance band and, above all, had the inhabitants had security and a decent standard of life, the exile would never have exiled himself. Unless we make life in the Highlands worth living for the Highlanders there is no solution to the Highlands problem. Until we solve that problem, Scotland will be neglecting one of its finest assets. We believe that it will not be difficult to solve if it is tackled with vigour, foresight and the accepted fact that Highlanders are ordinary Scottish people entitled as much as the rest of us to a full, free and happy life.
    Scottish Labour Party, *Plan for post-war Scotland* (1941)[2]

---

[1] Fulton, *Iain Crichton Smith* (1981), pp 135–8. The translation was by the author and the original was published in *Lines Review* (1969). For a critique of Smith's work, consult Nicolson, *Iain Crichton Smith* (1992). [2] SLP, *Post-war Scotland*, p. 13.

Iain Crichton Smith's 'Shall Gaelic die?' offered a baleful reflection on many of the tensions in the Highlands and Islands life during the post-war decades. It captures the essence of what, for Scottish Gaeldom, the Highlands now represented: struggle and loss.³ Such sentiments were far from unique to the poets and bards; their essential message was popularized and made accessible through a wide variety of Gaelic songs and folklore. The essential point, however, was that the idea of a special 'way of life' was founded upon an interwoven and spiritual uniqueness of place; a view that required the commitment of the believer or the knowledge of the insider. By contrast, the Scottish Labour Party provided a more hard-headed materialist assessment of the region's plight. These polar views in some ways encapsulate the very problems of philosophy that dogged the region's fortunes throughout our period.

While the culturalists mourned an age of decline, the Second World War ensured that this would be a pivotal moment in Highland history in more ways than one. The watershed was of course more profound even than its Highland implications might suggest, for this conflict had seen the British peoples and the last remnants of empire brought together in a titanic struggle against a common enemy. As such, this inevitably had implications for Scottish political life. One major problem was that nationalism had become stained by the excesses of Nazism in Germany. But the period offered hope for the Highlands, as it did for Britons elsewhere and Scotland's political parties emerged from the war keen to rebuild the economic and social life of the country. The Highlands was high on their agenda. The Labour Party's optimism was evident in its *Plan for post-war Scotland*. Here the party was pushing the idea of developing hydro-electric schemes in the Highlands, with the energetic wartime Secretary of State for Scotland, Tom Johnston, proving to be a driving force.

The agencies set up by post-war governments, including the North of Scotland Hydro-Electric Board (NSHEB), are a vital part of the post-war scene in the Highlands and Islands. They are afforded detailed treatment in the next chapter. The present chapter, however, focuses upon the attitudes and policies of the main political parties in Scotland towards issues that affected the Highlands and Islands. One of the major aims of the chapter is to record and comment upon the subtle changes in emphasis that are evident during the period 1939 to 1965. Our starting point is the immediate post-war period, when following the

3 The sense of an unchanging tradition, a practice of settlement and occupancy with Gaelic roots stretching back over 1,000 years is represented by the line 'They built a house with stones'. Their 'Highland world' represented a sense of place, the Gael's place contrasting with the industrial world to the south. The 'barometer of history' relates to the changing fortunes of the Gael with the central expropriation of the Clearances. The 'strangers' who came with their 'altered gaze' are seen as alien to the *Gàidhealtachd*, but Smith is also aware of the Gaels losing their language. By the mid-twentieth century, Gaels are in danger of not engaging with the Gaelic names all around them – of places, glens, hills, corries. The map has just become a 'string of words'.

years of decline, which were exacerbated by the exigencies of war; the immediate aim of politicians was simply to reconstruct the region. From that basis, the emphasis gradually shifted towards regenerating the area and making best use of its natural resources and traditional industries. By the 1960s, planned regional development was the dominant approach favoured by politicians and their advisors as they wrestled with the difficulties of stemming depopulation and social decay (see Table 2.1). This they did, in part, by granting government assistance to induce economic growth.

Yet the Highlands and Islands were not immune to the vicissitudes of government policy. As policies failed, or new initiatives were tabled, the region experienced different fortunes. Overall, however, the failure of successive governments, both Labour and Conservative, to adequately ameliorate the region's problems, ensured that the Highlands and Islands would continue to loom large in nationalist discourse. Before analyzing the ways in which the nationalist agenda impacted on the Highlands, let us turn to the peculiarities of Highland politics.

Table 2.1 Percentage population change by decades in the crofting counties (figures taken from Cameron, 'Objective one' (1996), p. 155).

	1900s	1910s	1920s	1930s	1940s	1950s	1960s	1970s
Argyll	−3.8	8.4	−18.1	−1.9	−2.6	−6.3	1.0	2.7
Caithness	−2.7	−11.6	−9.2	0	−11.7	20.7	1.5	−1.5
Inverness	−3.2	−5.5	−0.5	−1.2	4.8	−0.7	7.3	24.1
Orkney	−9.8	−6.9	−8.3	−2.3	−1.4	−12.2	−8.6	11.7
Ross	2.6	−8.5	−11.0	−1.3	−2.4	−4.8	1.2	18.5
Shetland	−1.1	−8.6	−16.1	−7.0	−3.0	−7.8	−2.8	57.8
Sutherland	−6.5	−11.8	−9.6	−5.0	−10.5	−1.4	−3.0	8.4

A TRIPTYCH OF NATIONALISMS: HIGHLAND, CELTIC AND SCOTTISH

The voting behaviour of the Highlands and Islands electorate is regarded by psephologists as atypical in comparison with the rest of the United Kingdom. The personality of the candidate has always been a key factor for the constituents and, consequently, the Highlands have not been the sole property of any one party.[4] All the main parties, with the exception of the SNP, represented Highland and Island constituencies between 1939 and 1965. Highland politicians felt a collective responsibility to work together in order to focus attention on the region.[5] In cultivating this close relationship with his constituents, the Highland MP was often at odds with his party's policy with regard to the region as a whole,

---

4 Grimble, 'Caithness and Sutherland' (1966), pp 230–1. On p. 284 there is a table with the Highlands and Islands election results between 1945 and 1966.   5 Kellas, *Scottish political system* (1984), p. 243.

especially when it was in government. David Robertson, Conservative MP for Caithness and Sutherland between 1950 and 1964 was one such example resigning the whip in 1959 in protest at the Conservative government's failure to alleviate the concerns of his constituents.[6] Highland politicians also acted as conduits of information from the peripheral community to the core, connecting the local political arena with the wider forum.[7] Others also played a vital role in shaping and expressing Highland opinion in the post-war era. As with the 1880s, poets continued to exert influence in their communities and their work is a useful barometer of views within the Gaelic intelligentsia.

The poet Iain Crichton Smith, whose work set the tone for the major theme of this chapter, was but one of a coterie of Gaelic literary figures whose prodigious talents heralded something of a renaissance in the artistic world of post-war Gaeldom.[8] The seeds of this revolution in Gaelic culture lie in the 1930s, but Sorley MacLean's collection of love poems *Dain do Eimhir agus dain eile*, published in 1943, is regarded as the inspiring catalyst.[9] MacLean and his younger contemporaries, Derick Thomson and George Campbell Hay, were keen to move beyond the sentimental and romantic poetry and prose associated with the 'Celtic twilight' movement.[10] These Gaelic writers showed a deeper understanding of the wider political context which affected the Highlands and Islands and addressed issues relating to identity, language and nationalism.

In the period 1939–65, many Gaelic activists, unlike the political parties, continued to champion the cause of Scottish nationalism in order to affect a cultural *risorgimento* and root the particular situation of Scottish Gaeldom within the wider experiences of a war-torn world.[11] Sorley MacLean's early experiences as a school teacher in Edinburgh, against the backdrop of the rise of fascism in Europe, hardened his socialist beliefs. MacLean's universalist and internationalist tendencies stimulated his analysis of the Highlands and Gaelic culture. Thomson and Hay drew on their experiences in the war to illustrate their nationalist thoughts, but Hay differed from Thomson because of his more inclusive attitude to cultural nationalism. Hay's background as a Kintyre man, with Lowland and Highland ancestry and (perhaps crucially), someone who learnt Gaelic himself, heavily influenced his poetic offerings. Significantly, his use of the term *Alba*, as opposed to *Gaidheals* and *Galls*, reflects his desire for plurality in both linguistic and cultural terms.[12] But what makes Hay's work so

---

6 Kellas, *Modern Scotland* (1968), pp 190–1. 7 Kellas, *Scottish political system*, p. 247. 8 MacLeod, 'Renaissance' (1989). It was somewhat paradoxical situation that this revolution in Gaelic arts should coincide with the near destruction of the language. Those Gaelic activists that recognized the parlous state of this language, as young native speakers abandoned their language, elected to preserve the rich folklore of the Gaels by setting up the School of Scottish Studies. 9 MacLeod, 'Renaissance', p. 224. 10 For a critique, consult Smith's 'Poetry of Derick Thomson' (1986); Whyte, 'George Campbell Hay' (1988). All of these poets contribute to MacAulay (ed.), *Nua-bhardachd Ghaidhlig* (1976). 11 MacLeod, 'Renaissance', p. 223. 12 *Alba*, *Gaidheal* and *Gall* translate as Scotland, Gael and 'foreigner' (or non-Gael) respectively.

powerful and of lasting relevance is the way in which he resists the temptation to become entrapped by a Gaelic sense of Scottishness; although he uses the *Gàidhealtachd* for imagery and setting in many instances. Hay made use of the Arab world as an appropriate context for the affirmation of Gaelic and Scottish identity and to grapple with issues common to all nation-states experiencing ethnic tensions within their borders.[13] His other early poetry offered a progressive vision of a new Scotland, enriched by returning émigrés from overseas Gaelic settlements (the offspring of the cleared), no longer employing their energies for the bloody cause of empire, but now centred on trying to create a better civil society in Scotland. Hence, the early years of the war witnessed a resurgence in Scottish nationalism within Gaelic poetry; a phenomenon that would encourage the notion that Scottish Gaels were to the fore in the re-emerging pan-Celtic movement.

This desire for political self-determination from some Gaelic activists was mirrored in other Celtic areas of post-war Europe. However, there were major difficulties for Scots and Gaels aligning themselves with minority nationalist movements that had close associations with fascism during the war. In a sense, the claim of nationalists for secession or devolution was completely discordant with the dominant mood within post-war Europe. Unity and reconstruction were the order of the day, and those seemingly opposed to these concepts, such as Celtic nationalists, were much maligned. Indeed, as the 'Cold War' reached its zenith during the 1950s and early 1960s, Celtic nationalism struggled to maintain an identity. They were treated as dangerous reactionaries or dismissed as colourful cranks with dubious political credentials and espousing antiquated and irrelevant arguments. The tactics adopted by those who were prominent in campaigning for a closer Celtic union, such as Wendy Wood, tended to bolster the image of a movement riddled with eccentricity.[14] Consequently, the majority of Scots nationalists and Celticists had an ambiguous relationship with other Celtic nationalists, offering only vague endorsements of closer political ties between the Celtic peoples.[15] Despite the relatively poor response from Scottish Gaelic activists to these developments, the early years of post-war Europe did offer ideas and links which would be drawn from in the late 1960s and 1970s when the tide of public opinion had softened in its attitudes towards nationalism.

The early post-war years were important for later Gaelic activists in a number of ways. Perhaps the most abiding achievement of Celtic activists in the immediate post-war years was the foundation of the monthly publication *An Aimsir Cheilteach: the Celtic Time* (1947–54). This journal was important in developing a pan-Celtic identity and a common agenda to combat peripherality.[16]

13 Whyte, 'George Campbell Hay', pp 130–3, 123.   14 Ellis, *Celtic dawn* (1993), pp 98–9.
15 Ibid., pp 88–9, 99–100.   16 Ibid., p. 104. As with other initiatives, this was based in Ireland and, though enjoying only a brief lifespan (1947–54), it helped to forge ideas among people who

From the outset, the perilous state of the Celtic languages and the gravity of their political position were acknowledged, as this extract from the first issue shows:

> Far too long have Celtic matters been the privilege, almost monopoly, of an intellectual minority, partly living in the past and partly interested in the subject as a hobby. In these moving times we have reached the stage where the Celtic peoples will truly have to enter the struggle for life or death.[17]

However, the embryonic post-war consensus for European unity was regarded as an opportunity by some:

> the Celtic peoples [...] by its example and leadership [will] provide for Europe a way of recovery out of the morass into which European civilization is gradually sinking [...]. We Celts still have a mighty contribution to make to human civilization. Beneath our suffering and struggle there are deep stirrings.

Although their specific proposal for a 'union of Celtic peoples' did not materialize, the establishment of the Federal Union of European Nationalities (FUEN) inaugurated just after the 1949 meeting of the Council of Europe was enthusiastically supported by Celtic representatives. Despite endorsing the view that the 'national characteristics and cultures of European minorites' were to be preserved, and indeed cultivated, FUEN was never given consultative status. Notwithstanding this lack of official recognition, the beginnings of the 'unity in diversity' principle were being laid down.

Despite the ephemeral nature of some of the initiatives and publications, and the marginalization of organizations such as FUEN, the vision of pan-Celticism survived. Therefore, the main legacy of pan-Celticism in this period was to provide a base on which to build and develop a powerful lobbying group for European cultural minorities. Connections were made between Celtic, and other language activists; a process that would prove crucial in the late 1960s and beyond when the issue of protecting threatened cultures became more salient. By 1965, pan-Celticists were able to tap into a growing resentment of post-war consensus politics. Questions of ethnic identity or cultural values were no longer regarded as atavistic or superfluous to the developed world; indeed quite the opposite. This helps to explain the involvement of key, mainstream politicians within the Celtic movement; a situation which contrasts sharply with the immediate post-war years when a Gaelic renaissance and renewed interest in

---

would come to play a prominent role in the Celtic League (1961 to present day).   17 See ibid., pp 101–10 for this and subsequent material on Celticism and Europe.

pan-Celticism met with indifference or hostility from independence parties such as the Scottish National Party (SNP).

After 1945, there was to be no repetition of the marriage between Gaelic language and culture and the political nationalism of the SNP which had marked the inter-war period.[18] The reasons for the SNP's disavowal of cultural nationalism reside in the haemorrhage that afflicted the party in 1942. The war had created a schism in the party over the most expedient course of action to take. The growing dissatisfaction among the different factions was brought to a head at the 1942 conference. The resultant situation left the SNP fractured, with John MacCormick leaving to form the Scottish Convention, in effect a pressure group for 'home rule'.[19] Dr Robert MacIntyre became the new leader of the SNP and he insisted on a long-term strategy that was spelt out in detailed and comprehensive form in a policy statement in 1946 and ratified in the 1949 constitution. The reformed party also underwent a fundamental shift in economic and social policies that were reflective of a combination of influences such as New Deal Liberalism, guild socialism, and social credit, packaged together and transmitted in a populist fashion. Because of this shift in policy, MacIntyre insisted on rigid party discipline. Consequently, many of the more flamboyant members, who typically were sympathetic to or actively involved in the cause of Gaelic Scotland, were expelled. The reforms within the party did not lead to any electoral breakthrough; quite the opposite in fact. MacIntyre won a by-election in 1945 at Motherwell, but this was more a protest vote against the Coalition government than any endorsement of independence. Consequently the seat was lost at the forthcoming general election. The results of the election were disastrous for the SNP, with six out of eight candidates losing their deposits. Thereafter the SNP was eclipsed by pressure groups, the most important of which was MacCormack's Scottish Convention.[20] Despite the lack of electoral success, nationalism did play a role in influencing the two main parties, either pushing them towards a more unitary position, or making them take defensive action.[21]

The Labour Party's attitude towards Scottish home rule has always been an ambiguous one; largely dictated by the economic and social situation in Scotland and by Labour's role at Westminster. Traditionally, when in power, the Labour Party has been reluctant to implement proposals for home rule. Similarly when the Scottish economy fared well, the issue slipped down the agenda. But the Labour Party was riven with disagreement over many key policy areas; and none more so than its stance on devolution. The attitude of the Labour Party in the

---

18 For a discussion on the history of the SNP, see Brand, *National movement in Scotland*; Finlay, *Independent and free*; Lynch, *History of the Scottish National Party*. 19 See Hanham, *Scottish nationalism*, pp 166–75 for more detailed analysis of events. 20 For information of the range of nationalist political groups within Scotland in the period 1939–65, see Thayer, *British political fringe* (1965), pp 189–202. 21 Finlay, 'Nationalist impact on Scottish politics' (1993).

period 1939–65 contrasts with its earlier support for home rule, and its vacillation did cause tension within the Scottish labour movement. Tom Johnston was an early supporter of home rule, indeed in 1935 he helped form the Saltire Society and, through groups like the London Scots' self-government committee, he continued to press the case for greater recognition of the Scottish dimension to British politics.[22] As Secretary of State for Scotland, he was not immune to using the 'spectre' of Scottish nationalism to intimidate Westminster and gain further concessions from Churchill's wartime coalition government.[23] Hence the legacy of Johnston is somewhat confusing in relation to Scottish devolution: pushing the boundaries of administrative devolution ever further, yet supporting the Union, albeit a flexible and a more responsive one.

Johnston's successors were vehemently opposed to home rule.[24] Therefore, once Labour had secured victory in 1945, their commitment to home rule for Scotland wavered.[25] The spoils of electoral victory, allied to the paucity of quality Scottish Labour MPs seriously undermined the Labour Party's commitment to Scottish home rule. This dismissal of home rule was confirmed at the Scottish Labour Party's 1958 conference when they rejected a motion calling for devolution.[26]

Historically, the Conservatives were implacably hostile to home rule. During the inter-war period, Conservative MPs attacked the notion of Scottish independence, questioning the view that Scotland contained a homogenous population.[27] Judging by the electoral returns of the inter-war period, these arguments stressing the economic suicide which would be committed by Scottish home rule seemed to find favour with the Scottish electorate. Despite this disapproval of home rule, there were some Conservative supporters who were keen to devolve more administration to Scotland, and others who chose a more strident position because they resented English insensitivity on matters affecting Scotland.[28] The appointment in 1936 of Walter Elliot as Secretary of State heralded a fresh approach from the Unionist Party. He wanted the Conservative Party to be progressive and occupy the centre ground, rapidly being vacated due to the demise of the Liberals. His reforms strengthened the powers of the Secretary of State and led to streamlining of the administrative machine into four departments: Agriculture, Education, Health, and Home Affairs. In installing a virtual 'government in waiting', Elliot had made immense symbolic changes, not least returning to Edinburgh capital city status. The

---

22 Johnston, *Memories* (1952); Walker, *Thomas Johnston* (1988); Pottinger in *Secretaries of state* (1979), pp 87–99.   23 Lynch, *Scotland*, pp 436–7; Harvie, *No gods*, p. 103.   24 According to Lynch (*Scotland*, p. 441), they distinguished themselves 'only in their hostility to what they called "nationalistic" discontent in Scotland'.   25 See Ellis, *Celtic dawn*, p. 103; Fry, *Patronage and principle*, pp 193–4.   26 As Lynch (*Scotland*, p. 443) puts it: 'the process of becoming a British party, begun in the mid-1920s, was complete'.   27 Hanham, *Scottish nationalism*, pp 105–6.   28 Fry, *Patronage and principle*, pp 179–80.

Secretary of State would now be the 'mouthpiece of Scottish opinion in the cabinet and elsewhere', though admittedly this would be dependent on the calibre of the appointee.[29] Despite this qualification, the increased status of the Secretary of State meant disaffected interest groups had a focal point to formulate national policies and wrest concessions from London.[30]

The Conservative Party had to wait until 1951 to regain power in Britain, but their critique of the Labour administrations of 1945–51 indicated their attitudes towards nationalism and administrative reform. At a hustings meeting in Edinburgh before the 1950 general election Winston Churchill warned that the Labour government posed a serious risk to the 1707 Treaty of Union because it was drawing Scotland towards the 'serfdom of socialism'.[31] As an antidote to this threat he promised 'guarantees of national security and internal independence' which would take the form of a Royal Commission to examine the constitutional arrangements between Scotland and England and a second Scottish representative in the cabinet. Following the defeat of the Conservatives a week later, these promises were quickly forgotten, but Churchill's exaggerated fear of Scottish nationalism would continue. Back in government in 1951, Churchill instructed Lord Home to 'go up to Scotland and see if you can get rid of this embryonic Scottish nationalist thing'.[32] In contrast to Churchill, James Stuart, the Secretary of State for Scotland between 1951 and 1958, was relaxed about the nationalist challenge, an approach that typified his lacklustre period in office.[33] Throughout the 1950s, the two main parties came to a sort of consensus with regard to devolution. But the nationalist challenge ensured that they had to recognize the Scottish dimension to British politics.[34]

No longer a dominant force at Westminster in the post-war political theatre, the Liberal Party cultivated the support from their strongholds, one of which was the Highlands of Scotland. The party itself had long associations with the concept of devolution, but a lack of electoral support meant that it was often peripheral to the debate. The end of the war witnessed the complete loss of independent Liberal MPs, Sir Archibald Sinclair from Caithness and Dingle Foot from Dundee both losing their seats.[35] In the 1950 election, they captured two seats including Jo Grimond's success in Orkney and Shetland, but they lost their deposits in thirty other constituencies. The Liberals then had to endure similar internal ructions as the SNP, but following Grimond's accession to the leadership in 1957, the party attempted to put its rancorous past to rest. However, the Liberals were still going through a difficult period and their pamphlet, *The new Liberalism* (1958), made scant reference to Scottish issues, let

---

29 Ibid., pp 184–6; *Committee on Scottish administration* (1937), p. 680.   30 Fry, *Patronage and principle*, p. 186.   31 Cited in Lynch, *Scotland*, p. 442.   32 Young, *Sir Alec Douglas-Home* (1970), p. 82.   33 Fry, *Patronage and principle*, pp 196–7, 223–5.   34 Miller, *British politics*, pp 22–3; Fry, *Patronage and principle*, pp 197–8.   35 Fry, *Patronage and principle*, pp 141–2.

alone the Highlands.[36] By the time of the 1964 general election, the party, particularly in Scotland, was keen to reassert its identity.

Therefore, the main political parties' attitudes to home rule in the post-war decades were largely dismissive. Not only had the SNP disavowed itself from the cultural nationalists, but also the other parties were all focused on regenerating the Scottish economy. In relation to the Highlands, the key consideration was to integrate the region, economically and socially, into the rest of Scottish society. The methods of achieving this modernization caused intense debate during the Second World War.

VISIONS OF THE POST-WAR HIGHLANDS

> Discount as much as you will the sentiment behind the numerous bewailings against the depopulation of the Highlands of Scotland, the fact remains that alarming depopulation has taken place and the reasons for it are economic and therefore within the power of the nation to reverse.
>
> Labour Party Scottish Council, *Plan for post-war Scotland* (1941)[37]

> The Roman Empire's method with the Celtic nations was mordauntly recorded by Tacitus in a phrase of our spiritual ancestor Calgacus, 'They make a wilderness and call it peace'. I would metapoiethize [sic] this in the form, *Solitudinem faciunt, reconstructionem post bellum appellant*, the London bosses perpetuate a depressed area and have the impudence to call it 'Post-war reconstruction'.
>
> Douglas Young, *Fascism for the Highlands* (1943)[38]

Tom Johnston's appointment as Secretary of State for Scotland in 1941 marked a significant departure from earlier years, as he wielded his new-found powers to devastating effect.[39] In keeping with the pre-war consensus on social policy, he believed integration and centralization offered Scotland the opportunity to improve her standing *vis-à-vis* the English regions. An advocate of planned economics, Johnston used the powers of the new Scottish state apparatus based in St Andrew's House to dramatic effect.[40] In keeping with this purposeful attitude, the Scottish Labour Party's *Plan for post-war Scotland* (1941) offered hope for the Highland population. Despite its internal difficulties, the SNP

---

36 Harvie, *No gods*, pp 111–12.   37 SLP, *Post-war Scotland*, p. 11.   38 Young, *Fascism for the Highlands*, pp 6–7.   39 Harvie, 'Tom Johnston' (1981).   40 During the war, he pressed Scotland's case with great vigour and his brief period in office has been summarized by Lynch (*Scotland*, pp 436–7) as follows: 'It was centralization without tears, devolution without anxieties. The intricate mechanisms of the new Union were a solution for a collectivist age'.

provided a consistent critique, both to the wartime coalition and the Labour government of 1945–51. Before an analysis of their criticisms, we turn to the Labour Party's proposals for reconstructing the Highlands.

The Labour Party Scottish Council, the authors of the *Plan for post-war Scotland* (1941), noted that the coalition government had two possible courses of action available with regard to the Highlands and Islands. The first approach, based on the 'defeatist outlook', claimed that 'geographically and climatically', the Highlands and Islands were not an 'economic national asset except for their scenic advantages which might conceivably be developed as a minor industry'. The alternative, the 'realist' position, argued that 'this country cannot afford to neglect any part of its surface and, whatever the obstacles, it is not beyond our wit and ingenuity to conquer and harness them'.[41] The authors claimed that the Labour Party supported the latter attitude, claiming that the region could provide 'rich and glorious products unequalled elsewhere except at considerable cost and the economic disadvantages of importation'. For the Labour Party, there were sinister forces at work denying this potential, claiming that '[I]t has too long been assumed that the Highlands are a romantic asset but an economic liability. We believe that this assumption has been carefully nurtured by selfish interests'.[42]

These 'selfish interests' were obviously in mind with the Labour Party's proposals to nationalize the key industries of the Highlands and Islands – agriculture, fishing and tourism. The *Plan for post-war Scotland* was certainly radical in its proposals, stating:

> Surely there is such a weight of evidence to prove that private landlordism has proved disastrous to the Highlands that all who have any love for their country will be with us in our advocacy of public ownership. Our policy is that the Scottish people should take over all Scotland north of the Highland line as a great State Farm and National Park. The crofters and the farmers could be given security and the status of servants of the state.[43]

The authors of this pamphlet certainly had clear ideas on how to achieve this transformation: farmers were to be supplied with seeds and implements and their produce being collected at 'strategic points' before being transported to the urban markets. The fishing industry would also benefit from proper regulation and direction, with state-owned canning and by-product factories helping to 'bring back vigorous life to the Islands'.[44] The pre-war tourist industry was criticized for failing to market the beauty of the Scottish Highlands, 'a world-asset',

---

41 SLP, *Post-war Scotland*, p. 11. 42 Ibid. 43 Ibid., p. 12. 44 Ibid. A similar planned approach was outlined for the tweed industry, the value of which was only properly recognized by the exigencies of war.

and make it a more affordable place to visit. The Labour Party's aim was to overturn these failures:

> In the post-war years we visualize the establishment of vast centres in selected beauty-spots to which groups of workers will come by state arrangements, for recreation and recuperation. We foresee the planned and encouraged development of facilities for the tourist whilst effective and unobtrusive safeguards prevent the spoliation of the Highland countryside.[45]

In keeping with their 'sensitive' approach to the Highlands, the Labour Party argued that only 'light and clean industries' would be relocated north. They believed that these ideas, along with state-controlled electricity distribution and a state-owned and controlled transport system, would help repopulate the region and make it viable. It was proposed to build communal centres for these mixed rural communities, but 'incomers' would have to adapt to the needs of the local community. The *Plan for post-war Scotland* envisaged that 'Communal centres must open up a *modern* social life whilst at the same time encouraging and invigorating the [Highland] Games, mods and other traditional forms of native culture'.[46] As will become evident in later chapters, these initiatives to modernize the Highlands while trying to retain the cultural attributes of the region were naive, though well-intentioned.

In May 1945, a Labour Party activist from Port Ellen, in Islay, offered another vision for the future. Alastair MacNeill Weir's *Highland plan* highlighted the difference between labour activists who were from the Highlands and Islands and the actual policies that were implemented by a government centred in London. Weir echoed the earlier criticisms of previous government approaches to the Highlands, saying that 'After 200 years of "free enterprise" and unrestricted landlordism, the Highlands are semi-derelict, poverty stricken, and lacking the amenities of modern life'. He continued: 'Only common sense, energy and large-scale planned development will save the Highlands in the post-war years. We must plan or perish. The choice is develop or evacuate'.[47] Central to this planned approach, and discussed in more detail in the next chapter, was the setting-up of a Highland Development Board. Weir envisaged this coordinating body initiating measures to repopulate the region, including a scheme to put ex-servicemen, 'suited by temperament and experience', into Highland communities to work the land.[48] These wartime Labour Party publications were not the only ones that referred to the Highlands. But while the Labour Party's proposals to reconstruct the Highlands and Islands emphasized the importance of planning and state control, the SNP were suspicious of any involvement from a London government.

45 Ibid., pp 12–13. 46 Ibid., p. 13. 47 Weir, *Highland plan* (1945), p. 3. 48 Ibid., pp 4–5.

Despite the upbeat assessment from the Labour Party on the future of the Highlands, Scottish nationalists were sceptical of their motives. The wartime government's approval for hydro-electric development in the Highlands was the background for some forceful criticisms from SNP members. One activist, Oliver Brown, attacked the dismissive attitude of English MPs, ridiculing the continued assumption that Scotland was a province of England. Brown took quotes from a variety of sources for his wartime publication *Scotlandshire: England's worst-governed province*, including this one from Commander Locker-Lampson on 15 May 1941: 'Is not Scotland England?'[49] The SNP often drew on Highland MPs to embarrass the main political parties. The Conservative MP for Argyll, F.A. MacQuisken KC, was quoted from a speech made in February 1939:

> It will take a generation of immense sums of money to undo the enormous wrongs of the last two hundred years since the Act of Union and the Battle of Culloden. (Laughter) It is no use laughing about that. It is a very recent wrong in the minds of our people. The wrongs are beyond all mention.[50]

The contrast between this indifference on general Highland matters and the intense interest in hydro-electricity development is discussed in the next chapter. But in highlighting the sense of disaffection felt by some Scots towards their parliamentary colleagues, the SNP sought to galvanize support in Scotland.

Another SNP tactic to rouse support, evident in their wartime publications, was to evoke the tragedy of Highland history to stir-up the passions of fellow Scots. With that in mind, Donnachadh Mac'illedhuibh in his pamphlet, *Death to the Highland Scot*, played down the racial distinction between the Highlands and the Lowlands, blaming the destruction of the Highlands on the 'British government and the Anglo-Quisling elements in Scotland itself'.[51] This native Highlander tried to place the governments' treatment of the Highlands in a broad context:

> What lies behind the relationship of the government to the Highlanders? Has there been a conscious purpose on its part – the destruction of the Highlanders as an obstacle to the unification of the 'British' peoples in a Greater England? or is it merely a case of criminal neglect unparalleled under any civilized government?[52]

In his skeletal history of the Highlands, Mac'illedhuibh cited the classic texts of the nineteenth century (used in chapter two) such as Donald MacLeod's

---

49 Brown, *Scotlandshire*, pp 6–7.   50 Brown, *Hitlerism in the Highlands* (1941), p. 3.
51 Mac'illedhuibh, *Death to the Highland Scot* (1944), pp 2–3.   52 Ibid., p. 3.

Gloomy memories and Alexander MacKenzie's *History of the Highland Clearances*. His conclusions were critical, particularly in relation to the distortion of the Clearances and the betrayal of Highlanders' military service for the empire. He asked: 'What has been the Highlanders' reward for their part in building Britain's Empire? Blood and tears, broken lives and homes and hearts, an empty desolate land and a dying folk'.[53] Oliver Brown expressed similar ideas, when he claimed that

> Since 1745, the clan feuds have disappeared and the Highlanders have fought the French, the Chinese, the Indians, the Americans, the Germans, the Turks, the Russians, the Boers, the Kaffirs, the Zulus, the Egyptians and the Japanese among others! That is known as PAX BRITANNICA.[54]

Mac'illedhuibh's sense of anger was typified by his attack on 'Balmorality':

> Following Victoria's occupation of Balmoral, deer stalking became fashionable and the possession of a Highland estate essential to social prestige. The English occupation began. The county ceased to produce food. One export remained – men and women. The county was derelict, the playground of wealthy aliens.[55]

Brown agreed, saying that 'anglicization has always meant "Anghillicization" – the expression of native traditions of social equality by encroaching Balmorality'.[56] These criticisms of previous British governments were used to highlight what the SNP regarded as the British state's continued mistreatment of Highlanders and the mismanagement of the region in general. Douglas Young, again writing in the war attacked the changes within the governance of Scotland. According to Young, Tom Johnston's actions had led to a reduction in democracy, and despite Johnston's earlier condemnation of government boards, the policy of appointing 'outsiders' to dictate Highland policy had increased.[57] Condemning Labour in similar fashion to the Conservatives, Mac'illedhuibh argued that the governments' attitude towards the Highlanders seemed to be emigrate or assimilate, in marked contrast with their dealings with other 'minority' groups across the world.[58] These visions for the future of the postwar Highlands from sections within the Scottish Labour Party and the SNP highlight the importance they attached to the region and its people. With Labour's dramatic victory in 1945 and the beginning of a 'new dawn' for the British public, we now turn to the actual implementation of the 1945–51 Labour

[53] Ibid., pp 3–4. [54] Brown, *Scotland* (1943?), p. 19. [55] Mac'illedhuibh, *Death to the Highland Scot*, p. 14. [56] Brown, *Scotland*, p. 18. [57] Young, *Fascism for the Highlands*, p. 7. [58] Mac'illedhuibh, *Death to the Highland Scot*, p. 14.

administration's policies to analyze the extent to which the rhetoric matched the reality.[59]

RECONSTRUCTION

Once in power, the Labour Party began its process of reconstructing the region, aiming to realize the potential that they felt the Highlands offered. Because of the structural changes within the British social and economic spheres, Labour politicians increasingly regarded the Highlands as being part of the underlying British problem. This was because the Highlanders were often dependent on seasonal labour in the industrialized Central Belt, but there was also a recognition that they had their own inimitable difficulties stemming from the poor record of indigenous economic activity. Within the ranks of the Scottish labour movement, there were still individuals who felt a keen sense of responsibility for the Highlands, though strictly on the level of economic and social improvement, and as we have seen none was more influential than Tom Johnston.[60] His legacy meant that the region could no longer be ignored, and the Labour government of 1945–51 responded in kind.

The Labour administration's *A programme of Highland development*, published in 1950, was taken as the blueprint for successive government's approaches to the 'Highland problem' up to the 1970s.[61] This white paper also sheds light on what the Labour government implemented during their first full term of office. In this publication, the following definition was used to outline the nature of the problem facing politicians and administrators concerned with the region:

> Fundamentally, the Highland problem is to encourage people to live in the Highlands by making it possible to secure there, in return for reasonable efforts, proper standards of life and the means of paying for them. The depopulation of the Highlands has long been viewed with concern. Commissions and committees of enquiry into the Highland problem or into particular aspects of it have been numerous, but the action taken by successive governments has been designed to preserve rather than to construct and has been motivated by social rather than economic considerations.[62]

As we saw in chapter two, this interpretation of government policies in the 1880s and 1890s is open to debate, but the report argued that since the 1940s new

---

59 The sense of a 'new dawn' was something of an exaggeration in Scotland both in terms of electoral success and the calibre of MPs returned. See Lynch, *Scotland*, p. 441. 60 Labour Party, *Forward Scotland* (1949), p. 5. 61 Gillanders, 'Gaelic Scotland today', pp 95–6. 62 *Programme of Highland development*, p. 1.

factors had emerged to allow a more radical approach to the Highland economy. For example, the prohibitive and dilapidating effects of the previous era (that is, the depressed nature of the agricultural and fishing industries) were no longer regarded as an impediment to economic growth because of the increased importance of home food production, the necessity for a large-scale programme of afforestation, the development of hydro-electric power in the Highlands and the greatly increased importance of the tourist trade. This provided the basis for a more constructive approach to the Highland problem and for treating it effectively as one of economic development; hence the need for a reassessment of the situation in the Highlands and the framing of plans to secure the full benefits presented by these fresh factors.

It is significant that the first government publication on the 'Highland problem' since 1938 should make scant reference to the Gaelic language or culture either as an important factor in the overall resolution of the problem, or as a policy aim in itself. Instead, the focus of the paper was on economic measures designed to maintain the population in the *Gàidhealtachd*, a general approach that could find few detractors; though, as we shall see in chapters six and seven, both Highlanders and Gaels found fault in the actual process and implementation of it. The government's comprehensive position in relation to the Highlands was stated as being

> to continue and extend the provision of basic services, with special financial assistance to Highland local authorities, and to encourage the development of the principal industries of agriculture, forestry, fisheries and tourism, the exploitation of natural resources and the growth of manufacturing industries, particularly those based on local resources.[63]

Since 1945, a major component of successive government initiatives has been the desire to improve the infrastructure of the Highlands and Islands to try and alleviate the disadvantages stemming from geographical isolation. The *Programme of Highland development* reiterated that commitment because of the recognition that without decent lines of communication all aspects of the Highland economy, from manufacturing to tourism, would be adversely affected and standards of living would suffer consequently.[64] Moreover, the crippling freight and transport costs of the ferry services were also seen as potentially damaging and following the prompting of the Advisory Panel on the Highlands and Islands (hereafter Highland Panel) there was a commitment to offer financial assistance to rectify this situation and improve ferry and fishing boat terminals.[65]

63 Ibid., pp 21–2.   64 Ibid., p. 10.   65 Ibid., pp 7, 22.

The main plank of the white paper was to bring the social amenities of the Highland region up to the standards enjoyed elsewhere in Britain, but underlying this desire was the aim of developing economic initiatives to stem the problem of depopulation.[66] The government pledged financial assistance for local authorities to provide basic services such as housing, water supply and drainage, health services, education and transport. Two years earlier, a new system of equalization grants was introduced to ensure that poorer local councils were able to improve their provision of services to the standard of local authorities with wealthier resources.

This state assistance allowed local authorities to embark on a significant housing programme, including the importation of over 1,000 of the once ubiquitous Swedish timber houses. The net result of this more focused and sustained strategy was the completion of over 6,000 houses between 1945 and 1950 compared with around 9,300 in the twenty-year-period from 1919 to 1939.[67] The report also noted the early successes of the grants made available to crofters under the provisions of the Agriculture (Scotland) Act of 1948. This enabled crofters to modernize their distinctive black houses as well as farm buildings; a practice that the authors believed would reap more benefits as the tourist industry developed.

The Labour government of 1950 put the provision of adequate water supplies and drainage as 'perhaps the most important single improvement which can be made in the amenities of the Highlands'.[68] Though these developments would benefit all inhabitants, dairy farming and tourism were singled out as areas that would notice the most marked difference. Bearing in mind the 'immense arrears to be overtaken', the government pledged further help for Highland authorities. They already received the maximum rate of grant available (85 per cent) through the Rural Water Supplies and Sewerage Act of 1944, but the possibility of extra funding for those in the Highland Development Area under the Distribution of Industry Act (1945) was also raised.

The 1947 National Health Service (Scotland) Act incorporated the special assistance given to the region from the Highlands and Islands (Medical Services) Scheme of 1913. The earlier act was designed 'to overcome the geographical obstacles to the provision of medical services for the people of the Highlands'.[69] This allowed for domiciliary medical care, with financial and other assistance provided for doctors and nurses to cover their rural practises. Hospital facilities at Inverness and Stornoway were to be extended, and the government had accepted that their isolated locations should not be seen as a barrier to the supply of the various specialist medical services through consultancy. The distinct problems facing Highlanders were also recognized by the setting up of an air ambulance service. The 1947 act consolidated and improved on these measures,

66 Ibid., p. 10.   67 Ibid., p. 8.   68 Ibid.   69 Ibid., pp 9–10.

with a new maternity department in Inverness and an extension of specialist services. It was hoped to build new general hospitals for Skye and Shetland, and an institution for the mentally impaired, but there was no set timetable. The possibility of using helicopters for those islands unable to be reached by the air ambulance service was mentioned, and experiments were being conducted with this in mind.

The Labour government was mainly satisfied with primary and secondary education, qualified by the need to improve some buildings and to address the shortage of teachers; problems that affected the whole of Scotland to varying degrees. The Education (Scotland) Act of 1946 had much to commend it, according to the Labour government, as it gave local authorities statutory powers to overcome the difficulties faced by isolated communities. The extra finance for the transport, bursaries and hostels required came from equalization grants and the Education (Scotland) Fund. The situation for the other educational sectors was not as complete, however; in particular the provision of technical education within further education was regarded as inadequate, though this problem was being investigated. According to the *Programme of Highland development*, the likely recommendations would include the founding of a central technical college at Inverness and more farm schools operating on similar lines to those in Sutherland and Ross and Cromarty. The report noted the explosion in evening classes throughout the Highlands since 1945, and promised to consider the issue of extra-curricular activity and communities requirements when building new schools.

Perhaps the most crucial problem facing government during the period 1939–65 was the need to end the isolation of the Highlands and Islands caused by the paucity of transport links. The Labour government of 1945–50 recognized that without a fundamental overhaul of the transport network, 'the maintenance of proper standards of life' would be impossible. This was all the more important bearing in mind the concerted efforts to reinvigorate the traditional industries of agriculture and fishing as well as hopes afforded to the manufacturing and tourist sectors; both wholly dependent on a modern and efficient communications system. The Trunks Road Act of 1946 paved the way for five more arterial roads to be built, including the 'Road to the Isles' (Fort William to Mallaig) and an important connection from Glengarry to the port of Kyle. All these roads were already included in the 'Crofter Counties Scheme', but because of the slow progress the Labour government decided to take on the sole responsibility for their maintenance and reconstruction.[70] The report recognized the difficulties that Highland councils faced in trying to upgrade the numerous unclassified roads scattered throughout the region, let alone the many communities with no viable road connection at all. The government therefore

70 Ibid., pp 10–11, 24.

pledged additional funds to be made available through the Department of Agriculture for the construction of roads and bridges.

Another salient deficiency of the Highlands and Islands transport and communications network was in the area of piers and boat slips. In their *Programme of Highland development*, the Labour government referred to the recent report compiled by the Highland Panel. Working on the principle that each island should have access to at least one pier, the members of the Highland Panel concluded that a detailed list of essential transport piers and boat slips should be compiled, local authorities should take over responsibility for their upkeep and the government should assist in matters relating to finance and maintenance. Accordingly, the Labour government had requested that local authorities fulfil the first of these recommendations in order to evaluate the financial commitment needed. The government, in customarily bureaucratic language, pledged to assist in the construction of the agreed essential piers 'to the extent that the general economic position of the country allows'.[71] This qualification was also used in relation to developing the ferry services of the region, with the government unwilling to act immediately on the recommendations of the Committee on Ferries in Great Britain. However, the vital role of the terminal at Kyle merited improvement to enable the new passenger and vehicle ferry to operate in all tidal conditions.

The excessive transport costs for both fare and freight charges were undoubtedly a hindrance to industry, both existing and potential plants, as well as to the realization of the government's stated aim of advancing the living standards of Highlanders. With this in mind, the government, working in conjunction with the Highland Panel, had established a joint committee to investigate the effects of transport costs on Highland development. The government's acceptance of the need to cushion the high transport costs was demonstrated by their commitment to David MacBrayne Ltd to subsidize the steamer services in the Western Highlands, a policy that also included the expansion of the fleet. The air services were run by British European Airways, and though they provided a vital lifeline for remote communities, they were not subsidized. Hence, the likelihood of these services being expanded was remote, due to the high costs of maintaining the necessary infrastructure in relation to the low density of traffic, but the report did offer the optimistic view that further technical developments may help alleviate these debilitating costs.[72]

The report reaffirmed the government's commitment to the main industries of agriculture, forestry, fishing, textiles and tourism. Various measures were announced to facilitate this general policy; some of these, such as an extensive programme to build more piers, were designed to benefit both industry and the local populations, but there were other, more focused schemes to develop lobster

71 Ibid., pp 11–12.   72 Ibid., pp 12–13.

fishing and extend afforestation schemes.[73] The issue of agriculture will be discussed in the next chapter, but it is worth noting the government's reluctance to set out clearly defined policies concerning crofting. The report highlighted the continuing importance of the Forestry Commission in providing employment to the region – a long-term vision of extending afforestation to another 750,000 acres of land, corresponding to 7,500 permanent jobs solely in the forests themselves. The forecast for the fishing industry was not an optimistic one, but the recommendations of the Highland Panel would be considered, again with the proviso of funding being made available from the exchequer according to the wider economic picture. One significant departure from past approaches was the encouragement of the shellfish industry through grants and loans distributed under the terms and conditions of the Inshore Fishing Industry Act of 1945. The main problem for lobster fishermen was in marketing the product, but the government rather meekly stated that further investigations would be made to try and overcome this difficulty. For those involved in white fish and herring fishing, the prospects were rather bleak. The act of 1945 and the Herring Industry Act of 1944 allowed fishermen to obtain extra finance to modernize their boats and equipment, but the real threat lay in the fierce competition from the growing number of bigger trawlers. On this issue, the government remained silent, consoling itself with the guarantee that handling facilities would be improved.

The industries of textiles and tourism had proved to be very valuable in maintaining the population in some of the Gaelic heartland and the Labour government was keen to develop them, especially the tourist sector. Textile production in the Highlands fell into two categories: the manufacture of hand-woven tweeds and hand-knitting. The former trade played a dominant role in the economy of the Outer Hebrides, particularly Lewis and Harris. After an initial upsurge in demand during and immediately after the war, this industry was now facing considerable difficulty in the face of foreign competition, the vagaries of fashion and the introduction of a purchase tax. The government was unwilling to exempt these islanders from this burden, unlike the hand-knitters of Shetland. Instead, the government offered the hand-weavers the opportunity of entering the tax free utility market, but the most important section, the Harris Tweed trade, decided against this option. The report indicated that the government viewed these developments as very much the concern of the industry itself, though it added that they would give assistance if appropriate.[74] The overriding concerns of the government in relation to tourism were to prolong the season and increase and improve the accommodation facilities.[75] The report noted that the Scottish Tourist Board had already proposed ways of encouraging tourists by lowering fares for the off-peak season, but other measures were being consid-

---

73 Ibid., pp 14–18. 74 Ibid., p. 17. 75 Ibid., pp 17–18.

ered. These included: a more concerted effort to stagger holidays; hoteliers reducing prices for the quieter periods; the construction of new hotels and holiday camps; the renovation of existing hotels; special priority for hotel licenses specifically geared for the overseas market; and augmenting the availability of accommodation in private dwellings. The government hoped that the drive to upgrade the Highlanders' quality of life through better housing, water and drainage would enable a growing number to provide bed and breakfast facilities. The siting of all but one of the National Parks of Scotland in the Highland counties was considered to be a welcome development, because as well as benefiting the tourist industry, these projects would also provide valuable employment; mirroring the activities in the two National Forest Parks situated in the Highlands.

In their desire to bring employment to the Highlands and Islands, the Labour government were on firmer ground with the projects mentioned above. However, the 1950 report also raised the prospect of using the natural resources of the region for commercial gain, especially minerals, seaweed and peat.[76] The government had provided aid for the quarrying of slate, limestone, silica sand, talc and diatomite, but although the Mineral Resources Panel of the Scottish Council felt that these developments were important for the social and economic structure of the Highlands, considerable difficulties remained in making them viable and sustainable schemes. The same could also be said for projects centring on seaweed and peat. The ongoing investigations into the use of both these resources indicated the experimental nature of these developments, despite the optimistic noises emanating from specialist government bodies. The report was enthusiastic in describing the potential uses of these resources and the benefits that could arise for Highland communities. In the case of peat exploitation, for example, there would be power generation, useful by-products, employment and the reclamation of fertile land. As the report said, 'Agricultural communities, it is hoped, would grow progressively as the peat is removed and would inherit the roads, services and social facilities provided for the peat-winning operations and the persons engaged on them'.[77] History has proved that the potential of these projects for substantially improving the Highland social and economic structures remained unfulfilled, but there was no mistaking the eagerness among government officials to investigate all prospective opportunities.

The report felt that despite the overwhelming rural nature of the Highland economy, ancillary industries derived from the various sectors mentioned earlier could continue to expand and make a significant contribution to the region. These ancillary occupations would be composed from a variety of industries; examples being hosiery making, distilling, fruit and vegetable canning, boat building, and the extraction of chemicals from seaweed, to name but a few. The

76 Ibid., pp 18–19. 77 Ibid., p. 19.

location and nature of these jobs could be regarded as contradictory because, on the one hand, the government extolled the virtues of rural work but, on the other, it also sought to develop the Highland Development Area centred on Inverness. The small-scale projects were deemed particularly appropriate for Highlanders: 'The development of rural domestic industries based on local products also fits in with the Highland way of life and can be complementary to seasonal occupations such as fishing and catering for tourists'.[78] The measures initiated by the Scottish Committee of the Council of Industrial Design to improve the quality of souvenirs were cited as a case in point. The government indicated that it would positively encourage private firms who wished to utilize the raw materials of the region, and assistance had been forthcoming for the aluminium factories at Kinlochleven, Fort William and Foyers.

The government's willingness to assist private ventures where it was regarded as beneficial to the local area as a whole, was consolidated in March 1949 when the Highland Development Area was established, covering the district between Inverness and Tain.[79] Under the powers of the Distribution of Industry Act, departments could contribute towards the costs of providing basic services necessary for the efficient working of the plant. Before this could be given, however, the private company had to prove the viability of the project in terms of a return on employment and production for the assistance given. The government hoped that local authorities would publicize the favourable terms offered by this initiative, despite the disadvantages in comparison with older Development Areas. To offset the high costs likely to be incurred if transporting goods from the south, the government advised companies to utilize the natural products of the Highlands, or industries already established there. The parameters applied elsewhere, in terms of the overall aim of reducing imports, would also be present in the Highland Development Area. By 1950, the report was able to announce the beginnings of industrial development at Inverness, Dingwall and Muir of Ord, along with the likely acquisition by Inverness Town Council of the Longman district, a zone that in time would bring considerable investment into the Highland economy.

This focus on developing the Highlands and Islands through economic and social means, as outlined in the Labour government's *A programme of Highland development*, was the basis on which governments attempted to resolve the difficulties affecting the north of Scotland. In the hustings to the 1951 general election, the focus was on regenerating the region, building on the much-needed capital investment of the Labour administration. The next section examines the 1950s, a period in which the Conservative Party governed Britain.

[78] Ibid.   [79] Ibid., p. 20.

REGENERATION

> In former wars, though the men went away, the women remained and where women live, life goes on. The last war took the girls also away, and many of them refused to return from life with modern amenities to the wilds of the Highlands with no roads, no wheel transport, and even no proper water supply. Without its women the Highlands will perish.
>
> Labour Party, *Forward Scotland* (1949)[80]

During the build-up to the 1951 general election, the Labour Party was keen to extol its achievements in the post-war Highlands. The above quotation from their 1949 publication demonstrates a realism in relation to the central issues of the 'Highland problem' as it stood in the mid-twentieth century. But by referring to the war, and hinting at the damage inflicted by six years of conflict and the difficulties in readjusting to peacetime, the Labour Party was able to offer a rebuke to those who criticized the lack of progress in the Highlands and Islands. The pronouncements from the Conservative governments of the 1950s were rather muted in relation to this northern area, taking issue with the degree of state involvement rather than the general intentions of the previous regime. Before examining the record of the Conservative governments, we need to analyze the background to the 1951 election to gauge the response to the Labour administrations record in office.

Despite the severity of the difficulties in the Highlands, the Labour Party felt a sense of achievement after four years in government. In *Forward Scotland* (1949), they listed the new projects underway in the key areas of forestry, housing, hydro-electricity, agriculture and fishing. Their two-pronged approach was to 'contribute assistance to the day-to-day problems which arise for solution' and 'to lay down a course of assistance towards progress in the Highlands which will help to lay a foundation of prosperity on which Highland life can flourish and reach final independence of outside aid'. They noted that much of their work was 'steady constructive work which attracts little notice' but, they continued, 'in the aggregate it will remake Highland life'. Keen to distinguish their record of government with previous administrations, the authors of the 1949 pamphlet said that

> The problems of the Highlands have never been solved in the past. Attempts have been spasmodic and sporadic. The Labour government has tackled the problem comprehensively and with vision. The Labour Party considers that the well-being of the Highlands and

---

80 Labour Party, *Forward Scotland*, p. 24.

Islands is a vital matter in the planning of Britain as a whole and that the Highlands produce among the finest of our British manhood.[81]

Although they realized that more needed to be done, and in a realistic and cost-effective manner, nevertheless the Labour Party remained optimistic about the future. With regard to agriculture they said that

> The Highlands at present support a small population on a very meagre and primitive standard of life. If its people are to enjoy a higher standard of living they must themselves produce more for the markets. The government are confident that the Highlands is one part of Britain where a large degree of expansion in agriculture is possible.

By the time of the 1951 general election, it was obvious that the Labour Party felt that its accomplishments in the Highlands, a 'minor revolution' they called it, had been ignored. There was a sense of anger at the lack of recognition accorded to the 'unparalleled progress' in the Highlands under Labour, particularly in relation to hydro-electricity. Although they felt that this 'historic moment' had gone largely unnoticed, the Labour Party was able to console itself with two ringing endorsements from the *Inverness Courier*. Although they were first published in September 1948, they appeared in Labour's 1951 campaign literature. The first report from 3 September considered it

> only fair to state that the present Secretary of State for Scotland and his two predecessors in office – all of them socialists – have proved themselves much more genuinely interested in the welfare of the Highlands than any of their predecessors for the last 50 years.

Four days later, the same publication confessed that

> In the Highlands today, even among those of us who like ourselves are not socialists, there is a feeling that at long last a genuine and sustained effort is being made to deal with the Highland problem in all its adversities and complexities and for that reason the Highland people who have never lacked faith in themselves look on the future with confidence.[82]

Therefore, Labour felt that under its stewardship, and the preferential treatment given to the Highlands and Islands, a sense of hope had returned to the region – was this a fair assessment?

81 Ibid., pp 23–4. 82 The original sentiments were expressed in the *Inverness Courier* of 7 Sept. 1948. They were then included in the Labour Party publication *Campaign quotations* (1951), p. 52.

During Labour's tenure in office, an incident occurred in the west Highlands that tested the rhetoric of the Labour Party. In November 1948, men from the crofting community of Knoydart occupied part of the landlord's estate.[83] Lord Brocket, the landlord, was not a popular figure due to his blatant mismanagement of the estate and his well-known Nazi sympathies. Indeed, in 1940 the government requisitioned his land to improve its productivity, increasing the number of sheep by over 2,000. After the war, the estate was returned to Lord Brocket, who, once again, allowed his stock to run down to below 1940 levels. At a time of reconstruction and a drive to maximize agricultural production, Brocket was facing the possible takeover of his estate by the state. But the Labour government prevaricated. Too long, in fact, and the people of Knoydart raided Brocket's estate.

The Labour government's reluctance to act in 1948 contrasted sharply with their avowed dislike for private landlordism, particularly in the Highlands. As we have seen, the Labour Party's *Plan for post-war Scotland* (1941) was radical in its proposals for land reform. Indeed, they were emphatic: 'We state bluntly that the first essential condition to the development of this half of our country is the elimination of private ownership of land. If any dare challenge this let them observe what ruin private interest have wrought'.[84] The 'seven men of Knoydart', as the original raiders were proclaimed, found little comfort in Labour's response. They set up a commission, headed by a member of the Highland Panel, John Cameron. The Cameron Report did little to redress the balance and the opportunity to tackle the issue of private ownership of land in the Highlands was lost. The outcome of the Knoydart raid was regarded by locals as an abrogation of responsibility on an issue that many regarded as at the heart of the problems in the Highlands.[85]

The SNP was the only political party to express any forceful criticism of Labour's handling of the raid on Knoydart. Their new leader, Robert MacIntyre, attacked the Labour government in a pamphlet entitled *State subsidies for private tyrannies: the lessons of Knoydart* (1949). By accepting the recommendations of the Cameron Report, MacIntyre argued that the Labour government

> Intimates to all similar Highland estate owners that so long as they neglect their estates, tyrannize over their people and generally pursue a policy calculated to destroy social life and encourage depopulation, they will be backed by the London socialist government against any just demands from the people.[86]

---

83 Starmore, 'Knoydart alternative' (1980). 84 Labour Party, *Forward Scotland*, p. 24.
85 Hunter, *Claim of crofting*, pp 70–1. 86 MacIntyre, *State subsidies* (1949), p. 3.

For MacIntyre, the judgment of the Cameron Report 'puts the "rights" of the of large-scale alien property ownership over the human and social rights of the people whose moral claim to the land is incontestable'. If the logical conclusion of the report was followed, the SNP believed it would lead to the ruination, indeed the evacuation, of Highland communities. This 'ideological prejudice' and 'narrow materialism', according to MacIntyre, 'finally leads to economic disaster by not considering human and social values'. In its conclusion, the pamphlet indicted the Labour government in scathing terms:

> Like Lord Brockett and his kind the Socialist government prefer the people to be defenceless and without independence. They must be employed by some agency under central control. The materialism of Victorian Capitalism of which the Brockett Estates provide a working example is upheld by the materialism of the newer central state power. The action of the men of Knoydart is symbolic of the need for free people to fight against both evils if they are to survive.[87]

These scathing comments demonstrate a deep unease among some sections of Scottish society towards the Labour administration, and despite its activism, it performed badly in the elections.[88] However, it was the Conservatives, not the SNP, who were to capitalize on the perceived weaknesses of the Labour Party in the 1951 general election.

The definition of the Highland problem as outlined in the Labour government's *A programme of Highland development* was taken as the template by successive governments, but was there a change in emphasis during the period up to 1965? The Balfour Commission was set up by the Conservative government of 1951–5, keeping part of a promise made by Churchill in the hustings.[89] In its section on the Highlands and Islands, the subsequent report reiterated the uniqueness of the region in terms of administrative difficulties stemming from the topography of the area and the dispersed nature of the population.[90] Because of these special considerations, successive governments had contributed disproportionately to the Highlands and Islands. The Conservative government continued in that vein; in the financial year 1953–4 the estimated expenditure of the four Scottish departments and the Forestry Commission amounted to over £11 million. The significance of this figure can be ascertained by examining the proportion of the monies spent in this region in comparison with Scotland as a whole, 9.7 per cent, while the population of the area concerned amounted to only 5.5 per cent of the total Scottish population.[91]

---

87 Ibid. 88 *Labour Party Scottish council report* (1952); Hutchison, *Scottish politics* (2001), p. 91. 89 *Royal commission on Scottish affairs* (1954). 90 Ibid., pp 81–6. 91 This expenditure did not represent all of the financial resources spent in the seven crofting counties, an area populated by 282,935 persons. See ibid., pp 122–4 for a full breakdown of the money spent during 1953–4.

The members of the commission acknowledged the depth of support for a single administrative body to oversee the Highlands and Islands area. Criticism of the existing set-up centred on the multiplicity of departments and organizations having an input into the region and the resultant lack of an integrated and purposeful plan for Highland development.[92] Nonetheless, the Conservative government believed that the existing arrangements allowed for an overall coordinated strategy for the region, despite the theoretical rationale for having a single authority. In practical terms, the government felt that there were a number of problems with the proposal for a Highlands Development Authority. The foremost concern from the government was the difficulty of adapting existing local and central government arrangements to one dominant organization. Other potential difficulties related to the possible duplication of duties between agencies, the likelihood of conflict and the debilitating effect on the calibre of local councillors by enticing them to the new body. The final argument against the founding of a Highland Development Agency was rather illuminating: 'The Highlands as a whole are not in every particular to be regarded as a special reserve which requires measures differing in genus as opposed to differing in degree from those applicable elsewhere'.[93] This appeared to contradict their concluding comments on the merits of the Crofters Commission:

> In our view, some such authority is essential in order to fulfil what will be perhaps their most important task – the balancing of economic factors with social, humanitarian and ethical considerations. We believe that the country is prepared, and rightly so, to pay a high price – in harbours, roads, transport facilities, water supplies, enclosure, land reclamation etc. – for the continued existence of a scattered population in the Highlands, a people whose contribution to the common good of the United Kingdom is acknowledged and cannot be measured in terms of money.[94]

Though typical 'one-nation' Conservative rhetoric, it was largely symptomatic of the sentiment that the crofter of the north-west Highlands should be able to remain in his/her homeland, but denying real power to the inhabitants of the region to resolve their difficulties themselves.

This unwillingness to tackle the nub of the problem and introduce radical measures to offset the particular disadvantages facing potential business enterprises in the Highlands and Islands was exemplified by the Royal Commission's comments on 'New Developments'. The Royal Commission report offered no fresh strategy to resolve the Highland problem, with the lack of success of the Development Area to entice new industry into the Inverness to Tain district

92 Ibid., pp 81–5.   93 Ibid., p. 84.   94 Ibid., p. 86.

being put down to industrialists focusing on economic concerns and coming to negative conclusions about siting their new factories in the Highlands. It was certainly not the result of any administrative shortcomings from government officials.[95] Instead, the Conservatives chose to praise the North of Scotland Hydro-Electricity Board (NSHEB) and the Forestry Commission for their 'strenuous efforts' in creating employment opportunities, and improving the social facilitates and natural assets of the region. Although these groups were already proving successful in arresting depopulation in some localities, the report stated that the full impact of their programmes, as with the attempts at power generation in the north from peat and nuclear resources and the development of the tourist industry, would take longer to register.

Although *The Royal Commission on Scottish affairs, 1952–54* was written by civil servants, its terms of reference were fashioned by the Conservative government. The general impression of Highland policy from this publication is of continuing the work started by the previous Labour administration. In their 1954 publication, *Scottish affairs*, the Conservatives were keen to emphasize *their* achievements since taking office. James Stuart, the Secretary of State for Scotland and MP for Moray and Nairnshire (1945–58), was quoted as saying:

> In the Highlands, there have been encouraging developments which, in our view, are on sound lines. Agriculture at present in the Highlands is deriving benefit from the effects of the Livestock Rearing Acts, the Hill Farming Acts, and other production grants, while the report of the Crofting Commission, which in my opinion is a very able one and is also a most interesting report to read, gives a helpful and hopeful line to follow up in the interests of the crofting areas [...].[96]

The few references to the Highlands in this 1954 pamphlet related to constituencies held by the Conservatives: Caithness and Sutherland and Argyll being the two areas singled out for praise.[97] This cursory treatment of the Highlands was also evident in other Conservatives literature during 1939–65. When the Highlands were mentioned, as in *Tory challenge* (1948), it was usually to caution against nationalizing industries or services that were involved in rural areas of Britain.[98] However, this relaxed approach from the Conservative government with regard to Highland development was not without its critics.

The SNP's internal problems did not prevent them from continuing to

---

95 Ibid., p. 85. 96 Ibid. 97 Ibid. In Caithness and Sutherland, the atomic energy plant at Dounreay, the peat plant at Altnabreac and the Shin hydro-electric scheme were all mentioned; Argyll was commended for offering factory space to potential investors. 98 In their *Agriculture and the Nation* (1959), the Conservative Party argued that state intervention in agriculture was something of a 'mixed blessing'.

attack, what they regarded as, London governments' indifference towards the Highlands. In their *Scotland in 1957*, the SNP reported on a meeting of Highland farmers at Dingwall, Easter Ross protesting against the Nature Conservancy's decision not to let cattle stock graze on Rhum. For the nationalists, this demonstrative neglect of the islands was coupled with a complete disregard for local sentiment.[99] The SNP was now less inclined to sentimentalize on the cultural damage to the region. Their more focused approach to Scotland's economic and social position reflected their wartime shift in policy and the resultant changes in personnel.[1] But the party was not content with complaining about the situation in the Highlands; they had their own policies to put across.[2]

In their *Policy of the Scottish National Party*, the SNP argued for state-owned forests, the development of local industries and a National Land Survey to reorganize the system of landholding in Scotland.[3] They continued to argue that hydro-electric schemes should be for the benefit of the community, not to further depopulation. According to the SNP, the potential of this new resource for Highland industry lay in the electrification of Highland railways and the supply of cheap electricity to households. They continued with a forceful plea for Scots to recover the ownership and control of their country in order to 'maintain therein a free community in association with the people of other nations'. Their policy document ended: 'The Scottish people will only attain full spiritual and moral stature in these difficult times and Scotland prosper material development when the power of the nation is in the hands of the Scottish people through a fully elected parliament in Scotland'.[4] Unfortunately for the SNP, the Scottish electorate was not listening, but that did not deter them from putting the nationalist case. In so doing, the SNP often drew comparisons between the British government treatment of Scotland with other 'minority' groups or postcolonial countries, 'from Canada to Ceylon'.[5] For the SNP, the 'massive combination' of English domination in Scotland threatened to 'liquidate the Scottish nation by forcing its thought and habits into an alien pattern; by distorting the economic fabric of the nation to meet the needs of [the] English economy, and by treating Scotland's social problems with remedies designed to suit those of England'.[6] For the SNP, the consequences of this approach for Scotland, and the Highlands, were disastrous.[7]

The Labour Party in Scotland was also keen to make capital out of the Conservatives rather lacklustre performance. In the lead-up to the 1959 general

99 *Scotland in 1957*, p. 10. 1 Hanham, *Scottish nationalism*, p. 175. 2 SNP, *Province or nation* (n.d.). 3 SNP, *Policy of the Scottish National Party* (1950), p. 9. 4 Ibid. 5 SNP *Scotland's present position* (1952), p. 3; *Scotland in 1957*, p. 7. 6 *Scotland's present position*, p. 2. 7 As well as arguing that 'every encouragement must be given to the teaching of Gaelic in schools', the pamphlet promised that a future Scottish state 'will adopt all appropriate methods to foster the native languages, games, music, dancing, arts and crafts and will establish radio and television services and a cinema-film industry suitable to the Scottish ethos'. SNP, *Policy of the Scottish National Party*, p. 15.

election, their pamphlet *Let Scotland prosper* (1958) criticized the incumbent Conservative administration for failing to secure Scotland's economic future. With regard to the Highlands, Scottish Labour contrasted their previous successes with the stalled progress of the Conservatives during the 1950s. A sense of pride was evident in the continued development of hydro-electric schemes. Disproving their earlier critics, Scottish Labour claimed that

> The Perthshire town of Pitlochry fought the [North of Scotland Hydro-Electricity] Board's plans, because they said a dam would ruin their tourist amenities and particularly the angling. Today, Pitlochry is an international tourist centre visited by distinguished people from all over the world. And the principal attraction is the dam with its famous fish ladder for protecting the salmon![8]

According to Labour, delays in linking remote areas to the national grid were due to mismanagement and financial parsimony.[9] The Conservative government, particularly its Secretaries of State for Scotland, was regarded as being weak in its resolve to tackle landowners and vested interest groups on fundamental issues in hydro-electricity, agriculture and afforestation.[10] Labour believed that this failure of nerve also applied to the new Crofters Commission, an organization with inadequate powers. Therefore, for Labour, the legacy of Conservative rule in Scotland had been to lessen the pace of regeneration.

Against what Scottish Labour perceived as the failure of Conservatism, *Let Scotland prosper* championed the socialist case. In the pamphlet, they claimed that

> The Highlands and Islands present one huge argument for the socialist approach to social and economic problems. If the principles of private enterprise were applied to the Highlands, and things were done only because they could show a profit, and not done if they showed a loss, then the Highlands today would have deteriorated into a national tourist park, beautiful – and deserted.

In their opinion, it was the quick action and foresight of the post-war Labour government that saved the Highlands from further decline. For Labour, the Conservatives had undermined their role as the saviours of the Highlands: reconstruction had been replaced by stasis. Because depopulation over the period 1951–6 was worse than 'even the bad old days pre-war', Labour felt that only a return to socialist principles could help arrest the slippage in Highland development. But Labour also recognized the need for a modern approach to the

8 SLP, *Let Scotland prosper* (1958), p. 9.   9 Ibid., p. 10.   10 Ibid., pp 30–1.

Highland problem, one that took into account the various regional factors that influenced development and adapting them to the unique Highland 'way of life'.[11]

REGIONAL DEVELOPMENT

> Hitherto, the Highland people generally have never been able to gather the means of providing capital for industry. Long exploitation and neglect by 'Clearance' landlordism saw to that. Apart from this, the lack of good roads, of regular cheap transport by rail and sea, and of electric power and water supply have made industries steer clear of the Highlands and the Isles. Lack of big populations and markets, and of skilled industrial labour, are also obstacles.
>
> Scottish Labour, *Let Scotland prosper* (1958)[12]

Scottish Labour's recognition of the depth of the 'Highland problem' was an acknowledgment that, despite the advances made, much still needed to be done. The sense in which 'history mattered' was also readily apparent in the difficulties facing the Crofters Commission. The next chapter focuses on this and other government agencies set up to address specific issues in the Highlands and Islands, whereas this final section examines the moves towards regional development, a UK-wide policy, but one that had particular significance in the Highlands. Before turning to the implications for northern Scotland, we need to analyze the origins of regional development.[13]

Regional policy, 'in its modern form', originated with the Local Employment Act of 1960.[14] This new approach came on the back of renewed deterioration in the Scottish economy.[15] In comparison with the inter-war period, the overall performance of the Scottish economy during 1939–65 was encouraging. In relation to other 'regions' of the UK, however, Scotland continued to lag behind in a whole range of economic indicators. The post-war surge in demand for heavy industrial products continued during the early years of the 1950s due to the Korean War, but the latter part of that decade witnessed a resumption of the comparative decline of Scottish manufacturing output. Although initially the Conservatives would rail against the centralizing effects of Labour's planned approach to reconstruction, by 1960 they too had come round to the idea of regional planning. Therefore, the need for economic diversity was the basis to *The inquiry into the Scottish economy* (Toothill Report) of 1961.[16]

Following the recommendations of the Toothill Report, Scotland received a

---

11 Ibid., pp 35–6. 12 Ibid., p. 35. 13 See Harvie, *No gods*, passim. 14 Kellas, *Scottish political system*, p. 195. Products of this shift in policy were seen in *Central Scotland plan* (1963). 15 See Harvie, *No gods*. 16 Toothill, *Report* (1961).

disproportionate allocation of resources in the fight to reduce regional differences in economic strength. Initially, Scottish industrialists received the psychological fillip of direct government involvement, but more sober assessments have demonstrated that the regional policy was fundamentally flawed from the outset.[17] As a result, the attempts of the Conservative government to implement Toothill's proposals were often patchy and inconsistent. Scotland was seen to be disadvantaged by the policy-making process itself; decisions were taken with the considerations of south-east England being paramount. Moreover, within the nerve-centre of British political life, Scotland's underrepresentation meant that all too often she was following initiatives designed for other parts of the UK. Taking the period 1945–79, the effects of these weaknesses are all too apparent. For example, despite the growth in expenditure, the absolute size of the Scottish workforce had not changed much. In addition, while *per capita* income levels augmented, so too did levels of unemployment. This failure to initiate key decisions, set with the particularisms of the Scottish economic situation firmly in mind, had a cumulatively damaging effect. Given the peculiar problems in the north of Scotland, we need to examine how this shift in emphasis towards regional development affected the Highlands and Islands.

By June 1959, a new Conservative government was willing to concede that 'in certain directions, a fresh impetus should now be given', perhaps reflecting the fact that the general feeling of prosperity affecting other parts of Britain held a certain hollowness in the Highlands and Islands.[18] The authors of the *Review of Highland policy* (1959) were pleased to announce that over 11,000 houses had been built in the region, and advances had also been made in the provision of water and drainage supplies, health provision and in educational facilities.[19] That said, there were still problems in some of the more isolated communities, lacking adequate dwellings and the standards of living afforded by electricity and modern sanitation methods. Transport also remained a source of discomfort for policy planners, as the finance allocated for long-standing road programmes quickly became insufficient in the light of increasing projections of both the volume and the tonnage of transport.[20] Because of this, the government promised to augment both the speed of reconstruction and the money allocated for Class I and township roads. Reflecting the growing importance of tourism to the Highlands, the review paper announced a provision for £250,000 per year to

17 Harvie, *No gods*, p. 37.   18 *Review of Highland policy* (1959), p. 1. Lynch (*Scotland*, p. 443) believes this conflict was felt throughout Scotland, and was partially reflected in the 1959 election result.   19 From 1950 to 1958, over £6 million had been spent on upgrading water and sewerage supplies, and it was expected that in the next 5 to 7 years 'most' of the major supply works in the Highland programme would be completed. Hospital accommodation had been increased in the islands, new technical colleges had been built at Inverness and Thurso and facilities extended elsewhere. Perhaps most significantly, over 90 per cent of the consumers in the NSHEB's area were now connected to the grid. See *Review of Highland policy*, pp 3–4.   20 Ibid., pp 4–5.

be spent on new roads to make accessible areas of outstanding scenic beauty; this would also end the isolation of vulnerable communities in Moidart, Torridon and Cowal. More piers were to be built or improved, a strategy designed to increase economic opportunities and to pre-empt the Highland Panel's findings on sea services to the islands off the western seaboard.

In relation to the basic industries of the Highlands and Islands – agriculture, forestry and fishing – the perception given was one of gradual improvement.[21] Rather disingenuously, the authors noted the satisfactory progress made by the Crofters Commission in the three years since its inception, with no comment on the deep-seated unease within the crofting communities and the resultant difficulties faced by the commission. Where limited advances had been made, such as in the participation of land improvement schemes, the government announced an increase in the funding for the Crofters' Grants Scheme from £100,000 to £500,000. The cooperative movement was also making some headway in the agricultural communities of the Highlands and Islands; a project designed to provide essential supplies, market the produce of the area and encourage new initiatives. The development of the forestry industry continued to play a large role in government thinking:

> Apart from its commercial and economic value to the country as a whole, it is a means whereby viable communities are most likely to be retained and in some cases restored to rural areas. Moreover, the employment it provides is very often whole time and includes specialized work such as operating and servicing mechanical equipment that may well appeal to the younger man.[22]

The government warmly welcomed the recent opening of a chipboard factory in Inverness, as it fitted the aim of encouraging industries to utilize the local produce of the Highlands. In order to provide a diversity of employment opportunities and much needed social benefits in the more marginal areas, the government announced an increase in the acreage to be given over for forestry planting on upland for the years from 1959 to 1963. The government proposed to develop a modern fleet for the men of the western seaboard to resolve the increased competition in the fishing areas. This would form part of a wider strategy as proposed by the Highland Panel to educate these same fishermen in the modern techniques of their trade. To meet this enlargement of fishing activity off western Scotland, the government promised to continue improving harbour and anchorage facilities in order to cope with the larger vessels. But at a time when Highlanders were calling for protection from domestic and foreign competition, these pledges would not be enough to resolve the continuing

21 Ibid., pp 6–8.   22 Ibid., pp 6–7.

decline of the fishing community of the west Highlands and Islands. With these concerns in mind, we turn to the alternative proposals of the Liberals and the Labour Party.

Both the Liberals and the Labour Party captured the sense of a new era as Britain entered the 1960s. Labour's *Signposts for the sixties* (1961) was a confident proclamation that Britain stood on the brink of a 'scientific revolution', and Labour was more committed to deliver the fruits of these technological breakthroughs.[23] The Liberal Party was keen to emerge from the political wilderness. Their three stated aims, as outlined in *Partners in a new Britain* (1963), were to reshape Britain for modernization, initiate partnerships at home and abroad to reduce class division and encourage international cooperation.[24] But the Liberals were also determined to reclaim the 'Celtic fringes' of Britain and their deliberate targeting of the rural vote was evident in their *Partners in a new Britain*, with specific proposals for regional planning and a renewed emphasis on the rural economy.

Part of the strategy of the Scottish Liberals was to attack the record of the Conservative government in relation to the Highlands and Islands. In his address to the party's general council in March 1962, John M. Bannerman, the chairman of the Scottish Liberals, criticized the lack of direction over the past decade and warned that 'the social and economic fabric of the Highlands' was 'in danger of breaking up'.[25] Bannerman catalogued a list of grievances that he clearly believed would strike a chord with his fellow Highlanders. He condemned the mismanagement of the region's economy, citing the inadequacy of the communications network – 'second-rate or entirely absent' – as hindering the development of tourism in the Highlands. The failure to replace single-track roads on arterial routes was a specific complaint in this regard but he also believed that the poor condition of township roads, 'the lifeline of many crofting areas', was exacerbating the problem of depopulation. Other factors – high freight costs, the closure of rural schools, the failure to protect the region's fishing fleet – were additional burdens for those wanting to remain in the Highlands and Islands. However, Bannerman's previous role as president of *An Comunn Gàidhealach* was evident in his assessment that the land question was fundamental to the 'rehabilitation' of the Highlands. Criticizing those who misused this resource as a 'playground', he rounded on the landowners as preventing development: 'Many thousands of acres are used for grouse and deer, and the use of land for agriculture or tourism is discouraged by the owners. The Tory today regards the Highlander as a hero in war and a gillie in peace'. In his concluding comments, Bannerman offered a simple solution:

---

23 Similar sentiments were expressed in Phillips, *Labour in the sixties* (1960).   24 Liberal Party, *Partners in a new Britain* (1963).   25 *GH*, 'Danger of break-up in Highlands: Mr Bannerman's warning on lack of direction', 5 March 1962, p. 10.

> There will be no redress for the Highland area until the Tories have been bundled neck and crop out of the north of Scotland. Their dead hand of privilege has reduced the north to an area where the people must leave if they are to employ their native energy to effect.

Two years later, another Highland Liberal set out, in great detail, the party's alternative plan for the future of the region.

The Scottish Liberals publication of Russell Johnston's *Highland development* (1964) was a particular attempt to reawaken the party's historical associations with the Highlands. Johnston's willingness to listen to the concerns of Highlanders paid dividends as he won the Inverness-shire constituency for the Liberals in the 1964 general election.[26] Johnston argued that though the Highlands merited special treatment, they could not be treated in isolation, nor should a local be made to sacrifice a career or expectations 'for the sake of a patriotic attachment to his homeland'.[27] Echoing the sentiments of the Highland Panel, Johnston called for a Highland Development Association (HDA) to be set up immediately. This was an essential element in the plan for strong regional development. The first task of the HDA, according to Johnston, would be to undertake a 'comprehensive survey of the Highlands with a view to the establishment of growth points which can trigger-off the development of whole areas'.[28] Despite the shortcomings of the Toothill Report, especially in relation to the Highlands, Johnston felt that one positive outcome was the realization that certain key areas merited concentrated government development. Given the increase in Highland unemployment since the region was designated a development district under the terms of the Local Employment Act (1960), more needed to be done. It was said that 'Industries based on natural resources such as the Pulp Mill [near Fort William] will be of tremendous value not merely intrinsically, but as "Corner Stone plants" in the Norwegian sense'.[29]

Throughout the pamphlet *Highland development*, a sound knowledge of comparable regions in Europe and further afield was evident. Norway, Switzerland and Japan are all cited as countries where regional development has worked despite local difficulties; the experience of France and Japan was an inspiration for a fresh approach to the key area of transport. No longer content to accept short-term financial considerations, Johnston believed that a strong railway network could be a 'potential instrument of regional development'. The growth of car ownership along with the stated aim of re-siting industry had clear implications for the Highlands, as Johnston pronounced:

---

26 Johnston, *Highland development* (1964). Johnston acknowledged that the pamphlet was written in full consultation with the Highland policy committee of the Scottish Liberals. The prospective candidates for other Highland constituencies were also involved as was the chair of the Scottish Liberals and one-time president of *An Comunn Gàidhealach*, John M. Bannerman.
27 Ibid., pp 5–6.   28 Ibid., p. 12.   29 Ibid.

> Now is the time to construct new roads, not only in the bleak bungaloid sprawls of the industrial south, but in the clear lands of the Highlands where a large proportion of to-morrow's Scotland will live in far better conditions.[30]

The need to establish a sound transport infrastructure was also crucial for the islands of Scotland. Given the extent of the task in hand, for all forms of transport, Johnston asked: 'why should the Highlands not lead in modernity?'[31]

The Irish experience offered strong parallels for the Highlands, particularly in relation to the land question and tourism. With regard to the former, the suggested reforms as outlined by the Liberals had specific implications for both the Forestry Commission and the Crofters Commission, on which more below. In relation to tourism, the Liberals had some harsh words to say:

> We do not accept that Tourism is the panacea of the Highlands, as has often been suggested by the Conservatives, but we do believe that as one industry among others, it has a most valuable and far from fully exploited part to play.

In Johnston's opinion, the 'professionalism' of the Irish should be drawn from to improve the standards and facilities of the tourism industry in the north of Scotland. Likewise, lessons could be learnt in terms of marketing and advertising the region, and developing cottage industries where local produce was used. Central to all these potential developments, irrespective of the suitability of comparative initiatives, was education. In emphatic terms, Johnston stated that 'We cannot urge too strongly the case for a University in the Highlands. This would serve as a magnificent focus for the spirit of constructive effort, of experiment and innovation which we seek'.

In *Highland development*, Johnston and his Liberal colleagues accepted that improvements had been made in the Highlands, but cautioned that much still remained to be done – this was especially apparent in the islands of north-west Scotland. In a specific section on the 'Island Problem', Johnston acknowledged the severity of the problems there by announcing that a separate study of the Scottish Liberal Party was being carried out. Johnston recognized that 'almost every island and indeed different districts within some islands have different potentialities and different problems'. The consequences of years of hardship and government neglect called for drastic measures. For Johnston, the first priority was to remember that

> there must be an overall solution which covers the encouragement of a satisfying way of life, the provision of employment, and in some

30 Ibid., pp 12–13, 14–15.   31 Ibid., pp 15–17, 23.

> cases the injection of new blood, but which is varied to meet the varying needs of different islands. For a satisfying way of life it is necessary to have a well-balanced community of a certain size. In some places this means deliberately encouraging immigration and paying for it.[32]

Though a laudable solution to depopulation, as will become evident in chapter seven, this was a slightly naïve position to take. But Russell Johnston's enthusiasm and commitment to redressing the failures of the past were readily apparent. He continued:

> Valuable experience and a boost to morale would be obtained by selecting certain islands, or areas within islands, for a comprehensive scheme of development [...]. In this way, it would be possible to see how best our new technical skills can be applied to the unique problem of harmonizing life in the far-flung isles with the material demands of the 20th century.[33]

In view of these proposals of the Scottish Liberals, what did the new Labour government enact?

Labour returned to power in 1964 enthused with the slogan 'the white heat of the technical revolution' and determined to make regional planning work. In their UK-wide publications, the concerns of the rural communities rarely featured.[34] In Scottish debates during the 1964 election, both main parties couched their economic policies, and criticisms of their rivals, in nationalist language. Once elected, the new Secretary of State for Scotland, Willie Ross, set about the task of regenerating the regions with a passion, and within two years various reports were published and measures implemented to offset emigration, improve the infrastructure, encourage research and development and entice industry with preferential grants.

The Highlands were an integral part of this new strategy of regional development. The Labour government's position on the Highlands was similar to the views expressed in their 1958 publication *Let Scotland prosper*. Continuity and change was the dominant approach from the new Labour administration, but the party was also aware that realism should replace sentimental perceptions of the Highlands. This was evident in their 1958 pamphlet:

> Crofting and fishing alone cannot, however, support the Highland population. We must plan for jobs in their homeland for the sons and daughters of crofters and fishermen who, at present, have to go south

---

32 Ibid., p. 23. 33 Ibid., p. 24. 34 Labour Party, *Signposts for the sixties* (1961); *Twelve wasted years* (c.1963).

to find the opportunities they seek. Labour realizes what is too often forgotten or ignored: that for many young folk in the Highlands the lure of the machine is greater than the lure of the land.[35]

Using the powers of the Distribution of Industry Act (1960), Labour would adapt the old Highland industries and encourage the new. If necessary, Labour promised to 'set up new industries under public control, with preference to those using local raw materials, like wool, timber, seaweed and hides'.[36] As with earlier statements of policy, Labour was convinced that their adherence to socialist principles was particularly suited to the exigencies of the Highlands. They pledged that

> within only a year of the election of the Labour government, the [Highlands and Islands] Board will be moving into action, proudly demonstrating to the whole of Britain that practical socialism offers new hope to men and women, crofts and communities forgotten for too long.[37]

These pre-election assurances to listen to the demands of Highlanders were at least partially answered in 1964 when the long-running campaign for some form of development authority was assuaged. The new Labour government set up a Highlands and Islands Development Board in order to meet the demands for redistributing industry and reviewing the region's transport needs. Despite the advances that had been made in the economic and social fabric of the Highlands and Islands since 1945, Labour were certainly aware of the gravity of the task in hand and the sense of history which hung over the region. In a telling statement, the authors of *Go-ahead Scotland* (1965) stated:

> For generations the crofting counties have cried out for action to revitalise their economy. They have cried out in vain. As the Secretary of State [Willie Ross] has said 'for 200 years the Highlander has been the man on Scotland's conscience'.[38]

CONCLUSION

There is a certain paradox in the period of 1939–65 in that while the Scottish National Party deliberately disavowed itself from the cultural nationalist dimension, Gaelic poets and writers of great stature were emerging to champion the

---

35 SLP, *Let Scotland prosper*, p. 39.   36 Ibid.   37 Ibid., p. 7.   38 Labour Party, *Go-ahead Scotland* (1965), p. 6.

case for independence in what Ruaraidh Erskine of Marr would describe as 'the heart of Scotland'. That said, in the immediate post-war years, Scottish enthusiasm for cultural and political connections between the Celtic countries came from those not directly involved in the quagmire of Highland politics. By the mid-1960s, however, a new generation of Gaelic student activists were keen to express their desire for closer cultural and political links between the inhabitants of all the Celtic nations. This ties in with the resurgence of the SNP and the folk revival that helped to stimulate interest in Gaelic culture in its multifarious forms.

The differences between what have been termed the 'Unionist experiment' and the 'informal home rule' of the Labour Party were not that significant.[39] The two main parties' policies were designed to reduce the disparities between inner and outer Britain. They had similar attitudes to the administration of Scotland, and by the 1950s their attitudes towards home rule were also close. Between 1945 and 1965, Scotland was virtually a two-party state, with each side 'content to leave Scotland in its condition of semi-Union'.[40] When problems presented themselves, there was a predilection to tie further strands to the gordian knot and add to the tiers of bureaucracy. Because of this creation of a 'state within a state', the Scottish public felt alienated and powerless in the face of an anonymous, omnipotent administrative machine. The example of David Robertson MP shows that there was a distinction between an indifferent Westminster and concerned Highland MPs. The false reading of the Scottish economy in the early 1950s was due to the short-term benefits of post-war reconstruction. Yet, the introduction of regional policy was not the 'lifesaver' many had foreseen. The enthusiasm for capital intensive, large-scale projects was reflected in the Highland region. As we shall see in chapter six, many Highland activists warned about the dangers of siting major industrial plants in the region or constructing tourist centres with little consultation or sensitivity to the physical and cultural environment. In effect, this made for difficulties, especially for those in the Highlands and Islands seeking to influence decisions taken at their expense.

As we shall see in the next chapter, the official response from government in the period 1939–65 was to establish specific agencies to address key aspects of the 'Highland problem'. Some bodies were designed to inform the state on the requirements of the region and to monitor the impact of legislation, while others were set up to administer specific programmes of development. Through examining the work of these government agencies, an insight can be gained into how government and its various public bodies viewed the wider problems in the Highlands and Islands. Certainly, tensions did exist between those empowered to investigate the ills of the Gaels and how their recommendations were interpreted

39 Lynch, *Scotland*, p. 436. 40 Ibid., pp 442–3.

or dismissed, and this will be examined in chapters six and seven. Whether the governments' efforts to improve the Highlanders' standard of living and end the physical isolation of many communities in the *Gàidhealtachd* would ultimately benefit the language and culture was more a matter of conjecture.

5

Government agencies and the 'Highland problem', 1939–1965

The days of a crofter living off his land are past, and not all the romantics in the Lowlands will make them return. It is from this understanding that the problem of depopulation can best be approached. People leave the Highlands because a reasonable living cannot be made in them. This may appear rather an obvious truth, but it cannot be overemphasized. It is too often said that the reasons for depopulation are the lure of the city lights, the poor housing, the lack of electric light or the poor transport. It is true that the lack of these things may drive people to the towns. But the lack itself is only a symptom of the main cause – poverty.

Scottish trade unionists submission to the Taylor Report (c.1954)[1]

We find the crofter, more particularly the younger crofter, utterly bored with the romantic conception of his life and what the city dweller thinks good for him [...] He has long since rejected the role of the noble son of nature who rejoices in homely fare and draws strength from stern privation. He now wants above all to be a citizen of this country as others are, not a curiosity or a 'character' [...] but a citizen [...] He prizes his Gaelic culture, but not to the extent of being treated as a museum-piece on account of it; he will assuredly prize it still more highly when it is no longer the bedfellow of poverty and underprivilege.

Crofters Commission, *Report* (1958)[2]

The ramifications of fighting a prolonged and exacting war gave renewed impetus to the notion of planned economics. As we have seen in the preceding chapter, the Highlands and Islands were not immune from these changes, and indeed in some measure this policy of reconstruction was more readily felt in this region, bearing in mind the difficulties surfacing before the war. The demands of Highlanders for more control in the administration and governance of their homelands accelerated during the first two decades after the war. Prior

---

1 NAS: AF81/4 Taylor Commission evidence.   2 CC, *Report for 1957* (1958), p. 7.

to the establishment of the Highlands and Islands Development Board in 1965, which brought partial realization of the call for more autonomy, the desire to improve the standard of living and economic and social well-being for the inhabitants of the *Gàidhealtachd* continued unabated. This became the overriding concern of policy-makers in the Scottish Office. Government agencies such as the North of Scotland Hydro-Electric Board (1943), the Advisory Panel on the Highlands and Islands (1947) and the Crofters Commission (1955) were established to further that aim. Moreover, the Forestry Commission, set up in 1919, received a significant fillip from the Labour government's legislation of the 1945 to 1951 period. Consequently, the Highlanders' traditional 'way of life' was being fundamentally challenged, even eclipsed, as improvements in standards of living ushered in a change of attitudes, as the opening quotations make clear. As a result of these changes, the difficulties facing the Gaelic language and culture were exacerbated, but without much in the way of wider recognition of the fundamental transformation that the *Gàidhealtachd* was experiencing. In some sense, the Gaelic language and culture were struggling to adapt to the new Gaelic society being created by the socio-economic improvements, and these changes themselves presented language activists with an arduous task in ensuring Gaels continued to cherish and uphold the language and culture of their forebears. Before analyzing the view from within the Highlands and Islands in the period 1939 to 1965 (which is done in the next two chapters), it is now necessary to focus on the three important public bodies established by government (the NSHEB, the Highland Panel and the Crofters Commission).[3] In addition, a fourth, the Forestry Commission, although not exclusive to the Highlands, played an important role there and must be considered. A closer examination of agencies such as these, and the process of creating them, reveals the complexity of the Highland problem and the reluctance of successive governments to offer radical and far-reaching proposals to overcome poverty and underprivilege.

The devolution of more administrative functions from London to St Andrew's House in Edinburgh just prior to the outbreak of the war resulted in the establishment of a virtual 'government in waiting' in the capital of Scotland. This machinery was used to good effect by the wartime Secretary of State for Scotland, Tom Johnston.[4] His adroit politicking and expedient tactics were vital in resurrecting the Scottish economy and providing the foundations for continued revival after the war.[5] Having established a 'Council of Ministers' composed of past Secretaries of State for Scotland, Johnston then proceeded to capitalize on the collective harmony instilled by the wartime spirit to press ahead with his vision for Scotland.[6] Johnston was instrumental in setting up a 'Council

---

3 The [Taylor] Commission of Enquiry into Crofting Conditions (1951–4), which preceded the Crofters Commission, will also be examined.   4 Hanham, 'Scottish Office' (1969).   5 Walker, *Thomas Johnston* (1988), pp 151–78.   6 Young, 'Scottish nationalism' (1970), p. 17; Hunter, *Claim of crofting*, pp 50–1.

of Industry' designed to analyze the needs of industry in Scotland, information which Johnston and the 'Council of State' could then use to redress the imbalance in war industry location and prevent the closure of Scottish plants which might otherwise have folded. In order to 'attract new industries or facilitate post-war development', Johnston was keen to play down the idea that the Highlands were a deprived area. This strategy was seen as integral to presenting a strong Scottish case to the London government.[7]

The Second World War undoubtedly had a dramatic impact on the Highlands and Islands of Scotland.[8] This related to the strategic importance of the region, the administrative changes taking place at a Scottish level and the renewed commitment to address the Highland problem of unemployment and depopulation. Moreover, as in previous military engagements, the inhabitants of the north of Scotland enlisted for active service in disproportionate numbers, particularly in the merchant navy. The exigencies of war actually resulted in a large number of military personnel coming to the Highlands and Islands, with important consequences for the population. The wild expanses of the Highlands and Islands offered a perfect environment for military training. The area known as the 'Rough Bounds', comprising Moidart, Knoydart and Glenelg, was heavily used by the newly formed commando units, while other 'behind the lines' groups were brought up to the Rothiemurchus estate and the Great Glen area. These units had a key role supporting the resistance movements across Europe, particularly Norway. Allied air crews also made extensive use of the region, particularly to improve navigational skills and for low-level flying to avoid radar detection. The navy bases at Kyle of Lochalsh, Invergordon and Scapa Flow were extended to cope with the increased activity centred on protecting the convoys of the North Atlantic. An aerodrome was built at Macrihanish on the Kintyre peninsula, and the ones at Benbecula and Stornoway were considerably upgraded. The establishment of prisoner of war camps throughout the region and the relocation of evacuees also hastened increased contact with the outside world.

These developments ensured that the lines of communication with the south were greatly improved.[9] But the wartime demands for key resources also heralded changes for the people of the Highlands and Islands. There was a short-term construction boom as defence spending brought much-needed employment opportunities to many parts of the Highlands and Islands, in addition to the developments in the aluminium, forestry and hydro-electric industries.[10] Moreover, the strategic demands for home-grown food and livestock also brought benefits to Highlanders through subsidized price policies

---

7 Hunter, *Claim of crofting*, pp 68–9. 8 For an insight into the effects of the war and its immediate aftermath, see Darling (ed.), *West Highland Survey* (1955) and the relevant county editions of the *Third statistical account of Scotland*. 9 Thomas, *West Highland railway*, pp 131–2. 10 For an insight into the difficulties involved in the latter, see Wood, *Hydro boys* (2002).

and requisitioning of deer farms. A number of committees were also established to investigate key aspects of Highland society – especially agriculture, fishing and hydro development.[11] As a result of these enquiries, and because of the Labour government's commitment to address the problems of the Highlands, a series of acts were passed which had a bearing on the region. For example, the Hill Farming Act of 1946, the Agriculture (Scotland) Act of 1948, and the Livestock Rearing Act of 1951 all gave financial assistance. Therefore, Tom Johnston's zeal and pragmatism was brought to bear on the Highlands of Scotland to signal a fresh approach to the region's difficulties. This 'vision' was especially apparent when harnessing hydro-electric power from the regions rich water resources became a reality.

THE NORTH OF SCOTLAND HYDRO-ELECTRIC BOARD

Under Johnston's leadership, the Cooper Commission was established to explore the possibilities of turning the vast water resources of the Highlands into practical use through hydro-electric power.[12] As a result, the Hydro-Electric Development (Scotland) Act was passed in 1943 and the NSHEB was given authority to conduct all future large-scale hydro-electric construction with a provision permitting the sale of surplus energy to the south. Johnson's rationale for pursuing this course of action was two-fold. First, the previously untapped water resources of this vast region would now be harnessed for the benefit of the nation as a whole. Secondly, it fulfilled part of his earlier vision of 're-establishing a self-supporting population in the Highlands and seeing the renaissance of the heart of "Scotia"'.[13] Thanks to Johnston (this time in his role as Director of the newly established NSHEB), the individuals involved in the nationalization of the electricity supply in Britain were fully informed of the peculiarities of the situation in the Highlands. Hence the board was exempt from the 1947 Act, which nationalized British electricity supply under the aegis of the one central body.

Special consideration was evident in the legislation itself, with a clause enabling the new body 'so far as their powers and duties permit, [to] collaborate in carrying out any measures for the economic development and social improvement of the North of Scotland district, or any part thereof'.[14] This 'social clause' was not repeated in other nationalized industries of the time and reflects the sensitivities of the area. This was apparent with regard to the natural habitat of the region and again provisions were written into the act to preserve the scenic beauty with the result that some schemes had to be curtailed or abandoned in the

---

11 *Hill sheep farming* (1944); *Land settlement committee* (1945); *Marginal farms* (1947). 12 *Hydro-electric development* (1942). 13 Cited in Walker, *Thomas Johnston*, p. 158. 14 Payne, *The hydro*, p. 45.

face of widespread public opposition, as with Glen Affric. The members of the Cooper Committee were quite scathing in attacking those opposed to the development of Highland glens for power generation as these comments from the committee's report demonstrate:

> If it is desired to preserve the natural features of the Highlands unchanged in all times coming for the benefit of those holidaymakers who wish to contemplate them in their natural state during the comparatively brief season imposed by climactic conditions, then the logical outcome of such an aesthetic policy would be to convert the greater part of the area into a national park and to sterilize it in perpetuity providing a few 'reservations' in which the dwindling remnants of the native population could for a time continue to reside until they eventually become extinct.[15]

The report went on to argue an alternative scenario in which hydro-electricity might act as a facilitator for 'initiative, independence and industry' to flourish. For the sake of 'a few localized interferences with natural beauties', they felt that 'solid benefits' would arise.[16] Thus, the 'new dawn' heralded by the end of the Second World War also coincided with an energetic campaign by the Scottish Office to improve the standard of living of the Highlanders, mainly by utilizing the plentiful and underexploited water resources – but tension remained.

The importance of developing hydro-electricity in the Highlands was reflected in the involvement of politicians and coverage given by the press in Scotland. During the war, the SNP were quite scathing in their criticism, especially when MPs, as they saw it, were so blatantly selfish and selective of their interest in Highland affairs. Oliver Brown in his *Scotlandshire* quoted from a range of different sources to highlight this contrast. The Conservative MP for Argyll, Major MacCallum, for example, was quoted as saying in July 1943 that 'We find cropping up in the Highlands today FOREIGN FINANCIAL ORGANIZATIONS acquiring large tracts of land in the Highlands for purely speculative purposes'. Arthur Woodburn, a future Labour Scottish Secretary of State suggested calling it 'a new form of Highland Clearances'. MacCallum agreed, continuing:

> The organizations acquiring this land have no intention of living on it or becoming responsible and respectable landowners. They turn out inconvenient occupiers and put the land on the market again, selling it at perhaps double the price which they paid for it. Then they come back and start again. They emanate from London and have no sympathy with the people of the country which they acquire.[17]

15 *Hydro-electric development*, p. 7. 16 Ibid. 17 Brown, *Scotlandshire*, pp 27–8, 11, 7.

Brown pointed out that between 1939 and 1943 seventy-four Highland estates had been bought over, the vast majority by the English. He then asked: 'When will the 51st (Highland) Division liberate the Highlands?'[18]

This image of an alien force invading the Highlands recurred in nationalist discourse. A key complaint was that the hydro-electric schemes did not benefit local communities; Mac'illedhuibh claiming that 'Irish labour monopolized the unskilled work; administrators and technicians were English'.[19] This criticism of the hydro schemes bypassing the local economy was part of a wider condemnation of government and private concerns exploiting the Highlands as a resource area for their own ends. At the outset, the appointment of Lord Cooper to head the inquiry team was questioned by the SNP. They regarded him as prejudiced and unsuitable given his earlier (mis)reading of the Scottish economy.[20] Scrutinizing the Cooper Report, the SNP came to the conclusion that selfish interests were behind the hydro schemes. Oliver Brown quoted from a section of the Cooper Report to highlight this point:

> It is, in our view, plain that the general provision of electricity to crofters or fishing hamlets throughout the Highlands for domestic and small power use is quite impracticable, the costs of transmission and distribution being prohibitive in relation to so small a demand.

For Brown, this admission that the economic viability of hydro development was fragile confirmed the involvement of big business and southern interests.[21] This background to the investigations of the committee made it all the more difficult for the SNP to accept the press coverage, with Douglas Young claiming that the Cooper Report 'was greeted by the regimented mass-press with manufactured enthusiasm'.[22] In his opinion, Johnston's actions had reduced democracy, and despite Johnston's earlier condemnation of government boards, the policy of appointing 'outsiders' to dictate Highland policy had increased. According to the nationalists, this 'Fascism for the Highlands' was symptomatic of deeper problems at the heart of Scotland's new system of government – a lack of scrutiny, accountability and democracy.[23] The SNP's cries of government corruption and sophistry left them wondering what Norwegian control of the Highlands would have brought, given their commitment to their rural areas.[24] These concerns remained throughout the 1950s, and the slower progress of hydro development in that decade mitigated any endorsement of the whole project from the SNP.[25]

18 Ibid., p. 28. 19 Mac'illedhuibh, *Death to the Highland Scot*, p. 17. 20 Brown, *Scotlandshire*, p. 34. 21 Brown, *Nation or desert*, pp 33–4. 22 Young, *Fascism for the Highlands*, pp 9–10. 23 Young also highlighted the irony that the man in charge of hydro development, Tom Johnston, had himself criticized this high-handed approach to Scotland by the National government in an article from May 1936 in *Outlook* entitled 'Fascist Boards for Scotland'. See ibid., pp 9–10, 15–16. 24 Brown, *Nation or desert*, pp 35–6. 25 SNP, *Policy of*

Needless to say, the Labour Party's perceptions of hydro-electric developments were quite different. Alastair Weir's *Highland plan* (1945) reflected the fears of some critics with regard to these schemes, but Weir was adamant that the unique Highland 'way of life' would not be compromised. He explained:

> The supplying of cheap power in the Highlands will permit, for the first time in our history, the industrialization of parts of the Highlands. But this must not be allowed to proceed in the haphazard, wasteful, ugly and unsightly methods, which have resulted in the horrible industrial townships of the Lowlands. Industry in the Highlands will give employment, but it must not also give tenements or factory-slums. It need not, for modern architecture and design have amply shown that although a thing is useful it need not be ugly.[26]

Reviewing their 1945–50 and 1950–1 terms of office, the Labour Party were particularly proud of the development of hydro-electricity in the Highlands. They quoted the approving words of the *West Stirling Gazette*: 'At Morar in Inverness-shire and at Lochalsh in Wester Ross the other day, a crofter's wife pulled a switch and the dim glows of the paraffin lamps were eclipsed by the flood of electric light. The first of the hydro-electric scheme had come into light'.[27] This sense of pride was tinged with resentment at the lack of recognition accorded to the Labour government for bringing about this 'historic moment' in Highland history. They claimed:

> Had it [hydro-electricity] happened in Russia, there would have been endless blurbs 'about the growing industrial might and improved living standards of the people of the great Soviet Union'. It happens in Scotland under a Labour government and it passes to the accompaniment of grudging comment and no credits.[28]

The party also responded to what they regarded as the unfair maligning of Tom Johnston and the jibes from the SNP that the schemes were for the benefits of private concerns.[29] They sought to justify the policy of selling surplus electricity to the Lowlands, pointing out that profits from hydro-electric schemes were, by law, reserved for the Highlands.[30] Rather than attack the NSHEB, the Labour Party believed that commentators should recognize that without this flexible arrangement the organization would struggle to survive. In emphatic terms, they pointed out that 'The Hydro Board sells to Lowland industry and

the Scottish National Party, pp 7–8.   **26** Weir, *Highland plan*, p. 8.   **27** Cited in Labour Party, *Campaign quotations*, pp 125–6. See also Labour Party, *Forward Scotland*, pp 4–5.   **28** Labour Party, *Campaign quotations*, p. 126.   **29** Labour Party, *Let Scotland prosper*, p. 9.   **30** Labour Party, *Forward Scotland*, p. 26.

housewives the electricity they need and uses its profits to bring light and power to Highland crofters who would otherwise still be using oil lamps – that is, if they were still living in the Highlands'.[31] Looking back at the end of the 1950s, the party were keen to blame any delays in linking up the rest of the Highlands on the Conservative government, claiming that it was the Conservatives who had reduced the hydro development programme and increased the interest rates for the necessary capital to expand.[32] On this issue, as with many others relating to the Highlands, the Conservatives were noticeably silent.

The Conservative government's failure to wholeheartedly endorse the expansion of hydro-electricity in the north of Scotland raised a serious concern that the board's commitment to expand the supply of this vital resource to the outlying areas would falter. Although Michael Noble, the Conservative government's Secretary of State for Scotland, informed the Scottish Board for Industry (SBI) in April 1963 that future schemes would have to wait until objections were heard at public inquiries, he also added that capital costs for hydro schemes were considerably greater than those for thermal power stations. The implication, recognized by George Middleton, the chairman of the SBI, seemed clear: 'cost was to be the only factor in determining whether there would be further hydro-electric development for Scotland'.[33] Indeed, the following year the Conservative government announced that they were cutting the NSHEB's island budget from £1.5 million to £500,000 for the years 1965–7.[34] The implications of this announcement were serious for those sixty out of the 137 inhabited islands in the NSHEB's catchment area with less than two hundred people. Because of the minimum cost of connection – £500 per customer – many regarded this as their 'last chance' to receive electricity directly, as several localities were suffering from acute depopulation. Certainly, those involved in the campaign 'yell for light' were desperately keen that their communities on the islands of Coll, Lismore and the north isles of Orkney (involving a total of 4,000 people), should not be excluded because of economic considerations.

Although these, and other, remote townships had to endure further procrastination before being connected to the national grid, the achievements of the NSHEB should not be overlooked. Indeed, their chairman, Lord Strathclyde, was keen to emphasize the progress made between 1943 and 1964 within the Highlands and the Islands. Though admitting that the boards job was 'by no means finished', he pointed to the recent announcement that work would soon be underway to connect the islands of Whalsay in Shetland, Shapinsay and Rousay in Orkney, and Barra, Vatersay and North Uist in the Outer Hebrides to the mainland by underground cable.[35] Thus, with nearly seven out of eight

---

31 Labour Party, *Let Scotland prosper*, pp 9–10.   32 Ibid., p. 10.   33 *GH*, 'No early start on hydro schemes', 20 Apr. 1963.   34 *GH*, 'Taking the load to the isles', 2 Mar. 1964.   35 Ibid. The NSHEB's network of underground cables was already the most extensive in Europe even before these schemes were completed.

islanders already connected to public supply lines, Lord Strathclyde 'doubted if even the most enthusiastic ever expected to see such a revolutionary change in the north of Scotland as had been brought about by the ever-wider spreading of electricity supplies'.[36]

Undoubtedly, the hydro board was held in high regard, evident in the broad support it received during proposals to merge the NSHEB with its southern equivalent. Lord MacPherson of Drumochter, a Labour peer, claimed that the board had brought 'tremendous social benefits' to the region and that their work had 'transformed the domestic and social life of the Highlands'. He complained that the current investigation was unnecessary, resulting as it did from the 'curious campaign' against the board, using the proposed development in Glen Nevis as a cover. He continued:

> The demand for reconsideration of present policy does not come from the people or from public authorities in the Highlands. The main objectors appear to be some local landowners and sporting interests whose objections we have been accustomed to ever since the idea of a hydro scheme was first mooted. The curious thing about the present propaganda is that much of it appears to be sponsored from London.

Lord Colville, the Conservative Party's former Secretary of State for Scotland during the inter-war period, was similarly resolute in his defence of the existing arrangements for power supply in Scotland. The NSHEB, he argued, was 'much more than an electricity authority' and its exalted status among the region's population had accorded it the role of being 'almost a godfather to the Highlands'.[37] Fortuitously for the population of the Highlands and Islands, this was not a valedictory send-off for the board, but the recommendations of the MacKenzie Committee to rationalize costs by amalgamating Scotland's two power authorities was an indication that economic pressures were never far from the surface in discussions about Highland development. The intervention of the Highland Panel in support of the NSHEB might give the impression that it was a formidable champion of Highland interests, with an ability to dissuade those keen to assert economic criteria as the main consideration in matters pertaining to the Highlands.[38] Before outlining the extent to which the Highland Panel was able to safeguard the interests of those living in the north of Scotland and convince politicians, civil servants and the population at large that the Highlands merited special treatment, the activities of another government agency utilizing the natural resources of the Highlands – the Forestry Commission – merit attention.

36 *GH*, 'Supplying power to the islands', 3 July 1964. 37 *GH*, 'Hydro-electric board defended', 17 Mar. 1961. 38 *GH*, 'Power board's future', 20 Apr. 1963.

THE FORESTRY COMMISSION

Although established in 1919, and not exclusively centred on the Highlands and Islands, the Forestry Commission was regarded by the political parties in Scotland as a crucial agency for facilitating economic and social well-being in the Highland region.[39] During the war, when competing visions of the future of the Highlands were being laid out, the SNP criticized the mishandling of the forestry resources. Their arguments were similar to those expressed in relation to hydro development, with Mac'illedhuibh claiming that

> As the forests have apparently been planted from consideration of Britain's wartime timber supplies rather than from any interest in the welfare of rural Scotland, probably most of the employment has been given to the Hondurans, Canadians and Newfoundlanders who are invariably imported into the Highlands for wartime forestry work while native workers are dispatched to the early battlefields.[40]

Consequently, the nationalists believed that Highlanders were suspicious of the Forestry Commission, seeing it as 'a deep-laid plot between the government and the landowners to deprive them forever of the land their fathers had held'.[41]

During their first majority terms of office, the Labour governments gave a high priority to afforestation programmes, with the Forestry Commission regarded as a vital agency for enticing people back to the land and offering alternative sources of income for hard-pressed crofters. Indeed, the commission was brought under the control of the Secretary of State for Scotland under the terms of the Forestry Act of 1945, a piece of legislation which made provisions for an extensive policy of afforestation. Decrying the 'foolishness' of the 1931 National government for destroying fifty million small trees, Labour was pleased to point out that in 1949 'we are going forward once again and a great scheme of afforestation promises to bring people back to the Highlands'.[42] In their opinion, afforestation was 'changing the face of Scotland, physically as well as spiritually', and Labour pointed out that the number of forestry workers had increased from 1,500 in September 1939 to 6,110 by July 1948. With work already begun on the first model forest village, the Labour government was convinced that forestry development was helping to maintain families in Highland communities and offering the possibility of a return of population too. The Secretary of State for Scotland had a key role in bringing 'mutual advantage' to forestry and agriculture, which as well as securing these respective industries, would provide 'a means of hope and healthy livelihood for new generations of one of the finest

39 The Forestry Commission was established following the *Report of the Reconstruction Committee* (1919). 40 Mac'illedhuibh, *Death to the Highland Scot*, p. 17. 41 Ibid. 42 Labour Party, *Forward Scotland*, pp 28–9.

races of men in the world'. In 1949, the Labour government had high hopes for forestry development, aiming to establish two and a half million acres of forest land in Scotland by the year 2000, which would provide steady employment, mainly in the Highlands.[43]

In their 1958 publication, *Let Scotland prosper*, however, the Labour Party expressed disappointment at the lack of progress in the programme of afforestation. Responding to the Forestry Commission's 37th annual report, which blamed the stalled progress on the lack of suitable land, Labour said:

> There is plenty of suitable land available, without encroaching on good agricultural land, but the Forestry Commission seems unable to get it. There can be no doubt that, in Scotland at least, this is due in part to the desire of landowners to preserve sporting rights, and their refusal either to develop the land themselves or to allow the commission to do the job.[44]

A similar sense of disappointment was evident in the SNP's literature. They wanted to create 'national forest parks' to boost the local economies and present locals with opportunities in agriculture, tourism and forestry itself.[45] This should be properly organized and coordinated to maximize benefits, hence their call for a 'national land survey'.

These calls for further state involvement in forestry were dismissed by the Conservatives. Because the Forestry Commission's powers of compulsory purchase had to be sanctioned by the Secretary of State for Scotland, the tenure of the Conservative governments (1951–64) was disappointing with respect to further afforestation.[46] The Conservatives had previously expressed doubts on the merits of state-owned forests, though they were careful not give an outright denunciation of the Forestry Commission.[47] Financial support was given to private landlords for forest planting, recognized by the Zuckerman Committee of 1957 as essential for their further involvement.[48] But the Conservatives recognized that state control and intervention had its merits, with the Red Deer Commission (1959) set up to resolve conflicts over land-use and conservation. By the 1960s, various interest groups were making their concerns known and indeed, one of the reasons behind the establishment of the HIDB in 1965 was to coordinate the different programmes put forward for land-use in the Highlands. The HIDB's predecessor had a more difficult role, as we shall see in the next section.

---

43 Ibid., p. 5. 44 Labour Party, *Let Scotland prosper*, pp 30–1. 45 SNP, *Policy of the Scottish National Party*, p. 9. 46 For Labour (*Let Scotland prosper*, pp 30–1), these powers were not used enough during the period of Conservative rule. 47 Vane, 'Free enterprise in forestry' (1947); *Scottish affairs* (1954), p. 8. 48 Zuckerman, *Forestry, agriculture and marginal land* (1957), p. 32.

THE HIGHLAND PANEL

The previous chapter demonstrated the greater government emphasis on improving Highlanders' standards of living through developing the basic infrastructure of the region and providing the inhabitants with improved social services. The renewed enthusiasm with which government officials set about tackling the difficulties faced by the people of the north of Scotland demonstrated a determination to integrate this troubled region into the economy of Scotland. This laudable aim to develop the Highlands would seem to indicate a desire to empower the inhabitants of the region and allow them to initiate new policies designed to obviate and assuage the problems afflicting Gaelic Scotland. Indeed, the Labour government's 1950 white paper, *A programme of Highland development*, highlighted the necessity of a development policy, and the crucial role of local authorities' planning departments in drawing up different plans to reflect their individual characteristics.[49] The approach adopted by the new Labour administration reflected in large measure the continued support in the Highlands for similar schemes to those adopted by the American government during the Great Depression. However, much to the chagrin of Highlanders, any imitation of a Tennessee Valley Authority (TVA) type of organization was not forthcoming. This remained the situation throughout the period up to 1964, despite the undoubted enthusiasm among Highland councillors and appointees of the Highland Panel, both of whom had direct experience of the specific problems of the region and the relevance of a scheme similar to the TVA being adopted as a useful template.[50] The charged atmosphere in the post-war Highlands was fuelled by the bitter memories of tortuous and difficult times during the inter-war period. Consequently, the first issue that the Highland Panel had to face in early 1947 was the very nature of the organization itself and its lack of executive powers.

Demands for an all-purpose Highland authority to address the 'Highland problem' were growing in the 1930s due to the continued decline in employment opportunities and further out-migration.[51] The governments' responses to these appeals for a Highland Development Authority were cautious, obstructive and, at times, hostile. For instance, their rejection in 1939 of the Highlands and Islands Committee's proposals were couched in the language of prevarication and deferral; citing the added burden for staff, the duplication of existing agencies and the amount of parliamentary time necessary to enable this suggestion to become law as reasons to deny the proposal.[52] Nonetheless, the government did qualify their refusal by saying that the situation was under

---

49 *Programme of Highland development*, pp 6–7.   **50** Thompson (*Highland panel*, p. 4) discusses a resolution passed by Sutherland County Council in July 1951 on the need for a Highland Development Authority. This was presented to members of the Highland Panel when they visited.   **51** Quigley, 'The Highlands of Scotland' (1944).   **52** Thompson, *Highland panel*, p. 2.

review – a delaying tactic used throughout the period 1939–65, as illustrated in the various government reports, papers and commissions.[53]

As in the past, however, the British government miscalculated the depth of feeling among Highlanders. Not only were activists demanding a powerful organization be established to tackle the difficulties in the region, but that its membership should be reflective of the population to which it would report, and therefore including a Gaelic-speaking representative.[54] In 1946, it was suggested that the recently formed Highlands Committee should be commandeered to operate as an advisory body, but, in a crucial departure from previous manifestations of the proposal, there was a call for this new committee to have some executive powers and to act in conjunction with the Scottish Council to formulate schemes for industrial development.[55] Even Labour activists in the Highlands were expecting more. Alastair Weir from Islay had already envisaged the establishment of a Highland Development Board with wide-ranging powers to coordinate his party's expressed support for a planned approach to the Highlands.[56] Despite these demands, the Secretary of State overturned these more radical proposals in favour of forming a separate organization that would work in tandem and coordinate with the existing Highland administrative machine and then advise the Scottish Office as to the best policies for the Highlands.

Not surprisingly therefore, the announcement of an *Advisory* Panel for the Highlands and Islands was neither wholeheartedly supported nor enthusiastically acclaimed. Indeed, the Highland League wrote to the Secretary of State referring to a resolution passed on the 14 December 1946, which implored him to adopt some form of Highland Council with adequate powers and resources to undertake and coordinate the rehabilitation of the Highlands and Islands. Thus, the resolution stated that 'The league consider that the appointment of a merely advisory committee for the Highlands, without executive powers, would be most unsatisfactory'.[57]

The Scottish press was likewise unimpressed by the government's response to the calls for a comprehensive agency to execute innovative schemes to improve the area. The editorial in *The Scotsman* of 18 December 1946 welcomed the government's acceptance that the Highlands had special problems, but criticized officials for proposing an organization that would be large and unwieldy. The column also attacked the government's continued emphasis on trying to integrate the Highland economy into the national one. It was also noted that the Scottish Agricultural Organisation Society had expressed displeasure at the mere advisory status of the Highland Panel. The editorial went on to condemn the recurrent practice of producing government reports without effective action

---

[53] *Scottish affairs*, pp 81–5; *Review of Highland policy*, p. 3. [54] Hunter, *Claim of crofting*, pp 41–6. [55] Thompson, *Highland panel*, p. 3. [56] Weir, *Highland plan*, pp 4–5. [57] Thompson, *Highland panel*, p. 3.

following, fearing that the Highland Panel would continue in that vein, creating more reports for the Secretary of State's private consumption. The editor highlighted the need to attract industry to the region and mentioned the possibility of utilizing the Distribution of Industries Act in order to entice industries there with the proviso that this would not lead to further attempts at centralization.[58] Given the activities of the wartime cabinet and its erstwhile Scottish leader Tom Johnston, the content of the government publication, *A programme of Highland development*, and the support within the civil service for a small body to implement the proposals, it is perhaps surprising that the newly elected Labour government failed to take cognisance of the increasingly vociferous demands for more autonomy and control to be vested in the Highlands.[59]

The Highland Panel was appointed by Joseph Westwood, Secretary of State for Scotland, on 21 January 1947, with the following remit:

> To keep under review and advise the Secretary of State on the carrying out of, the approved programme of Highland Development and to arrange in consultation with the Secretary of State for the investigation of further means of promoting the economic use and capacity of resources in the Highlands and Islands, and the social welfare of the Highland people.[60]

The members of the Highland Panel collated information from their visits to the various communities in the region and reported back to the Scottish Office with their thoughts on the most appropriate course of action. The other function of the Highland Panel was to assist the Secretary of State in coordinating the various schemes emanating from government departments, local authorities and other public bodies.[61] Because of the range of duties attached, the panel further divided into subcommittees on specific issues and working parties to investigate pressing problems. The Highland Panel was comprised of four Highland MPs, eight representatives from Highland local authorities, two from the Scottish Council (Development and Industry) and four 'lay' appointees approved by the Secretary of State. The nature and role of the panel had its detractors, including some of the appointees themselves; indeed even the composition of the Highland Panel was a contentious matter. The appointment of two members of

58 *The Scotsman*, 'Editorial', 18 Dec. 1946. The *GH* (13 Jan. 1947) also carried an article by the Labour activist and author of the party's publication *Highland Plan*, Weir, where he criticized the Government's proposals. 59 Following the publication of *A programme of Highland development*, the Scottish Council (Development and Industry) sent a memo to the Secretary of State concerning the absence of an effective body to implement the proposals of the Labour government. See Thompson, *Highland panel*, p. 6. 60 *Hansard*, Commons, 21 Jan. 1947. 61 *Programme of Highland development*, p. 6. The establishment of the Highlands Committee in 1952 after prompting by the representatives from the Scottish Council was an acknowledgment that the existing arrangements were not working adequately.

the Scottish Council was regarded by *The Scotsman* as indicative of the government's reluctance to treat the Highland problem in complete isolation, insisting instead 'that the Highlands should be organized as an integral part of the national economy of Scotland'.[62] However, the members of the *Royal commission on Scottish affairs* (1954) felt that the diversity of personalities on the panel ensured impartiality and objectivity.[63] Although the composition of the Highland Panel caused some debate, it was the nature and role of the organization itself that proved to be the most contentious issue.

Some members of the Highland Panel were unhappy with their near clandestine position, caused by the uncertainty about expressing their own thoughts on the situation in the Highlands. They argued that they should campaign on behalf of the Highland people and not be seen as mere functionaries of the government.[64] The lack of publicity surrounding the activities of the panel also meant that little credit was apportioned to them for schemes which had a positive effect on the socio-economic concerns of Highlanders.[65] But the ambiguity concerning the task of the Highland Panel is not surprising when one considers the difficult position it was placed in. The actual views of the panel are difficult to ascertain as no reports were published save one on land-use, and the extent to which their recommendations were adopted or ignored is hard to detect because it was government departments and agencies which executed policy in the Highlands. Nonetheless from studying the papers relating to the activities of the Highland Panel, it can be discerned that the group was restricted in expressing any direct criticism of government policy, in keeping with the clandestine concordat to spare government embarrassment. This was certainly the approach adopted by the panel in its early years of existence under the chairmanship of Malcolm MacMillan, Labour MP for the Western Isles. This fear of incurring the wrath of the government seemed to derive from an uncertainty among some panel members as to their role in the governance of the Highlands. One of the more active participants in the Highland Panel, Naomi Mitchison, believes that many were only appointed because of their social standing and not from any expressed desire to resolve or alleviate the difficulties faced by the inhabitants of this region.[66]

The rather submissive nature to the Highland Panel can be illustrated by examination of the group's earliest meetings. For example, a meeting of the Highlands committee (a subcommittee of the Highland Panel founded in 1952) in October 1958 had as the main item on the agenda the proposal to include a 'Lowland' MP on the Highland Panel in order to moderate the demands made of the government. Another illuminating instance was when members of the

62 *The Scotsman*, 18 Dec. 1946. 63 *Scottish affairs*, pp 84–5. 64 Thompson, *Highland panel*, p. 20. 65 Ibid., p. 39. The Highland Panel issued progress reports from 1951 to 1964 to try and rectify these problems. NAS: SEP12/5 Highland Panel: Highland development programme: progress reports, 1–12. 66 Interview with Naomi Mitchison, Aug. 1995.

panel were deliberating on the content of a memorandum to be forwarded to the Secretary of State on the issue of Highland development. The then vice-chairman, John Cameron (later Lord Cameron), warned the members that it was not the function of the panel to instruct the government on what policies it should enact. He felt their role should be a supportive one to the government's professed policy of stemming migration to the industrial centres of the Central Belt by extolling the benefits of the Highlands as a whole and concentrating their energies on crofting, fishing and textiles.[67] Although one commentator regarded Cameron's ascension to the chair of the Highland Panel in 1954 as leading to a more robust attitude, other factors need to be considered.[68] The constant hectoring by individual members like Naomi Mitchison, and her eye-opening observations on Norway in 1961, were perhaps more influential in awakening the panel from its state of torpor. Their more aggressive stance culminated with the embarrassing and politically damaging prospect of a unanimous resignation by the appointees if the proposed Beeching rail cuts for the north of Scotland were allowed. The ineffectiveness of the Highland Panel in the face of widespread concern at long-standing social, economic and cultural problems continued to sour relations with central government in the years before 1965. However, before examining the transformation of the Highland Panel and the reasons for it, we need to focus on what this body actually did in order to gauge its impact on the Gaelic language and culture.

The Advisory Panel on the Highlands and Islands had a thankless task due to its role as a sounding board for what policies might be suitable to implement, for it lacked the necessary powers to execute government legislation. As a result, it was an easy target for derision and abuse, made evident at the frequent meetings they held throughout the region. The multifaceted nature to the 'Highland problem' often meant that these meetings degenerated into a cathartic exercise for Highlanders and Islanders disillusioned by what they regarded as the lack of action or misplaced decision-making. One such occasion was in 1961 on the Isle of Mull, where representatives from the panel were in attendance ostensibly to advise the locals as to the best course of action for economic development.[69] The original idea was to formulate a ten-year plan for the Isle of Mull based on an analysis of its assets and liabilities, and then to prioritize the various issues. However, the packed audience ignored this 'grandiose' scheme and opted to air their grievances, the most pressing of which revolved around transport difficulties and tensions over land-use. As with most of the Highland Panel's meetings, Gaelic was very rarely mentioned, but the issues that focused on the maintenance of the population were of crucial importance for the preservation of the Gaelic-speaking community.

67 Thompson, *Highland panel*, p. 22.   68 Ibid., p. 3. Cameron's earlier views on what the function of the panel should be are quoted as: 'it should be a sounding board, a gadfly and a safety valve'. See ibid., p. 25.   69 Mitchison, 'Debate on island's future', *GH*, 6 Oct. 1961.

Despite the criticisms, the Highland Panel did have its supporters. It has been remarked that because it was ostensibly established to counsel government departments and others involved in legislating on Highland affairs, its true value and impact has not been fully acknowledged.[70] Certainly, the Labour Party, writing in 1949, were convinced that the Highland Panel was playing a key role:

> The Highlands and Islands Advisory Panel established by the Labour government, keeps a watch on the possibilities for new developments and improvements, and the creation of new communities in the Highlands and Islands is regarded as a matter of the highest importance. Labour aims at Highland repopulation and prosperity.[71]

This body, 'representative of the major Highland interests', was praised for its promotion of schemes to retain the population. *Forward Scotland* continued:

> New villages for Scotland are as important as new towns, and it should be possible to set our Scottish architects to work to design communities for the new people who are going to be brought into the lovely, if deserted, places of the Highlands of Scotland.[72]

A Political and Economic Planning (PEP) report, written in 1960, praised the Highland Panel on the Highlands and Islands for its effectiveness, a feature that stemmed from its knowledge of Highlanders' desires and the strong links made with the various government officials engaged in Highland matters. The report went on: 'In short, the panel has succeeded in becoming in some ways part and parcel of the governmental and administrative machine without sacrificing its position as an independent body'.[73] Similar comments were made during the Highland Panel's last years, described after their one hundredth meeting in December 1963 as the Secretary of State for Scotland's 'accredited advisors'. Certainly, in this capacity, they helped to prevent 'administrative blunders that would have discriminated against the Highlands'. Despite the fact that they were regarded more as '"licensed critics" rather than as radical reformers', they were able to exert influence on issues ranging from excessive telephone charges in isolated areas to the protection of air services in the Northern Isles. These tangible benefits, coupled with their lack of executive responsibility, tended to 'insulate' them from 'the usual range of partisan criticism'.[74]

Perhaps unsurprisingly, these favourable views had been raised earlier by Lord Cameron, the Highland Panel's chairman between 1954 and 1965. Writing

---

70 Thompson, *Highland panel*, p. 36.   71 Labour Party, *Forward Scotland*, p. 5.   72 Ibid., p. 29.   73 P.E.P. *Report* (1960).   74 *GH*, 'Highland Panel's century', 6 Dec. 1963.

in 1957, he applauded the achievements of the Highland Panel in its ten years of existence, stating that it had

> acted and acts as a centre of informed discussion where the problems of the Highlands and Islands as a whole can be focused and examined, where local interests and projects can be concerted and fitted into an overall pattern. It is a testing ground for ideas and theories. It is a means of bringing pressures to bear in support of local authorities and regional bodies upon such important factors in the Highland economy as the national transport authorities of land and air in order to secure effective recognition of and provision for the peculiar needs of the Highlands and Islands.[75]

The ability to offer a distinctive Highland opinion on the themes which emerged from an analysis of the Highland problem was also regarded by Cameron as a success: 'It is noticeable, too, how rapidly the panel learned to speak with one voice, the voice of the Highlands, with local interests subordinate to the interests of the Highlands as a whole'.[76] Because of this approach, Lord Cameron was in no doubt that all the major post-war development programmes in the Highlands (for example, pier, harbour and road construction) owed a debt to the 'persistent and reasoned advocacy' of the Highland Panel.[77]

Cameron supported the Highland Panel's strategy of focusing on the particular rather than attempting to present an overall strategy for Highlands, because he believed that 'august brooding on generalities tend to be an unproductive occupation'.[78] The Highland Panel was instrumental in establishing the Committee of Enquiry into Crofting Conditions, and although there was close contact between the panel and the Crofters Commission, the former concentrated more on developing ancillary occupations to crofting. By adopting that approach, Cameron believed that this diversity would allow Highlanders to share the improved standards of living enjoyed by fellow citizens in the rest of the country – he explicitly stated that crofting by itself would not achieve this.

In trying to better the lives of Highlanders, the Highland Panel was mainly concerned with subsidiary industries that utilized the natural products of the region, complemented the occupational characteristics of crofting and were compatible with the Highland 'way of life'.[79] The decline of the fishing industry, particularly herring, represented a damaging blow to this policy. The Highland Panel, rather than engage in recriminations, sought to develop inshore fishing, by offering advice on the logistics of marketing the produce and campaigning for modern facilities that were essential for the industry. Forestry and other local

75 Cameron, 'Ten years in the Highlands' (1957), p. 20.   76 Ibid.   77 Ibid. They certainly generated a large body of literature.   78 Ibid., p. 21.   79 Ibid., pp 21, 66.

industries, such as tweed manufacture and seaweed processing, also offered opportunities for employment and the Highland Panel were enthusiastic champions of these industries. By the late 1950s, it was clear to members of the Highland Panel that tourism offered the best opportunity for ancillary work. But Lord Cameron was straightforward in his assessment of how best to proceed: 'Highlanders start with a notable asset in their worldwide tradition of hospitality, but there is room for a more professional outlook in this matter of the holiday and tourist industry'. This involved ensuring uniform standards of catering and accommodation, and quality assurance practices as used in the Harris Tweed industry. While Highlanders could do much in attaining 'a very real and substantial permanent increase in prosperity' by helping themselves, Cameron believed that they also needed the government to introduce a comprehensive and modern transport system, with assistance in freight charges and transport costs in general. The Highland Panel did campaign for these measures, and as government white papers and reports make clear, their lobbying efforts were successful in squeezing greater financial commitments out of the various governments.[80]

In calling for more resources to be ploughed into the Highlands and Islands, the Highland Panel was not compromising its impartial status. Naomi Mitchison's attacks on government did cause some consternation in official circles, as the next chapter demonstrates. Other appointees were more muted in their criticisms. Their calls for greater urgency and action were invariably tempered by moderate language, and, though admitting that they would like to do more, they argued that money was limited. Moreover, they pointed out that even the money that was being spent took some time to register, due to the poor state of the Highland economy. Taking this as their baseline, Lord Cameron pleaded for other members to remain resolute, diligent and united.[81] In fulfilling these aims, the members of the panel continually sought solutions from similarly placed regions in Europe. The deputation who went to Norway in 1961 experienced an education showing what could be achieved with adequate resources and a long-term and rational strategy.

The success of the Norwegian government in stabilizing its rural population was made apparent to the members of the Highland Panel during their visit. Indeed, the significance and catalytic effect of the visit can be measured by the more purposeful and dissenting tone of the Highland Panel's correspondence with central government on returning from Norway.[82] The delegates from the Highlands were so impressed by the Norwegian government's approach to rural areas and the maintenance of its population, that they brought sections of the Highland Panel's 'Norway report' (which was never published) to the attention of their own government at the time when it was outlining the powers and remit

---

80 Thompson, *Highland panel*, p. 37. 81 Cameron, 'Ten years in the Highlands', p. 20.
82 Thompson, *Highland panel*, pp 45–6.

of the proposed Highlands and Islands Development Board.[83] One key passage focused on the prerequisites for successful expansion of rural industries and decentralization from large industrial centres. The gist of the argument was that financial assistance from the government was vital in the embryonic stages of industrial development, and those firms enticed to the region should be part of the master plan. These businesses should be fully primed on the local conditions and continuous contact with officials from a Highland Development Board would ensure that potential difficulties were addressed before they became a hindrance. The type of industries envisaged were large, modern manufacturing firms, not traditional homecrafts. The other highlighted extract dealt with the difficulties of importing schemes from other countries with different forms of government and administrative systems. Nonetheless, the formula by which the Norwegian government dealt with its rural areas was worthy of imitation. The overriding emphasis was on planning, generated from *within* the region. Hence the need for an integrated public transport system, development of tourism as part of a coordinated and sensitive scheme, and establishment of selected area growth points to stem depopulation. Above all, the report emphasized the need for central government to recognize the unique problems of marginal areas such as the Highlands and Islands, and consequently empower local government in the region to take the initiative based on their expert knowledge of the local conditions.

This position on economic development, as outlined in the Highland Panel's 'Norway report', was in marked contrast to their earlier reception to the Toothill Report of 1961 – a government publication that advocated the establishment of 'growth zones' to stimulate economic development.[84] In March 1962, bolstered by the information garnered from their trip to Norway, the Highland Panel set out a series of plans designed to improve Highland development.[85] The main features included improving financial incentives for industry to locate in the region, the selection of targeted 'economic growing points of industry and tourism', statutory supervision of Highland transport to improve efficiency and cost effectiveness, and monitoring and vetting the standard of tourist accommodation. The panel also stated that they favoured new administrative arrangements to oversee these initiatives, particularly the establishment of growth zones, the purpose of which would be to stem depopulation and relieve congestion in the Central Belt.[86] The Conservative government's positive response to the Highland Panel's proposals for planned and targeted development in the Highlands was also something of a reversal in outlook.[87] The new administrative support being offered to the Highland Panel was eagerly welcomed in the national press:

83 Ibid.   84 Toothill, *Report* (1961).   85 NAS: DD15/3/30 Highland Development Files: note of Highland Panel's visit to Norway.   86 *GH*, 'A new policy for the Highlands?', 3 Mar. 1962.   87 *GH*, 'More Support for Highland Panel', 5 Mar. 1962.

The possibility that the Highland Development Group and its secretariat will produce for the Highlands the first regional economic plan in Britain is an exhilarating thought, as well as an ironic commentary on the vehemence directed from those quarters at the Toothill Report, which first canvassed the idea of 'zones of growth'.[88]

By 1964, Fort William and the Inverness–Invergordon area were being championed as the most suitable locations to implement the policy of 'growth poles'.[89] Despite the upbeat atmosphere, many recognized that a number of difficulties had to be overcome if industry was to be enticed north – the poor communications infrastructure being of primary concern.

The abrasive tone adopted in the 'Norway report' signified that the members of the Highland Panel had experienced a harsh lesson in the failings of Highland development. Although there were a number of ways in which this more aggressive attitude was made manifest, the fact that their visit occurred during the considerations of the recently convened British Transport Commission, headed by Dr (later Lord) Richard Beeching, was propitious in that it helped to galvanize a burgeoning anti-closure campaign. Broadly speaking, activists used three interrelated and overlapping elements covering future economic development, the inadequacies of the existing transport network and the social needs of Highlanders to convince Beeching and others of the merits of their case amid constant rumours of wholesale closure of the region's railway lines.[90]

Following the deputation's summary of the Norwegian visit, delivered at a meeting of the Highland Panel in October 1961, Lord Cameron reaffirmed their opposition to any line closures in the north of Scotland. He expressed their commitment to the Highland railway network in economic terms, arguing that 'any substantial industrial development' was dependent on the existing lines being retained.[91] Two months later, the *Glasgow Herald*, also focusing on the financial aspects, claimed that the line from Inverness to Kyle should be retained, irrespective of improvements to the road network.[92] The correspondent argued that the expected increase in the volume of road traffic, bringing a range of economic benefits from small-scale tourist ventures to the large forestry plantations, would be better managed if the railways were retained:

> An attempt to tap new markets ought certainly to be made. Railwaymen did, after all, establish the Highlands as a touring ground for well-healed Victorians. Their great-grandsons, by sharpening

---

88 *GH*, 'Editorial: Highland policy', 5 Mar. 1962. 89 *GH*, 'Economic base for Highland expansion', 2 Mar. 1964. 90 For more detail on the proposed closure, including statistics on passenger levels and density of freight traffic see Beeching, *Reshaping of British railways* (1963). 91 *GH*, 'Highlands taking lessons from Norway', 28 Oct. 1961. 92 *GH*, 'West Highland portents', 19 Dec. 1961.

their wits, might do equally well in what remains of the twentieth century.

This gentle reminder of the enormous difficulties involved in establishing the railway in the Highlands, and the remarkable engineering feats that made such problems surmountable, helped to stress the significance and finality of following the recommendations of the Beeching Report.[93]

The economic case was certainly a factor in the commission's deliberations on which lines were to remain open, as explained when the Beeching Report was published in March 1963. Hence, Lieutenant-Colonel D.H. Cameron of Lochiel, chairman of the Scottish area of the British Transport Commission, said that considerations with regard to freight weighed heavily in terms of deciding which lines were reprieved. Thus, the line between Fort William and Mallaig was saved because of the pulp mill and the plans of David MacBrayne's Ltd (the ferry operators) to build railheads in Mallaig for their revised steamer service to the islands. This, in turn, had positive implications for the lines to Oban, with Crianlarich becoming a link between the Glasgow lines to Fort William and Oban. Despite these favourable comments in support of keeping certain Highland lines open, economic criteria were ruthlessly applied elsewhere in the decisions on which routes were recommended for closure. Mr James Ness, general manager of the Scottish region of British railways, said that 'no one who had seen the traffic studies published last year would be surprised at the proposal to close the lines north of Inverness to Wick and Thurso'.[94] Despite these criticisms, others were not persuaded that the financial argument necessarily meant that the recommendations of Beeching could not be reversed. Lord Polwarth, chairman of the Scottish Council (Development and Industry), adopted a retrospective stance, positing that if the Fort William line had been closed ten years previously, the pulp mill at Corpach would not have gone ahead. He warned against a hasty response to Dr Beeching's proposals, arguing that it was important to take the wider picture of Highland development into account when discussing the region's transport requirements.[95] Furthermore, the Scottish railway development association argued that Beeching's report was 'derived from narrowly based criteria in many respects contradictory to Scotland's present and future needs' that ignored 'the now recognized necessity for certain uneconomic public transport services'. The organization also claimed that the function of the railways was to complement the road network and not to act as an alternative.[96] Nevertheless, the proposal to close the Wick and Kyle routes represented failure, at least in the first instance. However, the campaign had built up a considerable head of steam, and activists in the Highlands were unwilling

---

93 Thomas, *West Highland railway* (1970).   94 *GH*, 'Freight the factor in closures', 28 Mar. 1963.   95 *GH*, 'Lord Polwarth's concern', 28 Mar. 1963.

to accept the termination of the railway network at Inverness in view of the economic and social case being put forward.

The Highland Panel, and other individuals and groups such as the Scottish Vigilantes Association, expended a considerable amount of energy in their determination to overturn the recommendations of the Beeching Report.[97] The initial reaction to the publication of the report in March 1963 was dramatic. Lord Lovat, speaking at a meeting of the Highland transport conference attended by around eighty delegates from local government and commercial interests from the north of Scotland, said that if the recommendations of the Beeching Report were carried out, the Highlands would be 'faced with a situation which would be the gravest of its kind since the Clearances'.[98] Though Lovat accepted that 'in theory' the report was 'clear, concise and confident', the practical implications of its proposals 'could only be described as rough, ruthless and reckless as far as the Highlands are concerned'. The other delegates clearly agreed, as was evident in the resolution passed that 'deplored the proposed closures' and in another that listed mitigating circumstances for the north of Scotland. Although the campaigners did not go as far as Lord Lovat's call for the construction of 'double-carriageway roads ringing the north of Scotland' before the railways could be closed, his suggestion was indicative of the strength of feeling that the Highlands were already disadvantaged in terms of the transport infrastructure without the recommendations of Beeching being implemented. The Beeching Report had laid great stress on the improvements to the British road network:

> after the post-war growth of competition from road transport, it is no longer socially necessary for the railways to cover such a preponderant part of the total variety of internal transport services as they did in the past, and it is certainly not possible for them to operate profitably if they did so.[99]

However, the inadequate condition of the road network, and therefore the lack of alternative means of travel for both Highlanders and visitors to the region, was a major cause of resentment and a recurrent line of defence in the campaign to save the region's railways.

Matters came to a head at the one hundredth meeting of the Highland Panel,

---

96 *GH*, 'Electrification of Gourock line urged', 19 May 1964.   97 The Scottish Vigilantes Association, which helped spearhead the anti-closure campaign, 'grew out of the determined action of a handful of Ross-shire farmers and business to prevent the withdrawal of rail services North and West of Inverness'. They also took an active interest in other aspects of Highland development. For a brief outline of their proposals, see Martech, *Highland opportunity* (1964), p. 5 for quotation.   98 *GH*, 'Highland protest at effect of closures', 12 Apr. 1963.   99 *Reshaping of British railways*, p. 4.

held in Inverness on 6 December 1963. Despite government assurances made in June that no lines would be closed without alternative means of transportation being made available, the panel had not received any further and definite confirmation that the lines north and west of Inverness would remain open after the implementation of Beeching's report, set for March 1964.[1] Consequently, at this symbolic assembly, Lord Cameron announced that if the passenger services north and west of Inverness were closed in March 1964, they would resign en masse as they felt that the government's stated role of developing the region would be seriously compromized, and therefore the panel's advisory role would be made redundant. This drastic measure brought sharp criticism in the editorial columns of the *Glasgow Herald*. Having praised the panel for 'their capacity for dispassionate but never dispirited judgment' on the day of their one hundredth meeting, the paper now felt that their positive portrayal of the agency was less valid, owing to the fact that the panel had chosen 'to brandish claymores in a totally uncharacteristic way' with their threat of resignation.[2] The editorial felt that the campaign to save the threatened railway lines based on the argument that the future of the Highlands itself was dependent on the outcome was misguided. Although their claim that it was 'hard to believe of a countryside so densely motorized as the Highlands' was heavily debatable, the views expressed did reveal the tensions within the country over the favourable dispensation granted to those living in the Highlands. This was clearly evident in their statement that 'if the Highlands insist on keeping the railways at the taxpayers' cost, the Highlands should use the railways more than they are using them today'.[3]

The government eventually bowed to the pressure being exerted by Highland groups such as the Highland Panel and reprieved the passenger lines from Inverness to Wick/Thurso and the Inverness to Kyle route. For his part, Beeching responded to these criticisms with vigour, attacking those 'forces of reaction' in Scotland that had sought to overturn his railway review instead of concentrating on securing additional funding to improve the road network.[4] He rejected the argument that the economic criteria used were too narrow, claiming that in applying certain conditions he was only following the logic of his remit. Insisting that he was not 'really emotional' about the government's decision to reject his conclusions with regard to the Highlands, Beeching did warn that those celebrating this 'hollow victory' should not prevent 'a constructive approach to this problem of rationalized transport' from taking place. He had a special mention for the Highlands when he visited Scotland on 21 May 1964:

---

1 *GH*, 'Highland Panel ultimatum', 7 Dec., 1963.   2 *GH*, 'Highland Panel's century', 6 Dec. 1963; *GH*, 'Editorial: The '63', 7 Dec. 1963.   3 *GH*, 'Editorial', 7 Dec. 1963.   4 *GH*, 'Dr Beeching criticises his "closure" critics', 21 May 1964.

It is my firm conviction as a lover of the Highlands and a too infrequent visitor that the future depends more on the development of a proper roadway system there than on the perpetuated use of railways, which I am afraid will always be uneconomic [...]. I think there is a great need for road improvements in the Highlands, and I only wish some of those people who concentrate their efforts into preventing closures of railways would devote more of their time to insisting that the roadways should be improved.[5]

Certainly, successive governments in the post-war period had made a commitment to improving the road network in the Highlands and Islands, but clearly the existing programmes of enlarging and building new routes were insufficient to cope with further expansions in vehicular traffic. Moreover, the restructuring of the ferry routes to the Outer Isles that occurred in the early 1960s only underlined the need for a greater financial commitment to the road network. This reorganization of sea traffic – another development advanced after the Highland Panel's Norwegian visit – also highlighted the need for a regional organization to oversee the various developments in transport to avoid duplication, maximize efficiency, integrate the different modes of public transport and ensure value for money for the significant amounts of public money being spent by central government.

The issues of how to plan, fund and operate an effective communications network were indeed the very reasons behind the government establishing the Highland Transport Inquiry under the joint chairmanship of Lords Cameron and Kilbrandon in 1960. Their initial recommendations, which laid the ground for a single coordinating transport authority, echoed the thoughts of Highland Panel members ruminating over what lessons could be learnt from their visit to Norway.[6] The inquiry team was assisted in its task by the Glasgow University academic, Dr W. Iain Skewis. His analysis of the function of transport in the Highlands and Islands, including an inventory of the region's transport resources, was certainly germane to the work of the inquiry team, though some of his findings on profiteering among sections of the Highland business community made for uncomfortable reading.[7] Rather than attack those who used the high freight charges for financial gain, Skewis suggested turning these unfavourable circumstances to the advantage of Highlanders by forming a tariff barrier to protect local industries from competition. Furthermore, he maintained that towns in the north of Scotland, such as Stornoway, should become centres for producing and distributing a range of commodities to offset the high freight costs and improve both the quality and quantity of consumer

5 Ibid. 6 *GH*, 'A new policy for the Highlands?', 3 Mar. 1962. 7 Skewis, 'Transport in the Highlands and Islands' (1962).

goods. Although these ideas were not endorsed by other groups, the general thrust of his argument regarding the need for subsidized transport was a key element in the report of the Highland Transport Inquiry, published in February 1963.[8]

The report called on the government for a commitment to Highland transport in the form of subsidies, investment and the establishment of a permanent Highland transport authority.[9] As reported in the *Glasgow Herald*, the 'kernel of the inquiry' was the reality that 'most public transport operating scheduled all-the-year-round services in the Highlands is unremunerative and cannot exist without assistance'. The authors of the report also addressed the ongoing concerns regarding the Beeching Report, deploying a range of arguments that addressed the 'critical dilemma' of an unprofitable service providing essential services. They claimed that if the railways were closed, without adequate replacements by way of alternative forms of travel, 'the Highland economy would be gravely crippled and all hope of Highland development would practically disappear'. If, however, the case for closure proved to be too compelling to ignore, the inquiry team called on the government to delay such action until bus and freight services were able to operate the routes 'in safety and with regularity'. This would require additional investment because the condition of the roads, according to the report, was totally inadequate for the needs of the region. The report's main recommendation, calling on a single transport authority to be established, was based on the 'viewpoint that Highland circumstances are widely recognized to be different from those in the rest of the country and to require and justify treatment on their own'.

This claim for 'special status' was frequently made, and indeed it underpinned the different facets to the campaign to save the Highland railway network, but paradoxically the improvements to the transport infrastructure, set alongside the raft of other social and economic measures, was undermining this contention, at least in cultural terms. The extent to which the cumulative effect of these changes was regarded as a threat is addressed in Part Three, but press coverage from the period offers a clear impression of the expected scale of the transformation:

> The end which the nation has willed for the Highlands [...] is the maintenance of viable communities. The report of the Highland transport inquiry points unequivocally to the means. It is no longer primarily the development of hydro-electricity. It is not alone the pursuit of a tourist industry. What will determine the rate of

8 *GH*, 'From ferry to flight', 10 Apr. 1962. 9 *GH*, 'Coordinating Highland transport', 5 Feb. 1963.

economic progress in the Highlands for the rest of this century is the extent to which transport is progressively developed.[10]

Given the region's terrain, developing sea links was a key element in the overall strategy of improving the transport infrastructure. Moreover, the necessary investment and levels of subsidy involved in the provision of new ferries acted as a fillip to those who argued that a Highland transport authority was needed to supervise and oversee the distribution of government funds to ensure efficiency and financial probity. Once again, the Norwegian visit had acted as a catalyst to these developments, but the Highland Panel's determination to improve sea transport was consistent with their stated aim of building an integrated and comprehensive transport infrastructure that would serve all the needs of the Highland population.

By the spring of 1963, new routes, including the triangular connection between Skye, Harris and North Uist, were being promoted by Lord Cameron, officials from the Scottish Office and representatives of David MacBrayne's in a tour of the Hebrides.[11] These new ferry services were regarded as a virtual extension of the road system linking the mainland to the Hebrides, bringing a range of opportunities for the local population. The main benefit arising from the improvement in communications was the promotion of tourism, and the berths available on the ships were regarded as important in enticing tourists to visit the islands because of the lack of adequate accommodation in the Hebrides. Phrases such as 'floating hotels' and 'amphibious tourism' were being used to convince potential visitors that the Hebrides was a suitable location to include on their north of Scotland itinerary, while MacBrayne's, the ferry operators, were offering concessionary 'run-about' tickets for private motorists to augment the number of travellers.[12] Surveying island communications in April 1963, Lord Cameron was determined to market the region to potential visitors, hence his declaration that 'Scotland's new western mainland', as he was now describing the Hebrides, were no longer a 'prison, strongly guarded by the sea'.[13]

In their review of the impending developments, the members of the Highland Panel were convinced that the impact of these improvements to island transport, and the related economic opportunities, was nothing short of 'revolutionary':[14]

> The passage of time, and, soon, of the MacBrayne vehicle ferry, bring into prospect a degree of social change, the limits of which are still

---

10 *GH*, 'Editorial: Transport in the Highlands', 5 Feb. 1963. 11 *GH*, 'Survey of Hebridean communications', 16 Apr. 1963; *GH*, 'Paving new route to the isles', 17 Apr. 1963. 12 *GH*, 'High hopes for isles ferries', 19 Apr. 1963; *GH*, 'Editorial: Wheels to the isles', 19 Apr. 1963. 13 *GH*, 'Wheels to the isles'. 14 *GH*, 'Lord Cameron urges road improvements', 19 Apr. 1963.

> beyond comprehension [...]. Inevitably the amount of new revenue and expansion of tourism involved will have an impact on islands noted for their tenacity in holding on to an independent culture [...]. How much of it will succumb under the pressure of modern communications remains to be seen and it is premature to speculate on the effect upon language and custom.[15]

The new ferries, the *Hebrides*, the *Columba* and the *Clansman*, took their maiden voyages in November 1963, exposing the population of the Western Isles 'to a powerful influence for social and economic change'. The newspaper's correspondent continued:

> They [the Western Isles] need no longer be regarded as remote. A network of interlinked road and sea services creates routes that were hitherto impossible – for the 'hopalong holiday' by car from island to island, for heavy lorries to replace the coastwise crawl of the cargo steamer; and for the islanders to become part of the mainland society while at the same time adding a tourist industry to their natural heritage of crofting.[16]

The extent to which previous economic and social change, stemming from developments in hydro-electricity and welfarism for example, had already transformed the culture of the western seaboard will be addressed later, but the *Glasgow Herald* report was correct in its assessment that 'The islanders, having equipped themselves with most of the desirable commodities of the twentieth century, are now impatient for communications to match'.[17] That much was obvious to the deputation from the Highland Panel, the Scottish Office and MacBrayne's, given the enthusiasm with which their Hebridean hosts awaited the opportunities afforded by the improvements to sea transport. Crofters in particular were already making plans on how to capitalize on the new opportunities afforded by the improvements in transport, with local tourist associations being established throughout the islands in order to improve facilities and monitor the standards of tourist accommodation.[18] As the *Glasgow Herald* correspondent noted, 'The reaction of the Outer Isles to the prospect of losing their isolation betrays neither regret nor resistance. More so than on the mainland or in Skye, the evidence is that the islanders are alert to events'.[19] This degree of readiness, as expressed by islanders, to the likely economic benefits from the new ferries was tempered by their concerns over the quality of the roads to the ports – a sentiment shared by members of the Highland Panel.[20]

15 *GH*, 'Survey of Hebridean Communications'. 16 *GH*, 'Floating road to the isles', 20 Nov. 1963. 17 *GH*, 'Wheels to the isles'. 18 *GH*, 'Hebrides await tourist influx', 18 Apr. 1963. 19 Ibid.

The need to press for further government support to facilitate these changes would be the primary objective of the Highland Transport Board (HTB), which met for the first time in December 1963. The delay in establishing this particular government agency stemmed from the unwillingness of the Ministry of Transport to cede control of the communications network in the Highlands and Islands to the Secretary of State for Scotland. Moreover, due to the strength of feeling aroused by proposals to alter the status of the NSHEB, Michael Noble was also thwarted in his plan to merge the NSHEB with its southern counterpart, transferring the 'social remit' of the hydro board to the newly constituted HTB in the process.[21] Once these issues were resolved and the HTB was launched, it was immediately faced with a 'baptism of fire' due to the threat still hanging over rail services. The members of the new board – which included two representatives from the islands – set about their task with the same determination now being shown by the Highland Panel, but using more temperate language. After their first meeting the chairman, Mr R.H.W. Bruce (a crofting landlord from Shetland and member of the Highland Panel since 1958), spoke about the challenges ahead: 'in view of what the government and others had said about the need for development of the Highlands, it was axiomatic that there must be a general improvement in transport conditions'.[22]

Therefore, the activities of the Highland Panel, in conjunction with other concerned parties, had overseen the campaign to protect the Highland's air services, the more efficient regulation of the bus services, the introduction of new ferry routes and the reprieve from the Beeching railway closures. Moreover, their continual lobbying of central government had ensured the establishment of the Highland Transport Board in July 1963, stemming from their belief that future economic growth was predicated on this vital aspect of the region's infrastructure being properly supervised.[23] The anticipated impact on the region's population from further improvements in communications, particularly on the western seaboard, was regarded as considerable – the new ferry routes alone were perceived as part of a wider scheme 'unprecedented since the Railway Age in its objective to use mass transport as an economic tool'.[24] Despite the fact that the islanders expected, even welcomed, a further alteration in their lifestyles due to the overhaul of transport arrangements, one key element in Highland society – land – would be a much more difficult issue to address given the emotional investment associated with this vital resource.[25]

---

20 *GH*, 'Wheels to the isles'.   21 *GH*, 'Board proposal a compromise', 24 July 1963.   22 *GH*, 'Crofting landlord is chairman' and 'Editorial: Highland transport', 6 Dec. 1963. Examples of this more measured tone were evident in the HTB's first public statement, in which they said that they 'stand firmly aside from the campaigns to save the Highland railways at all costs' and 'No area in Britain ... can claim it must for ever have a railway regardless of how little it is used'. See *GH*, 'Transport board explain position', 21 Dec. 1963.   23 *GH*, 'Highland Panel perturbed', 20 July 1963.   24 *GH*, 'Survey of Hebridean communications'.

The more assertive stance adopted by the Highland Panel after the visit to Norway was also in evidence in their long-awaited report into *Land-use in the Highlands*, eventually published in 1964.[26] In March 1962, the panel felt that a study was needed because, in deliberating on the wider issues of Highland development, they increasingly had to deal with questions concerning land-use. The fact that it took so long to deliberate on the crucial area of land reform was symptomatic of the Highland Panel's unimpressive record. Therefore the report considered the way in which land-use was administered and whether improvements could be made; taking into account other important issues in order to provide a large and thorough investigation of the problems and meaningful recommendations. The report, which contained radical proposals, seems to bear the impressive stamp of Naomi Mitchison.[27] It emphasized the need for integrated development in the four most important sectors of agriculture, tourism, forestry and industry. The report also reiterated the almost universally accepted argument that the region required administrative rationalization and a powerful development agency to tackle the difficulties afflicting the Highlands and Islands in a comprehensive and holistic manner. Their main conclusion was that land was being underutilized, or at times grossly misused. The solution put forward was for the state to take control of large tracts of land for farming and forestry, if necessary by compulsory acquisition.

The Highland Panel also proposed the expansion of cooperative projects for crofting communities, with further state aid to improve these schemes, and an extension of credit facilities, possibly in the form of a 'land bank'. The Crofters Commission, discussed below, was to be given more powers and work in conjunction with the government to reclaim more land and create family farms. The report envisaged state deer forests that would cater for the tourist market, part of a general scheme to make scenic areas of the Highlands more accessible. Public and private involvement was seen as crucial in developing salmon and trout farming and fresh water fisheries in general. In the case of industrial development, the report believed that the most fruitful option was for the newly established National Resources Council to produce a detailed survey to assess the viability of mineral and other resource exploitation. Finally, the Highland Panel called for further afforestation projects, making use of statutory powers and compulsory orders if necessary and irrespective of opposition from various special-interest groups. The forceful tone of this report gives the impression that the Highland Panel was keen to get involved in the land question. Others have not been so convinced, however.

Throughout the period of its existence, the Highland Panel was dogged by

25 *GH*, 'Hebrides await tourist influx'. 26 Highland Panel, *Land-use in the Highlands and Islands* (1964), p. 1. 27 The contention that Mitchison was the dominant influence in the drafting of the report is put forward by Gillanders, 'Gaelic Scotland today', p. 118.

questions surrounding land, and it was perhaps symptomatic of these difficulties that the report into *Land-use in the Highlands* took six revisions before finally being published in 1964.[28] In the setting up of the Highland Panel, it was hoped that this body would take on board the land question. Certainly, the Department of Agriculture was keen to shift the responsibility on this emotive issue, especially in a climate when maximizing agricultural returns was a priority. Given that crofting was of marginal economic value, and declining, the Highland Panel was reluctant to get involved, especially on the issue of absenteeism on crofts.[29] The procrastinating tactics of the Highland Panel continued in response to the 1948 Agriculture (Scotland) Act, but, by 1950, they accepted that land reform was necessary. With some encouragement from the Secretary of State and the Department of Agriculture, the Highland Panel issued a press statement expressing support for a commission of enquiry to examine the state of crofting.[30] Although the Highland Panel was the organization that called for the setting up of an inquiry team into crofting conditions, research has revealed that the motives were not altogether altruistic.[31] Within the Scottish Office, it was regarded by some civil servants as a shrewd tactic, relieving the members of the panel from making decisions that would not be universally popular.[32] The compliant attitude within the Highland Panel, referred to earlier, was once again in evidence during the drafting of the inquiry team's remit. The members of the Highland Panel were certainly aware of the many obstacles faced by crofters, not just on agricultural matters, but they acquiesced in the government's desire to focus strictly on land issues; an approach regarded by many commentators as a significant failing.[33] The next section explores some of these issues and examines what the members of the Crofters Commission were trying to achieve.

THE CROFTERS COMMISSION

Even in the twentieth century, land reform has been an issue fraught with difficulty as far as the Highlands and Islands were concerned. The agitation and

---

28 NAS: SEP12/481 Land-use in Highlands report: drafting, 1963–1964. 29 Hunter, *Claim of crofting*, pp 75–6. 30 Their statement read 'The panel feel, therefore, that the time has come when serious attention must be directed to the difficult questions involved in strengthening a community largely dependent on the soil'. See 'Condition of crofting communities', *The Scotsman*, 20 Dec. 1951. 31 Hunter, *Claim of crofting*, p. 77. 32 This suited everyone, including the Highland Panel, because it removed 'the onus of suggesting a solution' from them. See NAS: AF81/1, 'Notes for the Secretary of State', 16 Jan. 1951. This disclosure undermines the sense of pride which members of the Highland Panel felt after the inquiry team was established. See Cameron's article on 'Ten years in the Highlands' where he cites this as one of the achievements of the Panel. 33 The agricultural problems were mainly infertile land and absenteeism, but the lack of ancillary employment was also fundamental to the difficulties faced by crofters. See Hunter, *Claim of crofting*; Gillanders, 'Gaelic Scotland today'.

subsequent reforms of the late nineteenth century did not resolve the problems; they only shelved them. Indeed, many believed that in making crofters' security of tenure a sacrosanct matter, any attempts to 'modernize' land legislation would meet with failure. With this in mind, and the noted reluctance of the government, its civil servants and the Highland Panel to intervene, Hector MacNeill, the Labour Secretary of State for Scotland, introduced a commission to investigate the crofting condition. The actual terms of reference for the Commission of Enquiry, as outlined in the House of Commons on 25 April 1951, were:

> To review crofting conditions in the Highlands and Islands with special reference to the secure establishment of a smallholding population making full use of agricultural resources and deriving the maximum economic benefit therefrom; and to report.[34]

The team was led by Thomas Taylor, principal of Aberdeen University, and the more notable of the other members included Neil Gunn, Alec Cairncross and Margaret MacPherson.[35] They spent three years gathering evidence before publishing their report, a publication that produced a fairly sober general impression of the region:

> All of them [crofters] alike share in the evil results which flow from the wasteful exploitation of natural resources by land and sea, from deforestation and soil erosion, from years of neglect and improvident management. All of them suffer from lack of employment with resulting depopulation, from poor communications, and the terrible cost of all forms of transport. These conditions are not likely to be dissipated by any magical remedy or in any short space of time. If the process of decay is to be arrested and reversed, it will require a serious political decision that these communities are not allowed to perish; a settled policy well conceived and resolutely maintained for many years; and a substantial expenditure of public money.[36]

---

34 *Hansard*, Commons, 25 Apr. 1951. 35 Comparisons with the earlier Napier Commission are inevitable, but the one led by Taylor was noticeably different in two key respects. Firstly, the meetings of the 1950s were held in private, because it was felt that some informants might feel inhibited by the public attention. Secondly, rather than rely on the crofters themselves for the majority of evidence, the Taylor Commission took representations from public or government sponsored organizations such as the Department of Agriculture, Highlands and Islands county councils and the Forestry Commission. This more extensive investigation was undertaken because in marked contrast to the politically turbulent years of the 1880s when crofters were organized, well informed and hopeful for the future, their counterparts in the post-war era were disorganized, demoralized and lacking in conviction that crofting life could be sufficiently improved to entice the younger generation to stay. See Hunter, *Claim of crofting*, pp 80–1.

Despite the gloomy picture presented by the report, however, there were some changes for the better.

The members of the Taylor Commission were pleased to note the improvements that had taken place in the Highlands over the previous twenty to thirty years. Crofters had gained from the 1940/1 livestock subsidies and the legislation of the 1945–51 Labour governments.[37] But the development of hydro-electricity was perhaps the most obvious change. The report was pleased to record the advances, saying that 'There is no more heartening a sight in the Highlands than to come on a distant crofting township and see the wires carrying power and light even to remote holdings maintaining a precarious existence on the edge of the wild'. This not only made life more convenient and less arduous, but it also reduced the cost of light and fuel.[38] The report also recognized the advancements in crofter housing arising from inter-war legislation and the grants given by the post-war Labour administration.[39] Despite these improvements, however, the members of the enquiry team were aware of the difficulties that still remained, especially the lack of piped water supply and the continued existence of the old blackhouses. These problems were more apparent in the isolated communities of the western seaboard and Outer Hebrides. But even here, the changes ushered in by the post-war Labour government, particularly with regard to welfare reform, were proving beneficial. Malcolm MacMillan, Labour MP for the Western Isles, pointed out that many elderly crofters were dependent on welfare support, but this was welcome because 'nobody in the Highlands can be said to feel the cold, hard edge of poverty as sharply today as in the pre-war years'.[40]

Despite these measures of advancement, those giving evidence to the enquiry team were clear in articulating what was wrong with the crofting communities. The main complaint related to the underuse of crofts due to problems of absenteeism or the elderly make-up of the crofters. There was resentment at the way in which landlords allocated vacant lets, taking little account of the feelings of the local community. In their report, the enquiry team said:

> it is alleged that, instead of letting the ground to a deserving applicant, the landlord sells the croft over his head, without giving him a chance to purchase, or uses it to augment the holding of another crofter who has already several crofts in his hand, none of which may be properly worked [...]. [I]t is complained that the croft is let or sold to a city dweller as a holiday house, instead of being granted to a *bona fide* crofter who would reside in the township and work his place as an agricultural subject.[41]

36 Taylor Commission, *Report*, p. 8. 37 Grants were given for drainage, water supply, bracken control and supplying lime fertilizer. See Hunter, *Claim of crofting*, pp 53–6. 38 Taylor Commission, *Report*, p. 20. 39 Ibid. 40 *Hansard*, Commons, 27 Jan. 1955.

The Taylor Report gave one example of a township with thirteen crofts, twelve with houses modernized through state grants. But seven of the crofts were rented by absentee crofters with homes in Glasgow, Motherwell, the United States, Edinburgh, Conon Bridge, Greenock and Australia. Though admitting that this was an extreme case, the Taylor Commission pointed out that this was a general trend evident in the majority of cases they investigated.[42] Therefore, absenteeism was a problem recognized by the crofters, agricultural bodies and the local press. The diversity of experience was also brought out by the commission's investigations. Some areas witnessed overcrowding and congestion, while others were suffering from vacant lots. In the latter, a sense of despondency and decay was evident. There was a feeling that the communities were disintegrating as the social and economic fabric imploded.[43]

Given the hardship and the difficulties of sustaining a decent standard of living, the members of the Taylor Commission wanted to understand why people remained. They found an explanation in the Highlanders' deep attachment to the land, based on sentiments embedded in the Gaelic tradition. The expression 'dùthchas' (which roughly translates as 'a right to land'), sums up this emotional bond to the land, and the continuance of this concept was evident in the 1950s. The Taylor Report stated:

> Some stay because they are satisfied with the kind of life which a crofting township affords. They are free to do what they like in their own time and in their own way. They are not at any man's beck and call, nor are they slaves of clocks. They like the place, its customs and entertainments, its habits of social intercourse, its forms of religious devotion and practice. They are among their own people to whom they are bound by ties of blood and kinship. These are motives which exercise a strong compulsion on a Highland society.[44]

Another crofter spoke of his moral ownership of the land because 'It is the four small acres my family broke in from the wild morass and rock, drained, manured and fed, over the years, with no help from the proprietor'. This helped to explain the paradox that despite the hardship and toil, significant numbers remained. As one Skye crofter reported to the Crofters Commission in the early 1950s: 'If I was not born there and the very dust of the place dear to me ... I would quit tomorrow'.[45]

For others, the sense of 'duty and obligation' that came with caring for elderly relatives, or taking into consideration the desire of future generations to retain

---

41 Taylor Commission, *Report*, p. 38.   42 Taylor Commission, *Report*, pp 40–1.   43 NAS: AF81/7 Taylor Commission evidence. This despondency was regarded by the commissioners as the main reason for township apathy: not because of an innate conservatism.   44 Taylor Commission, *Report*, p. 35.

the croft, encouraged them to stay. A final reason, demonstrating the importance of the financial inducements that governments had given since 1945, was 'economic advantage'. The Taylor commissioners reported that

> They [crofters] know that living on the croft is cheap and secure, that while they may earn less than many town workers they will save more. They realise that, in terms of money, the house, stocking and implements of a croft are now assets of real value and not lightly to be given up. They may have discovered that in times of depression both parents and children will fare much better in the crofting townships than in the tenements of a great city.[46]

Although there were tensions and fears within the crofting community about the future, the vast majority of those interviewed during the course of the inquiry team's deliberations wanted to retain this form of land settlement in the Highlands and Islands. For it was, they believed, the embodiment of the 'Highland way of life'.

Despite this expressed desire to maintain the crofting communities, the need to secure a reasonable standard of living was regarded as a crucial factor in retaining future generations. In the inter-war period, crofters also felt a deep attachment to the land, but they were financially penalized in comparison with other regions of Britain.[47] The war had brought some respite, but as integration with rest of British society increased, so did Highlanders' expectations with regard to the 'quality of life'. Discussing the situation in the post-war Highlands, the Taylor Report drew particular attention to the needs of women:

> If it is a question of comfort, convenience or entertainment, crofting life compares unfavourably with urban conditions, especially for women. The crofter's wife has to take a hand in all the operations on the croft and over and above the cares of house and family which she shares with her sister in the town she may have to carry water from the well, often some distance away, and to bring her household supplies along township roads which in winter may be not only inconvenient but actually dangerous. It is no great exaggeration to say that the key to the whole crofting problem lies in the hands of the women,

---

45 Ibid., p. 31. This statement was taken in the Taylor Commission evidence, along with the opinions of Robert MacLeod from Carloway in Lewis who talked about this 'strong bond of affection for the croft' which had more to do with 'instinct' than 'rational thought'. See Hunter, *Claim of crofting*, pp 33–4.   **46** Taylor Commission *Report*, p. 35. This view was confirmed in an interview with James Shaw Grant (Sept. 1995).   **47** However, for the majority of crofters in the 1920s and 1930s the earlier battles to win and extend traditional rights to the land had been largely accomplished. See Hunter, *Crofting community*, p. 208; Hunter, *Claim of crofting*, p. 36.

especially the young women. If they elect to stay in the township, there is hope for the future. If they leave, they will probably never return.[48]

But the region had long suffered from the fact that in order to advance socially, the Highlander had to leave. The Taylor Commission recognized that the church and the education system had always encouraged the most gifted young talent to migrate. This growing challenge to the emotional pull of the land made the need for some alternative forms of income all the more apparent.[49] Although it went beyond their remit, the Taylor commissioners were all too aware that this problem of finding auxiliary employment had to be addressed. For the inquiry team, crofting was in a very precarious and parlous state by the 1950s, and the reality of life in the crofting counties had brought the crofting communities close to ruination, struggling as they were in 'a losing battle against the social and economic forces of the day'.[50] This was the background against which the members of the Taylor Commission published their report.

The report of 1954 recommended the break-up of hereditary succession to the croft, a principle established in 1886 and regarded by the act's detractors as hindering economic development in the Highlands and Islands.[51] The ensuing report supported the view that the 1886 act was fundamentally flawed, while recognizing its merits in terms of rectifying the parlous and fragile condition of the crofting community before the 1880s.[52] The major problem of crofting in the Highlands of the post-war period, as identified by the team, was that most crofts were too small to allow for a reasonable existence. They were also aware that this concern regarding the magnitude of the smallholdings had always bedevilled the inhabitants of this region, but a crucial difference now was that the inhabitants of the crofting areas were no longer 'content with the modes of life which were acceptable to their ancestors'.[53] They found that this inertia in the crofting communities did not appeal to those people of working age unable to gain access to a croft. Even when the young did work the croft, the difficulties in making their holding an economic proposition made this way of life increasingly unattractive.[54] The inquiry team felt compelled to extend the range of its investigation. They moved from treating crofting merely as an agricultural concern (as their remit had instructed), coming to the conclusion that the demise of the crofting system also stemmed from the failure of the auxiliary industries, such as fishing and manufacturing, to survive or to regain a foothold in the Highlands.

48 Taylor Commission, *Report*, p. 33. 49 NAS: AF81/8, AF81/14 Taylor Commission evidence; Hunter, *Claim of crofting*, pp 34–5. 50 Taylor Commission, *Report*, p. 9. 51 Ibid., pp 12–13. 52 In giving evidence to the commissioners, the Scottish Landowners Federation, the Agricultural Colleges and the Scottish Agricultural Organisation Society all called for an overhaul of the 1886 Act. See NAS: AF81/7 Taylor Commission evidence. 53 Taylor Commission, *Report*, p. 9.

The report recognized the numerous difficulties that enterprising crofters faced; such as lack of development capital, poor advice from agricultural colleges, and the lack of an efficient and responsive support system for the marketing and selling of produce. Because of the diversity of problems affecting crofters, the report felt that no single solution existed.[55] It was argued that what was needed was an administrative body designed to improve crofting conditions and suitably endowed with sufficient finance and executive powers. Thus, the most important recommendation of the forty-two contained in the report of the Commission of Enquiry was the creation of a crofters' commission. The commission would oversee the implementation of the loans scheme, designed to provide crofters with working capital. Those smallholdings left vacant (due to absenteeism), or in a state of disrepair (due to infirmity or old age), were to be redistributed to those crofters already cultivating the land. In using these discretionary powers to terminate tenancy agreements, the commission did not intend to make people homeless, and provisions were made to ensure those who relinquished their crofts would still retain their croft houses and a small plot of land.

Because of the wide range of views held in relation to the future of crofting, from land nationalization to a fatalistic dismissal of reform, producing recommendations that would receive approbation from the crofters proved arduous. Margaret MacPherson, a crofter from Skye, agreed with the local Shetland Labour Party branch in calling for the land to come under public ownership, but given the political situation of the time, the Conservative government was unlikely to support such a measure.[56] The members of the enquiry team were similarly reluctant to abandon any hopes of a viable alternative being implemented. In the end, the enquiry team opted for the creation of a crofters' commission, whose initial purpose was to produce a register of all croft land in the seven crofting counties. This was to be done with a view to ridding the system of absenteeism, inertia and the lack of economic opportunities afforded by small-holdings. A significant inclusion in the report was the acknowledgment that crofting in itself would only provide for bare subsistence, and therefore the Crofters Commission should be given wide powers and the government should give a clear commitment to augment auxiliary industries. Thus, given the existing situation, the findings of the report were far-reaching and were arrived at with the long-term future of the crofting system uppermost in mind.

The manner in which the problems were addressed and the dilution of the proposals by the Conservative government in the Crofters (Scotland) Bill of 1955 were bound to provoke a strong reaction among the crofters of the north-

---

54 MacCuish, 'Reform of crofting tenure', *TGSI*, 48 (1974), 557–83.   55 This diversity of experience within the crofting counties was matched by the different reactions to the commissioners when evidence was being given. See NAS: AF81/15 'Note on Shetland Visit'; NAS: AF81/16 'Note on Western Isles Visit'.   56 MacPherson recorded her disapproval of the report's recommendations, see Taylor Commission, *Report*, pp 89–94.

west Highlands and Islands and their political representatives in Westminster. The passions generated by the issue of land in the Highlands guaranteed friction and some argued that by introducing an element of market pressure, bitter memories of the past were being stirred up.[57] The grassroots reaction in the *Gàidhealtachd* is considered in chapter seven, but within parliament, doubts over the legislation were expressed. Malcolm MacMillan (Labour MP for the Western Isles) and Jo Grimond (Liberal MP for Orkney and Shetland) though supporting the bill, did not hold much faith in the Crofters Commission delivering the necessary changes to stem depopulation or enthuse the crofting population. Their cautionary comments related to the prevaricating tone of the bill, the ensuing bureaucracy and the deliberate focus on purely agricultural matters.[58] Their respective constituencies reflected the differing reactions to the need for change (both during the investigation of the Taylor Commission and the bill reaching the statute books). Shetlanders largely welcoming the proposed reforms, while meetings in the Western Isles organized by the Taylor Commission provoked feelings of suspicion or indifference that anything positive would come of the enquiry team's investigations.[59] The consensus of opinion on the Conservative government's bill from Highland politicians was that the dilution of the Taylor Commission's recommendations would be a mistake. However, given the sympathies of the Scottish Secretary of State, James Stuart, for landowners and the involvement of the Department of Agriculture in drawing up the legislation, it was perhaps not surprising that the bill reflected their concerns about wholesale change to the crofting areas.

The reluctance of the government to implement radical changes to the crofting system, which would harm land-owning interests, was demonstrated clearly when the Crofters Commission was established in 1955. Based in Inverness, the commission was led by Sir Robert Urquhart, a former career diplomat. Their first task was to compile a 'comprehensive and reliable register', upon which their strategy to eradicate absenteeism and consolidate working crofts would be based.[60] Despite their undaunted optimism, it soon became apparent that the powers of the commission were largely illusory. The forceful stance taken by the commission was largely a token gesture and they soon encountered difficulties in trying to push through reform. The problems of lack of finance and executive powers were due to the Conservative government's reluctance to introduce a powerful body to resolve some of the thorny issues of land settlement; but the commission's other difficulties stemmed from the crofters' deep mistrust. The basis of this suspicion was the feeling that the

---

57 According to Kellas (*Modern Scotland*, p. 156), the act of 1886 had favoured the crofter over the speculator with regard to the setting of fair rents and this achievement 'has always been cherished in the Highlands'. **58** Hunter, *Claim of crofting*, pp 92–3. **59** Ibid., pp 81–2. **60** Crofters Commission, *First report* (Edinburgh, 1956), p. 7.

commission was going to evict ageing crofters from their land, and indeed so potent was this fear that within half a year of being installed as chairman, Sir Robert Urquhart felt compelled to issue a public statement refuting these allegations. The perception of the Crofters Commission was undermined further by its role, or perceived role, in the assignation of crofts. The commission had the power to refuse a tenancy transfer if it deemed the move harmful to the wider interests of the community. Inevitably, some crofters were caught out by the commission's intervention, causing annoyance to both the crofter and his intended replacement. But part of the problem was the high-handed manner in which the commission conducted its business. Note the patronizing tone from this extract of the *Annual report for 1960*:

> The first reactions of those who presumed to interpret crofter opinion were typically defensive and resentful of change or innovation, always the safe line to take in the Highlands and Islands; but by the end of the year it was already apparent that the more thoughtful and active elements of the crofter population were beginning to understand the commission's purpose.[61]

In the various disputes, the commission often served as a 'whipping boy' as crofter and landlord sought to offload blame for the collapse of the transfer.

The Crofters Commission's frequent ebullience sometimes clouded their judgment, in particular their misplaced reading of the economy of the Highlands and the prospect of future capital investment. Writing in 1956, Sir Robert Urquhart proclaimed:

> The time is ripe [...] for restoring prosperity to the Highlands and Islands. Economic conditions are changing in our favour. The fates, so long unkind, have smiled at last upon the crofter; the rain has turned to electricity, the peats to power and bracken can yet become arable. New techniques are at hand when most needed and now the people, too, are promising to come with us.[62]

The infectious enthusiasm pervading the corridors of Abertarf House in Inverness, home to the Crofters Commission, was soon undermined by the difficulties involved in reforming the crofting system. Their second annual report, published in July 1958, heralded a more sober and sensitive approach from the Crofters Commission, reflecting the difficulties encountered by its members in its formative years. The appeals to businessmen to invest in the Highlands and

---

61 Crofters Commission, *Annual report for 1960* (Edinburgh, 1961), p. 9.   62 *The Skye Clarion*, Nov. 1956, cited in Hunter, *Claim of crofting*.

Islands based on 'a sense of patriotism' proved totally fruitless, hence the commissioners renewed focus on purely agricultural matters. The problems on the land stemmed from the time-consuming efforts needed to compile a comprehensive and accurate register of crofts in the north-west, largely due to landlord interference and haggling over the value of certain holdings. Moreover, even where detailed information was available, the hoped-for land reorganization was difficult to enact due to the 'bureaucratic morass' contained in the legislation.[63] The primary reason for this was the reluctance of aged crofters to relinquish their rights to the land, despite assurances that they could continue in their croft houses.[64] The commissioners put the problem in these terms:

> the main weapon in our armoury, as provided by the act of 1955, has several defects: it contemplates measures which the crofters in a decayed township seldom favour, and requires old people to face abrupt changes when they want to be left undisturbed. It empowers as inactive majority to outvote an active minority and so is self-defeating.[65]

Various attempts at land reorganization foundered, as the commissioners found that crofters did not relish the prospect of taking land from long-standing members of the community (be they absentee or otherwise inactive), even if it was sanctioned by the Crofters Commission.[66] Notwithstanding that factor, it also made economic sense for both parties to resist changes in crofting tenure. For, with the approval or complicity of the inactive crofter (who would retain his crofting rights), the other members of the community could gain access to the grazing and inbye land without having to pay rental.[67] Therefore the commission's stated desire of encouraging ageing crofters to relinquish their holdings was proving to be a fractious process.

There was more success with their aim of ridding the region of absenteeism, because the commission carried powers to compulsorily dispossess those absentee crofters who showed no inclination to work the croft or come to an agreement with the commission. However, even with this policy, the commission's popularity continued to dissipate, as they themselves only too readily recognized:

> this process [to eradicate absenteeism] is by no means universally popular. We have felt the full measure of the tenacity with which the

---

63 Ibid., p. 106. 64 Crofters Commission, *Annual report for 1960*, p. 11. 65 For a discussion of the need for reform, consult Crofters Commission, *Annual report for 1959*, pp 16–24. 66 For more detail on the Big Sands in Gairloch scheme, see Hunter, *Claim of crofting*, pp 106–8; Gillanders, 'Gaelic Scotland today', pp 102–4. 67 Crofters Commission, *Annual report for 1959*, pp 16–24.

absentee clings to the family croft, not only the home but the land too, even although he may have little prospect of working it himself. Even in the townships, popular sympathy may favour the absentee and oppose the operation of this section of the act. Township loyalty may count for more than progress, particularly when the majority are aged.[68]

Thus it was that the prelude to further state-intervention in crofting – the Crofters (Scotland) Act of 1961 – witnessed a marked deterioration in what were already fragile relations between the Crofters Commission and the crofters themselves.

What is not in dispute is that the 1958 and 1959 reports marked a turning point in the commission's attitude towards reforming the crofting communities. Their intended aim was to gain government support for more powers to gradually eliminate those crofters (two-thirds of the total) who neglected their holdings, and push forward with a policy of rationalization of crofts, even if it meant a short-term decline in the number of croft homes in the Highlands and Islands. Driving this change was a determination that the failed land reorganization schemes of the past would not be repeated, and as their popularity could not get much lower, they set out to convince parliament.[69]

Despite this broad sympathy for the Crofters Commission's point of view in the corridors of Westminster as the 1961 bill proceeded through its reading stages, one MP in particular, Malcolm MacMillan, took a forceful stand against the legislation.[70] MacMillan was simply reflecting the deep anger within his own crofting constituency of the Western Isles at the proposed reforms. Drawing on examples from his own constituency, he contrasted the arbitrary and clandestine manner in which the Crofters Commission operated with the Scottish Land Court, held in much greater esteem by the crofters. The widespread unease which MacMillan referred to had resulted in the establishment of a Western Isles Crofters' Union in January 1961, following months of heated discussion. Almost immediately, similar organizations sprang up throughout the *Gàidhealtachd*, culminating in setting up of the Federation of Crofters' Unions in 1962. This reaction from within the *Gàidhealtachd* is discussed in the penultimate chapter below; suffice to say for the moment that in the face of this opposition, the measures sought by the Crofters Commission were diluted during the passage of the bill. In particular, the commission's desire to dictate the subletting or merging of holdings was circumvented by the legislation. The

---

68 Ibid., p. 10.   69 Crofters Commission, *Annual report for 1960*, p. 8. Such was the commission's unpopularity, it felt it necessary to reassure crofters that the commission had no role in drafting the 1961 Crofters (Scotland) Act – they merely submitted proposals, as did other interested groups.   70 Hunter, *Claim of crofting*, pp 120–3.

main concession granted to the commissioners was that the rather cumbersome procedures by which they operated under were streamlined.[71]

Although the Crofters (Scotland) Act of 1961 did not deliver the powers that the Crofters Commission were calling for, it did allow crofters to receive compensation for any improvements to their small holding upon a reallocation. The commissioners hoped that this would encourage tourism, though as their *Annual report for 1961* demonstrated, the pace of change was slow. They shared

> the unease which is spreading in the Highland area at the apparently slow rate of progress; a ski-lift here, fresh paint there, locks restocked elsewhere make hopeful beginnings but the Highlands still await convincing evidence of a purposeful drive to reap as quickly as possible the maximum benefit from the tourist industry and, in particular, to try to attract more of the 'quality tourists'.[72]

In pushing for auxiliary employment for the Highlands and Islands, the Crofters Commission was showing signs of a more realistic approach to the diverse needs of the region. But the lack of progress on this issue made Urquhart all the more determined to improve the agricultural performance of the crofting communities.[73] This ensured that relations between the crofters and their Commission remained tense.

The appointment of James Shaw Grant as chairman of the Crofters Commission in 1963 heralded a marked improvement in relations with the crofters. Grant, a Lewisman and editor of the *Stornoway Gazette*, was more adept at gaining the trust of crofters. Consequently, the commission was able to act with more authority. Grant had been on the board of the commission since its inception in 1955, but his elevation laid to rest the notion that the agenda for the seven crofting counties was wholesale amalgamation of holdings. The report for 1963 contained a significant passage that affirmed Grant's belief that many crofts would, of necessity, remain small. Where mergers did take place, it would be with the wholehearted support of the crofting township involved.[74] The imbalance between the economic viability within the seven crofting counties was clear from the take up of the governments' generous financial packages, all of which were specifically designed with agricultural improvement in mind. Grant was firmly of the opinion that other economic developments would have to be augmented in order to sustain the population of the west Highlands and Islands, an area where the fertility of the soil and climatic conditions were unfavourable for large-scale agricultural schemes. The timing of his chairmanship was impor-

---

71 Hunter, *Claim of crofting*, pp 117–18. 72 Crofters Commission, *Annual report for 1961*, pp 20–1. 73 Hunter, *Claim of crofting*, p. 109. For an insight into Urquhart's views on crofting reform, see his 'Highland crofting, seen in its national and international contexts' (1964). 74 Crofters Commission, *Annual report for 1963* (1964), p. 22.

tant, because the Highlands and Islands Development Board was keen to introduce industrial schemes in the region which would complement the traditional way of life of Highlanders. Crofting was one such activity, and Grant's ability to work with the Federation of Crofters' Unions would prove decisive in winning concessions from government. His spirited defence of crofting as a lifestyle that was not necessarily at odds with economic development meant that crofting as a part-time occupation would survive. From 1965, the onus for maintaining the population rested with the Highlands and Islands Development Board; an organization with unprecedented power and specifically charged with developing the economy of the Highlands and Islands. It is significant that it set itself the specific task of maintaining the population in 'the true crofting areas'.[75]

By 1966, Grant was a vociferous advocate of the 'crofting way of life'. He argued that it was now more suited to the needs of the modern world than at any other time, saying:

> We believe that this willingness of crofters to work in industry combined with a desire to own their own homes and cultivate or stock a piece of land which they regards as their own [...] gives us an opportunity in the Highlands of working towards a new form of industrial society which will be healthier and more stable than any community which is completely urbanized. This is the true value of the small croft, and it will increase rather than diminish.[76]

CONCLUSION

The Highlands were a key element in the British post-war reconstruction programme. The opportunities offered by the introduction of hydro-electricity brought hope to those policy makers aiming to secure employment for the inhabitants of the region, and help alleviate the social problems which derived from the economic malaise. A realization that something had to be done to overturn the desperate situation was countered by the reluctance of government to empower the Highlanders themselves. The overriding approach was still top-down and externally imposed. Crofting was also in a desperate situation and the establishment of an enquiry team was an act of recognition: something needed to change if crofting was to become a viable form of agricultural tenure. These developments signify that though the maintenance of the Gaelic language was not recognized by officialdom as an asset in the fight for economic regeneration, there was an implicit realization that the Highland 'way of life' (whatever that

---

75 HIDB, *Report* (1965–6), p. 5.   76 Crofters Commission, *Annual report for 1966* (1967), p. 11.

actually meant) had to be maintained. Highlanders themselves became more demanding of central government as their self-confidence augmented.

Although the Labour government's 1950 white paper, *A programme of Highland development*, was taken as the blueprint for successive government approaches to the Highland problem in the post-war years, there was a fundamental difference of opinion between the political parties during the general election of 1964. Both Labour and the Liberals recognized the need for a more powerful coordinating body to address the ongoing difficulties faced by Highlanders, to meet the demands for redistributing industry and reviewing the region's transport needs.[77] The establishment of the Highlands and Islands Development Board in 1965 *was* a major breakthrough for Highlanders, representing the realization of a long-cherished aim for a powerful executive body to initiate and administer government policy with the specific interests of the region in mind.[78] Regarded at the time as an organization similar to the TVA in its potential for economic and social development, it was dismissed by the Conservatives as 'undiluted marxism'.[79] The fact that it existed at all was largely due to the cumulative pressure from activists within the Highlands and Islands, including the Highland Panel. But it also reflected a realization that the complexity of the Highland problem had led to a proliferation of organizations, the diffuse nature of which tended to inhibit rather than promote economic development.[80]

In his valediction for the Highland Panel in June 1965, Willie Ross, the new Secretary of State for Scotland, said that although the new board would 'inherit some of the panel's virtues and traditions, they would not be subjected to the same frustrations'. His vision for the new Highland development body was one that would combine the positive elements of the Highland Panel with the necessary powers to effect change. He continued:

> What we propose in the Highlands is a natural follow-on to the work of the panel, to their efforts to break away from romance and get realism into tackling the problems of the Highland area [...]. We can tackle these problems only through vigorous people on the spot, helped by wise leadership, but the actual attack must come from the people of the Highlands on their own.[81]

---

77 Scottish Council of the Labour Party, *Go-ahead Scotland* (1965), p. 7; Labour Party, *Let Scotland prosper*, pp 39–40. In his pamphlet, Russell Johnston argued that 'we cannot look at the Highland problem in isolation, indeed the habit of doing so has obscured the fact that it could contain the solution to the Lowland problem as well'. See Johnston, *Highland development*, pp 5–6.   78 See Levitt, 'Highlands and Islands Development Board' (1999), 85–105.   79 Quoted in Lynch, *Scotland*, p. 442. Later assessments of the HIDB were not complimentary, see Carter, 'Six years on' (1973).   80 It was estimated that 47 such bodies were in existence by 1965. See Thompson, *Highland panel*, p. 1.

The extent to which the HIDB represented the 'voice' of those in the region was a moot point, not least during its early years when criticisms were made regarding the personnel involved.[82] This was a reflection of the depth of feeling associated with Highland development, the diverse character of the Highlands and Islands and, therefore, the difficulties associated in cultivating a unified purpose – from crofting to industrial enterprise. Lord Cameron, in delivering the Highland Panel's 'last will and testament', rejoiced in the fact that one of the panel's achievements had been 'the creation of Highland public opinion'.[83]

In a sense, the next two chapters will explore that claim in more detail as the disparate nature of Highland society is explored. James Shaw Grant was not alone in upholding a vision of a vibrant and workable Highlands, a view that challenged the gloomy assessment of some external observers. Before examining what Gaels thought of government approaches to the 'Highland problem', we turn to those Highland intellectuals who were, in a sense, 'inside' the bureaucratic machine.

81 *GH*, 'Mr Ross's farewell to Highland Panel', 12 June 1965; *GH*, 'Highland Panel ends 18 years' work', 11 June 1965. 82 Grimble, 'The poet and scholar as journalist', pp 164–5. 83 *GH*, 'Farewell to Highland Panel'.

PART III

*Voices 'within', laments from 'below':
the Highlanders themselves, 1939–1965*

6

'The English way and the wrong way': social philosophy, political policy and the 'view from within'

> The scene is a crofting township in the north-west Highlands. Rushes are growing on what had once been good arable ground; head-drains are choked; sheep are dotted about a landscape that seems to be declining into the never-never land like the few aged men moving here and there. The absence of children foretells a steep fall in the vital statistics graph. An old lady with bright eyes and an ironic lift in her voice like the cry of a seabird answers us: 'Bachelors, is it? We thatch the roofs with them!'
>
> Neil Gunn, 'The Highlands today' (n.d.)[1]

> While it is always necessary to remember the peculiarities of the physical environment in the Highlands, the essential differences are those of social structure, and still more, of outlook: the 'problem' of the Highlands really arises out of a clash of social philosophies. It lies in the persistence into new circumstances of an ancient mode of life and thought, adapted to its own environment and with its characteristic form of social organization. The problems and difficulties of last century and of today have arisen mainly from the impact upon this society of a different way of life and thought, the product of the Industrial Revolution. It is a problem for the Highlands because of the disparity in power and persuasiveness of the two cultures.
>
> Adam Collier, *The crofting problem* (1953)[2]

It is perhaps ironic, but nevertheless true, that the period between the conclusion of the Second World War and the establishment of the Highlands and Islands Development Board (HIDB), was marked both by increased government interest in the 'Highland problem', and by continued decline in the Gaelic region of north-western Scotland. The malaise may have been less precipitous than in the 1920s and 30s, but economic contraction and social decay was, by the later 1940s, impacting broadly upon the Gaelic community, as is evident in Gunn's description of a typical Highland township.[3] This deep-seated and continuing

---

1 NLS: NMG, Dep 209/8.   2 Collier, *Crofting problem* (1953), p. 4.   3 James Shaw Grant also

decline, which, for example, threatened Gaelic as a living language, provides essential context for the material examined in this chapter. The previous discussion illustrated how during the period from 1939 to the 1960s, successive governments – both Conservative and Labour – attempted to address the problems of the Highland 'way of life' by introducing measures to gather information as to 'native' feelings in the Highlands and Islands. Thus, the primary initiatives saw the establishment of the Advisory Panel on the Highlands and Islands and the Crofters Commission. Both were meant to furnish central government with insights into the region's unique cultural legacy. Yet, these agencies often simply exacerbated tensions between Gaels' desires and governments' intentions. Indeed, so great was the tension between the position of the Highlanders' representatives on these agencies, and the proposed policies of government, that it has been described by Adam Collier, a former member of the 1938 Hilleary Committee, as a 'clash of social philosophies'. The gap between government orthodoxy and Highland mentality was not, however, simply enunciated by intellectuals and writers. A contributor to the *Stornoway Gazette* surely captured the views of fellow islanders when declaring that the government saw only two ways of tackling the Highlands issue: 'the English way and the wrong way'.

On first reflections, there would seem to be real problems ascertaining the thoughts and motivations of those 'regional' representations on the Highland Panel or the Crofters Commission. However, the task of analyzing the 'view from within' is made easier by two distinct sets of sources. The first is the writings of the Highlands representatives: especially the prodigious output of Naomi Mitchison and Neil Gunn. The second is the body of records generated by the Gaels themselves. The next chapter concentrates solely on the latter material and the views of local Gaelic activists who encapsulated the feelings on the ground. At this point, however, we turn to what we might term the 'middle rankers' – characters such as Neil Gunn, Naomi Mitchison, Adam Collier, Fraser Darling and James Shaw Grant – whose writings were the conduits through which wider Highland views passed.[4] Their trenchant views and reflective commentaries on various government policies and initiatives left a deep imprint. The first task, therefore, is to say something about the personalities involved.

---

mentioned the socially damaging gender imbalance in many parts of the Highlands during the inter-war period. Personal interview, Sept. 1995.   4 For some discussion on another 'insider', Roderick MacFarquar, who was involved in the Highland Fund, see McCrorie, *Highland cause* (2001).

THE 'VIEW FROM WITHIN'

Neil Miller Gunn (1891–1974), the son of a fisherman, was born in the Caithness village of Dunbeath.[5] In his early adult years he joined the civil service, working in different parts of England before being posted to Edinburgh. After further training, Gunn was appointed a customs and excise officer and in 1911 he was able to return to the Highlands. Although stationed in Inverness, Gunn's job enabled him to travel extensively throughout the region. He drew on these experiences, along with his own considerable knowledge of Highland history, in *The grey coast* (1926), his first novel, and *The lost glen* (1932). Gunn combined his interests in Zen Buddhism and ancient Scottish history in several of his fictional works, for example *Sun circle* (1933). But his idyllic portrayal of ancient pre-Celtic Scotland led one contemporary critic to cite 'Fiona MacLeod' as a 'dangerous inspiration' to Gunn.[6] Sentimentalism was certainly absent in *Butcher's broom* (1933) and *The silver darlings* (1941), both set against the backdrop of the Highland Clearances: '*The silver darlings* is a magnificent tribute to the indomitable spirit of the Gael, yet at the same time an adventure story with the terrible pace and authority of authenticity. It is a vast canvas of a book, packed with human insight and the smell and sound and touch of Highland life'.[7] Gunn dealt with other aspects of Highland life, particularly emigration, in *The serpent* (1943) and *The drinking well* (1946). By the end of the 1940s, his creative energies took him back into mysticism, but these publications never had the dramatic impact of his earlier works. Despite his changing literary fortunes, Gunn's appreciation of the diversity and complexity of Highland life did not go unnoticed, and in 1951 he was invited to join the Commission of Enquiry into Crofting Conditions (1951–4). Gunn described himself as 'a writer who knows the Highlands from the inside', and he used this inside knowledge to furnish numerous articles for a variety of publications until ill health forced him to retire from writing.[8]

Naomi Mitchison (1897–1998) also contributed to the inter-war renaissance in Scottish literature and arts.[9] Like Gunn, Mitchison's political beliefs were a mixture of socialist principles tinged with strong support for Scottish nationalism.[10] After many years in England, Mitchison returned to Scotland in 1937. Because of her husband's political connections (Dick Mitchison was Labour MP for a Birmingham constituency) and her growing involvement in local, national

---

5 See Hart and Pick, *Neil M. Gunn* (1981) for further details on Gunn, including his published works. See also Price, 'Gunn and the Gaelic idea' (1997), 85–102. 6 MacDonald, 'Modern Scots novelists' (1933), pp 161–2. Hart claims that Gunn's early fictional works 'evoke, with a sometimes burdensome poetic pathos, the doomed Celtic soul'. See Hart, 'Hunter and the circle', pp 66–7. 7 Lindsay, *History of Scottish literature*, p. 425. 8 Gunn, 'Drains for the Kraal', *GH*, 1 Jan. 1941. 9 For a fuller discussion of Naomi Mitchison's life history see Calder, *Naomi Mitchison* (1997). 10 Murray, *Beyond the limit*, pp x–xii.

and international campaigns, the 'Big House' at Carradale in Kintyre was a hive of activity.[11] Once settled in Carradale, Mitchison started to research the history of her family, the Haldanes, using the material for her historical novel, *The bull calves* (1947), set in her ancestral homeland after the 1745 Jacobite Rising. Mitchison was elected to Argyle County Council in 1946, and invited onto the Highland Panel in 1947. Others did not match her enthusiasm and conscientiousness on the panel and consequently she was a frequent adversary of both the Scottish Office and her colleagues on the Highland Panel.

Throughout her term of office, Mitchison campaigned vociferously to improve Highlanders' standards of living and empower them to initiate schemes that could benefit their communities as a whole. She contributed to a variety of newspapers, magazines and journals on a range of topics during her working life, drawing on her personal knowledge of local government in the Highlands, her activities as a member of the Highland Panel and her eclectic and well-travelled lifestyle.[12] In 1954, she published *The Highlands and Islands*.[13] She claimed this represented the 'voice' of those with a clear interest in the area:

> This policy was written after much discussion with various people having intimate knowledge of the Highlands. Most of them would, I think, rather remain anonymous, especially as many of them would not necessarily agree with more than a part of this pamphlet, nor are they all of one political party; yet all have, as I have, the welfare of the Highlands passionately at heart. The reason that, in general, and especially in the recommendations, I write 'we' rather than 'I' is that I feel I am writing as their mouthpiece and representative. I have taken space to go into some detail, as well as to chase a few of my own perhaps unacceptable hares. Where I have gone into detail, I have some first-hand knowledge.

Her background enabled Mitchison to offer a deep insight and awareness of the varieties of local problems that existed and an appreciation of the nature and severity of the difficulties compared with other 'marginal peoples' throughout the world.

James Shaw Grant was editor of the Lewis based *Stornoway Gazette* for over thirty years (1932–63), and second chairman of the Crofters Commission from 1963 to 1978. During Grant's tenure of office, there was some progress in relations between the crofters and the commission. Grant's literary achieve-

---

11 The house was especially busy during the Second World War with refugees, evacuees and an assortment of other 'guests'. 12 Mitchison, 'Living in Scotland to-day'. She says through her work with the Highland Panel, and fisheries subgroup in particular, 'one gets to know the Highlands in a deeper way than anyone living in any single place or, for that matter, interested in any single thing ... can ever know'. 13 Mitchison, *Highlands and Islands*.

ments, though not of the stature of Mitchison's and Gunn's, nevertheless provide a useful social commentary on the transformation taking place in the *Gàidhealtachd*. His reminiscences of life in the islands, particularly Lewis, reflect some of the underlying tensions and peculiarities that existed in the Highlands and Islands and the extent to which social and economic developments were taking cognisance of the Gaelic culture.[14]

Mitchison, Gunn and Grant must be seen in context, for none of them was the first, or the only, to express grave concerns about the activities of London governments and the very real problems of maintaining a viable Highland way of life. In fact, Mitchison and her peers were very clearly influenced by both earlier and contemporary writers – witnesses to the hardship, migration and economic contraction of the interwar years. After the Second World War, two seminal works on the Highlands were published: Adam Collier's *The crofting problem* (1953) and F. Fraser Darling's edited book *West Highland Survey* (1955).[15] These research projects broke new territory in their scope, perceptiveness and comprehensive analysis of the 'Highland problem'. They were the founders of the 'philosophy of difference' propagated within Highland intellectual circles. Something must, therefore, be said of them.

Collier, though born in the Central Belt of Scotland, took an active interest in Highland affairs. An economist at Glasgow University, Collier was an important member of the Hilleary Committee and took an active role in the publication of its report, entitled *The Highlands and Islands* (1938). A keen mountaineer, Collier's life was cut short after a climbing accident in the north-west Highlands in 1946. At that time, Collier had been working on a research project analyzing the reasons for the problems in the Highlands and remedial action that could be taken. His former lecturer at Glasgow University, Alec Cairncross, edited the existing manuscript to produce the well-received book, *The crofting problem*. Cairncross described Collier as having 'a mind scholarly and balanced, with a profound knowledge of his subject and a rare sensitivity to the interaction of cultural and economic forces'.[16]

In 1943, Fraser Darling approached the Development Commission and the Department of Agriculture in St Andrew's House with a proposal to begin a 'social and biological investigation into the problems of the West Highlands'.[17] Darling was given approval to expand his educational work in a series of demonstration crofts in the north-west Highlands. Along with a 'succession of young Gaelic-speaking Highlanders', Darling was appointed to record the 'social and biological conditions [...and] the vital statistics and the way of life' in the survey area.[18] The results of Darling's survey were published in 1955 and, in a review

---

14 Of particular interest in capturing the changing circumstances of the Highlands and Islands are Grant's books *Highland villages* (1980) and *The hub of my universe* (1982). 15 Collier, *Crofting problem*; Darling (ed.), *West Highland Survey*. 16 Collier, *Crofting problem*, p. x. 17 Development Commission, 'Introductory note' in *West Highland Survey*, p. v. 18 Ibid., pp v–vi. Darling

of the book, Mitchison paid tribute to Darling: 'All cultures are a matter of secrets ... people from outside walk on the secrets; the trap springs, the heart shuts. But Fraser Darling is inside'.[19] Darling argued that the 'Highland problem' was of such a complex nature that no single solution could resolve the difficulties faced by the Highlanders; advice that unfortunately had been wilfully disregarded by successive governments.[20] The discriminating judgments made by both Collier and Darling are a testament to their scholarly approach and therefore mark a clear break with previous assessments of the crofting community. Earlier reflections on the difficulties affecting the Highlands and Islands were based largely on emotional attitudes and knee-jerk responses to particularly acute economic and social crises. This work therefore presented governments and officials with detailed information on the nature of the 'Highland problem', free from the customary emotive language and cursory analysis.

ADVOCATES OF A 'WAY OF LIFE'

The government, their Highland agencies and those who worked on them made little specific mention of the role of Gaelic culture in the resolution of the problems afflicting the *Gàidhealtachd*. However, the publications of the Highland Panel and the Crofters Commission did refer to the distinct values of the Highlanders and the Highland 'way of life'. Insiders were aware of the transformation taking place in the region, changes ushered in by improvements in communications, social services and material living standards. However, they were keen to maintain, as they saw it, the distinctive 'Highland way of life'. First, we need to ascertain what it was they sought to preserve.

For Adam Collier, the essence of the 'Highland problem' stemmed from a diametrically opposite set of values, assumptions and philosophies between the Highlander and the non-Highlander.[21] His words captured the seeming spiritual relationship, often sentimentalized, between the Highlander and his world:

> It is more than a mere sense of remoteness in space that strikes him; it is a sense also of remoteness in time. He has stepped from a modern highly industrialized society in which each man is producing for

---

had already begun his educational and demonstrative work by reclaiming land on the island of Tanera Mòr in Loch Broom. The survey area consisted of 1,040 townships in the north-west Highlands and Islands.   19 Mitchison, 'Highlands with love and anger'.   20 In his preface to the *West Highland Survey* (pp vii-viii), Darling stated that he was given government funding 'in order to examine the Highland problem in the spirit of scientific inquiry, to gather a solid body of facts for analysis and synthesis, which would serve as a foundation for a future policy for the region. The argument was maintained that if the problem were understood in its wholeness, a solution would be possible'.   21 Collier actually believed that the term 'crofter problem' was a more accurate assessment of the fundamental difficulties in this region.

> others rather than himself and dependent on others for the satisfaction of his own needs, to one more primitive in which, despite recent changes, the family group is much more self-contained and self-sufficient than in any town.[22]

For Collier, this different lifestyle bred certain distinctive values:

> The standards and values of a crofter living in a small community in a remote glen or island must necessarily differ considerably from those of a town-dweller, be he unskilled labourer or university professor. This difference in background and in unconscious assumptions and attitudes goes far to explain why Highlander and non-Highlander disagree so often about what should be done for, or in, the Highlands.[23]

After 1945, the people of the region had to readjust to further demobilization and contend with an accelerated rate of social, economic and cultural change. The realization that something tangible could be achieved through advances in technology, especially in the development of hydro-electricity, encouraged politicians and the mandarins of St Andrew's House in Edinburgh. Certainly the physical environment bred a distinctive outlook on life, but was this peculiar to the Gaels of Collier's generation?

Mitchison and Gunn also believed that the Highlands and Islands was an area with a distinct set of values, but that the unique lifestyle of the Highlanders was under threat. By drawing on their rich experience of other European and African cultures, they felt this 'way of life' could be preserved. They were loath to see the region become a mere appendage to Scotland's Central Belt. As with Collier, they recognized that, in a European context, the Highlands and Islands were different but far from unique, despite their greater dependence on home-grown produce gained from small-holdings or from a peasant class than elsewhere in Britain. They agreed strongly with Collier's warning to non-Highlanders that

> There is a temptation to dismiss them [that is, Highlanders] as characteristics of a primitive outlook and a backward type of society. To appreciate that there is a real conflict of social philosophies here, it is necessary to stand back and scrutinize the premises of contemporary society which it seems so natural to accept. And it is only by recognizing the dichotomy between the two cultures, between two different types of attitude and adjustment to the material facts of

22 Collier, *Crofting problem*, p. 6.   23 Ibid.

existence, that we can succeed in ridding ourselves of the long-standing confusion of thought about the Highlands.[24]

Both Mitchison and Gunn had a fundamental desire to preserve the 'civilization of the old Gaeltachd [sic]' from the dangers presented by 'the blind forces of advertisement – both straight capitalist and of state origin – which we call progress, and partly through well-meaning ignorance'.[25] Mitchison was the most obstreperous campaigner among the appointees of the Highland Panel for improving Highlanders' standards of living. She spelt out the following justification for her beliefs in repopulation:

> The answer to that is partly in history and partly perhaps that the Highlands can give those who live and work there a certain first-hand experience of some kinds of beauty and some kinds of stress which appear to us likely to produce certain human values. They will be different values from those of Glasgow or London. And without them the combined civilization will be a poorer thing. We also know that the Highlands can produce, and export to the rest of the country, valuable food and timber and electric power.[26]

Mitchison's argument is similar to Collier's in that both felt the physical environment would encourage a different outlook on life in general, and, therefore, foster certain values that would of necessity differ from areas more integrated into an industrial and uniform society. For Neil Gunn, the mission of the Commission of Enquiry into Crofting Conditions was much more fundamental than their official remit indicated. Gunn's main inspiration was the preservation of a unique society, imbued with Gaelic culture and respect for nature, because 'unless the Highlands had a distinctive way of life, that would enrich the human spirit today, why bother with a Crofters Commission or other bodies to keep the old highland stock on their own land and sea?'[27] This desire to preserve the Highland 'way of life' was not something which had suddenly become a contentious issue and the members of the committee were fully aware of the magnitude of the problem they faced as well as the significance of their findings for the Highlands and Islands.[28] The problem was not merely an agricultural one, but something that was interrelated with the wider social and economic malaise of the Highlands.[29] As Gunn said, 'We like to contemplate a

---

24 Ibid., p. 8. 25 Mitchison, 'Highlands with love and anger'. 26 Mitchison, *Highlands and Islands*, p. 4. 27 NLS: NMG Dep 209/10, typescript of a speech which has in pencil 'for Robert Wotherspoon', n.d. 28 NLS: NMG Dep 209/10', interview with Gunn', n.d., but *c.*1953. With regard to crofting, Gunn says 'We have been worrying that tough problem for some time. A whole way of life is a big thing'. 29 NLS: NM Acc 8503/2, 'Has crofting a future?' by Joseph F. Duncan, n.d., but *c.*1953.

kind of community where the ancient values of highland culture (including the attitude to time) may be perpetuated amid an economy which will give a good life to all'.[30]

As we have seen in the introduction, the region of the Highlands and Islands does not equate exactly with the *Gàidhealtachd*; nonetheless, for these policy informers, the message was quite clear. They argued that the Gaelic parts of the region are the *real* Highlands; Gunn's words are typical:

> I suppose it is an extraordinary land, and there are lonely lost places where at times the whole region seems like one of its own legends or traditional songs; and when you come on a couple of hill men talking Gaelic, the age and nature of the legend or song assume a strangely authentic air.[31]

For Gunn, this helped to explain 'the curious nostalgia that haunts Highland men and women who go – as they have always gone – to every part of the world'.[32] Discussing the situation in Kintyre during the war, Mitchison said that 'Many families are incomers from the mainland, not Gaelic-speaking, and among the pure Highland families even, Gaelic is dying out'.[33] There are numerous other examples from Mitchison and Gunn, especially in their travel writing, which they usually penned for consumption in the lucrative North American market, that highlighted their view that the 'authentic' Highlands had the Gaelic language and culture at the heart of the community.

Notwithstanding their inability to speak Gaelic, all of the commentators discussed here displayed an interest in the preservation of the Gaelic language and culture. Gunn, however, showed the greatest commitment to the language, whereas Mitchison, who was less exposed to it, had a more fatalistic attitude towards the survival of the culture. She wrote: 'When I first came [to Kintyre] there was still some ceilidhing, the small gatherings round the fire with home-made songs and music. But the wireless killed that'. She felt that the predominant attitude among the younger population was to tune in to the radio and experience other cultures rather than listen to relatives singing 'the old stuff'.[34] Because of this negative response, she felt that many of the older people denied their Gaelic inheritance and acquiesced in the eradication of the language.[35] Neil Gunn was also troubled by the declining fortunes of the language, and he drew the comparison with Ireland, where Gaelic seemed to be

---

30 NMG, 'for Robert Wotherspoon'. 31 NLS: NMG Dep 209/8, 'Above the Highland line', n.d. 32 Ibid. 33 Mitchison, 'Gaelic with an Oxford accent'. The article is subheaded 'A call for the education authorities to do more to promote Scots and Gaelic, by a leading novelist and socialist'. 34 Mitchison, 'Living in Scotland to-day'. 35 Ibid. Grant also confirmed the speed with which Gaelic became a threatened language once radio became widely accessible in the islands. Personal interview, Sept. 1995.

based on a more realistic assessment of the situation and carried greater relevance due to its tendency to shock because of the 'Troubles'. However, he exercised caution by saying: 'I am not even suggesting that An Comunn Gaidhealach should open yet a new subscription list in the columns of An Gaidheal for firearms'.[36] Another issue that troubled Mitchison was the ambivalence of the Gaels themselves towards the language. She attributed this to the cumulative pressure from 'English culture' to assimilate; a practice which had resulted in the 'real' beauty of the Gaelic culture being distorted and sanitized for a mass audience. 'Instead', she claimed,

> we sing and publicize our 'little music', love-songs mostly, which are easy to perform, to listen to, and can be marketed in the south and in the cities, where they arouse muddled and lazy nostalgia of a kind that can be simply exploited, and used for money making.[37]

This was just part of a wider problem of 'a curious ambivalence in the Highlands towards Highland things and the outward symbols of the national culture'. Taking the kilt as an example, she stated:

> The average Scots country worker laughs at it, will not wear it, unless he happens to be, say, a member of An Comunn [Gàidhealach], and yet he finds it attractive, and if the excuse turns up, he will be into the kilt and moving and looking as one long accustomed to the swing and feel of the folds.[38]

She felt the kilt could be worn as an everyday working garment, except by fishermen! Mitchison's conclusions, however, were pessimistic. She believed that the kilt would not be worn daily because it had become a symbol of derision, a situation wholly due to the dominance of English speech, grammar and culture.[39]

Despite this rather gloomy picture, both Mitchison and Gunn believed that Gaelic would return because of either 'the ever shortening swing of the pendulum of taste' or the appearance of a Sibelius in the Highlands to rediscover the richness and glories of the ancient Gaelic culture.[40] Gunn argued that this *risorgimento* may have arisen earlier but for parochialism within the Gaelic community and the deliberate decision by Gaelic-speaking parents to educate their children in the English language.[41] These two individuals in their capacity as policy informers to central government sought to preserve the traditional way of life and value system of the Highlanders because of its worthiness. They

---

36 NLS: NMG Dep 209/9, 'The one who will come', typescript, n.d. This was actually printed in *AG* (1949), p. 127.   37 Mitchison, 'Gaelic with an Oxford accent'.   38 Ibid.   39 Ibid.   40 Mitchison, 'Living in Scotland to-day'.   41 NMG, 'The one who will come'.

never actually stated that it was to maintain the Gaelic language, but reading between the lines, one can discern that this was certainly a consideration. This desire to protect the Highlanders from further mismanagement resulted in Mitchison and Gunn continually agitating and criticizing central government on their behalf. But they were also masterful in the art of propaganda and self-publicity – talents that were in fact needed to overturn the erroneous depictions of life in the Highlands and Islands.

'THIS GREAT WHITE COW': GOVERNMENT AND THE HIGHLANDS

Highlanders often had to contend with gross misrepresentation from those with no clear understanding of the 'Gaelic way of life', nor of the day-to-day existence that living in such an environment produced. As Collier himself said, 'The general impression is that crofters struggle individually with their common problems of land scarcity, distant markets and lack of capital in conditions which are virtually uniform and unchanging'.[42] Reacting to a description of the simple dwellings of Highlanders as African Kraals, Gunn chided the 'distinguished and earnest politician', comparing him to those commentators who feign to 'live it rough' in the urban slums and then produce work to shock their intended audience, the middle class:

> It is no more than the description of a partial subjective reaction to unaccustomed phenomena, prompted in some measure by a distaste that is touched by fear. For the well-to-do have always found in the slums a certain menace. In a word, it is the point of view of the observer, not the point of view of the slum-dweller observed, to which we are treated. As an inner description of slum life, for all its appearance of objective truth, it is mostly false, a sentimental inversion.[43]

As with the Highlands, Gunn argued that these 'voyeurs' did not understand the notion of relativism because the observer 'tends to put into the mind of the slum-dweller the feelings that he himself would experience had he to live in such a milieu'.[44] Unfortunately, these false images tended to oscillate between contemporary depictions of Highlanders suffering from extreme privation to mythical representations based on the romanticized and mythical world of Scott, Landseer and Robert Louis Stevenson. Consequently, the inhabitants of this region were not deemed as 'responsible' enough to be empowered with sufficient machinery to resolve their difficulties.

Because of the predominantly negative attitude from 'outside' the

---

42 Collier, *Crofting problem*, p. 1.   43 Gunn, 'Drains for the Kraal'.   44 Ibid.

Gàidhealtachd, many Highlanders had continually to challenge the policies and programmes emanating from Westminster and the civil servants in St Andrew's House. The lack of detailed knowledge of the people of the Highlands and their lifestyles led to misconceptions and contradictory perceptions that proved harmful when governments tried to press forward with economic and social legislation. Collier believed that this failure to acknowledge the core of the problem meant that many government officials were unwilling to invest time and effort to reassess radically the manner in which the Highlands were administered. Collier believed that this isolation created distinctive difficulties:

> Because it raises fundamental political issues in odd guises, controversy on Highland matters is apt to be both bitter and ill-advised in the full sense of that word; and the issues have come to be recognized by politicians and civil servants as potential booby-traps which they have naturally tried to avoid.[45]

One way of government 'avoiding' the issues was to set up commissions of enquiry. Neither Mitchison nor Gunn were enthusiasts of commissions, for both desired Scottish self-government and more democratic and accountable institutions of government, which a system of commissioners would not deliver.[46] But they also questioned the usefulness of repeatedly setting up commissions designed to pontificate on the 'Highland problem' but without the teeth to carry through their recommendations, however misguided:

> A gathering of dragons takes place unobtrusively and in connection with the disposal of treasure; it is usually presided over by some very senior, indeed battle-scarred, dragon of unimpeachable antiquity. In the absence of heroes all proceeds according to plan and the end-result goes up in smoke. It is usual to refer to such a gathering as a Royal Commission.[47]

Writing in 1939, Gunn cited the recently published 'Hilleary Report' on the Highlands as a case in point: 'I would merely suggest that the annual grant of £65,000 for five years spread over all the purposes stated is just absurd. The gillie's tip on a larger scale'.[48]

---

45 Collier, *Crofting problem*, p. 2. 46 NMG, 'And then rebuild it'. For Gunn the main problem with a further commission was that it 'would not be directly responsible to the people of the country in which it would be operating. Let it be responsible to the people concerned through the usual democratic channels and you have government'. He suggested that the recent upsurge in examining the state of Scotland was a consequence of the renewed interest in self-government. 47 NLS: NM Acc 8503/2, letter by Mitchison to *The Observer* on the subject of dragons, 3 June 1960. 48 NMG, 'And then rebuild it'.

'The English way and the wrong way'

The war acted as a catalyst for a new, more forceful attitude within Scottish political circles. A desire for redress was also due in large part to the bitter memories of the inter-war era of depression and emigration. The stirrings of activity within the Scottish Office merely added to the clamour for meaningful and decisive action. People were no longer willing to accept token acknowledgment of their problems with no fundamental change to their situation.[49] Again, Mitchison captured the essence of wider views. Her criticism of the commissions was trenchant:

> They are advisory bodies, appointed in arbitrary ways, with no power. By their very existence they proclaim that there is no real democratic power or government within Scotland capable of dealing directly and finally with our domestic issues. The utmost they can do is to beg that any scheme or plan that they have formulated may be sanctioned by an authority outside their country.[50]

Following the publication of the report of the *Royal Commission on Scottish Affairs* in 1954, Mitchison claimed that the lack of a coherent strategy to ameliorate the difficulties afflicting Scotland as a whole rendered the report inadequate. This was not surprising because most members of the commission 'are in some way involved in the enormous, benevolent and overwhelming machine of British government. One cannot expect them even to want to do more than tidy it up here and there'.[51] For these policy informers, self-government could resolve this 'democratic deficit', but any devolution of power was welcome. Hence their continued calls for a development body with substantial powers for the Highlands. Their argument was based on sound logic; empower those with knowledge of the area so that there could be a realistic appraisal of the magnitude of the difficulties concerned. '[M]en and women are happiest when they are building for themselves', Gunn wrote, and 'when they are conscious of being creative in their own land'. This, he averred, 'has to do with the essence of life itself'.[52]

Despite the repeated use of commissions of enquiry, governments seemed to display a lack of awareness of the nature and intricacies involved in the 'Highland problem'. 'Insiders' regarded this ignorance of Highland affairs as inevitable because of the drive towards centralization. This process increased considerably during the war, turning London into a vortex for political and economic control of Britain. Mitchison wrote: 'It's fantastic that so many decisions have to be sent down to London, where they simply don't know the conditions. And only two days a year in parliament for Scottish affairs!'[53] The

49 Ibid. 50 NMG, 'Awakening of a nation'. 51 Mitchison, 'Commission offers nothing to average Scot'. 52 NMG, 'Awakening of a nation'. 53 NLS: NM Acc 8374, 'letter from

post-war Labour government's continuation of that policy troubled Highland activists. Gaels themselves were demonstrating some bitterness at the lack of coverage of items of particular importance for the Highlands and Islands, such as fishing, and their ineffectiveness in resisting legislation or legal decisions which harmed the economy of the region. In response to a legal decision taken at The Hague on fishing in 1952 a letter in the *Stornoway Gazette* reflected growing bitterness: 'It has been well said that the English mentality can see only two ways of doing things – the English way and the wrong way'.[54]

Whether this led to a growing sense of national pride and a desire for political independence among some Gaels to resolve the country's difficulties is difficult to substantiate. In the eyes of Naomi Mitchison, however, it merely added to the long-standing problem of how Gaels viewed the institutions of government:

> Anyone who knows the islands will realize that the coming of [the] money economy there wasn't altogether a happy thing. There was this great white cow, the government – 'They' – which could be evaded and laughed at and milked. In relation to it, there was no such thing as dishonesty.[55]

In the context of the post-war years with a renewed interest in the problems of the Highlands and increased levels of funding, this was a worrying insight. Unless there was a shift in the way government was perceived, 'subsidies or any other payments are looked on as gratuitous blessings and not as something which must in any way be earned or deserved'.[56]

One other important and damaging effect of this negative attitude towards the institutions of government was the unwillingness of Highlanders to become involved in local decision-making bodies, in particular the county council. Mitchison explained: 'most of them don't even want to help because they feel that they will only waste their time and that their knowledge will be lost in a tangle of administration and interests which they distrust and perhaps rightly'.[57] Mitchison felt that the loss of people with local knowledge of the problems afflicting Highland communities would continue unless the image of local government as just 'agents' for enforcing orders or trying to gain as much in grant funding as possible was overcome. Unfortunately, she lamented, local authorities were continually thwarted by government interference, which just compounded the problem of trying to improve the calibre of local government officials.

The weakness of local government – the lack of power, transparency and local

Mitchison to Mr Simmons', n.d. but during the Second World War. **54** *Stornoway Gazette*, 11 Jan. 1952. **55** NLS: NM Acc 8503/2, 'The county council and the crofter' in *London Forward*, n.d. but it was a review of Collier's 1953 book. **56** Ibid. **57** Ibid.

knowledge – compounded the misallocation and misappropriation of public money. In a review of Dr Bowie's *The future of Scotland* (1939), Gunn made some perceptive comments on the misuse of government finance; the mere throwing of money at the problem without listening. Gunn recognized the central issue:

> For those of us who are aware of the enormous amount of state aid pumped into the Hebrides every week by way of pension and dole, his [Bowie's] figures certainly give us furiously to think. After all, St Kilda was evacuated. If there is not a livelihood in crofting-fishing for the average Hebridean head of family under the existing economic dispensation – what's to be done about it? And if nothing is done?[58]

If the inhabitants of the Highlands and Islands could not rely on their local councillors to shape government policy according to the needs of the locality or to use funds in a resourceful and considered manner, what was the answer for activists such as Gunn and Mitchison?

THE CASE FOR HIGHLAND DEVELOPMENT: THE INSIDERS' VIEW

Those who worked for government agencies from the late 1930s to the 1960s had a unique insight into what legislation might be appropriate for the region, the difficulties involved with implementing government policy and the attitudes of Highlanders to such action. Some of the people had their own thoughts on the most appropriate course of action to take to resolve aspects of the Highland problem. For Highlanders, such as Mitchison and Gunn, who were actively seeking redress for the damage inflicted on northern Scotland by past governments, officials or landowners, the beginnings of an answer lay in the establishment of a powerful, autonomous administrative body. For Mitchison, the future was bleak unless there was

> some kind of T.V.A. type of Highland authority with plans for scattered Highland industries, for a more thorough use of the fisheries, for local use of Forestry Commission timber, and for all the many things which men like Adam Collier could see were needed, but could not see any machinery for getting.[59]

In alluding to the deep problems facing the Highlands and Islands, Gunn's solution was the introduction of a powerful government agency to oversee the

---

58 NMG, 'And then rebuild it'.   59 Mitchison, 'The county council and the crofter'.

panoply of concerns afflicting the *Gàidhealtachd*. Gunn concurred with Mitchison, stating that

> Perhaps the major trouble in the north has been the absence of an overall authority that could fit the bits and pieces, the sporadic starts and stops, into some sort of reasonable pattern that would not only give the man of initiative a chance but would create the chance for him.[60]

Here, Gunn was underlining his argument that because of the desperate circumstances in the region, Highlanders should be given state assistance in order to break the vicious circle of unemployment–lack of confidence–emigration. These policy informers were convinced that with targeted and appropriate government action, the Highlands could reverse the sense of demoralization.

Both Mitchison and Gunn had an indubitable faith that the Highlands contained enough natural resources, many of which could now be exploited due to the harnessing of hydro-electric power, in order to sustain a significant population. Gunn asserted:

> The basic ingredients are certainly present, with an immense hydro-electric scheme getting past the blue-print stage and beginning to produce the power. The harvests of sea and land, with attendant small industries for by-products, tweed weaving, afforestation with its valuable subsidiaries, distilling with proper organization of trade mark and distribution, in fact all the kinds of labour that have long been native to the highlands but now require organization at a higher level to meet the controlled conditions in the markets of the world.[61]

Therefore, like Mitchison, Gunn was optimistic that the Highlands and Islands could sustain a sizeable population at the same level of comfort as in the rest of Scotland. While this was an attainable goal, it was dependent on government initiatives and the indigenous population adapting to the changing circumstances. As we have seen, throughout the period from 1939 to 1965, Mitchison and Gunn sought to influence policy decisions taken at Westminster in a way that would allow the way of life of the Highlands to be continued and indeed enhanced. Their stance derived, not from some romanticized or sentimental regard for the Highlanders, but from a realization that acute pressures were now impacting on this region.[62] They felt that those involved in the economic and

---

60 NMG, 'The Highlands today'.   61 NMG, 'Above the Highland line'; See also Mitchison, *Highlands and Islands* (p. 4), where she says: 'We also know that the Highlands can produce, and export to the rest of the country, valuable food and timber and electric power'.   62 Personal interview with Grant, Sept. 1995.

social development of this area had to take cognisance of the particular circumstances and set of attitudes in the Highlands and Islands, and only a sensitive approach would preserve the traditional lifestyle of the Highlanders in a rapidly changing environment.

It is ironic to note that in the period prior to the establishment of the HIDB (1965), with its enthusiasm for nodal growth points, policy informers such as Gunn and Mitchison cautioned against the development of large-scale industrial centres. Mitchison put her argument in these terms:

> It is no use writing in urban and industrial terms about the Highlands. The only large-scale industries which could sensibly be located there are the few which need large supplies of hydro-electric power; they do not necessarily give much employment, but if they do the result is the single-industry village, not the best type of community for free-minded people. These villages in turn depopulate the surrounding country and add to the Highland problem. Light industries are possible in a few places, usually only through the keenness, devotion and special ability of one or two people. Most Highland raw materials in the shape of minerals are remote or difficult to work or not of first-class quality; even with heavily subsidized transport costs they are of doubtful national value.[63]

Though development could be encouraged through the re-siting of factories that use the raw materials, Mitchison did not hold out much hope for 'that would mean real planning'.[64] This cautious outlook would be vindicated in the following years as the formation of 'Development areas', so called under the terms of the Distribution of Industry Act (1954), made little impact on the Highlands and Islands. Neil Gunn also believed that a Highlands replete with industrial parks would have a negative impact on the region as a whole. Indeed, both Mitchison and Gunn felt that this could exacerbate the 'Highland problem' in that the young population would continue to be enticed from the glens and straths, even though they might opt for Highland towns, such as Inverness and Fort William, rather than Glasgow or Edinburgh.[65] Aside from this pragmatic argument, they stressed the rather metaphysical effects of such an expansion in the Highlands: 'we don't want to turn that ancient land and sea, with all the human qualities that they have bred, into a mass industrial area, even if that were possible'.[66]

Their alternative suggestion, and the one in which both the Crofters Commission of Enquiry and the Highland Panel were preoccupied, was the

---

[63] Mitchison, *Highlands and Islands*, p. 4. [64] Ibid. [65] Ibid. [66] NMG, 'For Robert Wotherspoon'.

means by which opportunities for ancillary and part-time work for the crofters and others residing in the Highlands and Islands could be extended – all of which would complement the cultural mores of the Gaels:

> And perhaps here is the place for suggesting that the Highlands have long had a native culture of their own and that industrial planning should be geared to it. Not heavy industries, not individual estates, but the creation of small industries and particularly small industries that would deal with the varied harvests of land and sea right through to the processing of their by-products.[67]

With this in mind, both Mitchison and Gunn stressed the desire to utilize the natural products of the area, and, as we have seen in the case of Mitchison, their proper marketing, coordination and overall organization.[68]

'Insiders', such as Mitchison and Gunn, analyzed the 'Highland problem' in precise terms in their drive to maintain the distinctiveness of the Highlands and Islands. This considered approach allowed for comprehensive changes to occur at a more sedate pace and therefore more suited to the Highland psyche. Mitchison called on Highlanders to renounce the habit of applying wholesale to the Highlands and Islands unsuitable 'mainland' standards. Her extensive travelling experiences, for example, were always reflected upon with the problems of the Highlands in mind: 'Why [...] must we always insist on a bath when our Scandinavian neighbours of all classes enjoy a hot and cold shower, which cuts the size and cost of the house and uses less fuel?'[69] Mitchison's penchant for minute detail meant that she left no stone unturned. In one article, she could talk about household hygiene; in the next she was tackling the problem of centralized food production, or the Highlanders' abandonment of their 'standards of taste' to accommodate summer visitors.[70] What lay behind these attacks was a belief that, by accepting the norms of the rest of Britain, Highlanders would lose their own sense of identity. Mitchison feared they would be unnecessarily disadvantaged by adopting the lifestyle of the industrialized classes.

Mitchison's pleas for locals to retain a distinctive lifestyle, and for potential employers to respect the characteristics of the Highlands and Islands, proved difficult to realize, as external pressures to modernize augmented during the post-war period. The conflict between maintaining traditional work practices in the face of more modern methods was a topic that exercised Mitchison's mind. Drawing on the changes in the Harris tweed industry in Lewis, she asked:

---

67 NMG, 'The Highlands today'.   68 NMG, 'For Robert Wotherspoon'; Mitchison, *Highlands and Islands*, passim.   69 Mitchison, *Highlands and Islands*, p. 45.   70 NLS: NM Acc 8503/2, a letter to *The Scotsman* entitled 'Food production in remote places: "The key is marketing"', 2 Aug. 1957; Mitchison, 'Living in Scotland to-day'.

> Should we lament for the passing of the real hand-made tweeds? I do not know. There are still some weavers to make them, for the few special customers who want that extra beauty. But it is the other kind of tweed which has kept the population in the islands.[71]

Therefore, despite calling for the Highlanders to take into account their own special difficulties vis-à-vis the physical environment and resist the pressure to adopt the standard of living that the more industrialized areas were accustomed to, this was tempered by recognition that the Highlanders could not live in the past. They had to be dynamic and meet the demands of the market, but this should be achieved by the people of the Highlands themselves, and not from government diktat, and in a way that met the specific requirements of the Highlanders.

Underlying this philosophy, Mitchison emphasized the role of the population as a key resource in economic development. Drawing on her rich knowledge of other similar 'marginal' areas in Europe, she argued that

> Economy and efficiency are not everything. There are also people. Other countries, which may have the same temptation to centralize, have seen the necessity for small cooperatives and marketing schemes, and have put heart into their peasants, who were as discouraged as our crofters are now, and turned them into lively, progressive and hopeful communities of people.[72]

The special characteristics of the Highlanders, she claimed, were born out of living in its unique environment, and should be tapped, but not by imposing organizational structures from the industrial south.[73] However, capital was required in order to realize the goal of initiating small, locally based industries, indigenous to the Highlands, which were reliant on this region's natural resources. Investors were in short supply and it had long been claimed that there was a distinct lack of entrepreneurial spirit in the Highlands and Islands.[74] This was put down to structural imbalance, for example in the local population. This was a feature of the Highlands and Islands that was regarded as inhibiting the crofting community in particular, partly from the reasons mentioned in relation to examples of social conservatism but also for reasons that were harder to quantify.

Naomi Mitchison and Neil Gunn were not alone in emphasizing the importance of the people as a resource in the struggle to overcome the Highland problem and to induce some hope for this beleaguered community. Fraser

71 Mitchison, 'Action by the Highland Panel', *The Guardian*, 19 Oct. 1955.   72 Mitchison, 'Food production'.   73 Mitchison, *Highlands and Islands*, p. 4.   74 Smout, *History of Scottish people*, p. 98.

Darling's *West Highland Survey* had also placed great emphasis on the holistic approach to economic and social regeneration. This emphasis on localized community-led initiatives to generate economic growth would certainly have helped the maintenance of Gaelic-speaking communities, because the influx of non-Gaelic speakers would be minimized and the younger population may have taken some hope from the opportunities afforded by cooperative enterprises. But those involved in Highland affairs were familiar with the apparent lack of initiative in the crofting communities.

Entrepreneurial activity in the Highlands was concentrated in communities outwith the *Gàidhealtachd*. The success stories that existed in the 1950s were predominantly on the east coast; Brora for example, with its coalmine, brickworks, wool mill and distillery, was described by Gunn as 'a little hive of industry'.[75] Thus, entrepreneurs like these were to be lauded and supported in every way possible: 'It must be the care of every Highlander to support and encourage pioneers like these, for they are all too few'.[76] Though Gunn did not underestimate the value of these business entrepreneurs, 'the few who start things going, a sort of creative elite', he did believe that, 'taking crofting as an instance, the ultimate makers and creators are the crofters themselves'.[77] Gunn felt that if the crofters worked out among themselves the improvements which were needed, the Crofters Commission could act in the knowledge that their proposals would be accepted and implemented more effectively.[78] But this illustrates a crippling paradox facing campaigners like Gunn, for the crofters needed prompting to be innovative and entrepreneurial. Unfortunately, their position was also divorced from reality, as enterprising crofters keen to 'make things happen' found themselves thwarted by township diktat.[79] Although James Shaw Grant could recollect stories of individual initiative, he conceded that 'peer pressure' was sometimes a significant deterrent to change.[80]

Grant and others were aware that the historical development of the Highlands had left the region, particularly the crofting communities, without a middle class of any significance. Therefore, although many regarded the problems affecting the Highlands and Islands as being imposed from outwith the region, the social structure of this territory was also important. The almost complete absence of a middle class, for example, with those who did exist being in the professions, inevitably took its toll. As Collier had pointed out, writing in

---

75 NLS: NMG Dep 209/10, 'undated typescript', c.1956. 76 Ibid. 77 Mitchison, 'Living in Scotland'. 78 NLS: NMG Dep 209/8, letter 24 Jan. 1956. 79 Gillanders, 'Gaelic Scotland today'. 80 Grant argued that the stereotype of the crofter as lazy and lacking in initiative should be treated with caution. He pointed out the speed and willingness with which the crofters abandoned their old black houses when grant aid became available for new homes. He recalled a common occurrence in the isles known as the 'half house', where crofters would use the available grants to build what they could, boarding up the rest of the house until further funding could be secured whereupon the planks shoring up the gable end would be used as floorboards for the other half of the house. Personal interview, Sept. 1995.

the 1940s, 'what we have is a small class of land-owners, mostly non-native and partly absentee, a large and fairly homogenous peasantry, and few opportunities for individuals to climb the social ladder except in the professions'.[81] Therefore, the issue of encouraging industries into the Highlands and Islands had another indirect bearing on the vitality of the Gaelic language: an influx of non-Gaelic speakers. O'Dell put the matter in these terms:

> Changes in the economy of the Highlands and Islands since 1945 may mark a reversal of trends of a century. Once again, public enquiries on various topics have ventilated grievances and shown lines of possible deployment of resources, but it is by no means certain yet whether decline can be effectively arrested. The people have vanished over large districts, and if the north is to be revitalized there must be colonization.[82]

Discussing the development of a nuclear site at Dounreay in Caithness, Neil Gunn warmed to the prospect of employment opportunities and expressed little fear at the possible 'swamping' of indigenous culture by incoming workers as at Dounreay: 'All this (Dounreay and Caithness) has meant an influx of strangers, and you may wonder if it will change the old spirit, the ancient attitude to life'. He continued in an optimistic, and perhaps naïve, vein, stating 'that not even a whole New World can change what matters in the Scottish spirit'.[83] It is interesting to note, however, that he did not specifically mention Gaelic culture and, as we shall see in the following chapter, Gaels themselves were quite scathing about the lack of positive discrimination for them when funding and other government support was being distributed. This issue would become steadily more important in the following decades, as increased numbers of settlers born outwith the *Gàidhealtachd* moved north. These people, by the very fact of their deliberate step to migrate to the Highlands and Islands, were more likely to take a prominent role in the decision-making of their local communities. As such, they could be deemed to be a 'threat' to the indigenous population, a group largely wary of change and tinted with rather exclusivist aims and ideas.

Whether ancillary employment was anticipated as coming from within the indigenous communities or as a consequence of people coming into the region, their needs had to be catered for in order to retain a viable population. Mitchison, Gunn and Grant were certainly aware of the psychological needs of the community. Although the Labour government's *A programme of Highland development* (1950) made a cursory reference to the recreational needs of Highland communities, Gunn and Mitchison were in no doubt about the

---

81 Collier, *Crofting problem*, p. 5.   82 O'Dell & Walton, *Highlands of Scotland* (1962).
83 NMG, 'For Robert Wotherspoon'.

importance of addressing this dimension of the Highland problem, because it related to the psychological needs of the inhabitants of this area.[84] For both of them, the failure to recognize this element was a significant contributory factor in encouraging Highland out-migration. To try and offset the lure of the urban centres to the south, activists in the Highlands and Islands sought to address the psychological needs of the youth in particular. As yet, promoting various facets of Gaelic culture was not deemed a sufficient incentive or enticement for people to remain or return to the *Gàidhealtachd*, but, nonetheless, concern was expressed at the social needs of the community:

> anything that will make life more interesting, more vivid, for the young people will help to keep them in the Highlands, and not only keep them there but give them zest and initiative in what they have to do. Perhaps, after all, the basic problem in the highlands is a psychological one. However, that's a deep subject.[85]

The main culprits in impeding these projects, Gunn and Mitchison believed, were central and local government; although the stance of the Presbyterian churches also incurred their wrath. This idea that Calvinist dogmatism hindered the flourishing of the region's communities is a constant trait in Mitchison's and Gunn's work.[86] It is, however, worthy of note that in all the writings of Gunn and Mitchison, no mention is made of the possibility of the language being a cohesive force, though there is tacit acknowledgment of this factor when discussing the 'unique values' of the Highlanders.

The greatest incentive towards retaining the Highland youth was undoubtedly work; other factors such as the psychological requirements of the community were dependent on employment being available. The chairman of the crofting assessors, in 1958 at a conference on crofting, claimed that 'the assessors insisted that it is not just bright lights that young people chase after. They are confident that if there were a due variety of interesting and challenging ancillary employments, we would hold enough of the young men and women we need to stabilize the population'.[87] One of the ancillary employments increasingly regarded with optimism for fulfilling the lack of employment opportunities was tourism. Bearing in mind the pivotal role of this activity in the Highland economy today, and the role of Gaelic culture within the marketing strategy of the Scottish Tourist Board, the portentous warnings from policy informers make for interesting reading.

84 *Programme of Highland development*, parags 20–1, p. 10.   85 NLS: NMG Dep 209/10 interview with Gunn, no other details, n.d., but *c.*1953.   86 Mitchison, *Lobsters on the agenda*; Mitchison, 'Letters from a tribe', *New Statesman*, 16 Oct. 1964.   87 NLS: NMG Dep 209/16/2, which contained Crofters Commission reports & minutes of meetings from 1950 to 1958. Press statement by chairman of crofting assessors at conference 26–8 Nov. 1958.

TOURISM

One of the central problems of the Highlands was to sustain a viable population. Yet, as intimated in the opening epigraph of this chapter, depopulation had left the region with social problems. Various commentators acknowledged the need for some form of economic rejuvenation and many regarded tourism as a potential source of income for the region's inhabitants. The 1960s witnessed the beginnings of mass tourism in the Highlands and Islands but the difficulties faced by those trying to entice visitors to the region stemmed from the rather basic services available, coupled with the lack of accommodation and amenities, such as restaurants. The prospect of thousands of people descending on this ecologically fragile and scenic terrain caused apprehension among some commentators, especially with regard to the potential problems of noise and litter pollution.[88] Nonetheless, because of the region's great size, and the financial benefits that might accrue from tourism, the same commentators believed in the capacity of the Highlanders and local businesses to overcome the 'teething problems' caused by such a speedy growth of the tourist industry.[89]

Naomi Mitchison and Neil Gunn were vociferous in their calls for local crofters to adapt to the tourist market. The notion of adapting croft houses for summer visitors, for example, was often mentioned. Otherwise, it was argued that chalets could be built in order to meet the demand for accommodation and supplant the incomes of crofters. The wider problems involved in building these apartments was also recognized; hence an appeal for MacBrayne's (the main ferry company servicing the islands off the west coast) to introduce cheaper freight charges for individuals interested in capitalizing on the growth in visitors.[90] Citing Skye as an example, Mitchison noted the efforts being made to encourage tourists to visit and to continue to do so on a regular basis. By staying in one of the renovated croft houses, she believed that visitors could perhaps experience 'more of the ordinary life of the country'.[91] There was also the hope that some of these visitors may stay in the communities for a reasonable time (say, three months) or even settle there and make their visit permanent. For Mitchison, this introduction of 'warm young blood' offered the advantage of introducing new types of employment, which would in turn broaden the skills base of the local communities.[92]

Mitchison welcomed the prospect of tourists settling in parts of the *Gàidhealtachd*, as she believed that 'any kind of skilled man is welcome on an island'.[93] These incomers may provide the particular locality with fresh ideas and skills and enhance the community, but overall it would keep vital services viable; as on the Isle of Mull: 'Such people might meet their own need for a life

---

[88] Naomi Mitchison, 'Other happiness, other risks', *Guardian*, 18 May 1964. [89] Ibid. [90] Ibid. [91] Naomi Mitchison, 'Oh, Rowan Tree', *Good Housekeeping*, July 1959. [92] Mitchison, 'Other happiness, other risks'. [93] Ibid.

with other kinds of risks than those in a city and other kinds of happiness, and Mull's need for warm young blood, and the courage to look the world in the face and say "this is our way"'.[94] The development of holiday homes was already apparent in the early 1960s, and this element in the tourist industry was not particularly welcomed by Mitchison, though the issue of pricing young, local couples out of the house market would become more important in later decades.[95] It is interesting to note that despite her Highland ancestry (albeit Southern Highland), Mitchison herself mentioned that she too was considered a newcomer to Carradale by most of the older inhabitants.[96] She did not explain why this was, other than the length of time she had resided in Kintyre, but James Shaw Grant recalled how he felt an incomer to Lewis despite his much stronger lineage to Gaeldom. The discriminating factor for him was his inability to speak Gaelic in a stronghold of the language, but, despite that, he maintained that the population largely accepted him because he adopted a positive attitude and did not seek to proselytize the locals to his ideas on how their lives might be conducted.[97] Hence, the 'problem' of the intrusion of new blood into Gaelic-speaking communities was not a new phenomenon; only with the ever-increasing numbers did the emphasis change.

The emerging tourist industry was not greeted with universal acclaim. Gunn, while acknowledging the need to entice tourists to the area to offer employment opportunities, raised questions about the artificiality of a region maintained by visitors. He rightly placed the issue in context:

> Highlanders' are above all a social people, and a bright home means more to a young woman than an attraction to tourists. And where the girls are, there the young men gather together. Emigrating, like being a bachelor, is normally not an end in itself, not a human ambition. When thatching roofs with bachelors becomes a possibility, something has gone sour with more than the land.[98]

Another danger presented by a sudden mass influx of peoples was the pressure on the local population to adapt to the supposed desires of the visitors. Referring to Kintyre, Mitchison argued that

> Carradale isn't really Highland. It is mixed in blood and feeling. In summer it is full of visitors, mostly from Glasgow and thereabouts, so it is their standards of taste – or what are popularly considered to be their standards – which are aimed at.[99]

---

[94] Ibid. [95] Ibid. [96] Mitchison, 'Living in Scotland to-day'. [97] Interview with Grant, Sept. 1995. [98] NMG, 'The Highlands today'. [99] Mitchison, 'Living in Scotland to-day'.

The harmful effects tourism might have on fragile indigenous culture, Mitchison argued, were impacting on areas other than Carradale. She claimed that 'What has happened in Carradale is, of course, happening more or less quickly all over the Highlands. A culture insufficiently stable is being swamped in a great wave of tourism'.[1] Yet, Mitchison had a more stern observation to make. She believed the creation of a 'service industry' such as tourism was demeaning, especially in relation to what were perceived as 'noble' occupations which accorded with the Highland way of life, such as crofting and fishing. 'Some people', Mitchison claimed,

> may feel that to change crofters into waiters, fishermen into barmen, and the daughters of both into chambermaids, is not a terrific advance, or one which enhances the ancient dignity of the Highlander ... Nor is the man of the house, lurking about the back premises while his wife serves the visitors, an inspiring figure.[2]

It was felt that the Highlander could be further demeaned by their being misrepresented by tourist officials, or by unscrupulous individuals seeking to make a return on the new opportunities presented by the increase in visitors to the Highlands and Islands. Mitchison was clear on this point:

> One keeps on meeting social and aesthetic problems in connection with tourism. Does it, for example, demand the bogus traditional? I think of this every time I pass an hotel faced with sham stone and bedizened inside with tartan.[3]

Attempts to construct tourist facilities in a manner sympathetic to the local environment were, on occasion, thwarted by officials in the Department of Health. This was taken as an indication of the insensitivity of government officials despite the demands of local communities to respect their natural habitat.[4] Mitchison was not arguing against 'the culture export', but rather the presentation and content of what was being exported.[5] Drawing on her recent travels, Mitchison made the comparison that, unlike those in Denmark, Scotland's souvenirs were typified with ersatz and kitsch material charged at an excessive price.[6]

The 'improvements' to the region's infrastructure, designed to ameliorate the difficulties faced by tourists in the 1960s, were also regarded as detrimental if they were carried too far. Discussing the possibility of a corniche road

---

1 NLS: NM Acc 8503/2, 1955 bundle containing a letter by Dr W.A.S. Thom, from Rosebank, Peebles; Naomi Mitchison, 'Is Carradale Highland?', *The Scottish Field*, July 1955. 2 Ibid. 3 Mitchison, 'Other happiness, other risks'. 4 Mitchison, 'Home thoughts from Italy – II: Culture ... for export', *GH*, 18 Oct. 1958. 5 Ibid. 6 Ibid.

connecting the far north-west mainland, Mitchison questioned not so much the need, but the moral or ethical position of constructing such a thoroughfare. Without it, she argued, 'one must stop and be quiet, lay foot on the close turf, look and wait and breathe the soft-sea-smelling air, knowing it has been like this for a very long time and it is not for us that it will change'.[7] This type of project, therefore, raised the paradoxical situation that the very assets and appeal of the Highlands and Islands were themselves threatened by the resultant tourists, and the construction projects arising from their increased numbers. There were real dangers attached to making wholesale changes to the community, just for the sake of tourism. In these early days, holiday homes were more of a cultural curiosity than a serious economic threat, though there were some social repercussions. As Mitchison wrote, 'It can be depressing, though, to have too many holiday houses in a village standing empty half the year or more'.[8]

The strategy adopted to 'sell' the Highlands and Islands mainly focused on the superb scenery. Again, emphasis on the 'unique' way of life was prevalent, though references to Gaelic culture were limited, or cryptic in their presentation, as Mitchison's words illustrate: 'There is always beauty in the Highlands, and in the long evenings your hosts may be induced to shut off the radio and perhaps you will hear the real songs and stories that go with this far, rainbow country on the edge of the Atlantic'.[9] In this respect, the packaging of the Highlands and Islands was similar to that of Ireland, where de Valera famously attempted to mould the embryonic Irish Free State in the image of a bucolic, Catholic and Gaelic nation. Certainly the slow pace of life and the differing value system were brought to public attention, though with the effect of reinforcing the Highlander stereotype and consequently the butt of jokes in the towns and cities of the Central Belt.[10]

Tourism, so important to the economy of the Highlands and Islands today, was still in its embryonic stages in terms of a mass market. It was, therefore, still the preserve of the landowning class with their sporting estates or enjoyed by mountaineers seeking the challenge of the region's mountain ranges. There were also attempts to lengthen the tourist season, so that those crofters, who had responded to the potential of subsidizing their income through leasing their properties, would derive further recompense.[11] While regarded as potentially a 'life-saver' for Highland and Island communities in securing employment, of far greater significance was the need to introduce changes in the education system to ensure the youth of this region either remained in their localities or at least, no longer regarded this option as a symbol of failure.

---

[7] Ibid. [8] Mitchison, 'Other happiness, other risks'. [9] Mitchison, 'In a far, rainbow country', *Scotland's Magazine*, Dec. 1959. [10] Mitchison, 'Oh, Rowan Tree', in which Mitchison sells Raasay as an island where 'you can forget there was ever such a thing as time'. [11] Mitchison, 'In a far, rainbow country'.

EDUCATION

> Scottish education thinks it has been successful insofar as it has put a barrier of ignorance and prejudice between every generation of young Scots and the true history of the country and their heritage. This is demonstrable – it is not a question of opinion and so, insofar as during my years as a schoolmaster in the Gaidhealtachd, I was driving out the culture that was native to the children and substituting, not another culture but simply nothing. Insofar as I was doing that, as other teachers are doing that in these parts, I was a Quisling – in any self-respecting country I would have been put in prison had I done it willingly, but of course that didn't arise in this case.[12]

This damning indictment of the Scottish education system, with regards the Gaelic language and culture, was spoken by 'Fionn MacColla', the noted Scottish novelist and keen participant in the Scottish Renaissance of the inter-war period, in a BBC interview transmitted in 1972. Likening himself to a collaborator with officials in the Scottish Education Department for destroying Gaelic-speaking communities during his days as a teacher on Barra was undoubtedly severe, but 'MacColla' felt a strong sense of complicity and culpability by purposely failing to provide 'a continuous link between the historical heritage and the consciousness of each generation'.[13] It is perhaps no coincidence that he voiced this critique of the education system at the very time when language activists were making significant advances towards persuading the government to adopt a more supportive role vis-à-vis Gaelic. Naomi Mitchison and Neil Gunn both acquiesced with this critical assessment of the Scottish education scene, but Mitchison in particular wrote powerfully on the need for a fundamental review of education as a whole throughout the Highlands. From the primary to the secondary sector, she believed that schools should use their unique environment to teach the children the basics; but she also felt they should imbue pupils with a healthy respect for their surroundings and way of life. In order to persuade teenagers not to leave, she argued that secondary schools should be built close to the Highland and Island communities and continue to inculcate the youth of the Highlands in the ways of their forebears. These 'graduates', as she called them, would then become the future leaders of their respective townships, whether or not they went on to attend university.

At the same time, the ongoing debate over the need for a fifth university to be established in Scotland continued to inflame Highlanders. Mitchison and Gunn made vociferous calls for it to be stationed in the Highlands, arguing that it could

---

[12] Fionn MacColla's papers in NLS (real name Tom MacDonald), Dep 239/1b containing a partial transcript of BBC TV interview on Scope, 17 Jan. 1972, between Gordon Smith and Tom MacDonald. [13] Ibid.

act as a focal point for those enthused with the Highlands and Gaelic culture. They also felt that it might finally alleviate some of the sins of the past from the educational establishment of Scotland.

The education system, virtually unchanged since the 1918 Education (Scotland) Act, was regarded by many as a contributing factor in the depopulation of the Highlands and Islands. Mitchison believed that

> For three generations we have seen the educational siphoning off of the bright children from the Highlands of Scotland. There was no future at home, though after retirement the doctor or teacher or ship's captain might come back to the island croft.[14]

Mitchison often made strong claims for a reorientation in education policy and particularly the argument for bringing curricula at all levels of education more readily into line with the requirements of the Highlands.[15] This was something that many of those involved in different decision-making bodies and strata of Highland society could agree on. The contradictions in trying to empower Highlanders, or initiate new schemes, while simultaneously enticing the young and intelligent to leave, were readily apparent. Again, Mitchison writes:

> This is a very unsatisfactory position; if the Highlands are to hold their own they must have young, vigorous, intelligent people living there, capable of creating the bettering environment, socially and economically, which will hold or increase the population instead of letting it gradually drain away, as it is still doing in spite of all sorts of schemes and inducements. You need intelligence and drive to take advantage of the help which is offered.[16]

This pragmatic response to the difficulties involved in trying to encourage the youth of the *Gàidhealtachd* to remain in the Highlands and Islands was a double-edged sword: to make the education system more adaptable to the lifestyle of this region; and to implement measures designed to arrest the decline in the Gaelic language.

This encouragement of talented youngsters to remain in the community could be secured by integrating the subjects of study at school level with the local environment. The advantages of this were multiple and self-sustaining. For instance, it would allow children to appreciate the skills inherited from their ancestors, ranging from general cultural and linguistic traditions, to more practical measures, such as navigation or crop husbandry in an environmentally

---

14 Mitchison, 'Checking Highland "brain drain"', *GH*, 9 Dec. 1964. 15 Ibid.
16 Ibid.

marginal and difficult region. Children, Mitchison argued, would also develop a healthy respect for the livelihoods of those who opted to stay and contribute to the local community as crofters, fishermen and the like. There would be those individuals who would continue to deride the efforts of those who chose a different career, but they would be making a wholly conscious decision, and not one heavily socialized through the education system.

In what ways could this be achieved? Mitchison believed that there were hopeful signs that the circle was being squared, such as was shown in the school system of Lewis. In Leurbost, boys in the mathematics class measured the common grazing land, which had never before been done accurately, but was needed then due to a land rehabilitation scheme. This encapsulated Mitchison's integrative and practical views of education with social and cultural purpose. She enthused:

> Those children were keyed into their environment in a thoroughly interesting way. In other junior secondaries, emphasis may be on weaving or bulb growing, not just as 'technical instruction' but as something which makes sense of the curriculum.[17]

By doing nothing more than involving the children in croft or weaving work, they may be amassing a powerful desire to leave. However, if education was aligned with the needs of the community, and the locals could see the importance of what was being done, as well as the skill levels involved, then Mitchison believed children would recognize the true perspective of what living and working in a crofting community entailed.

This change in emphasis vis-à-vis primary and secondary education need not be restricted to just these levels. Mitchison envisaged more further education colleges, such as that proposed by the Argyll education committee for the Isle of Mull, using the old Aros estate for ten-month courses for those who were unlikely to enter the professions but unsure as to the practicalities of embarking on a career in crofting, forestry or fishing. For instance, she argued that the work potential and diversity offered by crofting life were manifold:

> not necessarily in the strict field of agriculture but in associated or associable jobs and crafts. Hospitality to summer visitors might be put on to a more imaginative basis, linked to a way of life rather than to quick profits. And I have an idea that once National Parks are set up in Scotland, we shall have a rather different kind of visitor, who will need a guide or ranger knowledgeable about wildlife and plants, good on sea or mountain, entirely trustworthy. Am I too hopeful in seeing

17 Ibid.

here a thousand non-academic jobs to be prepared for through Highland education?[18]

This avenue could be developed, according to Mitchison, with the idea that there would be no formal educational requirements; the only stipulation on entry being that the pupil should benefit. However, Mitchison went on, this variation on the existing educational system should not be used as an excuse for poorly taught courses, but rather an opportunity to teach subjects that related to rural life, enriching students' experiences and making them appreciate their Highland environment. She did not envisage this to be necessarily an expensive project, even with a proposed four or five centres scattered throughout the north western Highlands. Some would definitely be located in the islands, perhaps with their own specialism related to the abilities of the teaching staff or the particular circumstances of the island on which the college was sited. Occasional 'outsiders', enthusiastic with contributions to effect a more imaginative crofting way of life, would be welcome. Their presence would introduce 'competition and excitement', which Mitchison felt was tolerable in limited amounts.[19]

For Mitchison, the most important tier was the third, as this was intended to create the 'leaders and inspirers' within the local communities.[20] The 'Institute of Highland Resource Development', which she proposed, was to be eclectic in its focus with the main concerns being research, experimentation, and courses designed to imbue former FE pupils with confidence and foresight in order to benefit their native areas. This institute, which Mitchison regarded as 'the seed of a Highland university', would initially be under the aegis of one or more of the existing universities. Neil Gunn also campaigned for a Highland university, which, he felt, in time, would 'assume a distinctive and progressive character that would give it a unique place among the other centres of teaching and research'.[21] Mitchison hoped that such an institution would be unique in its focus and facilities, enticing students from across Western Europe. 'I have an idea that a place like this', Mitchison wrote wistfully, 'firmly planted in the practical development of what is an "underdeveloped area", would be most useful for overseas students, whose problems of resource and community development are not unlike those of the Highlands'.[22]

Neil Gunn believed that the Highlands had an excellent case to be the fifth Scottish university. He argued that this region would be particularly receptive to a distinguished seat of learning because within the Gaelic tradition there lay

18 Ibid. 19 Ibid., note the difference in emphasis from her earlier comments on incomers. For Mitchison, education was a vital element in resolving the problems in the Highlands, and consequently she argued it should be handled in a sensitive manner. 20 Ibid. 21 NLS: NMG Dep 209/9 containing a typescript from 'Gunn to Provost Wotherspoon' who was to present a copy to representatives of the University Grants Commission, c.1960. The typescript was arguing the case for a university in Inverness. 22 Mitchison, 'Checking Highland "brain drain"'.

'a very high respect for learning and scholarship'.[23] He also held that the facilities at the Dounreay nuclear atomic plant could be used in tandem with the universities, benefiting both the nuclear industry and the research of the university. Moreover, natural resources such as water, land and forestry could also be studied at first-hand, and a significant contribution made to their development and improvement for the unique environment of the Highlands and Islands. The benefits to students would be that along with textbook instruction, their laboratory would be the vast expanse of the Highlands and Islands. Therefore, he was also of the opinion that, given time, this university would 'assume a distinctive and progressive character that would give it a unique place among the other centres of teaching and research'.[24] Moreover, Gunn felt that locating a university in the Highlands would stimulate demographic and economic growth, which in turn would encourage novel approaches to regenerate this region.

Where did Gaelic fit into the question of education for these policy informers? Campaigners such as Neil Gunn believed that a Celtic department should be at the forefront of the University of the Highlands:

> Our Gaelic culture is a national heritage, even if in the past it has taken foreign scholarship to bring the fact home to us. We think it is time that this whole realm of study was integrated in a native centre that would be recognized everywhere as thorough and authoritative, and that would attract students from foreign countries. Here special or post-graduate courses might well be instituted, and teaching be combined with research and field work. At the same time, we consider that scholarship might well find its creative outlet in stimulating the arts, especially literature and music where the gaelic heritage is rich.[25]

Gunn felt that this would be a tremendous success, owing to the urgent need for such facilities but also due to the very high respect for learning and scholarship within the Gaelic tradition.[26]

In the 1950s, Naomi Mitchison wrote with some experience and authority on her native Kintyre, a place, she believed, where the schools system had already eradicated Gaelic, and was now seeking to expurgate the local dialect of Lallans from the children's speech.[27] She was well aware of the negative and long-lasting

---

23 NMG, 'Gunn to Provost Wotherspoon'. 24 Ibid. 25 Ibid. 26 Ibid. 27 Naomi Mitchison, 'Murder in our Scottish schools', *The Scotsman*, 23 June 1956, which is an extract from an article she wrote in the last number of the Argyll teachers' magazine *MacTalla* where she asks of the teachers: 'But what are you [the teachers] doing to our readers? You are teaching them as far as possible only to understand and respect the southern dialect spoken in the neighbouring island, with spelling cribbed, cabined and confined by such anti-Scots as Dr Johnson. Meanwhile, the Scots writers are trying to get away from just this dialect, to enlarge and enrich it with versions, idioms and spellings which you red pencil when you meet them in the innocent primary stage. You have killed the Gaelic already ... Now you are killing Lallans, at any rate

effect that this form of social control had on the children, both in the school and in their chosen careers:

> But it means that the children learn to despise their own language and the language of their parents. The fact that they end their school days with a respectable school language, such as is to be seen in the newspapers, makes them look down on the spoken home language. When they try to express themselves in public speech, or even in writing a letter, they get muddled between the two; they cannot speak from the heart in the school language, and dare not use the despised language of the home and the ancestors.[28]

She refused to accept the teachers' excuse of blaming the examiners, and she chided them from not sending deputations to St Andrew's House in protest, instead leaving the fight to people like Mitchison who care for the preservation of language that has 'poetic qualities'.[29] According to Mitchison, the net result of teaching this sanitized school language meant that the children used Americanisms in order to enrich their speech. In an ironic vein, she says that schools should teach the children American-English from infancy so that they could at least speak it correctly. She claimed:

> These children's children will speak a kind of wishy-washy BBC American. They won't be able to understand Hugh MacDiarmid. And doubtless their Burns will have to be retranslated for them from the Russian. Think it over![30]

Mitchison deplored the eradication of Scotland's indigenous languages; which to add insult to injury were being replaced by 'the gutless dialect of the Home Counties', itself heavily influenced by 'American slang'.[31]

Mitchison's views on the lack of recognition for Gaelic in education were also forthright. She attacked the notion that Highland children should be pressurized into learning French at the expense of Gaelic, because she doubted whether a certificate in French would teach children much about modern European culture.[32] Writing in 1942, her assessment of Gaelic was somewhat gloomy: 'The Gaelic-speaking areas are rapidly diminishing; it is almost certainly too late to save the language as a living means of culture'.[33] The incessant drive for genteel English, exemplified by the BBC, was also responsible for the disappearance of Gaelic idioms. The net result of this was very damaging for young Gaels: 'It means that in the tongue they speak naturally, they feel that they are inferior.

written and genuine Lallans'. In Mitchison's papers at the NLS, Acc 8503/2, 1956 bundle. 28 Ibid. 29 Ibid. 30 Ibid. 31 Mitchison, 'Gaelic with an Oxford accent'. 32 Mitchison, *Highlands and Islands*, p. 23. 33 Mitchison, 'Gaelic with an Oxford accent'.

Conversely, they feel that anyone who speaks with the clipped vowels and south English idiom of the BBC is superior'.[34] Echoing the sentiments of 'Fionn MacColla', she wrote 'all this represents a triumph for the English and the anglicizing Quislings, unconscious enough of what they were doing, many of them!'

Mitchison, due to her nationalist beliefs, baulked at the thought of so many Scots adopting the 'acceptable' language of English and trying to immerse themselves in the culture of her larger neighbour: 'That', she believed, 'is bad for people; it means that they can have no genuine pride and self-confidence. Everything must be measured by an alien standard. Nor can they probably even arrive at the best of what they are aiming at'. She also felt that these Scots would be caught in a kind of cultural purgatory; willingly abandoning their traditional languages, yet always 'slightly outside, out of tune with' English culture. In a sense, Mitchison was repeating the argument used in the context of Highlanders' imitating mainland standards: a policy she believed to be detrimental to their well-being. But unlike the latter case, the aping of everything English stemmed from the lack of a national capital: hence the reason for so many writers and artists pursuing the case for Scottish independence, because: 'this provides a spiritual capital; dear City of God, failing any City of Cecrops'.[35] She campaigned for the restoration of both the Gaelic and the Scots language in order to liberate the people of Scotland from what she regarded as a 'stream of mediocre English culture'. Mitchison was particularly concerned with the Highlands because she believed it contained the remnants of a 'Scottish civilisation'. Lamenting the 'disintegrating acid' eroding the Gaelic culture, she looked, perhaps naively, to the education authorities to rectify the situation.[36]

CONCLUSION

> If it be the case that 'Gaelic alone is not enough to keep a man alive' and that therefore the Hebridean world of oral tradition must yield to the encroachment of mass semi-sophistication and anglicized education, so that the islanders be not cheated in the labour markets of the south, that does not mean that victory is going to the 'better' of the two contestants in the struggle, but simply that the material progress of the Islands is being achieved at the cost of cultural impoverishment, which makes one envy the more the Icelanders and the Faeroese who have contrived to make the best of both worlds, and are retaining their ancient languages as instruments of modern culture and education, while bringing their material way of life up to date.[37]

34 Ibid. 35 Ibid. 36 Ibid. 37 Campbell, 'Introduction', *Tales of Barra* (1960), p. 25.

John Lorne Campbell's comments encapsulate the central thrust of Mitchison, Gunn and Grant's views on the 'Highland problem'. For these policy informers, there was undoubtedly much sympathy for the Gaelic language and culture, but their stance was also tempered by the belief that successive governments and their political mandarins in the civil service were largely indifferent to the plight of the Highlander, and in particular the Gaelic-speaking communities therein. As subsequent events demonstrated, their criticisms of government policy went largely unheeded; especially with regard to large-scale industrialization, the development of urban centres, the role of education and the marketing of tourism. The lack of understanding of the true nature of the 'Highland problem' had led to repeated failures over many years, which, in turn, instilled in the Gaels a negative perception of government and its motives. For Collier, this produced the most harmful effect of all: 'the cultural integrity of the people has been invaded and their faith in the soundness of their way of living impaired'.[38] Therefore, because of the manner in which the 'Highland problem' was tackled, the vitality of the Gaelic culture continued to be placed in serious jeopardy.

Perhaps the more worrying tendency among those involved in crucial decisions vis-à-vis the situation in the Highlands and Islands was a misplaced optimism in the durability of Gaelic. Neil Gunn, charged with the overhaul of the crofting system and, like the other members of the commission, keen to preserve the 'unique Highland way of life', adopted an optimistic and perhaps unrealistic faith in the Gaels to preserve their language and culture in the face of immense social and economic turmoil:

> Fashions in life and art change but the fundamental things remain deep. The real tragedy of the Highlands were [sic] the brutal onslaughts like the final enactments that followed the '45, directed deliberately to break up the Highland way of life, shash [sic] its culture. But you can't rub out a people's unconscious by government order. Nothing is surer then [sic] that the Highlands will be fruitful again, and as for the songs, the actual songs, they will be the thematic riches out of which future native artists will create their symphonies.[39]

This misplaced optimism was symptomatic of the widespread complacency regarding the indigenous tongue. As the next chapter shows, Gaelic language activists of this period themselves identified lethargy as a source of concern. Where these policy informants and agenda setters differed from fellow

38 Collier, *Crofting problem*, p. 1. 39 NLS: NMG Dep 209/10, 'For BBC', n.d., corrected typescript; Gunn, 'The one who will come'; Gunn, 'Above the Highland line'.

'The English way and the wrong way'

appointees was in their deep concern for the welfare of the Highlanders and the need to create a viable and secure economy that would alleviate the pressures to migrate. In arguing this way, they raised many criticisms of the attitude of both government and the Highlanders themselves. Mitchison and Gunn were not mere romantics; when they emphasized the different value system, and the uniqueness of the Highland way of life, they did so with viability and sustainability in mind. Where they can be criticized, however, was in their naïve failure to appreciate the extent to which the Gaels were becoming assimilated into the cultural norms and values of those beyond the *Gàidhealtachd*.

Naomi Mitchison and Neil Gunn each highlighted certain failings of the official approach that they believed would harm the unique character of the Highlands and Islands. Theirs were voices in the wilderness that testified to the indifference and insensitivity of external forces. The measures that they sought to overturn eventually came to pass. In the process, the fortunes of the Gaelic language and culture declined with alarming pace. The greatest charge that could be directed at these policy informers is that they failed to appreciate that the very phenomenon they were seeking to maintain, the 'Highland way of life', was fast disappearing regardless of their attempts to lessen the impact of British policies. The increasing integration of the Highlands and Islands into the wider Scottish, and British, economies meant that the yearning for the maintenance of 'Highland values' was always threatened by failure. The 'clash of social philosophies', which accelerated during the post-war decades, was in many ways facilitated by these government agencies, proposing, as they were, measures designed to alleviate the isolation, hardship and associated problems that underlay this distinctive lifestyle. However, in seeking to fully explain and understand the reasons behind the continued decline in the Gaelic language and the changing nature of 'Highland' culture during the post-war decades, we must turn to the Gaels themselves.

7

'Cùm a' Ghaidhlig beò': the Gaels' response to the 'colossus of advancing materialism'[1]

> Twenty-odd years ago [*c.*1940], Barra was an island where, one felt, time had been standing still for generations. It is always extraordinarily difficult to convey the feeling and atmosphere of a community where oral tradition and the religious sense are still very much alive to people who have only known the atmosphere of the modern ephemeral, rapidly changing world of industrial civilization. On the other hand there is a community of independent personalities where memories of men and events are often amazingly long (in the Gaelic-speaking Outer Hebrides they go back to Viking times a thousand years ago), and where there is an ever-present sense of the reality and existence of the other world where people live in a mental jumble of newspaper headlines and BBC news bulletins, forgetting yesterday's as they read or hear today's, worrying themselves constantly about far-away events which they cannot possibly control, where memories are so short that men often do not know the names of their grandparents, and where the only real world seems to be the everyday material one.
>
> J.L. Campbell, *Tales of Barra told by the Coddy* (1960)[2]

> We need new industries suitable to the country and to the Highlanders themselves. When these are procured, the Highlanders will be engaged in occupations in their own glens, speaking their own language, for the language will flourish best in its own native environment.
>
> *An Gaidheal*, 'President's English address' (1947)[3]

In post-war Scotland, the task of galvanizing interest in the fate of Gaelic rested with *An Comunn Gàidhealach*. Established in 1891 to promote the Gaelic language, culture, history and heritage, *An Comunn*, as it is generally known,

---

1 The Gaelic phrase translates as 'keep the Gaelic alive', *An Gaidheal*, [*AG*] (1950), 61–2. The other quotation was given by *An Comunn*'s President, John Bannerman, *AG* (1950), 138–9. *An Gaidheal* was the magazine of *An Comunn Gaidhealach* [ACG], replacing its previous publication, *An Deo-Greine*, in 1923. 2 Campbell, 'Introduction' (1960), pp 24–5. 3 *AG* (1947), 15.

developed over the inter-war years as the principal 'pressure-group', not only for the promotion of Gaelic language and culture but also for the furtherance of the cultural dimension of the 'Highlands' as the *Gàidhealtachd*. It retained this preeminent position throughout the period 1939–65, although dissent within the ranks on policy and direction in due course provided an opening for future Gaelic promotional groups to emerge.[4] Within the pages of its bilingual magazine *An Gaidheal*, the policies affecting the Highlands and Islands were given considerable exposure and, as befitted the organ of an organization which bilingually proclaimed itself as 'The Highland Association', the publication also sought to act as a 'voice-box' on various topics emanating from within the Highlands as a whole. Despite its self-appointed role as the unofficial 'voice of the Gael', and therefore by the same token the 'voice of the Highlander', the membership and leadership of *An Comunn Gàidhealach* always represented only a particular and limited strand of the Gaelic-speaking community and an even more limited element within the resident Highland population. Nonetheless, as effectively the only organ in Scottish civil society within which Highland affairs and issues were reported and discussed from a specifically Gaelic perspective, *An Comunn*'s house journal, *An Gaidheal*, acted as an important prism through which the latter were reflected. It provides a useful indicator on attitudes within the Gaelic-speaking community on issues as diverse as the Knoydart land-raid and support for Breton culture.[5]

As the Highlands emerged from the war, the fundamental issue affecting the *Gàidhealtachd* was how to preserve the culture and language of the Highlands against what the 1950 president of *An Comunn*, John Bannerman, described as the 'colossus of advancing materialism'. The effects of modernization were felt to be spreading rapidly at this time and, as the prominent Gaelic campaigner and scholar, John Lorne Campbell saw it, 'the atmosphere of the modern ephemeral, rapidly changing world of industrial civilization' was not necessarily benign. How the Gaels reacted and adapted to the initiatives of governments and their agencies in the period 1939–65, while addressing a wide range of social and economic changes, forms the basis of this chapter. Whereas the previous chapter was primarily concerned with the *Highland* 'view from within', as articulated by middle-class intellectuals such as Mitchison, Gunn and Grant, this chapter focuses on the *Gaelic* 'view from within' – the specific attitudes of Gaelic speakers and activists to the social and economic transformation of the

---

4 Thomson, 'Gaelic in Scotland', p. 7. 5 This point cannot be left without a qualification regarding the fact that the readership of this magazine was fairly limited if judged on subscription rates, and the extent to which the editor filtered contributions is also a point for conjecture. That said, in addition to other publications from within Gaeldom, of which there were few, it is the best barometer of attitudes among Gaels regarding events in the Highlands. Moreover, *ACG* had a large number of branches throughout the region, and in the urban centres to the south, that would act as the forum of discussion of issues reported in the pages of *AG*.

Highlands and Islands and the perceived consequences for Gaelic culture and for the Gaelic/Highland 'way of life'.

As in the past, Highlanders responded to the onset of war by joining the British armed forces in significant numbers. Many were already in the Merchant Navy, and because of the nature of the war in its early stages, casualties were high. While these losses were keenly felt in the islands, it was events in France that were to captured the imagination and soon thereafter rouse feelings across the Highlands as a whole. The brave conduct of the 51st (Highland) Division, guarding the retreat of allied troops at Dunkirk, was regarded as testimony to the fighting prowess of successive generations of Highland soldiers. However, the pride of fellow Highlanders was tempered by the view that Churchill had sacrificed the Highland troops to assuage French sensitivities over their abandonment to the full force of the axis powers. As the full story of subsequent imprisonment and associated hardships duly emerged, the feeling developed that a not insignificant debt was owed to the Highlands for the perceived injustice of events at St Valery. It was an issue that served to add extra poignancy and edge to campaigns within the Highlands to secure state development aid in the years immediately after the war.

Given the long association of Scotland and the Highlands to military service, it was virtually inevitable that the war would have an impact on the activities of *An Comunn*. One consequence was that fund-raising assumed a different focus. The primary emphasis was now on supporting the war effort rather than on specific Gaelic language promotion projects. In effect, the war had acted as a brake on the propagandist efforts by *An Comunn Gàidhealach* to inject interest in the fate of the language.[6] This shift in policy was not greeted with universal approval. Derick Thomson, the poet and soon to become a prominent language campaigner, reflected certain unease at the course of events in a letter to *An Gaidheal*: 'A natural – if unfortunate from the point of view of Gaelic – patriotic enthusiasm has led An Comunn out of its true path. Will it be bold enough to find its way back again?'[7] Thomson was not arguing for the abandonment of wartime support, but rather that it could be done in such a manner as to promote the interests of the Gaelic language simultaneously. He used the example of including Gaelic books and a propaganda letter in the parcels sent to POWs, which would boost the spirits of the Gaelic recipients and further the interests of language campaigners. Although *An Comunn* did not go as far as Thomson suggested, they did take on board some of the complaints and certainly letters from Gaels in the Stalags demonstrated their immense gratitude for these morale-boosting efforts from *An Comunn*. The net effect of the various wartime ventures left *An Comunn* in a reasonable position – low in funds but assured in the knowledge that Gaels had not been abandoned by their own 'kith and kin'.

---

6 Thompson, *An Comunn Gaidhealach*, pp 76–8.   7 *AG*, Oct. 1941.

As we have seen in the preceding chapters, the end of the war heralded a number of key changes in the governance of Scotland. The Highlands and Islands would also experience considerable changes in the years up to 1965, especially in the fields of economic reconstruction and social policy. From a specifically Gaelic perspective, the greatest concern was that running in parallel with these initiatives was a continued fall in the numbers of Gaelic speakers. The hiatus in census recording caused by the war helped to mask the dramatic downturn in fortunes of the Gaelic language. Across Scotland as a whole, the actual numbers of speakers fell from 136,135 in 1931 to 95,447 in 1951, with a further slip to 80,978 in those registering their ability to speak the language in 1961. The report pertaining to the number of Gaelic speakers recorded in the census of 1961 highlighted the continued decline in the numbers of both monoglot and bilingual Gaels.[8] The respective figures in 1961 were 974 and 80,004, the total number of Gaelic speakers representing just 1.7 per cent of the Scottish population. A further breakdown of the statistics in relation to the Highlands and Islands indicated that the language continued to recede to the Outer Hebrides though areas of the Inner Hebrides retained a healthy number of speakers (up to 80 per cent Gaelic-speaking in some districts of Skye, though Mull had fallen to under 40 per cent). The only mainland areas to show percentages of 60 per cent or over of Gaelic speakers were the sparsely populated western peninsula districts of Applecross and Ardnamurchan, though significant numbers resided in some cities of the Central Belt; Glasgow being by far and away the greater with 11,165. The most disturbing feature of these statistics in relation to previous ones was the parlous figure for monoglot speakers, especially when one considers that the vast majority of these people were in the 3–4 age-group, being thus only transiently monolingual. Hence, these decades marked a significant transformation within Gaeldom as the existence of monoglot Gaels almost disappeared.[9]

The data presented in the 1951 census returns did not surprise those who had kept abreast of developments in the *Gàidhealtachd*. Throughout the 1940s, *An Gaidheal* had repeatedly foretold the extent of post-war depopulation and language loss facing the Highlands.[10] Indeed, in 1949 a rather sombre warning

---

8 GRO, *Census 1961 Scotland vol. 7*, 'Gaelic' (1966). 9 Obviously, the census data does not offer any insight into the actual usage of Gaelic. Do speakers use it habitually or on an infrequent basis? Moreover, where do speakers tend to communicate in Gaelic? Is it confined to the domestic situation or are there specific occasions such as religious services, ceilidhs, workplaces and the like where Gaelic can be spoken? Other considerations involve the degree to which the self-acknowledged Gael can read and write in the language, their proficiency in doing this or fluency in speaking, and lastly the extent of mutual interference between Gaelic and English. The only means of analyzing the data more thoroughly is through detailed survey of specific locales. Unfortunately, for the period in question, 1939–65, no such projects were undertaken. Thus, one has to rely on contemporary accounts from those people living in the Gaelic-speaking areas, and in different capacities. See MacDonald, 'Gaelic language' (1968), p. 179.   10 *AG* (1949), 31.

had already been given that the future of the Gaelic language itself could well be in doubt, given the pace and the extent with which the transformation of the *Gàidhealtachd* was occurring.[11] The figures acted as a catalyst for *An Comunn* to engage in some self-examination. This was to be done in an objective and coherent manner, ignoring defeatist and alarmist perspectives, with appropriate and urgent action to follow. An analysis of the Gaelic situation revealed that out-migration and the failure of the Gaelic population to renew itself due to a fall in marriage rates and a residual elderly population were major concerns. As we shall see, the resolution of these problems was a cause for debate within *An Comunn Gàidhealach*: while some members were content to remain in a cultural organization, others wanted the association to take a more political stance.

POST-WAR HIGHLAND RECONSTRUCTION

The post-war reconstruction in the Highlands led to renewed appeals for the connection to be made between language regeneration and economic and social development. The initiator this time was Finlay J. MacDonald, a Gaelic activist who would play a key role in the development of Gaelic broadcasting. At the 1949 AGM of *An Comunn*, he proposed that the organization should 'encourage and promote industries in the Highlands where such industries shall in any way tend to arrest the depopulation of the Highland areas and the subsequent decline of the Gaelic language'.[12] MacDonald was of the opinion that Gaelic's only hope of survival was for it to be concentrated in a specific area, such as the Highlands, because there was no likelihood of the language securing converts in English-language-dominated communities. Thus, he argued, the issue for Gaelic organizations such as *An Comunn* was to lobby the relevant public bodies and government to ensure that these people were given opportunities to remain in the Highlands and Islands, the prime concern being employment. He contended that in the past, *An Comunn* had placed too much emphasis on the culture of the Gaels without realizing that without a Gaelic population the culture and language that they endeavoured to promote would be 'still-born'. Therefore, he called on members of *An Comunn* to turn their attention to the issue of Highland depopulation and use every means at its disposal to encourage industry into the *Gàidhealtachd*. The seconder of the motion also felt that this had always been a grave weakness of *An Comunn*, because without the people in the Highlands, Gaelic was heading for further decay and possible death.

The arguments against the motion were themselves persuasive, focused as they were on events in the Highlands which had failed to reverse the ailing fortunes of the language. One who opposed the motion argued that 'It was [...]

11 *AG* (1951), 83–4. 12 *AG* (1949), 159, 161.

a fallacy to say that where there are people, there they would have the language. They had brought industries into the Highlands in the past but they had not kept the Gaelic language where these industries had been brought'.[13] The Revd Tom Murchison, editor of *An Gaidheal* from 1946 to 1957 and informed activist in the Highlands throughout the 1940s to 1960s, admitted that the issue was complicated. Although he conceded that 'cultural recovery and progress could not be divorced from economic recovery' and that he was once of the opinion of the proposers, nevertheless he no longer believed that *An Comunn* should become directly involved in the economic debate: 'rather, it was in the long-term interests of *An Comunn Gàidhealach* if it adhered to its present objectives'. In clarifying this view, he said that because *An Comunn* was the sole organization directly concerned with the task of preserving the language, its remit should not be expanded to incorporate issues such as the economic and social health of the *Gàidhealtachd*. Certainly, he believed that *An Comunn Gàidhealach* could pressurize those bodies established to resolve the political and economic problems of the *Gàidhealtachd*, but he was not sure if *An Comunn* could do a better job, especially as its resources were already stretched with their present tasks. In arguing to successfully defeat the motion, Murchison pointed out that membership of *An Comunn* was not mutually exclusive. Indeed, participation in other organizations would allow for a broader and more diverse range of opinions with which to offer constructive criticism within *An Comunn* and on the Highlands.[14]

With this affirmation that their sponsoring body's cultural role remained intact as its primary purpose, *An Gaidheal* nonetheless continued to publicize expressed apprehensions about economic and social development in the Highlands and Islands. The worrying statistics presented by Fraser Darling's *West Highland Survey* and the unsatisfactory outcome of the Knoydart land-raid were the catalyst for some scathing attacks by prominent Gaels on successive governments' negligent and indifferent approaches to the resolution of the 'Highland problem'. Government inaction fuelled feelings of contempt for the frequent outpourings of 'sympathetic consideration' – '*moran ga radh is beagan 'ga dheanamh!*' ('much said and little done').[15] Rather than just accept this 'negligent indifference', Gaelic activists put forward their own vision for the economic future of the Highlands and Islands.

The basic premise for the concerted attack on government policy and lethargy was that better management and usage of the Highlands and Islands' natural resources could sustain a larger population than existed at that time. The raid on the estates of Lord Brocket by the 'Men of Knoydart' in 1948 focused attention on the issue of land, regarded by many Gaels as 'the basic Highland question'.[16] Responding to the raid, the Scottish Secretary of State, Arthur

13 Ibid.   14 *AG* (1949), 31–2.   15 Ibid.   16 *AG* (1950), 103–4. Knoydart, in the 1940s, was a

Woodburn, appointed John Cameron, the then vice-chairman of the Advisory Panel on the Highlands and Islands and former member of the Scottish Land Court, to conduct an investigation into the situation in this north-western community. His recommendations highlighted the different approaches to aspects of the Highland problem between policy informers, the government and those articulating the voice of the Gael.[17] The latter felt betrayed and said that his report disappointed those who believed that '"the new Highlands" should be based on agricultural family holdings rather than on factories and power stations'.[18] Dismissing the cases put by the Knoydart people and the government, Cameron recommended that the Knoydart estate should remain a single unit because family or part-time holdings were unfeasible given the infertility of the soil, the cost of providing housing and other services and the resultant insecurity. However, to many within the Gaelic community it seemed that his knowledge of the subject had not stopped him from proposing something reminiscent of the Clearances. As one contributor to *An Gaidheal* put it,

> The question is, surely, not the best method of rearing the maximum number of sheep and cattle on the 50,000 acres comprising the Knoydart estate, but rather the best method of maintaining in Knoydart a reasonable level of population in a reasonable standard of living.[19]

In essence, the responses to the Knoydart raid reflected the different attitudes on the issue of crofting. The position of the Gaels as outlined by Murchison was that the government's reaction to Knoydart demonstrated an unwillingness or inability to listen to the people of that community or to respect Highlanders' desires to settle on the land. The Labour government's decision to exclude Scotland from the planned development of small holdings in England and Wales on a limited scale, with the intention of enticing more people onto the land, met with a terse response from the Gaelic leadership: 'Can it be that a "government of the people" prefers large estates to small holdings, large-scale capitalist farming to an independent peasantry?'[20] Gaels were entitled to some answers because the Labour government appeared to be making ad hoc decisions based on political expediency. On the one hand, the government gave financial assistance to crofters to build new houses and farm buildings or to replace and improve their stock; but against this stood the decision not to introduce large-scale land settlement in Scotland because it was regarded as too difficult and not economically viable.[21]

predominately Gaelic-speaking community which had suffered from the prevailing ailments of the Highlands, including limited accessibility to the fertile land. **17** It should be noted that the dominant 'voice' of the Gaelic-speaking community in this period was male. **18** *AG* (1949), 42. **19** Ibid. **20** *AG* (1949), 74. **21** Ibid.; *AG* (1949), 71.

For the Gaelic leadership, the Department of Agriculture's dire predictions for the economic and social future of crofting communities need not necessarily come true. In these immediate post-war years, Gaelic spokespeople continued to press for a combination of increasing productivity, capital assistance for buildings, equipment and stock, and improving the market by developing the tourist industry and cultivating an export trade.[22] They recognized that crofting was a part-time occupation, and was therefore dependent on the availability of ancillary employment, but they were enthusiastic and optimistic about the potential offered by the advent of the hydro-electric schemes or significant development. What these committed Gaelic commentators and activists wanted was for government officials of different persuasions and capacities to reciprocate by improving the deficient transport infrastructure and to realize the full implications of this new energy source.[23]

Such was the excitement and the potential offered by hydro-electricity that the Gaelic leadership endorsed the view, outlined in the previous chapter, that the Highlands and Islands could become a model for other countries seeking to rehabilitate their rural areas.[24] What was needed was an integrated approach, radical in both outlook and action. This imaginative and comprehensive approach was evident in an investigation set up by the North of Scotland Hydro-Electricity Board into the development of raw materials through the harnessing of hydro-electricity. It was hoped that the new technical processes would lead to commercial extraction of minerals, which would bring industries in and increase employment. *An Gaidheal* also reported on the decision of the Secretary of State to set up a committee to advise on the potential of peat resources to be commercially exploited for power generation.[25] The hydro report also examined the possibility of establishing factories to finish the products by reducing the costs of freight and gearing products for the requirements of Highland industries.[26] Gaelic spokesmen were only too well aware that transport remained 'the crux of the Highland problem', affecting the region's economic and social viability.[27] However, with appropriate and remedial action on transport and other barriers to development, the Gaelic leadership believed that the Highlands and Islands could become a fully integrated region of both modern Scotland and Britain, contributing to the economy as a whole and maintaining the social and cultural fabric of the *Gàidhealtachd*.

In view of the debate within *An Comunn* as to whether it should be involved in matters of a political nature, it is useful to note that many of the committees or organizations established to explore specific aspects of the Highland problem often contained prominent Gaels. Indeed, the hydro investigation was super-

---

22 Although most of the contributors during this time were men, it is difficult to determine if all the anonymous reports in *An Gaidheal* were actually penned by men.   23 *AG* (1948), 50.   24 *AG* (1949), 113.   25 *AG* (1949), 167.   26 *AG* (1949), 82.   27 *AG* (1950), 90; *AG* (1949), 71.

vised by a committee member of *Clann Albainn*, the body set up to repopulate parts of rural Scotland.[28] Three members of *An Comunn*'s executive committee also served on the Scottish National Parks Committee, and were instrumental in producing the publication *National parks and the conservation of nature in Scotland* (1948). The proposed five national parks to be sited in the Highland region would act as a 'lung' for urban visitors and provide development opportunities for the inhabitants of the Highlands. *An Gaidheal*'s reviewer, who was involved in the publication itself, argued that the five designated areas should not be regarded as wilderness or as a playground for the rich or the 'urban proletariat'. Instead of being treated as a 'museum-piece', he said that each park must be a working area where local communities could thrive.[29] Therefore, Gaels supported the proposals emanating from Highland activists keen to develop tourism, intensive agriculture, afforestation, hydro-electricity and associated rural industries, while also recognizing the difficulties involved in trying to convince government to act. As one commentator said, 'it is undeniable that men are decaying, and this in spite of the potential wealth of the area'.[30] For the Gaelic leadership, as with policy informers like Mitchison, Gunn and Grant, there was a sense of frustration that this rich reservoir of opportunity was being squandered by government negligence and inactivity. The preliminary work of the 'West Highland Survey' demonstrated that where new industries were introduced, afforestation projects extended or small holdings created, the population could be maintained and, indeed, augmented.

The economic neglect of the Highlands and Islands had immense implications for the Gaelic language and culture. Without tangible projects to entice industries into the Highlands, many in *An Commun* believed the language would die:

> Some of us feel that, while Gaelic may survive as a field of study for scholars, as an accomplishment for those who like it so, and as a concomitant of what is known as 'Highland music', the battle will have been utterly lost and the aims of *An Comunn* will have been wholly frustrated if the Gaelic-speaking (or, indeed, the non-Gaelic-speaking) Highlanders totally disappear from their native parishes.[31]

Despite these understandable concerns, contributors to *An Gaidheal* also recognized that they had no right to preach to fellow Gaels in the Highlands and Islands to endure a lower standard of living for the sake of the language and culture:

---

28 *AG* (1949), 82; *AG* (1949), 39.   29 *AG* (1948), 50–1.   30 *AG* (1949), 31–2.
31 *AG* (1949), 1.

> Those who live in the Glens and in the Islands have decided and are deciding that the road of their improvement is the road to the cities. Many of you have so decided, and you cannot ask others to remain when you yourselves have refused to do so. As long as conditions in the Highlands remain as they are, so long will the people stream to the towns or emigrate to other countries.[32]

Thus, implicit in *An Comunn*'s clarion call for jobs to be brought to the Highlands was a rarely uttered demand that these jobs should be reserved for Gaelic speakers.

This call for positive discrimination stemmed from a recognition that even in places where Gaelic was still strong, groups like *An Comunn* faced a difficult task in retaining the same levels of usage and knowledge of Gaelic. With an influx of non-Gaels, it would be rendered nearly impossible to ensure that the language remained in its 'homeland'. Thus, schemes by *Clann Albainn*, founded according to a contributor to *An Gaidheal* 'as a practical effort to recolonize the Highlands', were cautiously welcomed. On the front page of their January 1949 edition, the voice of *An Comunn* noted that it was already 'a hard fight to keep Gaelic in the ascendant' in areas where the language had endured over centuries but it would be 'infinitely more difficult to plant it anew among a newly settled population drawn from different parts of the country and mostly with a non-Gaelic background'. The reporter continued: 'In a reconstructed and repopulated land we must see to it that the continuity of Gaelic tradition is not broken. That is why we ought to be concerned, even genuinely alarmed, at what is now happening before our very eyes in the west mainland parishes and in some of the islands'.[33]

Therefore, in sharp contrast to Neil Gunn's welcoming comments on the influx of population to the Highlands, outlined in the previous chapter (p. 203), Gaelic activists were already forewarning of the need to preserve potential new jobs for Gaelic-speaking Gaels. One said: 'If there is to be planned redevelopment of the Highlands, let it be based sensibly on suitability of personnel as well as being along the lines of industries indigenous to the countryside of lochs and bens and moorlands'.[34] Only a few years later, these central issues of who should benefit from Highland economic development and what form the latter should take raised themselves in the starkest and most challenging of terms with the revelation of a plan by the Ministry of Defence in London to construct a major missile-testing range in the Outer Hebrides, with an implicit acknowledgment that the resultant dramatic rise in the island population would comprise incoming non-Gael servicemen and construction workers.

Given the tensions between the fragile status of the language, and the

32 *AG* (1947), 15.   33 *AG* (1949), 1.   34 *AG* (1951), 98, 108.

desperate need for any form of ancillary employment, the proposals to establish a rocket range in the Gaelic heartland of Uist, the southern part of the Outer Hebrides, created heated discussion. Initial reaction from the Gaelic movement was less than enthusiastic. The advisory committee of *An Comunn* wrote to the Secretary of State for Scotland in 1955, stressing its 'grave concern' at the potential impact 'on the cultural and social well-being of the community'. This was compounded by the uncertainty attached to the project, and the letter pleaded for adequate safeguards to protect the Gaelic population to be put into place beforehand.[35] Despite these fears, other Gaels were less perturbed by the prospect of 1,500 army personnel basing themselves in the Uists. Writing in the *Saltire Review*, the Gaelic commentator Finlay J. MacDonald contended that

> The Gaelic language is, fundamentally, the element which blends the 35,000 people who live between the Butt of Lewis and Barra Head into one single community. It transcends differing ways of life and differing creeds and integrates a race [...]. In the Hebrides there is no language panic because people are too busy talking it.[36]

He pointed out that in the last fifty years, the fall in percentage terms in the number of Gaelic speakers in the Outer Hebrides had only been about 4 per cent, down to approximately 86 per cent of the archipelago's population; whereas in Mull, during the same time span, the incidence of Gaelic speakers fell from $c.$79 per cent to just over 34 per cent. However, he did acknowledge that if the proposed range stationed 1,500 personnel on Benbecula then immediately the percentage figure for South Uist and Benbecula would drop from $c.$89 per cent to 64 per cent. Despite that, he noted that the majority in Uist was in favour of the initiative and most of the opposition came from outside the islands. With that in mind, another Gaelic correspondent warned that 'lamentation combined with apathy will achieve nothing'. The writer went on to say:

> There is plenty of evidence that the Western Isles have survived invasion in the past by absorbing alien influences into their own peculiar pattern of living. Atmosphere, environment and custom are on our side, but the Gaels must show enthusiasm and endurance in the face of indifference, ridicule, and opposition.[37]

So, although some Gaels were relaxed about the potential cultural impact from economic and social changes taking place around them, others were much more mindful of the threats posed to the language and culture, hence the calls for positive discrimination and affirmative action.

---

35 *AG* (1955), 114–15.   36 MacDonald, 'Last days of Gaelic'; discussed in *AG* (1956), 10. See also Burnett, *Benbecula* (1986).   37 *AG* (1956), 10.

As might be expected given the intensity and scope of the transformation taking place in the Highlands and Islands, divergent, conflicting even contradictory views were a regular feature in the columns of *An Gaidheal*. Although Tom Murchison was keen for *An Comunn* to concentrate solely on matters pertaining to the Gaelic language, he ensured that under his stewardship (1946–57) the publication reported on a variety of economic and social issues that indirectly had a bearing on the well-being of Gaelic. Murchison, a noted Gaelic stalwart, was himself a key member of the Highland Development League, being reappointed president in 1949. This organization, established in the 1930s, had already expressed dissatisfaction at the government's decision on the Knoydart land-raid and the imbalance between land policy in Scotland and in the rest of Britain. Because of the involvement of strong-willed Gaels such as Murchison, its pronouncements were often echoed within the columns of *An Gaidheal*.[38]

The periodical also reviewed the activities of all manner of organizations pertaining to the Highlands. For example, it kept its readers informed as to the activities, or more often than not, the prevarications of the Highland Panel and joined with other members of this body in calling for more devolution of power: 'What is wanted is thorough and comprehensive reconstruction of the Highlands and Islands by "unified resource development" on the lines indicated by the great TVA enterprise in the United States of America'.[39] Many of the proposals had been mentioned before; indeed looking back over press cuttings for the last twenty years, one contributor to *An Gaidheal* expressed amazement that there had been so few advances.[40] That said, others hoped that the cumulative effects of research into the different aspects of the Highland problem would eventually make the government act in a decisive fashion.[41] Nonetheless, given the widespread frustration of Gaels and other Highland activists at the perceived indifference of Westminster governments to the many difficulties faced by the region, there was no heightened sense of anticipation from Gaelic commentators when the Labour government launched its white paper, *A programme of Highland development*, in 1950.

Murchison's reaction to this government publication was predictable and blunt: 'Quite frankly, this is a disappointing document'.[42] Absolving the Highland Panel from any blame, he specifically targeted the government due to its failure to give this body adequate power, autonomy and control. If this deficiency was resolved, then 'the "castles in the air" of the white paper might have a better chance of taking shape in the form of thriving Highland communities'. Encouraged that the 'powers-that-be' were beginning to treat the many Highland problems as aspects of one big problem, nonetheless he argued that the

---

38 *AG* (1950), 97. 39 *AG* (1948), 50, 168. 40 *AG* (1950), 66. 41 Ibid., 50. 42 Ibid., 103–4.

existence of a comprehensive plan was a redundant strategy given the lack of enforcement powers that Highlanders had. He expressed disappointment that the Highland Panel only acted as a liaison between the local authorities and the state departments and bemoaned the dominance of the treasury in all matters of government policy. Further worries were compounded by the prevarication in setting up a clear timetable for reconstruction. He ended his article with an impassioned plea for definitive government action:

> One is not so foolish or unpatriotic or so selfish as to suppose that the country's money must be poured out in the Highlands, without regard to the state of the country generally. Nevertheless the situation in the Highlands and Islands is so clamant and urgent that a policy for rehabilitation and development there demands the highest possible priority.

Therefore, in the columns of *An Gaidheal*, the failure to establish a powerful government agency in the Highlands was seen as a cause for concern. Even when the Labour Party committed itself to a Highland Development Agency in the 1964 general election campaign, this particular organ of Gaelic opinion remained sceptical. However, there was a marked contrast between the externally imposed economic policies of successive governments and the much more responsive and exciting decrees emanating from the Scottish Education Department (SED). In this sphere, *An Comunn* was more hopeful that at least one element of government had come to realize the importance of maintaining the Gaelic language and culture.

FORMAL EDUCATION IN THE *GÀIDHEALTACHD*

As the Highlands emerged from the war, the membership of *An Comunn Gàidhealach* increasingly returned to a position in which education was recognized as the crucial field for the preservation and promotion of the Gaelic language and culture. Moreover, as post-war reconstruction across Scotland intensified, the crucial relationship between educational policy and the economic redevelopment of the Highlands was underlined, as emphasized at the 1950 National mod by John Bannerman:

> There are brains in Gaeldom of the most desirable quality that are compelled to keep their contents latent because of the great economic limitations that have hitherto prevailed [...]. The Gael is a valuable product of a valuable special nursery, as Glasgow and other cities of our country and empire know [...]. It would be blind folly on the part

of the powers-that-be not to develop and give opportunity to the acclimatized Highlander in his own land.[43]

Certainly in the post-war era, the 'powers-that-be' in the form of the Scottish Education Department [SED] did take a more supportive attitude towards the Gaelic language, evident in various publications produced between 1946 and 1956.[44] The fragile state of the Gaelic language and culture, reflected in the virtual disappearance of Gaels as a monoglot entity, undoubtedly helped a shift in approach from those in authority, but *An Comunn* deserve recognition for their persistence in highlighting the need for action and their determination to extract concessions from the government on language policy.[45]

Not content with pressurizing successive governments for action, members of *An Comunn* went to extraordinary lengths to try and stem the tide of language decline. This reflected the depth of feeling among some Gaelic activists that the dramatic changes being ushered in during the 1940s and 1950s were threatening the very existence of the language itself. In this energized atmosphere, different initiatives were proposed and subjected to critical appraisal.[46] Thus, in February 1947, the 'special reorganization committee' established by *An Comunn* reported back with a number of recommendations on the organization's future strategy on how to promote the Gaelic language and culture. Education, in its broadest sense, was clearly seen as a priority.[47] The report called for the adoption of teaching of Gaelic throughout all the schools in Scotland, and it believed that *An Comunn*'s primary aim should be to ensure that this was implemented. This proposal was in response to criticisms that *An Comunn* was concentrating its attentions only on those areas where Gaelic was still spoken, particularly the islands and western seaboard, thus abandoning those communities where the language was weaker or recently moribund. *An Comunn* was also anxious to provide a platform from which some of the misconceptions or negative attitudes towards the language – from within as much as outwith the *Gàidhealtachd* – could be countered.

The publication of the Advisory Council on Education's detailed and comprehensive reports on primary and secondary education in 1947 provoked further reflection by Gaelic's leading advocates. Farquar MacRae, effectively responding on behalf of *An Comunn*, welcomed the recommendations 'with regard to the Gaelic-speaking areas' though he expressed a number of concerns

---

43 *AG* (1950), 138–9, 144. 44 See John A. Smith's contribution on 'Schools, Gaelic teaching in' in Thomson, *Companion to Gaelic Scotland* (p. 261), where he cites the 1945 Education (Scotland) Act as being of major indirect importance in facilitating a shift in attitude towards Gaelic in education. Because the new Act was more 'child-centred' than previous measures, it allowed for a more positive attitude towards Gaelic. The reports emanating from the SED in the decade following the act reflect this different approach and helped stimulate developments such as bilingualism in the Highlands. 45 *AG* (1951), 3, 6. 46 *AG* (1951), 98, 108. 47 *AG* (1947), 63–4.

about provision in the rest of Scotland.[48] Besides being upset that Gaelic was classified as among 'other foreign languages', MacRae criticized the difficulty in obtaining a qualification for those learning the language. Bristling at the suggestion that Gaelic had a low 'utility value', he urged the members of the Advisory Council to reflect on their own stated view 'that Gaelic literature (for all Scotsmen) enshrines the experience of their race and will come home to them with an intimacy of appeal no other could rival'. Indeed, MacRae suggested that the practical application of Gaelic was readily apparent when logically considering their section on 'arts and crafts':

> Any native art or craft or industry founded on native soil and tradition will tend to retain in the glens happy contented speakers of Gaelic. Their presence and example and activity will make the place more interesting and attractive for others, and in the cumulative result we may well have the influence which is going to reverse the drift to the cities and overseas, and so establish on prosperous holdings and in fishing and forestry villages families who will speak Gaelic as naturally as they breathe their native air.

However, as we shall see, others were perhaps less convinced than MacRae that their fellow-Gaels and Highlanders would be so supportive of the language.

Certainly, the more sympathetic attitude from the SED towards Gaelic encouraged *An Comunn* to press for further reforms including the adoption of more modern methods of teaching and Gaelic to be made available where the demand merited it.[49] At the secondary education level, they wanted parity with the other languages taught, resenting the difficulties learners faced and the assumption that Gaelic was somehow less useful than French or German.[50] While the deficiencies of Gaelic provision within the secondary sector continued to exercise the minds of Gaelic activists, it was on the critical early phase of primary education when the child moved out of a Gaelic-speaking household into a non-Gaelic school environment that most attention was directed. This was regarded as the critical area on which to secure a stable bedrock foundation on which to build for the future. One of the major problems in this sector – the lack of suitably qualified teachers – was exacerbated by the omission of Gaelic as an examination topic on leaving primary education. *An Comunn* urged that Gaelic should be taught at least two-and-a-half hours per week, and they called for additional Gaelic-speaking inspectors as there were only three in Scotland and none situated in Inverness-shire. The SED responded by saying that they would

---

48 *AG* (1947), 101–2. 49 *AG* (1949), 157–8. In the President's address of November 1950, John Bannerman said: 'That is why An Comunn Gaidhealach is making the keystone of its efforts the child in the Highlands'. 50 *AG* (1949), 18; Thompson, *An Comunn Gaidhealach*, pp 81–2.

do their utmost to make the situation more satisfactory, but though the possibility of relocating the existing Gaelic-speaking inspectors over the whole of the *Gàidhealtachd* was mooted, in reality the budgetary constrains within which the SED had to operate, allied to residual prejudices against Gaelic within St Andrew's House, meant that such ideas were never a realistic or feasible option. It also presupposed that the Gaelic-speaking HMI would be willing to be relocated. On the evidence of the teachers themselves, this was a moot point.[51]

Throughout the immediate post-war period, the problem of insufficient numbers of Gaelic-speaking teachers suitably interested and willing to return to the *Gàidhealtachd* to work would continue to plague the efforts of *An Comunn* and the SED to maintain and promote the language. During the early 1950s, many editions of *An Gaidheal* recognized that while there was no shortage of suitably qualified Gaelic-speaking teachers in Scotland overall, the problem was that in ever increasing numbers, these selfsame Gaelic teachers were taking up posts outwith the Highlands and Islands.[52] Certainly, as *An Comunn* itself acknowledged, an inadequate supply of Gaelic teachers and the lack of up-to-date resources were fundamental difficulties during the period. An examination of the reasons for these problems revealed a deeper predicament facing those trying to preserve the language and culture.

While many Gaels, Highlanders and Scots recognized the richness, cultural value and indeed usefulness of the Gaelic language, others were less convinced.[53] The perception that Gaelic was a handicap to schoolchildren was seemingly reinforced by results from intelligence tests as publicized by the press in 1952. Finlay J. MacDonald felt that some teachers shared this negative view of Gaelic. He believed that it was necessary to release a statement saying that the fault lay with the unsuitability of the test, not with the Gaelic of the children.[54] Later research would vindicate MacDonald's view, but during the period 1939 to 1965, Gaelic enthusiasts faced an uphill struggle in enticing learners of the language to persevere. As early as 1948, the then president of *An Comunn*, Dr John Cameron, gave a moving lament to the continuing drain on the Highland population and the uncertainty regarding the social and economic prospects for the region. As for education, he stated:

> It is [...] our duty and right as Highlanders to demand that our language be adequately taught, and we have a right to ask from our own people that there be an end to indifference. If our land, our homes or our resources were taken from us, we should call down heaven as a witness to the injustice of it, but when our language – a much more precious thing – is neglected, some of us are prepared to

51 *AG* (1948), 72. 52 *AG* (1950), 162; AG (1950), 41–2; *AG* (1952), 83–4. 53 *AG* (1948), 15–16. 54 *AG* (1952), 61.

sit by and watch it crumble to decay. The road is long and hard, but the years are passing, and the chance will not come again, for the accent and idiom of spoken Gaelic will, as things are, soon pass away.[55]

This bleak and honest assessment highlighted the scale of the problem and the sense of exasperation that some Gaelic activists had with the indifference or complacency from 'their own people'. In order to break the negative mentality and kick-start a revival, it was felt that a more fundamental and holistic approach was required to galvanize Highland and Gaelic youngsters.

EDUCATIONAL EXPERIMENTS FOR THE *GÀIDHEALTACHD*

Realizing that the fate of the language lay largely in their own hands, members of *An Comunn Gàidhealach* proposed a range of devices to meet the needs of non-Gaelic speakers. One such strategy was to use *An Gaidheal* as an educational tool by devoting some space each month to assist learners. One correspondent argued that this would address the problem of a lack of Gaelic resources in education, aid learners and boost the sales of the journal at the same time.[56] In 1955, the executive council of *An Comunn* agreed that back numbers of *An Gaidheal* be made available to secondary schools where Gaelic was taught. Following his visit to the Celtic Congress in Dublin in 1954, Donald Grant (later to be an editor of the magazine) suggested that he follow up his contacts there and ask about the possibility of producing a Scottish Gaelic edition of certain illustrated Irish school readers. Both these proposals illustrate the problem of the paucity of materials for the teaching of Gaelic in schools, but they also demonstrate the relative weakness of Scottish Gaels to resolve their own problems. Indeed, this was made apparent in the same edition of *An Gaidheal* when, due to the increasing costs involved, it was recommended that the supplement *An Gaidheal Og* (The Young Gael) be reduced from four pages per month to two. Although justifying this proposal by saying that half of the magazine would continue to be in Gaelic, few of the members welcomed the move.[57]

Despite the rich body of Scottish Gaelic literature, many of the young learners were not being exposed to it; hence *An Comunn* sought to encourage the Gaelic youth to identify with their culture and appreciate its value in the face of modernizing forces. One of the main vehicles for accomplishing this was through *Comunn na h-Òigridh* (the Gaelic youth movement) and in the 1947 report of the 'special reorganization committee', several recommendations centred on this body. One suggestion was to strengthen the links *An Comunn* had

55 *AG* (1948), 15–16. 56 *AG* (1948), 147. 57 *AG* (1955), 13.

with Gaelic youth, as *Comunn na h-Òigridh* only catered for children up to the age of fourteen. Following the example of Ireland, the argument was put for the links with the young to be prolonged into their twenties in order to consolidate their learning process and strengthen their interest in the plight of the language and culture. Coupled with this proposal was a call for the structure of the youth wing to be reorganized to improve efficiency and target specific geographical locations. This tied in with the final recommendation to make the reformed *Comunn na h-Òigridh* an autonomous body under the aegis of *An Comunn Gàidhealach*.[58] Hence, even before the 1951 census revealed the extent of Gaelic's decline, one can detect a sense of urgency within the ranks of *An Comunn*, and a desire that the sons and daughters of Gaels be given the opportunity for instruction in their language.

In 1950, the first learner's school was held at Swordale in Easter Ross, the home of John M. Bannerman, who was the president of *An Comunn Gàidhealach* from 1949 to 1957. The children were given instruction in handicrafts and nature studies and participated in drama, dancing and song. The enthusiasm for this venture was demonstrated by a report of the second school in 1951, with the correspondent praising the 'fine crowd of girls who showed by their manner and deportment that they were proud of the people from whom they are descended – *gu robh iad moiteil as na daoine bho tainig iad*'.[59] In the following few years, the school developed into three levels of learner with children attending from the Highlands and Glasgow. The emphasis was very much on enjoyment, but also on facilitating the usage of Gaelic, and every progressive step was welcomed: 'An innovation this year was the setting apart of one table at mealtimes for those who were fairly capable of making conversation in Gaelic. No English was permitted and there was no desire for it'.[60] After establishing a camp for native speakers in 1955, *Comunn na h-Òigridh* established a permanent residence the following year at Cnoc nan Ros, near Tain in Easter Ross.[61]

The existence of these learners' camps testified to the lack of resources available for the Gaelic language, but the content of these annual jamborees demonstrates that those in the higher echelons of the Gaelic language movement wanted the learners to appreciate the various aspects to the 'Gaelic way of life'. The traditional music and song of the Gael was a key cultural component of this idealized 'lifestyle' and consequently contributors to *An Gaidheal* supported the establishment of music schools in the Highlands and Islands. Again, the SED was making heartening comments on the desirability of teaching children 'the haunting beauty of Gaelic songs'.[62] In 1949, through the columns of *An Gaidheal*, the case was put to establish a rural music institute to nurture the talents of Gaels, especially in their traditional music. The familiar difficulty of

---

58 *AG* (1947), 22–3.   59 *AG* (1951), 94. The Gaelic quotation translates as 'they are proud of the people from whom they came'.   60 *AG* (1952), 78–9.   61 *AG* (1955), 56; *AG* (1956), 124.   62 *AG* (1952), 53.

finding qualified teachers was apparent but, rather than accept less able tutors or inferior instruments, a stop-gap measure of teaching during the holidays was proposed. A survey of the needs and potential of such an institute, taking into account the resources available or potentially available, was also suggested.[63]

This survey of the musical needs of Gaelic children proved to be unsatisfactory, but the proposal did excite comment on what such an institute should teach. Two learned Gaelic scholars, John Lorne Campbell and Margaret Fay Shaw, responded with the following warning: 'We believe that it is on the traditional music of the Highlands that the musical education of the highlander ought to be built in the first place, and not upon the non-Gaelic musical idiom'. This cautionary note mirrors the worries of policy informers identified in the previous chapter who feared that the Highlands would be transformed into a 'Brigadoon'-style fantasy land. As prominent members of the Folklore Institute of Scotland, Campbell and Shaw appealed to fellow Gaels to assist in the recording and tuition of the ancient traditional music of the Gaels. As well as preserving this rich, but diminishing, reservoir of material, the act of recording skilled exponents of Gaelic music and song would ensure that 'the apparatus of education' was utilized for positive reasons – 'to perpetuate and not to obliterate' the rich musical heritage of the Gael.[64] Unfortunately, this proposal fell on deaf ears and the lack of a central Music Institute in the Highlands and Islands only encouraged those with talent, or even those just wanting to improve their abilities, to seek expert tuition elsewhere, such as the Army School of Piping in Edinburgh Castle.[65] Within the *Gàidhealtachd* itself, the paucity of qualified music teachers worried organizers of provincial mods, and as they were regarded as the 'lifeblood' of *An Comunn Gàidhealach*, their propaganda committee endeavoured to rectify this problem.[66]

The recognition of the psychological aspects to the maintenance of Gaelic culture led *An Comunn* to pursue a novel enterprise. The initial success of the *Comunn na h-Òigridh* summer camps encouraged the executive committee of *An Comunn* to establish a 'Gaelic informal committee' in December 1950. Heralding the launch of this policy, John Bannerman said:

> It is our ambition that there should be established in our Gaelic Highlands permanent educative and recreational establishments

63 *AG* (1949), 36.   64 *AG* (1949), 88.   65 Many Gaels adhered to the martial tradition of their forebears by joining the army. Tuition would be given in the individual battalions, but opportunities were available for those with exceptional talent to attain the rank of Pipe Major by completing a course at Edinburgh Castle. The Glasgow city police pipe band also had strong Gaelic connections, and fond memories are held for the 'gentle Highland bobby' who walked the beat in some of Glasgow's more colourful districts. Other Gaelic musicians also migrated to Glasgow, where the healthy numbers of Gaels provided a supportive network for those keen to improve their abilities. Interview with Ronald Morrison, Uist and Barra Association and member of the Piobaireachd Society, Aug. 1996.   66 *AG* (1955), 102–3.

where children and adults may meet for the common purposes of friendship that actuate us all.

In conjunction with this new venture, *An Comunn* also pledged to build on the *Comunn na h-Òigridh* summer camp in the north with one in the south and to extend the Gaelic learners' camp.[67] Eventually, the 'committee for informal education' was established after long negotiations between representatives of *An Comunn*, the SED and the county education committees of Sutherland, Ross-shire, Inverness-shire and Argyll. They all shared the costs for the project, which included appointing three full-time officials. They were entrusted with the task of

> developing social, recreational and cultural activities and to foster Gaelic language and culture, crafts and handiwork, local tradition, folklore and history, and generally foster the sense of belonging to a community bound together by a common language and tradition.[68]

An Comunn was appreciative of the 'vision and ready cooperation' of the other two participants, but the recent attitude of the SED was singled out for praise as its commitment to this project had 'gone far to atone for former neglect of, and indifference to, the language'. *An Comunn* believed that this initiative was 'probably *the* most important' enterprise that it had undertaken, and indeed it was cited in 1951 to offset criticism that it had done little to stem the continued depopulation from the Highlands and Islands.[69] At the launch of the 'Gaelic informal committee' it was hoped that 'the Gaelic and Highland people would rally round and support this immensely important and potentially very rewarding enterprise'. This anticipated support proved to be unforthcoming.

The first annual report of the joint committee (1952) contained very depressing news for Gaelic enthusiasts, with examples of complacency, indifference and even hostility among the indigenous population of the Gaelic heartland. As for the desire to establish a centre for music in the Highlands, the authors of the report noted that although there was 'considerable enthusiasm' for Gaelic music, this did not translate into a desire to study the spoken language of Gaelic. The report also contained a 'strong plea' for the further diffusion of more effective Gaelic teaching, and called on the Gaelic-speaking community to be more supportive of the scheme. Despite the setbacks, including the failed attempt to recruit local community leaders, the article acknowledged that the benefits of such a scheme would not be apparent for several years. It ended on a rather telling note:

---

67 *AG* (1950), 138–9, 144. 68 Ibid., 163. 69 Ibid.; *AG* (1951), 75.

> It is saddening to be told that some who profess to be supporters of *An Comunn Gàidhealach* have not only been uncooperative but definitely discouraging in this enterprise. We can do without such 'supporters'.[70]

It is quite wrong to regard the Gaelic-speaking community as a monolithic block; divisions and tensions existed. By 1955, the lack of suitable organizers and the apathy from the host communities led to the suspension of the 'Gaelic informal committee'.[71]

Given the support of the SED for this venture, it must have been acutely embarrassing for those in *An Comunn* who had been demanding government assistance for the needs of the *Gàidhealtachd* that their own people had not responded in a positive fashion. *An Comunn's* emphasis on the indigenous Gaelic-speaking population was not surprising, given the difficulties this group had faced from officialdom over the years, but *An Comunn* was not completely dismissive of those non-Gaels who wanted to learn the language. In the immediate post-war period, the signs were hopeful. As Dr John Cameron said,

> It will not be lost on the many able Gaelic scholars who do such valuable work for our language in schools and colleges that, if Gaelic is to make up lost ground, our approach and methods must be designed to meet the needs of pupils who are not Gaelic speakers, and they will realize that much remains to be done in this sphere.[72]

In view of their endorsement for Gaelic in education generally, the SED's response on the specific issue of learners was disappointing.

This tempered enthusiasm for allowing Gaelic to be a partial medium of instruction stems from the more child-centred approach of the education authorities following the 1945 Education (Scotland) Act.[73] The 1947 report from the SED was not acted upon until the late 1950s, when the so-called 'Inverness Experiment' witnessed Gaelic medium schemes being introduced into primary schools of the remaining bilingual areas in Inverness-shire; then followed to a lesser degree in Ross-shire and even less in Argyll.[74] This scheme evolved out of two surveys of the bilingual situation in Highland counties in 1957 and 1959, emanating from the reformed bilingualism committee of the Scottish Council for Research in Education.[75] The actual workings of this 'experiment' involved several schools being designated as suitable for the early teaching of Gaelic

---

70 *AG* (1952), 52. 71 *AG* (1955), 73. 72 *AG* (1949), 157–8. 73 Thompson, *An Comunn Gaidhealach*, p. 87. 74 Although the SED's support for bilingualism has not been viewed as totally altruistic, see Mackinnon, *Gaelic* (1991), pp 100, 102. 75 These results formed the basis for the Scottish Council for Research in Education's book *Gaelic speaking children in Highland schools* (1961).

reading and writing, and in general Gaelic was used more often in these schools. In all county schools, Gaelic was given enhanced status and an overall supervisor (later advisor) was appointed. Although enthusiasm waned at times and there was a lack of a coherent and common approach in all the schools, it was nevertheless an important stepping stone in that it heralded the beginnings of the fight against 'what was a serious flaw in the educational system: its "English-primacy" assumptions'.[76] The research into bilingualism certainly helped *An Comunn* convince the SED of the usefulness of Gaelic studies, and a learner's certificate at secondary level was introduced in 1962.

SCOTTISH UNIVERSITIES AND THE *GÀIDHEALTACHD*

The post-war expansion in higher education stimulated Gaelic studies at the various Celtic departments of Aberdeen, Edinburgh and Glasgow universities and helped to give this subject a greater sense of purpose. By the 1960s, there was an understanding and agreement among academics on the parameters of Celtic studies with an implicit consensus that the degree course in Gaelic should incorporate the 'more strictly "Celtic" dimension' as it had emerged in the late nineteenth century, while also being responsive to the changing needs and pressures within academia and beyond. However, given the widespread and far-reaching social and economic developments occurring in the *Gàidhealtachd* during the 1940s and 1950s, it was inevitable that the issue of what the university departments 'were doing *for* Gaelic' would provoke commentary.[77]

The problem of a gap between the 'professional Gael' in the urban centres and their fellow Gaels back in the *Gàidhealtachd* surfaced in *An Gaidheal* in the late 1940s. While there was a general appreciation of Celtic and Gaelic studies as a branch of scholarship, in addition to the sense of pride afforded to Gaels to study in *their* language, murmurings of discontent were being voiced at a senior level within *An Comunn* of a feeling within some sections of Gaeldom that Celtic scholars were not doing enough for the language.[78] Responding to the frequent suggestion that *An Comunn* should do more to recruit 'able Celts' from the various Gaelic societies in the Scottish universities, a correspondent from the University of Edinburgh agreed that recruiting from this group would certainly benefit the cause of Gaelic in its heartlands, their perceived 'distance' from the core problems being seen as an actual advantage. The contributor was, however, not unaware of the tensions to be overcome. In a thinly veiled criticism of Gaelic

---

76 Thomson, 'Gaelic in Scotland', p. 7.   77 These points were initially made at what was Willie Gillies' inaugural lecture as the Chair of Celtic Studies at Edinburgh University, Gillies, 'Gaelic Studies' (1989), pp 24–6; Also within academia, the work of the Scottish Gaelic Texts Society continued to develop: see Thomson, 'Gaelic in Scotland', pp 8–9.   78 Gillies, 'Gaelic Studies'; *AG* (1947), 15; *AG* (1948), 16.

academia, he noted: 'Much as I appreciate the genius of my fellow-Gaels, I have not yet found among them an inordinate readiness to widen their sometimes closed and attenuated ranks'. Within Edinburgh, he estimated that only around two per cent of the university's Celtic Department held membership of *An Comunn* and in his letter he expressed amazement that so few of his colleague 'professional Gaels', showed such a lack of interest in the activities and publications of *An Comunn Gàidhealach*, including the Gaelic platform of *An Gaidheal*.[79]

Though some of the people in and around *An Comunn* were appreciative of the contribution some academics were making to the language and culture in terms of teaching, research and publishing, they were keen to draw in both strands to work together for an ostensible common cause. Unfortunately, despite these efforts, there was something resembling a 'dialogue of the deaf' – with damaging consequences for Gaeldom as a whole. Firstly, the research that was being conducted in the various Celtic departments did not meet some of the needs of the wider Gaelic-speaking community, especially those concerned with the shrinking base of Gaelic speakers in Scotland. Secondly, the bursaries provided for higher education were not geared to the new professions opening up in the Highlands. Thirdly, the campaign for a Highland University was not coordinated by the disparate groups who cherished this ideal. One Gaelic correspondent to *An Gaidheal* had the following vision of such an institution: 'A Gaelic rural university, combining science and the humanities, where Gaelic is as is Hebrew in the University of Jerusalem'. Similarly unheeded was Cameron's idea of establishing 'a central body of the best brains in Gaeldom to examine our resources, both human and material, arrange for their expansion and determine to what extent and by what stages we can offer instruction in the old tongue to our Gaelic Youth'. Finally, and as a consequence of the other factors, the widespread complacency that numerous Gaelic commentators alluded to in this period was in some ways encouraged – both sides were largely uninformed of the other's situation.[80]

One organization that helped in the development of greater understanding and engagement between academic Gaels and the wider community was the School of Scottish Studies, established in 1951 at the University of Edinburgh. From the outset, it was slightly divorced from the elitism of the Celtic Studies departments. The people involved in the setting up of this institute recognized the warning signs for the survival of Gaelic and the likelihood that the number of speakers and the quality of their language and cultural capabilities would soon place the capacity for self-renewal under severe threat. The initial move to preserve the rich folklore of the *Gàidhealtachd* followed the 1947 Perth mod and a suggestion from the distinguished Irish writer Pádraig Ó Siochfhradha that

79 *AG* (1948), 51–2. 80 *AG* (1948), 51, 87; Gillies, 'Gaelic Studies', pp 25–6.

Scotland should establish a Folklore Institute of Scotland (FIS) (*Comunn Beul-Aithris na h-Albann*), along the lines of the Irish organization.[81] The school was of major importance for Gaelic because it meant that for the first time there was a coordinated and systematic attempt to collect the rich folklore and music of the Gaels and preserve this material for posterity through taped sessions, many of which have been made available in a variety of different formats through the years.[82]

The urgent need to record the range of material extant in the *Gàidhealtachd* was reflected in the inaugural lecture by the holder of the new Chair of Celtic at Edinburgh University, Professor Myles Dillon.[83] The Scottish *Gàidhealtachd* undoubtedly still contained folklorists, *seannachies* and musicians of the highest quality, but those in the FIS were also keen to keep an account of the different dialects and in 1947 they worked with the Linguistic Survey of Scotland to record Gaelic speakers in Oban.[84] Their intent was clear, and the difficulties involved can be appreciated from this statement from one of their members writing for *An Gaidheal* in 1949: 'It is hoped to arrange for future collaboration of a similar nature, when cattle and sheep sales bring in Gaelic speakers from outlying districts to centres where electric power is available to operate modern recording apparatus'.[85]

A further indication of the pace of change in the Highlands and Islands since 1939, and the desire to preserve the 'authentic voice' of the *Gàidhealtachd*, can be discerned from review articles in *An Gaidheal* from the 1951 and 1955 respectively. The musicologist Francis Collinson feared for a loss of depth to aspects of Gaelic culture in his review of folklorist John Lorne Campbell's *Seann orain a' Bharraidh: Gaelic folk songs from the Isle of Barra*.[86] Underlining the importance of this type of activity was the fact that two of the contributors died before the collection was published. Collinson hoped that these attempts to preserve 'the truth of the music of the Hebrides' would continue because they were an asset both to Gaeldom and to Scotland. Margaret Fay Shaw's book *Folksongs and folklore of South Uist*, though published in 1955, was collected between 1920 and 1935, at a time 'when social, economic and cultural change was only beginning to threaten it'.[87] Reflecting on the transformation that had affected this important Gaelic island, the reviewer commented:

> The picture presented is already somewhat out of date; that is part of its value. If it seems partly antiquarian, it is not falsely so, and it gives

---

81 Thompson, *An Comunn Gaidhealach*, p. 83; *AG* (1947), 38. 82 Initially made available on vinyl and tape, and discussed via its journal *Tocher*, the School has now digitized much of their archive on the *Tobar an Dualchais* website: www.tobarandualchais.co.uk, accessed July 2010. 83 *AG* (1947), 38. 84 Jackson, 'Linguistic Survey of Scotland'. 85 *AG* (1949), 44. 86 *AG* (1951), 37. 87 *AG* (1955), 74.

a picture, and an assessment of a mode of life which was common, in various degrees, to many parts of the Hebrides [...]. If it survives at all now, it is in corners even more remote than Glen Dale, South Uist, where Margaret Fay Shaw lived and worked in the early thirties.

These recordings were tremendously valuable, but the expense and labour needed could not be met from the School of Scottish Studies alone. In 1950, they appealed to *An Comunn* to assist them in preserving the rich folklore of the Gaels. This in itself demonstrates the speed with which the skilled exponents of the traditional arts and folklore of the *Gàidhealtachd* were disappearing. But perhaps the importance of this period for the language is highlighted by the fact that as attempts were being made to record and indeed resuscitate the language, the passing on of the tradition was faltering; if not ceasing.

Therefore, despite the advances made in Gaelic education, the language and culture were receding further back into the archipelago of the Outer Hebrides. Even in the heartland of Gaelic, parents and children were enjoying an improvement in their standards of living and being exposed to the 'outside world' in more comprehensive terms than before. *An Comunn* firmly believed that Gaelic education would assist in their attempts to maintain language levels, as John Cameron said in 1948: 'When our language receives the proper dignity in the educational scheme of things, then surely will we realize the heritage that is ours and pass it on in all its beauty and richness'.[88] The aim of achieving Gaelic medium instruction was partially and temporarily realized by the late 1950s, but problems remained, especially with the attitudes of parents and teachers. *An Comunn* made appeals but in reality these went largely unheeded by their intended audience in the Highlands:

> The person who is able to understand his language in a literary way is best fitted to understand anything in another language [...]. All that we ask for our own language is that each and everyone in the Gaelic area who may wish it be made intelligent in it.[89]

The enthusiasm for Gaelic instruction, and the expectation of further developments was in Glasgow and other urban areas where significant numbers of the Gaelic diaspora lived; less so in the heartland.[90] This paradox was also apparent between scholars of Gaelic and the language activists, and this resulted in poor coordination on issues such as the establishment of a strong, central body to direct policy and prioritize key developments. The acceptance of Gaelic as a valid and important part of the educational process would in time help to offset the image problem that Gaels had, but it was a significant problem and rendered attempts to demythologize the *Gàidhealtachd* somewhat forlorn.

88 *AG* (1948), 15–16. 89 *AG* (1950), 144. 90 *AG* (1952), 83–4.

So, while surveys were conducted, reports published and agencies and institutions established, the language and culture receded, the economy declined and the social fabric atrophied as depopulation continued across the Highlands and Islands. While a few extolled the stature of its culture and the importance of its language, to the many, and therefore in the popular mind of Scotland, the Highlands and Islands still had a serious image problem as a 'burden' and a place of doomed decline. In the context of accelerating economic and social intrusion in the Highlands and Islands, the intertwined issues of image and identity were, and indeed remain, important.[91]

THE IDENTITY OF THE GAEL

As successive governments increasingly turned to policies and strategies for economic development and social revival based on planned, centralized control, leading to a further expansion and intensification in the scale and pace of post-war change, Scotland's peripheral and economically marginal areas became increasingly irritated at what was perceived to be central government's failure to develop industrial projects that were sensitive to the specifics of their respective localities. Across the Highlands and Islands, there was a common exasperation at an apparent lack of the necessary political influence and a shared sense of frustration at the absence of any effective structural levers of power within the region. What gave the Gaelic perspective on this common claim of an apparent democratic deficit a distinctive edge was its cultural dimension and the framing of grievance in ethnic terms. The latter meant that discourse of development within the *Gàidhealtachd* over these pivotal decades was not only peculiarly complex – with its added subtext of ethnic identity and implicit questions of belonging – it was also increasingly sensitive.

The nub of the ethnic, cultural and identity subtext of the arguments relating to Highland development were succinctly summarized in 1956 by the Revd Kenneth MacKinnon at the concert of the local Oban mod: 'Without the knowledge of the Gaelic language', he told his overwhelmingly Highland and Gaelic audience, 'we cannot be true Highlanders or Islanders. And without a knowledge of Gaelic language and culture, no one can understand and appreciate fully the Highland background'.[92] The minister of Appin was not alone in this view. The belief that the language and cultural inheritance of the Gael were inextricably linked with the future of Highlands, with the latter, as the *Gàidhealtachd*, seen as

---

[91] As Willie Gillies, reflecting on the problems and possible ways forward for Gaelic and Highland studies in the 1980s, so tellingly remarked: 'There are so many vested interests with a stake in the Highlands that it is difficult to get room to grind one's own axe, and some of the old racial myths are so deeply embedded as to be taken as part of the "given" by professional historians'. See 'Gaelic studies', fn. 30, p. 42; also pp 27–39.   [92] *AG* (1956), 66–7.

the birthright of the Gael, was a recurring and overarching narrative in the pages of *An Gaidheal*. It was promoted as the claim of right of a noble people imbued with certain qualities, beliefs and values deriving from their distinct ethnic language and culture. Virtually every aspect of traditional life in the Highlands evoked a sense of an ancient heritage embedded in the land and the people as graphically encapsulated in a paean of praise for the popular Highland game of shinty: 'That it is part of our heritage is indisputable, and if we were to creep back to the deserted ground, when the moon is out, might we not see the sons of Finn playing, as tradition tells us, with silver clubs and a golden ball, under the watchful eye of Bran'.[93]

Nor was the argument simply based on the rich cultural landscape of Appin, Lorne and north Argyll or the popularity of shinty across the Highlands. For Scotland as a whole, as successive contributors to *An Gaidheal* frequently pointed out, the case for a Gaelic Highlands also had a national dimension. Sympathizing with a previous correspondent mistakenly taken for an Englishman despite wearing the kilt, Iain MacLennan suggested that the latter's mistake was in choosing the wrong identifier of national identity, arguing that 'Scottish Gaelic is unknown to foreigners, but they regard it as proof of nationality, even more so than the kilt'. The language needed to be maintained (*'cùm a Gaidhlig beò'*) not just for the sake of the Gaelic Highlands but for Scotland as a whole: 'The moral is that, if we wish to remain a nation, we must keep our language'.[94] Indeed, as *An Gaidheal* itself liked to demonstrate, the ethnic and cultural importance of the Gael and therefore of the implicit need for a Gaelic Highlands went beyond the national as well as the local. Throughout this period, *An Gaidheal* carried articles relating to the other Celtic countries and regions to demonstrate that Scottish Gaels regarded themselves as an integral part of a pan-European Celtic community. And while some tension between the more political stance taken by other Celtic regions, such as Brittany, and the conservatism of some members of *An Comunn*'s hierarchy is clearly discernible, the overall position was one of mutual admiration.[95] The positioning of the campaign for a Gaelic Highlands in such a transnational context could be exhilarating and liberating. Indeed, Gaels often imitated successful ventures originating in other Celtic countries and such was the empathy among these Celtic groups that invitations to attend their respective cultural events were a regular occurrence.[96]

---

93 *AG* (1960), 56–7. The account of the shinty cup final demonstrated the difficulties in maintaining such traditions: 'it is a great friendly highland occasion, with the personal touch that is so characteristic of the part of the world in which we live. It has survived numerous counter-calls of present-day life – T.V., National Service, and the never-ending struggle of clubs to pay their way'. 94 *AG* (1950), 1–2. It is worth pointing out that *An Gaidheal* did not wholly exclude the other minority language in Scotland – Scots. See *AG* (1950), 31. 95 *AG* (1948), 39; *AG* (1947–8), 63–4. 96 *AG* (1947), 9.

At the same time, attendance at the Irish *Oireachtas* or the Welsh *Eisteddfod* often left the Scottish guests despondent as the imbalance of the struggle, not least for the Celtic languages struggling to survive the encroachments of an increasingly dominant English language and culture, was all too dramatically exposed.[97] Even major European cultures such as French and German felt threatened by the latter. As Tom Murchison commented,

> One language, English, is irresistibly gaining the ascendancy in the scientific and commercial world and may well become the world language [...]. The conflict of world-languages and local languages is not confined to the Celtic countries, and it is bound to become more and more acute.[98]

In this context, the task of reinvigorating the peripheral and sparsely populated *Gàidhealtachd* as a predominantly Gaelic-speaking heartland was, to say the least, daunting. One response was to see the campaign for a Gaelic Highlands as a challenge of global significance. The Second World War had brought together Gaels from around the Commonwealth, some of whom were felt to have more fluent and purer Gaelic than their Scottish counterparts. Murchison was keen to ensure that these connections be maintained and strengthened, not least because the overseas Gaels would continue to contribute to the literature and culture of Gaelic Scotland.[99]

Occasionally, *An Gaidheal* would carry reports from overseas, for example the San Francisco mod, and cordial greetings were always exchanged to bolster the spirits of both parties.[1] Other than their historical or nostalgic aspects, in the post-war era these contacts were increasingly seen to have an inherent economic importance, not least in relation to the developing tourist industry in the Highlands and Islands.

THE IMAGE OF THE GAEL

For those grappling with the concomitant issues of post-war Highland development and the survival and regeneration of the Gaelic language and culture, the burden of history involved more than a long legacy of economic underdevelopment, linguistic and cultural marginalization and hostility. There were also the not insignificant consequences within Scotland and beyond of successive periods of the 'manufacturing' of the 'Highlands' and the 'Highlander' as cultural constructs with associated characteristics and attributes. Varying and

---

97 *AG* (1955), 43; *AG* (1952), 96–7; *AG* (1960), 7–8. 98 *AG* (1949), 56. 99 *AG* (1947), 37–8.
1 *AG* (1948), 120.

often contradictory, from the complimentary, through the patronizing, to the demeaning and hostile, the accumulation of cultural accretions in the manufacturing of the image of the Gaelic and the Highlander was substantial. The uncouth 'wild Hielander' of ancient times, the 'noble savage' of the Ossianic era, the warlike clansman of romantic Jacobitism, the faithful servant of Balmorality and empire, the gatekeeper to the mystical realm of the 'Celtic twilight', the crafty peasant confronting the overweening power of capital and authority, the listless dependent on government aid, were all images that permeated literature, the media and popular culture. Increasingly, they were also taken up in the new growth industry of Highland tourism.[2]

Within the Highlands and within Gaeldom, the reaction to this 'image problem' varied. For the most part, what were seen as positive representations were accepted, even enthusiastically endorsed. The more ambivalent or patronizing portrayals evoked a conflicting response. Some chose to treat the issue in a humorous way, as in a Gaelic pantomime entitled 'Whiskers galore' capitalizing on the popularity of *Whisky galore*, the Hebridean farce of Compton MacKenzie and its subsequent classic film adaptation, that played to packed audiences in Glasgow in 1951. The theme of the pantomime was to present the Highlands as they were felt to be seen through Lowlanders' eyes. This may involve misrepresentation, but there was no real harm in it. As the reviewer in *An Gaidheal* noted, 'There are many topical allusions, and some shrewd but kindly thrusts at the various gaucheries, anomalies and absurdities with which some of us in Gaelic and Highland circles are so familiar that we have ceased to notice them'.[3]

Others, perhaps conscious of the damaging impact caused by the perpetuation of longstanding and erroneous depictions of Highland and Island life, were less forgiving. In January 1952, the *Stornoway Gazette* reprinted comments made in a BBC radio programme broadcast a month earlier, in which a local man had attempted to correct the false depictions of Hebrideans that had appeared in recent newspaper articles, some of which later re-surfaced in overseas publications. In attempting to enlighten mainlanders on the harsh realities of island life, the Hebridean representative had lamented that seventeenth-century folklore was still being recycled as current twentieth-century practice. In doing so, he was of necessity taking part in 'a continual struggle against misunderstanding and misrepresentation' and the consequences of the recurring image problem of the Highlands and Islands:

> half the people of Britain think the Hebrideans barbarous and uncouth. The other half think that life in the Islands is too romantic for words. Barbarity is a relative term, and I am not convinced that

---

2 See McCrone, *Scotland the brand* (1995); Gold, *Imagining Scotland* (1995). 3 *AG* (1951), 10. The play was scripted by Finlay J. MacDonald and Alex MacKenzie.

dog-racing tracks or even tramcars are essential to civilization. As for romance, there is nothing romantic in the struggle for existence in these windswept islands. We live with hard economic facts, and Prince Charlie is long since dead.[4]

From this perspective, the image issue was far from innocuous. The fact that so many mainlanders, including journalists and politicians, were felt to be 'more interested in picturesque falsehood than in unadorned fact' was seen to have serious implications, not least in terms of government policy on Highland economic development. While such misconceptions could perhaps be tolerated if the islands were an independent entity, the fact that their survival was inextricably linked to policy decisions taken on the mainland meant that the persistent peddling of hoary old myths was insidiously harmful. However, such was the depth and extent of accumulated cultural misrepresentations that perhaps tellingly, the island observer concluded his observations on a pessimistic note: 'The most I hope for is a missionary enterprise to propagate the truth about the Hebrides'.

This idea of the need to educate the 'outside world' was increasingly seen by many as crucially important, particularly given the 1945 Labour government's stated commitment to integrate the Highlands and Islands into the rest of British society. The demand for the empowerment of Highlanders through a dedicated development agency was felt to be seriously undermined by all the mythical representations of Gaeldom. The widespread representation of the Highlands and Islands crofting communities as a 'begging bowl' dependency culture was particularly resented by those who were keen to promote the initiatives of the local development associations and the enterprising spirit of local individuals. To these advocates of Highland entrepreneurialism, 'as all of us know who are in touch with the north-west, it is not true to say that only the unenterprising "stay-at-home"'. Every effort had to be made to refute the damning popular image by publicizing the latter achievements as: 'There can be no better reply to those who sneeringly speak of the Highland people as ever begging for outside assistance than the increasingly numerous instances of local people taking in hand the betterment of local conditions'.[5]

The anger at these negative representations was further reinforced by a sense of betrayal, given the long history of the Gaelic Highlanders' dutiful service to the state. Speaking in the context of what he perceived to be a new post-war mood of empathy within the country, John Bannerman used his 1950 presidential address to the National mod to warn that government should not be allowed to forget their obligations to Scotland's Gaels. In an unambiguous reiteration of the notions of *dìleas*, faithfulness, loyalty and service that had been central to the

4 *Stornoway Gazette*, 11 Jan. 1952.   5 *AG* (1950), 90; (1951), 68.

core iconography of Victorian Balmorality, he declared that this 'minority people
[...] deserve consideration, if only because they are the proud source from
which this country and empire have received invaluable spiritual and material
benefit'.[6] Bannerman's invocation of a two-way sense of a reciprocal relationship
between loyal obedience and dutiful obligation derived from Gaeldom and the
Highlands long complicity with the British 'nation', crown and empire. The
echoes of this long history were further reinforced in 1953 with the coronation
of a new monarch when the old imagery of parallels between the monarch's
relationship to the 'family' of Britain and the Highlander's relationship to
Gaeldom's clans was recycled and orchestrated in the context of a fresh round
of royal visitations to the Highlands and the Hebrides.[7] The problem for
Gaeldom and the Highlands in appealing for 'special treatment' by evoking their
ostensibly distinctive 'values' was that the discourse of accumulated attributes in
which they were necessarily couched served only to reinforce the romanticized,
simplistic and 'manufactured' stereotypes of the Gael and the Highlander. As
other critical commentators recognized, this loaded discourse was integral to the
deep problems of image and identity that the Highlands faced. As in Scotland as
a whole, the irony of this process of self-colonialism was that the problematic
caricatures at the heart of the latter were often fortified and compounded by
cultural contributions from within the *Gàidhealtachd* itself.

The platform from which John Bannerman served notice on the government
that it had reciprocal obligations to meet the economic and social needs of the
Gaelic Highlands was the 1950 National mod, an annual cultural gathering that
was the premier showcase event promoting the Gaelic language and culture of
Scotland's Gaeldom and the Gaelic Highlands. Although some members of *An
Comunn* would dispute any claim that the National mod was their flagship policy,
it was the most visible demonstration of Gaelic activity every year and ostensibly
a useful 'litmus test' of the health of the language and culture. Akin to the
Eisteddfod in Wales or the *Jocques Flores* in Catalonia, this cultural event in some
respects can be viewed as a microcosm of the *Gàidhealtachd*. Issues and friction
over language and culture in relation to the mod were refractions of deeper, more
fundamental and therefore much more serious tensions and problems within the
avowed Highland heartland of Gaelic language and culture. Did the language
policy relating to the cultural competitions reflect or mask reality? Was the
cultural content of local and national mod programmes the fullest and most
appropriate expression of the 'true' richness and artistic achievement of Gaelic
culture? Was the format of an annual series of local and national mod competi-

---

6 *AG* (1950), 139. 7 *AG* (1952), 18, 20. These values of the Gael, and the late King George
VI were 'old and simple pieties, so scorned by the sophisticated and "emancipated" moderns'
but 'cherished and practised' by Gael and king; *AG* (1952), 58; *AG* (1956), 89; *AG* (1956),
106–7.

tions the most appropriate and useful forum through which to promote and develop the latter?

In relation to language, one of the complaints levelled by commentators on the National mod was the extent to which English was used as the medium of communication, especially when those involved were all capable of conversing in Gaelic. However, Murchison, the editor of *An Gaidheal* (1946–56) believed that many of these complainants were themselves limited in their Gaelic language skills, and these same people would suffer if Gaels conducted their business solely in their native tongue:

> The Gael, for all his many faults, is curiously loathe to express himself in a language which some of his hearers may not understand; he thinks, rightly or wrongly, that it is rude and discourteous to do so. Even our Gaelic children in Highland school playgrounds are ready, perhaps over-ready, to turn to English as soon as one non-Gaelic child happens to be present.[8]

Another observer of the 1949 mod took a harder line. Expressing concern that on numerous occasions groups of fluent Gaelic speakers would exchange a few sentences in their native tongue and then lapse into English for no apparent reason, he warned of the dangers of such a course of action for the future of the language within the Gaelic-speaking communities of the Highlands:

> Unless fluent speakers are prepared to make it the language of the home, the language of normal intercourse with their friends and, wherever possible, the language in which their work or business is conducted, Gaelic will soon be a memory of the past. Speaking a few words once a year at the mod – lip-service of this kind – will do nothing towards keeping it alive.[9]

In order to rectify what they perceived to be a fundamental weakness of the linguistic format of the mod, some argued that non-Gaelic speakers should be excluded from competing as most showed no inclination or desire to learn the language.[10] As one correspondent to *An Gaidheal* put it, those people who could only recite 'Parrot Gaelic' did not deserve to feature in the mod. *An Comunn*'s leadership, however, rejected the criticisms and such a sweeping exclusion measure was never enacted.[11]

Apart from the perennial debate about linguistic competency and fluency as criteria for participation, a more basic and frequently expressed reproach was

---

8 *AG* (1949), 151.   9 *AG* (1949), 155–6.   10 *AG* (1949), 151.   11 *AG* (1949), 156. It followed a similar complaint raised in the correspondence pages of the *Oban Times*.

that the mod wasted *An Comunn*'s energy and resources. Speaking at the organization's 1951 AGM, a member from Sunderland argued that instead of exerting so much energy on the mod, *An Comunn* should focus on and encourage local community initiatives within the Highlands, like the one on Mull, where Gaelic-speaking mothers had developed their own programme to train island children in the everyday use of Gaelic.[12] Others framed their criticisms at the perceived promotion of the annual mod at the expense of grass-roots language and cultural promotion within the Gaelic-speaking Highlands themselves in a wider cultural and political context. Writing of the need to emphasize the Celtic dimension to Britain's past in the face of the penetrative corrosion of a remorseless anglicization, a distant contributor to *An Gaidheal*, a sympathizer from Surrey (but whose 'heart' was in the Highlands), cited the relevance of the turn-of-the-century argument of the distinguished Celticist, Alfred Nutt. In order to bring to the fore this 'Celtic dimension', the various Celtic peoples of Britain needed a secure power base and the political conviction to realize this aim. Sadly, not even the Welsh, in the 'one part of Britain where the rot of Teutonization is beginning to be arrested', could stem the tide, the implication being that if *An Comunn* had the necessary conviction it would focus on establishing just such a base within the Gaelic-speaking Highlands, rather than in vain efforts to stem the tide through futile cultural showcase events such as the National mod.[13] Support for such a rethink of the cultural focus of *An Comunn* was evident in the subsequent contribution of a Welsh-language supporter to *An Gaidheal* who could bear witness to how the 'rot of Teutonization' could indeed be treated and prevented. Envious of the resilient cultural heritage still extant in the Gaelic Highland heartland of Scotland, he pleaded for a focus on the maintenance of Scottish Gaelic in the grass-roots communities of the latter rather than through the contrived format of cultural competitions:

> If there was no other reason for keeping Gaelic alive than that songs should continue to be sung in it naturally, and not as an artificially fostered pseudo-cultural 'stunt', this reason would suffice in any world where the sense of values was not already almost hopelessly perverted. For can anyone point to a corpus of folk song anywhere on the face of the globe that can hold a candle to that of the Scottish Highlands and Islands?[14]

As the most visible sign of *An Comunn Gàidhealach*'s existence, the National mod brought frequent derision and sardonic comment, with the criticism levelled at the running of the mod frequently implying a wider dissatisfaction with the organizing body itself. A recurrent criticism was that other than 'run a

---

12 *AG* (1951), 103. 13 *AG* (1956), 26. 14 *AG* (1956), 55.

sing-song once a year', *An Comunn*'s contribution to the development of the Gaelic language was minimal.[15] Such attacks not only evoked an exasperated and defensive reaction from the *An Comunn* leadership, they also revealed deep divisions within the Highlands' heartland Gaelic-speaking communities. The derisory dismissal of *An Comunn*'s premier event and of the effectiveness of the organization itself emanated from within the Gaelic Highlands by a Gaelic-speaking councillor seeking to dissuade his county council education committee from accepting a request from *An Comunn* to participate in the latter's 'Gaelic informal education scheme'. Clearly angered by this active opposition from within the *Gàidhealtachd* itself, the editor of *An Gaidheal* retaliated. Their critic, he declared, either displayed a singular ignorance or, worse, he refused to accept all the good work undoubtedly done by *An Comunn* since its foundation. The organization, he conceded, had made mistakes and could, perhaps, have done more for the language, but he felt strongly that attitudes such as that expressed, of which, he admitted, there were many, only served to continually undermine the positive work being done or proposed. Writing at the beginning of 1951, Murchison claimed that the opening of the new decade presented *An Comunn Gàidhealach* with 'splendid new opportunities' and counselled against failing to grasp them or acting in a timid manner solely because 'of the ill-informed and even ignorant attitude of some fellow-Gaels'.[16]

The timing of Murchison's optimistic assessment of the opportunities that lay ahead was not without significance. Both the Highlands and *An Comunn* were only beginning to finally emerge from the difficulties of the inter-war period and the dire readings from the just-published 1951 census returns had brought the work of the principal organization of Gaeldom in relation to the Highland communities it sought to serve under close and renewed scrutiny. As a consequence of the war, there had been no decennial survey of the number of Scotland's Gaelic speakers since 1931. Now, the distressing results of the first post-war census showed a massive 31 per cent decline in the number of Gaelic speakers over the two decades since 1931. It was a bleak revelation that placed *An Comunn*, its leadership and its policies under the microscope. In an upbeat stoic defence of its activities, Murchison sought to put the task of *An Comunn* in what he felt was the proper perspective: 'How could *An Comunn* adequately deal with the cultural problem', he pleaded, 'when the basic economic problem has baffled the politicians and administrators, with all the state's resources behind them, for a century past?'[17] The decline in Gaelic speakers may be dramatic, but without *An Comunn* and its efforts, he argued, Gaelic would have been in a far worse position: 'To put it at the very lowest, *An Comunn* has saved something from the wreck, it has established points of resistance, it has even established points of attack and "bridge-heads" from which new territory may be won or lost territory

15 *AG* (1951), 3, 6.   16 Ibid.   17 *AG* (1951), 83–4.

recovered'. Continuing in this vein, Murchison praised the efforts of *An Comunn* over the last sixty years as being invaluable in restoring to Gaelic a sense of self-respect and pride, a process which, he argued, also incorporated many non-Gaels. Nonetheless, a concluding caveat contained a telling qualification to this glowing eulogy, when he conceded and acknowledged: 'But we have not succeeded in doing this to a degree commensurate with the realities of the situation'.[18] Other commentators from within the organization were significantly more self-critical. While recognizing that outside influences had played a substantial role in placing Gaelic in a precarious position, the Revd Kenneth MacKinnon also warned of apathy and complacency within the Gaelic Highland community itself; 'If it is dying', he openly declared, 'it is because we are neglecting it, starving it, allowing it to fall out of use'. It was an honest criticism from within *An Comunn* that reflected a wider groundswell of opinion within Gaeldom that the latter's lead cultural organization was failing in its duty.[19]

RESPONDING TO MODERNITY

The issues and problems highlighted by the debate within *An Comunn* over the organization's focus and strategies in relation to the future of the Gaelic language and culture within the *Gàidhealtachd* were reflective of the deep and far-reaching changes within the Highlands and Islands as the post-war pace and reach of transforming social and cultural practices penetrated even the most outlying areas. Responses to this encapsulating and eclipsing modernity ranged from a ready and welcoming acceptance, through critical and hesitant ambivalency, to an emotive and ethnocentric retreat into an introspective essentialism.

At an individual, domestic and community level, most developments in enhanced communications, services and facilities were accepted with alacrity, notwithstanding the discernible impact such advances had on core aspects of the traditional Highland 'way of life'. As we have seen in previous chapters, the experience and upheaval of the Second World War, easier access to an expanded educational sector and improved transport communications had all combined to broaden horizons and open the Highlands and Highland residents to an ever-growing array of options, new tastes and fashions in individual and domestic lifestyle and communal social and recreational practice. For Gaelic culture, in particular the social and cultural practices through which the rich oral tradition of song, poetry, story and lore was transmitted and renewed, the resultant changes in social practice and personal taste had a deep and traumatic impact. More than anything, it was one single emblematic factor, as Morag MacLeod's informed and perceptive commentary on this key period makes clear, the arrival

18 Ibid. 19 *AG* (1956), 19.

of hydro-electric power, that had overwhelming and irreversible social and cultural consequences. In every household in every scattered township across the Highlands and Islands, people 'took to the machine and to an easier life'. The resultant shifts, modification and adaptations in the nature of work, social mores and expectations not only had a profound impact on Gaels' social habits – it had a marked influence on standards of living. The latter also, in turn, impacted severely on the dissemination and diffusion of the Gaelic language and culture.[20]

Developments at a national level also had a significant bearing on the acculturation process within the Gaelic Highlands. The expansion of the mass media had presented a fundamental challenge to those seeking to preserve the Gaelic language and culture. In the early years after the establishment of the Scottish Home Service of the BBC in 1926, Gaelic had only a token presence and the amount of airtime devoted to the language increased at a very slow pace. By the mid-1960s, with around three hours per week, the broadcasting output consisted of weekly and monthly religious services, monthly children's' programmes, a weekly talk and two programmes per week varying in content from Gaelic song, drama and literature to periodic material devoted to women's issues. Short news bulletins at midday followed by ten minutes of music and a weekly magazine programme broadcast on VHF covering the north of Scotland completed provision for the Gaelic language in broadcasting.[21] Although, in terms of broadcasting hours, this was a relatively small amount of Gaelic language coverage, astutely programmed it could have significant impact. In the early 1960s, under the guidance of Fred MacAulay, producer of Gaelic programming for the BBC in Glasgow, a marked shift took place in the range of Gaelic material broadcast, with the inclusion of a repertoire of singers and songs more reflective of popular taste in Gaelic communities throughout the Highlands and islands. As Morag MacLeod has noted, there was no doubt

> that the BBC had the greatest influence on the Gaelic public, and 'ordinary' people who had never left their island and rural homes saw the possibility of having their own repertoires featured on radio. Nothing could be better for the prestige of traditional song.[22]

This was obviously important psychologically, in terms of individual and collective wellbeing within the Gaelic Highlands, but it also had a percolating influence and consequence in relation to the form and performance of Gaelic song and culture. Parallel initiatives and happenings relating to the work of the School of Scottish Studies and the folk revival of the 1950s and 1960s were also loosely interconnected to these developments within the Gaelic content of the

20 MacLeod, 'Folk revival in Gaelic song' (1996), p. 128. 21 MacDonald, 'Gaelic language', pp 181–2. 22 MacLeod, 'Folk revival in Gaelic song', p. 131.

BBC. Indeed, it has been suggested that one indirect consequence was to help shift organizers and participants in the National mod to broaden out the repertoire of songs and the style in which they were sung to something 'more attuned to the indigenous culture'.[23]

A parallel, though often overlooked, development within Scotland's Gaelic community in this pivotal era that also highlighted the intertwining aspects of modernity and the diffusion of Gaelic culture was the warm embracing of the expanding medium of the gramophone record industry. In 1956, a new company, *Gaelfonn*, was launched, committed to producing and promoting recordings of popular Gaelic music. Six years on and the *Scottish Daily Express* was reporting on the company in stereotypical fashion: 'in a small soundproof room overlooking Glasgow's bustling dockland today, a stocky figure in a kilt and tweed jacket will be singing a soft melody of the Gaelic'. The occasion was the re-recording of Gaelic songs by Scalpay's Angus MacLeod and Islay's Donald MacLeod originally used to launch 'Scotland's only Gaelic recording company' in 'the big unfriendly world of the disc business'. Undoubtedly, the producer Murdo Ferguson, described as a 'fervid enthusiast of Gaeldom', hoped to build on the enormous popularity of the original releases:

> Gaelic records produced in Glasgow are selling to Scottish communities in Japan, China, America and Canada. There are even 'furriners' among their more enthusiastic customers. Like the languages specialist who travelled from Norway to collect their latest releases. The company still produces 78s on hand presses in the basement. But the demand is falling as the Highlands and Islands turn to the new record players and the small 45 discs. The Gaelic on record must keep up with the times.[24]

The Gaelic record industry now aligned itself with radio as having a seminal influence in the changes in social habits driven by improvements in standards of living, electrification and the material effects of the 'affluent society' of the late 1950s. When these were succeeded by the subsequent advent and spread of television, there was an even further toll on the traditional acculturation process associated with the diffusion of Gaelic culture in virtually every household in every township within the Highlands and Islands. By the 1960s, the communal gathering place of the 'ceilidh house' and all that went with it had become virtually obsolete and 'a very rare commodity'.

The popularity of Gaelic radio, the success of the Gaelic record industry and associated developments confirmed that the commodification of Gaelic culture

---

23 Ibid. 24 'Angus finds fame in Gaelic', *Scottish Daily Express*, 4 June 1962, p. 10. The records sold 78,000 and 72,000 copies respectively.

for individual and communal consumption by and within the Gaelic community was highly popular. The reaction to proposals for the commodification of Gaelic culture for 'external' consumption was much more lukewarm, critical and ambivalent. Previous chapters traced the development of the tourist industry in the Highlands and Islands and the degree to which an increase in visitors to the *Gàidhealtachd* was regarded by many as offering hope for Highlanders, crofters in particular, to supplement their incomes. In the period 1939–65, it was mainly the scenic beauty of the region that was being marketed, but increasingly the potential of the cultural element was being alluded to by influential Highland writers such as Neil Gunn. In the context of an embryonic Highland tourism industry, it was not a new suggestion. As early as 1934, the noted historian I.F. Grant had been pressing the case for a Highland Folk Museum similar to ones she had visited in Scandinavia. When her early initiative, *Am Fasgadh* (the Shelter), was opened in June 1944, many Gaels were satisfied that the cultural aspect to tourism was now being recognized, even though they appreciated that its merits may not be valued until later.[25] By the 1950s, the dearth of any other new cultural heritage centres continued to disappoint. In 1956, Kenneth MacKinnon asked disapprovingly:

> What is there distinctive about the Highlands today excepting the scenery? Half the fun of a foreign holiday lies in the distinctive character of the foreign nation and its people. I have no doubt that visitors to the Highlands are disappointed by the seeming anglicization of the Highlands and the positively non-Highland hospitality and fare of the hotels and inns.[26]

Calling on *An Comunn* and the Scottish Tourist Board to do more to distinguish the Highlands from the anglicized parts of Scotland, such as providing bilingual maps, street signs and shop signs, MacKinnon argued that the situation in the Scottish Highlands stood in marked contrast to the experience in Nova Scotia. He particularly envied the setting up of 'Highland villages' among the Gaels of Nova Scotia, arguing that similar projects in Scotland would demonstrate that the Highlands were and remained Gaelic, as well as acting as a focal point for cultural activity in the region and enticing visitors. Ruling out the possibility of asking the government for support, as their ideas 'seem inimical to our cause', he called on *An Comunn* to mobilize public opinion and act in a positive manner. When 1965 finally saw the construction of a visitor centre at Culloden, it was seen as perhaps a poor response in comparison with representations of the Gaels' experience across the Atlantic but it was nonetheless welcome as reflecting the beginnings of recognition in the merits of cultural tourism.

25 *AG* (1949), 148. 26 *AG* (1956), 89–90.

While many Gaels welcomed the potential opportunities that this source of income offered, others were more critical. For example, suggestions that crofters should diversify and earn some of the income from tourism were not universally welcomed by Gaels. In the 1959 winter edition of *Gairm*, a Lewis bard, Norman MacLeod, writing under his sobriquet *Am Bàrd Bochd*, responded in Gaelic verse (subsequently anthologized and translated) in typically caustic terms:

> Buy a mutch-like chef's tall hat
> white jacket and striped trousers;
> learn by practice how to point
> your bottom smartly upwards;
> wax and 'spittle' your moustache
> until it sticks out finely;
> so that no one twigs that you were born in these Western islands.
> [...]
> But I must sound a warning
> though the words will take some finding:
> somewhere behind the cornyards
> is no toilet for the strangers;
> there's a danger there of pimples
> where the skin is somewhat tender,
> and most of all when they don't know
> a docken from a nettle.[27]

MacLeod ended his bitter observations on a further sardonic note, predicting that the 'new' crofters would continue to sell their birthright and lose the independence and solid reputation that they once had. Alongside Mackinnon's pleas for more cultural tourism and Isabel Grant's initiatives in relation to museums and material culture, *Am Bàrd Bochd*'s scathing attack on the idea that crofters should make money from tourism, fuelled by the sense that the introduction of tourism on a mass scale was sanitizing the culture of the Gael, graphically underlines the ambivalency surrounding several aspects of the response to encapsulating modernity within the Gaelic Highlands. Other responses demonstrated a much deeper and humourless retreat into intransigence.

---

27 Thomson, *Gaelic poetry*, pp 262–3 for a partial translation. The Gaelic original was published in *Gairm* (1959), pp 152–3.

RETREAT TO ESSENTIALISM

Norman MacLeod's acerbic response to the expanding Highland tourist industry reflected not only an adverse reaction to one particular aspect of modernity. It also indicated an awareness of how the latter contained critical implications for the Gaels' sense of identity. The previous chapter showed how some policy informers argued for the improvements in the standards of living and the trappings of a modern lifestyle to reflect the distinct environment of the Highlands and Islands. However, on the whole, their advice went unheeded. Similar demands were made from within the Gaelic community, where an added dimension was a specific concern for the maintenance of Gaelic culture within the Highlands and the identity of the *Gàidhealtachd* as 'the land of the Gael'. One form in which these concerns were expressed was a mild generational conservatism. The president of *An Comunn* in his 1950 address warned of the dangers presented by 'the maze of modern distraction and invention all around us'.[28] He felt that as a result of previous apathy and neglect on the part of government, the transformation introduced in this immediate post-war period 'makes the new development almost as great a menace to our folk-culture as was the apathy which preceded it'.[29] By the mid-1950s, the difficulties involved in making Gaelic seem relevant for the youth of the Highlands and Islands was widely recognized:

> It is sad, though understandable, that many native speakers, on entering modern society, deny their heritage and model themselves on the Transatlantic ideal – not because it appeals to them more, but because they are afraid of seeming 'different'. If we could make Gaelic a popular fashion, it would achieve an enviable distinction and an assured future [...]. I am not suggesting that you hire a spot on Radio Luxembourg, get our medallists into the Hit Parade, and thus acquire a horde of 'fans'; but propaganda is undoubtedly one answer.[30]

As already noted, the shifts in individual tastes, standards of living and patterns of everyday life had a corrosive effect on traditional cultural performance and practice. The extent of the cultural decline in one of Gaeldom's strongholds, South Uist, can be gauged by the reaction of a local bard on his return from war service. At just 39 years of age and at the height of his creative powers, Donald Allan MacDonald was beginning to feel alienated from the people for whom he had already composed so many songs in the pre-war period. The bard felt culturally distanced from his own people, especially the younger

28 *AG* (1950), 139. 29 Ibid. 30 *AG* (1956), 19.

generation. Trapped in a cultural vacuum, he was unwilling to adapt to the demands and opportunities of a new social order that downplayed the oral tradition and its celebration and as the 'social structures and occasions which had sustained his composition [... and] the audience for his compositions went into ever decreasing decline, our bard ceased to practice his art'.[31] One of the reasons for this dilution in Gaelic culture was the decline of the ceilidh house or *tigh-ceilidh*.[32] The feeling of gratitude at the material benefits of modernity, of going forward, were now being balanced against a sense of regret at the cultural shifts within the Highlands, of going backward from a region once defined as 'the land of the Gael'. Thus, by the 1960s and the advent of electricity in places like Barra, 'despite its advantages', this new form of power was seen as having 'a strong adverse effect on the old social life'. It was observed that 'many people now prefer to stay at home and watch television instead of going to *ceilidhs* or attending the drama productions in the local halls and schools'.[33]

While researching the cultural scene for the 'West Highland Survey' of the 1940s, one Gaelic researcher had felt that while the scale of decline during the war was undeniable, it remained the case that, although 'Gaeldom as a culture is flowering no more and the plant is sick', the future would nonetheless turn out well as 'scions from the old stock grafted into a fresh environment bloom anew'.[34] For many, such confidence was seen to have been overly optimistic. The comprehensive surveys of every parish in the Highlands and Islands taken for the various county editions of the third statistical account of Scotland in the 1950s and 1960s serve to confirm the latter verdict. The individual parochial accounts capture beautifully the different emotions generated by the dramatic shift in the economic, social and cultural landscape of the Highlands. The fact that so many of the contributors from the various parishes were connected to different churches in the Highlands is also useful in terms of gauging a more widespread response given the connections between religion, Gaelic and a prescribed 'Highland way of life'.[35] The combined effects of war, welfarism and reconstruction did not stem depopulation from the Highlands and Islands. As we have seen, the reasons for this are complex and interrelated but, paradoxically, the measures introduced by the state to tackle the 'Highland problem' actually contributed to out-migration. Therefore, though welfare reforms and the improvements in the standard of living were warmly received in the region because they removed 'real want, which our forefathers knew about', these 'blessings of modern "civilization"' were not universally endorsed because of the impact they had on the culture of the Highlands and Islands.[36] Moreover, the

---

31 MacDonald (ed.), *Songs of Donald MacDonald*, pp 51–2.   32 MacDonald, *Echoes of the Glen*, p. 31.   33 Barron (ed.), *County of Inverness* (1985), p. 561.   34 Darling and Morley, 'The social situation', p. 281.   35 See Meek, 'Highland churches' for some reflections on these shifts.   36 Barron, *County of Inverness*, pp 586–9, 360–3, 561; Malcolm MacMillan, Labour MP for the Western Isles, *Hansard*, Commons, 27 Jan. 1955; Maclean, *The Highlands*, pp 17–18.

region's population became more aware of their 'relative deprivation', and while this generated criticism at the perceived inequalities in the reconstruction programme, it also facilitated a desire to move to those places where the trappings of modernity were more widely available. The pressure on the 'native Gaelic stock' was intense because, with depopulation, as in the west Highland township of Glen Roy, 'a language, a culture, a civilization passes into oblivion'.[37] This loss of 'native stock', along with the associated decline of the cultural fabric of the Highlands and Islands, helped to reinforce a number of negative attitudes towards the process of development held by some in the region and the 'Highland' communities further to the south.

This widespread tendency to contrast the Highlands with the 'south', the Highland 'way of life' to an 'alien' material culture and the spiritually uplifting and morally sound life in a Highland parish to demeaning mere survival in the degrading urban jungle of Scotland's Lowland cities is a recurring feature throughout the surveys, particularly those from the Gaelic heartlands of the west. A few took comfort in the belief that the changes in the post-war period had 'resulted in a more independent attitude to life' and 'an end to the fatalistic and gloomy religious attitude'.[38] But for the majority of the parish ministers who mainly conducted the surveys, it was the loss not the gain of an 'independent attitude to life' that was to be lamented as the harmful consequence in the increase of a pernicious 'welfarism', whereby 'the spirit of independence is killed and only more and more is demanded. There is a different spirit abroad everywhere, a spirit of restlessness and lack of discipline through want of supervision from the home'.[39] While some attributed the pervasiveness of these transformed attitudes on the combined effect of two world wars and the loss of men from the townships,[40] the preponderant tendency was to attack the growing influence of the city, often with the implicit understanding that industrialism itself was the greater threat:

> Those who have tried to graft certain aspects of city life onto the Highland way of life have not been very successful, for in most cases the poorer, rather than the better features, have been emulated and the result has been not to elevate but to lower the tone of the community. Gambling, especially on the football pools, is prevalent. Sunday as an 'odd-job-day' is still very much the exception. Sunday newspapers are delivered to certain homes. A considerable proportion of the younger ladies indulge in smoking.[41]

Within the parishes of the west, where, notwithstanding undeniable decline,

---

[37] Maclean, *The Highlands*, pp 17–18. [38] Barron, *County of Inverness*, p. 588. [39] Smith (ed.), *County of Caithness* (1988), pp 150, 153. [40] Ibid., p. 153. [41] Barron, *County of Inverness*, p. 166.

the Gaelic language and culture was still felt to be in better health than elsewhere in the Highlands, this sense of an invidious and threatening assault on a 'traditional way of life' by external and 'alien' values and forces was deeply felt. The combined impact of the war and welfarism, set alongside reconstruction policies and subsequent regeneration measures, were all identified as having contributed to a damaging alteration in the cultural balance of the region.[42] Even the improvements in the provision of education were viewed with suspicion. Some regarded it as a necessary evil; others as a danger.[43] And while there was an element of criticism at a perceived complacent attitude within the Gaelic community towards this threat to the language and culture, the more typical response was to externalize and demonize the menace through a simplistic ethnic essentialism. This deep resentment at the intrusion of mores felt to be associated with the 'alien' life of the urban communities to the south found expression in observations with unambiguous overtones of social and ethnic superiority, as in the observation that 'The less intelligent lower strata of society talk English with an accent more akin to that of Glasgow and the industrial belt than the soft Gaelic accent of the western seaboard'.[44]

Such derogatory comments were reflective of an attitude within Gaeldom that was more than simply an aversion to an urban and industrial way of living that was seen to be somehow inappropriate and incompatible with the Highlands. Such disdain for those who spoke the demotic Scots of Glasgow and Scotland's Central Belt had a class as well as an ethnic element as the accompanying explanation of the social roots of Lochaber's 'less intelligent lower strata' made clear:

> During the years of the Second World War, Loch Eil was full of tankers and other ugly naval vessels. On its shores at Annat and Corpach, squalid clusters of prefabricated houses sprang up and to them came the scum of the industrial midlands of England and Scotland.[45]

The roots of such disparaging contrasts between the Gael and non-Gael, the native Highlander and incomer 'scum' lay in the fundamentally essentialist way in which the case for Highland development was so frequently made. In a determination to try and retain a sense of the Highlands as 'the land of the Gael', economic progress in the Highlands was given qualified support from a very specific perspective. When *An Comunn* proclaimed that 'we welcome every effort that will give to our people a better standard of living and opportunities for happy work in their own land' as the context in which the organization 'must

---

42 Burnett, 'Cultural developments' (2005), pp 181–5. 43 See above, p. 215. 44 Maclean, *The Highlands* (1975), p. 19. 45 Ibid., p. 30.

work the harder to preserve the Gaelic language and all that it connotes', the telling qualifiers with which all enthusiasm was tempered were assistance 'to *our* people' living 'in *their* own land'.[46] It was a nativism and differentiating sense of ethnicity that drew on the *Gàidhealtachd*'s deep-rooted sense of social, ethnic and cultural injustice. It was, however, a differentiation from which even the most committed non-Gaelic Highland sympathizers were exempt, as evident in the observations of a correspondent to the *Stornoway Gazette* of 25 January 1952 on the work of Fraser Darling, the champion of crofting agriculture and the west Highland townships. In a letter entitled 'Crofters' rights', under the pseudonym 'Fearann Domhnaill', the contributor pointed out to his fellow Gaels, islanders and Highlanders: 'Dr Fraser Darling is "an outsider". He has had his look at the Highlands! But it is safe to say that he will live and die without ever knowing a lot of things which we know ourselves, who are Highlands born and bred'. The notion that any non-Gael had any genuine concern for the Gael was ridiculed: 'If others had their way with us we would have been driven into the Atlantic generations ago'.[47]

Attitudes within Lewis towards the non-Gael 'other' had already been hardening in the wake of the investigations of the Crofters Commission enquiry, a process that had brought to the fore a rather distasteful conflation of class and ethnicity in the attitude towards non-Gaels. In an argument over the rights of squatters on island crofting land, one member of a packed meeting in Lewis approvingly expressed the essential heart of the matter: 'The squatters are already with us [...]. They did not drop out of the skies; they are not foreigners – they are our own kith and kin'. No one objected to squatters who were fellow islanders, but a warning was put out that if squatters' rights were legalized, the position of the crofters may be jeopardized: 'I don't want any undesirables from the Gorbals or Galashiels to say they have as much right to the common grazings as I have. I can't see anything but chaos if we split up the island like this'.[48]

The expression of such essentialist ethnocentric 'kith and kin' attitudes within Gaeldom was not confined to those communities within the Gaelic Highlands where issues of access to land and housing were most acute. An examination of any of the exhortations delivered by successive presidents of *An Comunn* makes it clear that they were indicative of a commonly held belief prevalent within and throughout Gaeldom during the period 1939–65. What the Highlands, Scotland and Britain as a whole were experiencing, the context in which *An Comunn* was struggling to sustain the language and culture of the Gael, was 'the economic maelstrom causing depopulation and consequent loss to the motherland of her most able sons and daughters, many of whom are Gaelic speaking'. The tenor of the argument and the tone of the rhetoric were

46 *AG* (1950), 139.   47 *Stornoway Gazette*, 25 Jan. 1952.   48 *Stornoway Gazette*, 11 Jan. 1952.

unambiguous. Occasionally, the problem of Highland depopulation was presented in national terms as an issue facing the whole country: 'Numerous influential bodies are concerned to stop this loss of our lifeblood, and every Scotsman should be moved to work ceaselessly towards this end, if he cherishes the worth of his people both in the economic and cultural life of this country'. More often it was presented in the clear and exclusivist terms of Gaelic ethnicity and race as in the exhortation of *An Comunn*'s president, John Bannerman, in 1951: 'Let the planners save the present stock of men and women from extinction, and their schemes will be built, not on sand, but securely founded on the rock that is the faith and culture of a noble people'. It was the duty of the country to honour its historic debt to this 'noble people' and save the homogeneity of the Gaelic race from dilution: 'Their [the Gaels] stock is not easily replaced nor can the acclimatization of the ages be ignored with impunity'.[49] In short, as well as having the historic claim, only Highlanders of true Gaelic pedigree had the essential right to live and work in their ethnic homeland.

From this perspective, the potential of modernity in terms of economic development, an improved infrastructure or an enhanced standard of living could be readily assimilated, even welcomed. The social consequences in terms of a changing 'way of life', or the adoption of a new lifestyle, particularly by Highland youth, were a matter of regret and a challenge to reassert traditional values. The real threat was to the notion of Gaelic ethnicity and identity that was the essence of the belief in the Highlands as the *Gàidhealtachd*, As a cultural construct, the Highlands were only meaningful as 'the land of the Gael', the former being inconceivable without the latter. Examples of such 'inclusivist' thought not only pervaded the pages of *An Gaidheal*, but were also recurring in other publications based in the Highlands or concerning Gaeldom. The problems that such an ethnocentric notion of the Highlands posed in terms of a response to modernity for a region that was not only a geographical entity but also an ethnic homeland were neatly summed up by the assessment of the challenge as outlined by the president of *An Comunn*:

> today the long overdue development of our natural resources and native industries – together with the much needed transport improvements and the possible introduction of new industries [...] which will increase labour demand – may make the phrase 'Highland development' true territorially, but not necessarily true racially.[50]

One consequence was that for some Gaels there was a feeling that representations made on their behalf by others, including non-Gaelic-speaking Highlanders, were insufficient. This contributed to a widespread feeling of

49 *AG* (1951), 98, 108. 50 *AG* (1950), 139.

anger that *their* voice was not being heard or recognized by officialdom. In the context of the deep-rooted and pervasive economic and social transformation ushered in by war, welfarism and reconstruction, these concerns and grievances would continue to prove problematic as the Gaelic language and culture struggled to adapt to the reality of the modern Highlands.

CONCLUSION: THE FUTURE OF THE HIGHLANDS?

Morley's assessment that Gaelic would endure through the difficult times of the 1940s was partially accurate, though the 'scions' were now taking up residence in urban centres, Glasgow in particular, in growing numbers. The census figures for 1961 revealed a further fall in the number of Gaelic speakers, and the continued recession of the language to the western extremities of northern Scotland, with sizeable pockets in the urban areas to the south. Therefore, at first glance, *An Comunn*'s efforts to preserve the language and culture in what was regarded as its natural environment of the Highlands had proven to be ineffective. In a sense, this reflected a broader failure by successive governments and their agencies to resolve the longstanding 'Highland problem' of unemployment and depopulation. Despite repeated references by government bodies and policy informing individuals to the sensitivities involved in order to preserve the 'Highland way of life', various schemes foundered.

This chapter has demonstrated some of the reasons for this stasis, in particular the deep mistrust by many Gaels of initiatives stemming from outwith the *Gàidhealtachd*. The image of the Gael, subject to so much mythologizing, certainly did not aid those arguing for decentralization of economic and social policies. However, some prominent Gaels were themselves guilty of perpetuating the romanticized misrepresentations. The president of *An Comunn*, while welcoming the economic developments taking place in the Highlands of the 1950s, presented a number of caveats, one of which was the need to preserve and expand on 'the spiritual attributes of the people'.[51] However, as other, more astute commentators noted, the improvement in Highlanders' standard of living was exposing Gaels to a different value system to a far greater degree than ever before, contributing to further out-migration and a detachment from the 'Highland way of life' as embodied in crofting, the Gaelic language and its associated cultural 'traditions'.

By the late 1960s, many of the tensions deriving from this fundamental shift in the cultural matrix in the *Gàidhealtachd* were all too apparent. *The future of the Highlands*, an edited collection of essays published in 1968, offered some trenchant and prescient commentary on the difficulties involved in the ongoing

51 *AG* (1951), 98, 108.

process of readjustment caused by modernization. The economic problems of the period were regarded as being essentially the same as the ones facing legislators in the 1950s, as outlined in various parliamentary documents and reports by successive governments. However, the '*current* Highland problem' was viewed as the product of recent historical events, 'persistent parliamentary indifference' and 'an emotional attachment to crofting as a way of life' that caused Highlanders and administrators to conveniently regard land as 'the basic economic resource of the Highlands and Islands'.[52] In a controversial essay, and courting a response that would challenge his own view that euphemism was 'a way of life in the north', Farquhar Gillanders went on to argue that tourism was not the basis for the region's economy due to its poor return and indeed its incompatibility with the 'Highland character'. Mindful that the focus on crofting was distracting attention from the underlying economic problems, nevertheless he called for a review of the crofting system in order to bring more land into cultivation – and with incoming families taking up the crofts if necessary.

Reflecting the beginnings of a shift in policy towards more industry being situated in the Highlands, Gillanders called for 'urbanized Highlanders' and others to be enticed to the region with the prospect of sustainable employment. With this inflow of people,

> there may well be life and prosperity in the glens in fifty years time, but without new blood there will be a vast army of pious old-age pensioners in strategic control of the Highlands and Islands before very long. The social atmosphere in any community will affect fundamentally the economic development of the area. I have nothing against old-age pensioners – but if you have no youth, no young men or young women living *all the year round* in the Highlands, then as a race we have no future, nor do we deserve one.[53]

The claim that these migrants would be encouraged north with industrial jobs comparable to those available elsewhere in Scotland, wanting 'to run their own lives according to their own lights' was certainly open to debate. However, their very presence would provoke controversy given the sensitivities involved, evident in the demand by another contributor to the book for 'native' control of Highland culture, ecology and economy.[54]

The slight dissonance between the assessment and prognosis for the Highlands between the various writers naturally reflected the backgrounds, interests and expertise of the different contributors. For those more concerned

---

52 Gillanders, 'Gaelic Scotland today', p. 97.   53 Ibid., pp 106, 114, 115.   54 Grimble, 'Introduction', pp 24–5.

with the cultural implications of the economic and social transformation in the Highlands, the emphasis was more on education, literature and the organizations that played an important role in seeking to preserve the Gaelic language. Kenneth D. MacDonald, while acknowledging the criticism meted out to *An Comunn* and the perceived failings of the National mod, nevertheless offered a sympathetic and appreciative assessment of what this organization had been trying to achieve and the recent measures undertaken to broaden its activities. The stark reality of linguistic and cultural displacement and decline in the late 1960s was apparent with MacDonald's conclusion that perhaps the time had come for those in 'Gaelic conservation strategy [...] to concentrate all the effort on the Outer Isles [...] and to accept the fact that in other areas the battle is already lost'.[55]

The idea of pooling all resources to focus in on Hebridean Gaels, though based on a realistic assessment of the dramatic decline in the language, would perhaps have appeared as defeatist to Derick Thomson, resolute in guarding, nurturing and fostering the still active Gaelic tradition 'for the common weal'.[56] This Lewis-born Gael, editor of the Glasgow-based periodical *Gairm* since its inception in 1952, charted the way in which Gaelic literature and the arts had developed down to the late 1960s. Though certainly cognisant of the harsh realities of Gaelic Scotland, with an overall 'decline in racial pride and solidarity', Thomson nevertheless felt that the beginnings of a more assertive reaction by Gaels offered some hope for the future. After delineating the range of positions within the Gaelic-speaking world between the more rural-based 'local sector' and an urban-centred 'modern coterie', Thomson fixed his attention on how the metropolitan Gaelic 'artist' could take the language forward. Throughout his essay, the impact of modernization on the Gaelic community was evident, both as a contributory factor to the shifts in type, number and range of material and also as an inspiration for comment and critique. The resultant 'radical reappraisal' in literature and the arts over the previous twenty years had produced 'a very large cleavage of opinion'. In itself, that reflected both the difficulties and opportunities for Gaels across Scotland as they reacted, adjusted and adapted to the modern conditions now widespread throughout the Highlands.[57]

In a courageous and far-sighted contribution, John A. Smith focused on the need to factor culture and education into economic development policies. He argued that the authorities had a 'moral obligation' to ensure that the intended repopulation and revitalization of the Highlands now envisaged by planners, economists and politicians should have a Gaelic 'outlook'.[58] He urged these groups to recognize the suitability of graduates with a background in Celtic and

55 MacDonald, 'Gaelic language', pp 195–6. 56 Thomson, 'Literature and the arts' (1968), p. 237. 57 Ibid., pp 207, 210–14. 58 Smith, 'Gaelic culture' (1968), pp 84–5.

Gaelic Studies for administrative posts in central government or agencies like the HIDB to help realize this vision. Smith himself argued that the forces for change unleashed in the Highlands in recent years were not necessarily a malignant influence:

> Constructive use must be made by all concerned with Gaelic and Gaelic culture of certain forces which will otherwise help to destroy the Highland ways of life and the Gaelic language. The myth that it was the 1745 and forced clearances which began the process of change in the Highland way of life should be exploded once and for all. This process had begun long before 1745 and it was inevitable. The Clearances were not all forced on the people: many of them were voluntary movements by the Highlanders themselves. Furthermore, the clearance movement has become far more widespread and continuous in the last fifty years. The underlying forces which have been at work thus for centuries are mainly social and economic. They are not necessarily destructive in aim nor in result.[59]

These hard-hitting comments on the powerfully emotive topic of the Highland Clearances were part of a wider appeal to fellow-Gaels and Highlanders to embrace the 'modern forces' emanating from the new development agencies and the mass media and harness them for the benefit of Gaelic culture.

In a similar vein, Smith, though acknowledging that education had a 'double-edged' impact on the language, felt that the main responsibility for the continuance of the language 'must rest on those who were born into it and speak it naturally'. The perennial problem of losing the 'intellectual cream of the Gaelic-speaking areas' to further education and careers in the professions could be partially resolved if more jobs were made available to Highland graduates.[60] He called on Highland-based Gaels to demand further improvements in education provision, particularly in formerly neglected areas like the Gaelic heartlands themselves and with a broader approach than before, to encompass adult and youth groups. It was clear from Smith's comments that he believed that an attitudinal change was necessary to ensure bilingualism was made to work and Gaelic language activities in the now-threatened areas of the *Gàidhealtachd* were not regarded 'in some degree as alien or irrelevant to it'.[61] For this successful Uist-born Gael, the language and culture of the Gael were at a crossroads. Smith presciently anticipated some of the ways in which language regeneration could occur. Where some were resigned to further linguistic and cultural loss due to the detrimental impact of adverse government policies or complacency and division among Gaels, he identified opportunities to take both the language and

59 Ibid., pp 72–3, 90. 60 Ibid., pp 72–3, 81. 61 Ibid., pp 80–1, 88–90.

the Highland people forward. Without this type of approach, he warned that the future for the Gaelic language and culture was bleak:

> There is not the slightest doubt but that the position of Gaelic has been adversely affected by the general malaise which has lain for centuries over the area where it is spoken. Hundreds of thousands of Gaelic speakers have been lost through heavy emigration and continuous depopulation, the old ways of life which helped to protect the language have broken up, the urge is on Gaelic-speaking youth as elsewhere to break with the past – in all of these changes the language has grievously suffered. Its comparative isolation has protected Gaelic in certain areas from earlier disappearance, but nowadays with the improvement of transport, the threat of mass pressures like TV, from the outside world, and the deliberate planting of industrial centres in the Highland area there are new forces at work potentially more powerful and more strategically placed for the obliteration of the language.[62]

---

62 Ibid., p. 81.

8

Conclusion

The consciousness of the Gaelic mind may be described as possessing historical continuity and religious sense; it may be said to exist in a vertical plane. The consciousness of the modern Western world, on the other hand, may be said to exist in a horizontal plane, possessing breadth and extent, dominated by scientific materialism and a concern with purely contemporary happenings. There is a profound difference between the mental attitudes, which represent the different spirits of different ages, and are very much in conflict.

John Lorne Campbell, *Strange things* (1968)[1]

The evidence is not produced, and it is difficult to accept the statement that it [crofting] is a free and independent way of life when it is not self-supporting but dependent on substantial subsidies from the industrial civilization; nor can the intrinsic quality be distinguished when the largest auxiliary employment – weaving in the island of Lewis – is regulated by a trade union enforcing the closed shop. It is possible, however, to argue about a mystique, which must be either accepted or rejected. If accepted, it will have to be paid for by the rest of the country – a political decision.

Joseph F. Duncan, 'Has crofting a future?' (*c*.1953)[2]

The representation of the 'Gaelic mind' by Campbell and the critical assessment of the 'intrinsic quality' of crofting, seen by Duncan as being at the heart of the Highland way of life, reflect two very different perspectives. Yet, ultimately, these ostensibly differing internal and external assessments concur on their sense of the uniqueness of the Highlands. The 'conflict' referred to by Campbell corresponds to the 'clash of social philosophies' identified by Collier in the Highlands of the 1940s. It reflects an internalized assessment of the dramatic transformation taking place in the Highlands and Islands in the years after the

---

1 Campbell and Hall, *Strange things* (1968), pp 6–7. 2 NLS: NM Acc 8503/2, 'Has crofting a future?' by Duncan. Perhaps best known for his role in founding the Scottish Farm Servants' Union, of which he was secretary from 1912 to 1945, but at this time (the 1950s) chairman of the Scottish Agricultural Improvement Council and Governor of the North of Scotland College of Agriculture. Duncan was also a member of the team that produced the Hilleary Report (1938), but he subsequently resigned.

war and epitomizes the sense of struggle from those clinging to a lifestyle, a culture and a process of thought in the face of fundamental change. Duncan's attempts to inject a degree of realism into the debate on the recommendations of the Taylor Report on crofting reform reflects the sense of frustration held by those 'outside' the region at the difficulties encountered in the modernization of the Highlands and Islands.

Duncan's recognition of the politicized nature of Highland development was certainly evident in successive governments' treatment of the 'Highland problem' in the post-war era. The extent to which a vibrant Gaelic culture and a distinctive 'Highland' way of life could exist in a society that was by then heavily integrated into the rest of Scotland struck at the core of the problem for those 'within' and 'below' the Highlands. The exposure to an 'alien' value system vexed those determined to retain the Gaelic language and culture in their historic homeland. In order to fully understand the redefined post-war Highlands, we must take into account both internal and external discourses. Campbell, the Gaelic scholar and noted folklorist, was immersed in the culture of the Gaels; he was fully aware of their place in history and their sense of patria. This multi-layered contextualizing mechanism would also have applied to Duncan, even if only at a latent level. No one could escape the loaded history of the Highlands. It was a key element informing and shaping these conflicting views and, indeed, their legacy of increasingly paradoxical and irreconcilable positions.

THE CULTURAL PERSPECTIVE: HIGHLANDS AS *GÀIDHEALTACHD*

The process by which the Highlands became a cultural construction relates to past negotiations between, and within, internal and external images, motifs and icons. The 'voices' that conveyed these messages adopted many different accents. For Gaels, the collective consciousness was fashioned by what they thought, read and sang about. The particular carriers of the Gaels' collective consciousness were destined to perform different roles. Poets and songsters acted as the barometers of local feeling; they internalized the sentiments of the Gaelic people. Their legacy was to leave a rich repository of material that would be drawn from by future generations of Gaels. The decline in the oral tradition affected this particular transmission of collective thought, but the buoyancy of the urban Gaelic societies, the growing strength of the local and national mods and the continuation of the ceilidh, albeit in more of an artificial way, ensured that the most popular Gaelic songs continued to frame the experiences of the past within a particular context. In the nineteenth century, there were also writers who recorded for posterity the brutality of the Clearances and the misery of emigration. The powerful and emotive historiography that emerged acted in a similar manner to the poems and songs. But as well as shaping Highlanders' perceptions of the changing circumstances of their lives, these texts conveyed and interpreted the 'moment' for an increasingly inquisitive southern audience. Such polemical pieces of writing had an immense influence, not least because they enjoyed a wide circulation, evident in the constant reissuing of seminal texts that were circulated both within and outwith the Highlands. Crucially, they were still the dominant means of interpreting the history of the Highlands in the period between 1939 and 1965.

From such sources, certain dominant themes emerged. Given the wholesale and comprehensive nature of the changes that the Highlands witnessed after the 1745 Jacobite Rising, the initial reaction of Gaels was to grieve for the loss of their status, their respect and, ultimately, their homeland. The perception that their contribution to Highland, Scottish and European civilizations was being cast aside amid rapid changes to their physical environment instilled in the mentality of the Gael a feeling of being victimized. Moreover, it was people without any comprehension of the Gaelic world who carried out this maltreatment. These 'improvers' were internalized into the Gaelic consciousness as oppressors who were ultimately forcing Gaels to emigrate. Exile led the diasporic Gaels to romanticize their former life, preserving it in aspic as a fulfilling, idyllic experience. This tempered their attitudes towards the new, alien environment and created a strand of anti-industrialism that pervaded Highland society through to the post-war years. Within the context of the mid-nineteenth-century famine and destitution, an evangelical tradition came to permeate large parts of Highland society. This indoctrinated many of the people with a fatalistic acceptance of their economic hardship and cultural marginalism. This submissive attitude would eventually be overcome, but another response to the famine was dependency. Within the Highlands, there was an increasing reliance on government intervention, which brought with it an externalization of control over the local economy, and over individual and collective destiny. This notion that it was incumbent upon the state to provide assistance to the Highlands would increase in tandem with the growing contribution, and sacrifice, of Gaels for the 'glory' of the British Empire. Arguments based on the obligation of government to intercede in Highland society were used not just by Gaels, but also by politicians and commentators – then, and now.

One of the paradoxes of the religious fervour that swept through many parts of the Highlands and Islands in the nineteenth century was that it did provide a sense of fortitude in a beleaguered and dispirited community. The leadership of the resistance movement of the late nineteenth century tapped into this resurgent ethnic identity. Contrasts were drawn between kindly, virtuous and honourable indigenes and avaricious, profligate 'invaders'. The wastefulness of a system that created wilderness out of life, preferred sheep, then deer, to humans, was emphasized and then used by Gaels to justify the agitation of the

1880s. In launching their attacks on the injurious system of land holding, Highland activists evoked the past, but for a purpose. Crofting, initially regarded as a diminution of clanship, was now revalorized as the essential embodiment of the 'Gaelic way of life'. Publicizing the stand taken against cruel landlordism and an unyielding state helped to foster an image of the Highlands as a crofting, and Gaelic, community. Improved communications to the south enabled Highlanders to ally themselves with both their own urban diaspora and an emergent labour movement. These connections combined to further facilitate the successful passage of the 1886 Crofters' Act. The latter became a symbolic victory for Gaels, regarded as a triumph in adversity for an oppressed people against an all-powerful force. The retelling of these aspects of Highland history became a powerful and constant reminder of the hard-won struggles to retain any semblance of living with dignity in the twentieth century. But in these early years of the 'modern' Highlands, the boundaries were set for subsequent discussions on the future of the region and its people.

The mental, cultural and physical boundaries of the modern Highlands were fashioned both by internal perspectives and by external perceptions. Following the 'pacification' of the clans in the wake of Culloden, the region acquired a new, reinvented significance as a different 'Highlands' and 'Highlander' were manufactured. The Ossianic movement was the initiating moment that triggered a series of successive presentations and re-presentations of the cultural capital of the Highlands and the meaning and value of its cultural landscape. Their combined impact had a major bearing on the attitudes towards the region in the post-war era, and arguably, still exist.

Those who sought out certain attributes in the 'noble savages' of the north, and looked for inspiration in the physical landscape, were drawn mainly from outside the region. But the creation of Highland cultural icons was a fluid process. As one discourse influenced another, some Gaels also contributed to the production of a *Gàidhealtachd* pastiche, exemplified by the 'Celtic twilight' school. The extent to which the caricature became self-fulfilling is a moot point. Certainly, with the musical tradition of the bagpipes the military takeover of this particular aspect of Gaelic culture produced forms of music and a style of playing which was discordant with earlier versions – a practice only now being rectified. The same is true of Gaelic song, anglicized and sanitized for a wider audience, thus losing its essence in the translation. This deliberate gentrifying of Gaelic culture was also evident in a growing body of literature that falsified elements of the past for dramatic purpose. Even some of the dominant Gaelic poets and songsters of the era were drawn into this sentimentalism. In romanticizing about the pre-Clearance era as an idyllic existence, and contrasting that world with the alien, urban environment, their nostalgic reminiscences echo many of the sentiments of the 'Celticists'. This invective that was poured on the urban world encouraged an identification of the 'non-Highland' world to the south with destitution, decadence and industry. Thus, the key themes identified from the post-Culloden years filtered through into the discussion on the Highlands in the post-war period and although the gap between the myth and reality of the Highlands led to the rehabilitation of the Highlander, the damage inflicted was deep-rooted and pervasive.

THE ECONOMIC DEVELOPMENT PERSPECTIVE: THE 'HIGHLAND PROBLEM'

One of the most damaging effects of these redefining processes was a bolstering of the belief that the Highlands as a region were the antithesis of progress. Culturally, the Highlands had become an imaginary world, a place where one could return to for comfort, succour and inspiration – but not a model for modern development. The search for spiritual solace, which encouraged a valorization of the Gael, also thereby confirmed the domination of the 'real' world over the 'other', and in so doing rendered the Highlander effectively impotent politically.[3] Though Peter Womack pursues this line of inquiry with regard to the eighteenth century, arguably it continued well into the modern period. The process of appropriating the images of the region and refashioning its essential features was exemplified by the creation of a debased Gaelicized national identity. This condemnation of the Highlander to a role on the margins of society was perpetuated by the nationalist discourse. Despite the decline in cultural nationalism in the post-war years, the association between the Highlander and the 'heart of Scotia' endured. Therefore, the ascribed identity of the Highlander, imbued with certain values, continued to undermine the attempts of Highland activists to inject a degree of realism into the debate on Highland development.

During the Second World War, politicians and governments were keen to arrest the all-pervasive sense of decline, despair and fatalistic abandonment of hope that dominated the Highlands of the inter-war period. After the war, a new political order emerged. Tom Johnston's impressive stewardship of the Secretary of State's office showed what could be done. His drive and enthusiasm invigorated the Scottish state apparatus and signalled a fresh approach from government towards the Highlands with a raft of investigative committees set up to address different facets of the 'Highland problem'. But the emphasis on a planned and integrative approach to improve the material standards of Highlanders did produce dissent.

The criticism levelled at government economic policy in Scotland, and the Highlands and Islands in particular, was easily dismissed by central government

---

3 Womack, *Improvement and romance*, p. 166.

and the civil servants at St Andrew's House. A paradox emerged: the devolution of more administrative functions to Edinburgh with the simultaneous reduction in the powers of the Scottish public to influence policy. The growing state apparatus needed a strong Secretary of State to represent Scottish interests in the cabinet and to harness and control the mandarins at St Andrew's House. Johnston's decision to retire from politics in 1945 left the ship without a captain, and the calibre of subsequent ministers did not match him until Willie Ross took the helm in 1964. But, by then, much damage had been done and the administrative machine had grown immeasurably. Economic and social policy decisions were either taken with reference to overall UK policy or taken for political expediency, at a time when the state became increasingly intrusive in the lives of the Scottish public. Because of the blanket implementation of government policy, which stemmed from the way the 'Highland problem' was addressed and conceptualized, the perception among all the different sections of the Highland population was that central government was not listening to their specific needs.

Throughout the period from the war to the establishment of the Highlands and Islands Development Board, the population of the Highlands and Islands continued to decline, albeit at a much less alarming rate than the inter-war period.[4] A corollary of that process was the deep-seated malaise within the community that threatened to obliterate Gaelic as a living language. The momentous decision of Highland and Island MPs to establish an all-Gaelic lobby group in 1965 reflected a growing concern in the *Gàidhealtachd* that something needed to be done in order to save the historic tongue.[5] Governments had attempted, albeit indirectly, to maintain the cultural fabric of the region. Cultural aspects of the Highlands were somewhat feebly emphasized in relation to local industry and education. Commitments were made to continue encouraging local industry projects, especially those that utilized local products, as this was regarded as complementary to the Highland way of life. The ambiguity surrounding what government actually meant by the 'Highland way of life' was unfortunate. The failure to recognize the diversity of the Highlands, and therefore the complexity and multi-layered nature of the 'Highland problem', hindered progress in the region's economic and social development.

This fundamental weakness of government policy was evident in the

4 MacLean, 'Scottish Highland migration' (2000).   5 The indifference towards the Gaelic language from Westminster during the years 1939–65 is reflected in the complete omission from Hansard of any entry entitled 'Gaelic' until the parliamentary session of 1962–3. Certainly this would be symptomatic of wider concerns being paramount among politicians, but the fact that it took until the beginning of the 1960s for Gaelic to feature in parliamentary records would tend to support earlier comments on the development of a Scottish dimension to parliamentary affairs and the rumblings of nationalist discontent emanating from Scotland. The thorny issue of legal recognition for Gaelic was raised in 1965 by Malcolm MacMillan, the Labour MP for the Western Isles. But Willie Ross, the Secretary of State of Scotland, adopted a delaying tactic though he did agree to meet 'authentic Highland sources' to balance up the bald statistics of the 1961 census. See *Hansard*, vol. 718, pp 1011–12.

difficulties faced by a series of government agencies. Though primarily set up to address the socio-economic problems of the Highlands and Islands, the cultural fabric of the region was also recognized as an element worth preserving. But in trying to realize their stated aims, the agencies were thwarted by the impulses of the past. For example, the activities of the NSHEB were viewed with suspicion by Highlanders and with concern by those with a vested interest in preserving the Highlands as a recreational retreat. The establishment of a Highland Panel limited as an advisory body was regarded as a mistake by Highland activists fully aware of the magnitude of the task in hand and now denied the necessary powerful development body to implement and coordinate the different programmes. The failure to empower Highlanders and their agencies also restricted the activities of the Forestry Commission in its negotiations to buy more land from private landowners. This problem also burdened the Crofters Commission, but this particular agency had many more problems to face due to the subtle and nuanced history of the 'crofting way of life'.

Joseph Duncan's sober response to the Taylor Commission's report, with which this chapter opened, showed that if crofting was treated as a straightforward agricultural issue, then certain obvious solutions presented themselves. But, despite recognizing the diversity of experience in the crofting counties, the subsequent legislation failed to differentiate between the varied needs of crofters. It was no coincidence that the most vocal criticism emanated from the Gaelic-speaking crofting communities. Here, reverence for the victory of 1886 was strongest and a reluctance to sever ties with the Gaelic diaspora militated against attempts to eradicate absenteeism. There were also ethnocentrist views expressed by those seeking to ensure that the *Gàidhealtachd* was protected from an influx of 'alien' values. Therefore, by imposing blanket reforms, the region was treated as a monolithic entity: a crofting community. It meant that any proposed solutions to the long-standing and diverse problems would collapse under the weight of past battles.

CONFLICTING VIEWS ON 'THE COLOSSUS OF ADVANCING MATERIALISM'

The publications of those 'inside' the Highland agencies offer a fascinating insight into the problems inherent in modernizing a region with a strong sense of its own history while trying to preserve a distinct way of life. Despite the fact that these individuals were more aware than most of the complexity of Highland history, however, they were not immune to restating the cherished myths of the Highlands. Naomi Mitchison and Neil Gunn were particularly forceful in expressing the opinion that development should be in keeping with the physical and cultural landscape of the *Gàidhealtachd*. The mainstays of the Highland economy, as envisaged by these policy informers, were the primary industries of crofting and fishing allied to the potential of more modish opportunities, particularly tourism. Basically, any pioneer projects that helped to keep the young people in the Highlands were deemed acceptable, providing the unsightly sprawl of the industrial centres of the Central Belt was not replicated in the north. In a sense, and despite their internationalist perspectives, they were too close to the problem. Radical measures were put aside in favour of a gradualist approach that was seen as better suited to the Highland, or Gaelic, psyche. But in some of their proposals for regenerating the region, there was a certain misplaced optimism, and their understanding of the Gaelic Highlands was somewhat limited.

The notion that the crofters' or Highlanders' lifestyle was in some way cocooned from the more materialist and brutalized world of industry was decidedly naïve. Certainly, the outlying communities of the *Gàidhealtachd* with their distinctive oral culture and traditions offered a different perspective on the world, but they had never been totally isolated. What did happen after 1945, however, was that the pace and extent of external penetration quickened and intensified as the region was further 'opened-up' to a new wave of modernizing forces. A failure or an unwillingness to recognize the breadth, depth and significance of the impact of these changes by so many key policy informers within the Highland and Gaelic community made a realistic assessment of the fragility of both region and culture all the more difficult. The point that was recognized by all too few was that Gaelic had reached a critical juncture, whereby the younger members of the community were rejecting the old ways of life and being exposed to challenges from the English language of a scale and power that would have been barely comprehensible to their forebears. Moreover, as we have seen, this repeated emphasis on a different value system, and a unique way of life, fostered an unhealthy reaction among the population of the Highlands. In particular, a sense of injustice and superiority formed a useful breeding ground for overtly ethnocentrist sentiments. Prior to the war, the *Gàidhealtachd* clearly was a region with distinct characteristics, but it is disingenuous to refer to a 'unique way of life' during this period of rapid transition.

John Lorne Campbell's faith in a distinctive mental outlook was understandable, given his scholarly interest in recording the folklore of the Gael, coupled with the fact that he lived on the exposed Hebridean island of Canna. But the singers, storytellers and tradition-bearers that he was busy recording were dying out as the Gaelic world became integrated into the rest of Scotland and exposed to other value systems through mass communication and the influx of non-Gaels. Another perspective on the state of post-war Gaelic culture came from Averil Morley, a Gaelic research assistant with the 'West Highland Survey'. She perceptively pointed out that

> The Gaels are a people with deep roots which still hold fast to an earlier time, though the vine may climb by the support of other

cultures which it will cover and mask. But the plant and flower of Gaeldom have survived into a climate and environment no longer kind. Gaeldom as a culture is flowering no more and the plant is sick, though scions from the old stock grafted into a fresh environment bloom anew. We are concerned here with the sick but surviving culture of Highland Gaeldom. The attitudes of Scotland and of England towards the earlier and in some ways primitive culture surviving on their fringes are mixed. The pragmatists, a vocal crowd, say 'Let it die and the sooner the better'. The sentimentalists, equally vocal [...] look back over their shoulder, refuse to see the inexorable process of change in the Gaels' environment, and would have the culture stand still in time.[6]

Some of the more perceptive observers recognized the depth of the changes and the critical consequences in which economic development and cultural survival were inextricably, if sometimes confusingly, linked. This recognition that the edifice of the Gaelic world was breaking down and becoming even more dependent on an urban diaspora was written in the 1940s. Derick Thomson, writing in 1954, confirmed the break-up of the Gaelic-speaking communities due to the 'infiltration of the English language'.[7] Those Highlanders who lived through the period 1939–65 did experience profound changes in their everyday lives.

It was perhaps no mere coincidence that just over a decade later, in 1965, *An Comunn Gàidhealach* began publishing a series of pamphlets designed to inform their members, and others, on different aspects of Highland – and by implication – Gaelic society. They give the impression that the Highlander had to be instructed on what was inherent to his or her identity. For example,

> Who then are the Highlanders and who represent the Gael today? Residents in the Highland counties with surnames prefixed 'Mac' are almost always of the old stock but so are Campbells, Frasers and Camerons. It cannot truly be said that all with Highland surnames are Highlanders, for example Harold Macmillan, the former prime minister, is an Englishman of Highland descent. In the end, language is the surest test. For it 'identifies people'. Gaelic identifies the Gael. Included in this identification are Gaelic speakers bearing Lowland names, and the Gaelic-speaking Canadians of Nova Scotia. Residents in the Highland counties whose parents or remoter ancestors were Gaelic speakers are Gaels by residence and by representation.[8]

6 Morley and Darling, 'Social situation', p. 281.   7 Thomson, 'Gaelic oral tradition' (1954), p. 16.   8 Mackay, *Who are the Highlanders?* (1966), p. 3. This was no. 1 in a series published by *ACG*.

This ambiguity between Highlander and Gael was also evident in the second pamphlet, *Highland way of life: today*, which was published in 1966. Frank Thompson claimed that

> though no longer members of the isolated communities they used to be, the inhabitants still retain the characteristics which have distinguished them throughout the ages – almost living anachronisms. It is for this reason that many incomers to the Gaidhealtachd, though they may spend their whole lives in the area, are never quite able to merge completely into what is the Highland way of life.

Voicing sentiments redolent of the 'Celtic twilight' school, Thompson continued:

> The Highland way of life is many things to many people. To the true-born Highlander, it is the reason for an existence which brings the spiritual and material things of life together in a quite unique coalescence found nowhere else in the world.[9]

To what extent these 'characteristics' were 'unique' to the Highlands is a moot point, given the degree of change ushered in during the post-war period, but what these opinions do reveal is that ideas of Highland or Gaelic essentialism were prevalent.[10] However, whatever fundamental qualities had come to define the Highlands and its people were now in need of reconfiguration.

Others Gaels were keen for Highlanders to move forward and lay aside the problems of a bygone era; aware that regurgitating clichés that emphasized the exclusivity of the region removed the onus of responsibility from the population to act. Farquhar Gillanders, for example, argued in 1968 that the 'real hope for the Highlands today [...] is in the courage to implement proved economic principles'. A strong advocate of reforming the crofting system – 'It is not the possession of land that is important: it is how the land is being used' – Gillanders continued:

> The Highlander must cease to regard himself as a member of a chosen race to whom normal economic laws do not apply. If he – and the Highland administrators – accept this reorientation, then industrialists and others may yet become interested, positively, in the Highland economy and its problems. Neither cultural nor spiritual

---

9 Thompson, *Highland way of life – today* (1966). This was no. 2 of *ACG*'s series.   10 It is worth pointing out that this deep attachment to the land, history, language, customs and folklore was also evident elsewhere in rural Scotland. These regions await further research into how the post-1939 economic and social changes impacted on their cultural sense of identity.

distinctiveness can be maintained much longer unless a sounder economic basis to the community is devised. It is not enough for the Highlander to look back and bemoan his lot. He must assert himself.[11]

Sympathetic outsiders, primarily interested in the physical splendour of the Highland landscape, were also expressing concern on the dangers development posed for the land itself. In a 1961 study commissioned by the National Trust for Scotland, the author, W.H. Murray, concluded that his survey 'revealed that the face of the Scottish Highlands is changing greatly', primarily from the work of the NSHEB and the Forestry Commission.[12]

Within the Highlands, Murray's survey appears to have been received with little comment. Gillanders appeals for more dynamism within rural communities, free from the 'sentiment and emotion [that] persistently bedevil Highland economic analysis', were met with a more vigourous but mixed response by crofters – testament to the fact that this section of the region's population was not a monolithic entity, and that they were becoming increasingly non-representative of Highland society as a whole. The strongest resistance to change was, perhaps understandably, from those Gaelic-speaking areas witnessing such a fundamental transformation to their cultural being. Moreover, because the Highlands were, and arguably still are, viewed through the accreted layers of history, the influence of the past acted as the prism through which the transformation was viewed throughout this period of economic and social development.

While researching the background material for his polemical book, *The Highland Clearances* (1963), John Prebble received a letter signed 'an exile from Kildonan'. Referring to his old Sutherland township, a place where the most infamous clearances were captured by Donald MacLeod in his *Gloomy memories*, the émigré asked:

> What is the position in Kildonan today? Six alien proprietors owning land and water (where once hundreds of good, happy people lived), a red Post Office van, a score of gamekeepers and shepherds. In addition to deer, grouse and salmon, the proprietors do quite a sideline in sheep and cattle. They sometimes open baby shows and strut at Highland games, and the people think it fine.[13]

Thus, the defining moments of the Highlanders' inheritance were evoked to analyze Sutherland society in the 1960s. Therefore, the 'deep roots' of Gaeldom referred to by Morley ensured that the Highlands were conceptualized in a certain way. But, while her comments held true for the Gael, they were equally

---

11 Gillanders, 'Gaelic Scotland today', p. 148.   12 Murray, *Highland landscape* (1962), pp 9–19.
13 Prebble, *Highland Clearances*, fn., p. 102.

applicable to those 'outside' of the Gaelic world. It is only by recognizing these parallel processes and interactions that we can gain an understanding of the tensions incurred in the transformation of the Highlands and Islands of Scotland during the years between 1939 and 1965.

BURDENS OF THE PAST: LESSONS FOR THE FUTURE

Feumaidh mi dhol chun taigh-tasgaidh	I must go to the museum
as aonais duslach an fheòir	without the dust of the grass
air m'aodach,	on my clothes
dh'fhaicinn uidheaman m'eachraidh	to see the tools of my history
mus tèid an leth-shealladh	before the half-sight
den leth-sgeul	of the half-story
a th'agam	I have
a dhìth	is swept
leis an sguab th'air cùl mo shàil.	away by the brush at my heels.
Feumaidh mi leabhar bhith deas air mo shùil	I must have a book for my eyes
de bhriathran nan làithean a dh'fhalbh,	of the words of days gone by
feumaidh mi leughadh fa chomhair an àm	I must read it when facing the time
tha cànan an cunnart dhol balbh.	a language threatens to go dumb.
Feumaidh mi leabhar a dh'innseas dhomh sgeul	I must have a book that will tell me a story
nach eil idir air bilean an t-sluaigh,	that's not on the lips of the people,
a dhol gu fear eile 'son barrachd de dh'fhios	must go to someone else for more information
's de thuigse air adhbhar na truaigh.	and understanding of the reason for grief.
Màiri NicGumaraid,	Mary Montgomery,
'An taigh-tasgaidh 's an leabhar'.[14]	'The museum and the book'.

In 2007, the 'Highland year of culture' offered a justified moment for celebration, but also a useful opportunity for reflection. Undoubtedly, much had improved in the region since the establishment of the HIDB in 1965, not least the reversal of decades of demographic decline.[15] The intervening years had also seen a diversification in the economic sector as successive initiatives had struggled to overcome the challenges involved in trying to realize sustained growth. In social terms, the people of the Highlands had benefited from advances in areas such as transport, communication, housing and educational facilities to ensure parity in living standards with other parts of Scotland. However, these positive aspects are tempered by the knowledge that parts of the region remain susceptible to economic and social decay due to the fragility associated with living in a relatively isolated and marginal landscape, and depopulation continues at the margins. It is in these vulnerable communities that tensions over cultural

---

14 Mary Montgomery was born in Lewis 1955 and started writing poetry at Aberdeen University in 1974. This extract is published in Whyte (ed.), *An aghaidh na sìorradheachd* (1991), pp 174–7.   15 Burnett, '"Cultural museum"' (2001), pp 61–4.

identity are at their most acute. It is not insignificant that the opening essay in the flagship publication, *Fonn's Duthchas: land and legacy*, was entitled 'The Scottish Highlands: a contested country'.[16] It serves as an implicit recognition that the conflicts and tensions within the discourse summarized in this book linger as live and problematic issues within the region.

The processes at work in the 1980s when Mary Montgomery lamented the loss of the 'living tradition' and the consignment of her history and culture to commodification as heritage in a museum have continued and intensified. Although the ongoing Gaelic renaissance has created some grounds for optimism, the language remains in a parlous state with continuing decline in the number of Gaelic speakers and a further spatial retreat of the language.[17] Over the subsequent three decades, there has been a significant increase in the profile, promotion and recognition of Gaelic language and culture.[18] Yet, as recent research makes clear, what is involved is a complex process of context and contingency 'giving rise to questions such as, *who does Gaelic belong to?*'[19]

For some, however, a more fundamentalist approach is championed: 'As many Gaels self-consciously jettison the reminders of poverty from their lives in a headlong rush towards modernism and material wealth, there is a serious danger of violating the integrity of Gaeldom's cultural matrix'.[20] Imploring Gaels to reclaim their 'cultural resources [...] as their own and retell them to succeeding generations' raises the issue of who may assume ownership of the cultural capital of the *Gàidhealtachd*; or indeed the Highlands.[21] By underlining the shifting demographic profile of Gaelic learners, as well as the dramatic weakening of the traditional bounded concept of the Highlands as the *Gàidhealtachd*, this process also raises the implicit question: who do the Highlands belong to?

Yet although the tensions and paradoxes associated with the cultural ownership of the Highlands have become increasingly acute in recent years, issues of identity and belonging have often been integral to discussions on Highland development. Certainly, seminal publications by those with a Gaelic and Highland background in the 1930s and 1960s made the important, and welcome, connections between economic and cultural development. After criticizing

---

16 Hunter, 'Scottish Highlands' (2006).   17 This was reflected in the last census figures, where the number of Gaelic speakers reached a nadir of just 58,650. See GRO Scotland, *2001 Census: Gaelic report* (2005). While the Outer Hebrides may remain the one area where the language is mostly the first language within the community, the reality of contemporary Scotland is that the most populous part of the *Gàidhealtachd* in the sense of the Gaelic-speech community is in urban Scotland.   18 Certainly, the upsurge in support and resources for the Gaelic language and culture is evident in the fields of education, governance, economics and the media. See McLeod (ed.), *Revitalising Gaelic in Scotland* (2006), for examples of recent discussions on these matters.   19 Oliver, 'Scottish Gaelic identities' (2005), p. 3, emphasis in the original.   20 Newton, *Scottish Gaelic world* (2000), p. 286.   21 Newton, *The world of the Scottish Highlanders* (2009), pp 5–6.

'politicians and reformers' for failing to recognize the need to coordinate these two aspects, Sir Alexander MacEwen laid out his analysis of the Highland problem in 1932. Fearing 'the days of the typical Highlander' to be numbered, MacEwen looked to Scandinavian models of rural development for inspiration.[22] He hoped that the creation of a 'genuine Gaelic atmosphere' would galvanize the 'spirit of the people', which in turn would revitalize the economy and stabilize the social fabric of the region.[23] As we have seen in section three, MacEwen's prescient analysis and trenchant views would find support in the following years from Highland and Gaelic activists but his ambitions for cultural regeneration were not forthcoming.

Writing in 1962, the geographers O'Dell and Walton were tentatively optimistic about the future of the Highlands, not least because, as they saw it, the economic changes in the post-war 'may mark a reversal of trends of a century'. Undoubtedly, the exigencies of war and subsequent reconstruction policies had helped improve the region's infrastructure but they had also enabled many of MacEwen's proposals to be realized. By the 1960s, hydro-electric schemes were widespread, small- and indeed larger-scale industrial ventures were appearing, the primary sector was relatively buoyant, and the 'considerable environmental advantages' of the region were bearing fruit with numerous tourist initiatives and afforestation schemes.[24] Depopulation was still a problem, however, and though in-migration was gradually increasing in certain parts of the region, calls for wholesale colonization schemes from 'outside' demonstrated a certain naïveté and ignorance about the cultural sensitivities involved as perceived from 'within'. The alternative or 'native' approach was outlined by Ian Grimble, one of the editors of *The future of the Highlands*, in 1968: 'even at this late hour there is no reason why the Highlands should not be recovered culturally, ecologically and economically *by their native inhabitants, and under their own control*' [my emphasis].[25] This determined, perhaps desperate, response demonstrated a perceptive awareness of the cultural implications of the recent economic and social transformation in the Highlands, but the tone also hinted at the realities of a more diverse and fractured Highland region.

Since the late 1960s, the cultural matrix of the Highlands has profoundly altered from those earlier times when the slogan of *tir is teanga*/'land and language' was so proudly evoked as a combined rallying call for Highlanders and a resurgent *Gàidhealtachd*. And yet, for many, the tendency to elide Highlander and Gael remains. Indeed, the discourse of race, so prevalent and problematic in the nineteenth and early twentieth centuries, lingers on in certain quarters. To some extent, it is encouraged by the elevation of culture as an economic driver

---

22 A recurrent theme among those interested in Highland development. See Brox, *Modernisation without centralisation* (2006). 23 MacEwen, *Thistle and the rose*, pp 200, 204, 212–14. 24 O'Dell & Walton, *Highlands of Scotland*, pp 212, 326. 25 Grimble, 'Introduction', pp 24–5.

in local community development, or the way in which heritage and cultural tourism are promoted.[26] As a consequence, in the 'contested country' of the Scottish Highlands, important questions of 'place', identity, belonging and cultural memory continue to attract attention.[27] They are both cause and effect of the tensions and differing opinions evident on a range of issues relating to the economic, social, environmental, political and cultural development of the region. Calls for a 'reimagining' of what it means to be a Gaelic speaker, in recognition of the ambiguities and fluidities involved in negotiating 'a cultural identity that is embedded in the assumed boundedness of the traditional *Gàidhealtachd*' are to be welcomed.[28] Calls for a reimagining of what it means to be 'a Gael' are more problematic. It is in this context that a broader understanding of the realities and complexities of contemporary experience for residents of the Highlands and Islands is vital for the region's future.

The past should not be forgotten; nor should it be abused. During the period between 1939 and 1965, the Highland and Gaelic 'way of life' was forced to confront what was seen as 'the colossus of advancing materialism'. This intensified after 1965 as Gaels and Highlanders gravitated towards a standard of living and a set of values that reflected an urban 'way of life'. Their descendants are the Gaelic and Highland youth of today. It is to be hoped that they will mature with a more secure sense of their Gaelic, and Highland, identity. The changing economic, social and cultural configurations of the Highlands necessitate an appreciation that essentialist views and binary oppositional stances are not productive positions to adopt now, or in the future. If the Highlands and Islands are to become a more inclusive, viable and sustainable community in this new millennium and the renaissance of the *Gàidhealtachd* is to be achieved, then the lessons of the past must be learned. What I have sought to identify during the period of 1939 to 1965, namely the growing dissonance between the idea of the Highlands as the 'land of the Gael' and the realities of contemporary experience, is still with us today. It remains one of the central issues that needs to be addressed, but as this study has identified, this is not as simple as it seems. However, in recognizing the shifting cultural landscape, the hope is that further reflective research will emerge to take the debate forward.

---

26 Ray, 'Local rural development' (1997); Withers, 'Place, memory, monument' (1996); Basu, *Highland homecomings* (2007). 27 For a detailed discussion on the theoretical underpinnings of the concept of 'place', consult the essays in Massey and Jess (eds), *A place in the world?* (1995). 28 Oliver, 'Scottish Gaelic identities', p. 22.

Bibliography

PRIMARY

Archival
NLS   Neil Miller Gunn MSS Dep 209.
NLS   Naomi Mitchison MSS Acc 8503.
NLS   Fionn MacColla (Tom MacDonald) MSS Dep 239.
NAS   AF81/1, 'Notes for the secretary of state'.
NAS   AF81/ 2–5, 7, 8 Commission of enquiry into crofting conditions: notes of evidence.
NAS   DD15/3/30 Highland development files: Note of Advisory Panel in Highland development's visit to Norway.
NAS   DD 15/1–9 Highland development files.
NAS   SEP12/5 Highland Panel: Highland Development Programme: progress reports 1–12, 1951–60.
NAS   SEP12/481 Highland Panel: Land-use in Highlands report by Agriculture and Forestry Group: drafting, 1963–4.
NAS   SEP12/187 Highland Panel: Agriculture and Forestry Group: land-use report, 1964–5.

Government and related publications
A programme of Highland development (Edinburgh, 1950, Cmnd. 7976).
Advisory Panel on the Highlands and Islands (for the Department of Agriculture and Fisheries), *Land-use in the Highlands and Islands* (Edinburgh, 1964).
British Transport Commission, *The reshaping of British railways: part 1* [Beeching] *Report* (London, 1963).
Central Scotland plan, 1963 (Edinburgh, Cmnd. 2188, 1963).
Committee on Scottish administration (Edinburgh, Cmnd. 5563, 1937).
Congested Districts Board (CDB), *Annual report* (1897).
Crofters Commission, *Annual report* (Edinburgh, 1956–66).
Crofting conditions: report of the commission of enquiry ['Taylor Commission'] (Edinburgh, 1954, Cmnd. 9091).
DAFS, *Scotland's marginal farms: the Highlands* (Edinburgh, 1947).
GRO Scotland, *Census 1961, Scotland, vol. 7*, 'Gaelic' (Edinburgh, 1966).
GRO Scotland, *Scotland's census 2001: Gaelic report* (Edinburgh, 2005).
Hansard, *Parliamentary debates, House of Commons.*
Highlands and Islands Development Board, *Report* (Inverness, 1965–6).
Natural Resources (Technical) Committee, *Forestry, agriculture and marginal land* ['Zuckerman Committee'] (London, 1957).

Political and Economic Planning, *Report on advisory committees in British government* (London, 1960).
Report by the Scottish land settlement committee (Edinburgh, 1945).
Report of the committee on hill sheep farming in Scotland (Edinburgh, 1944).
Report of the reconstruction committee (London, Cmnd. 8881, 1919).
Report on hydro-electric development in Scotland (London, Cmnd. 6406, iv, 677, 1942).
Review of Highland policy (Edinburgh, 1959, Cmnd. 785).
Royal Commission on Scottish affairs, 1952–4 (Edinburgh, Cmnd. 9212, 1954).
Scottish Council (Development and Industry), *Report of the committee of inquiry into the Scottish economy* ['Toothill Report'] (Edinburgh, 1961).
—— *Report of the committee on local development in Scotland* ['Cairncross Report'] (Edinburgh, 1952).
Scottish Council for Research in Education, *Gaelic-speaking children in Highland schools* (London, 1961).
Scottish Economic Committee, *The Highlands and Islands of Scotland: a review of the economic conditions with recommendations for improvement* ['Hilleary Committee'] (London, 1938).
SED, *Primary education* (Edinburgh, Cmnd. 6973, 1946).
—— *Provision for Gaelic education in Scotland: a report by HM Inspector of schools* (Edinburgh, 1994).
—— *Secondary education* (Edinburgh, Cmnd. 7005, 1947).

BOOKS, PAMPHLETS, ARTICLES AND THESES

Alaya, Flavia, *William Sharp – 'Fiona MacLeod', 1855–1905* (Cambridge, MA, 1970).
Anderson, Iain F., *To introduce the Hebrides* (London, 1933).
Bannerman, John M., 'The Lordship of the Isles' in J.M. Brown (ed.), *Scottish society in the fifteenth century* (London, 1977), pp 209–40.
Barron, Hugh (ed.), *The third statistical account of Scotland: the County of Inverness* (Edinburgh, 1985).
Basu, Paul, *Highland homecomings: genealogy and heritage tourism in the Scottish diaspora* (London, 2007).
Black, Ronald, *An tuil, the flood: anthology of 20th-century Scottish Gaelic verse* (Edinburgh, 1999).
Blackie, John Stuart, *The language and literature of the Scottish Highlands* (Edinburgh, 1876).
—— *Gaelic societies, Highland depopulation and land law reform* (Edinburgh, 1880).
—— *The Scottish Highlands and the land laws* (Edinburgh, 1885).
Boswell, James (ed. F.A. Pottle & C.H. Bennett), *Boswell's journal of a tour to the Hebrides* (London, 1936).
Brand, J., *The national movement in Scotland* (London, 1978).
Broun, Dauvit, 'Scotland before 1100: writing Scotland's origins' in B. Harris and A.R. MacDonald (eds), *Scotland: the making and unmaking of a nation: volume 1: the Scottish nation: origins to c.1500* (Dundee, 2006), pp 1–16.

Brown, M.E., 'The study of folk tradition' in D. Gifford (ed.), *The history of Scottish literature: vol. 3, nineteenth century* (Aberdeen, 1988), pp 397–409.
Brown, Oliver, *Hitlerism in the Highlands* (Glasgow, n.d., but 1941?).
—— *Scotland: nation or desert* (Glasgow, n.d., but 1943?).
—— *Scotlandshire: England's worst-governed province* (Glasgow, n.d., but 1943?).
Brown, Terence, *Ireland: a social and cultural history, 1922–79* (Glasgow, 1981).
Brox, Ottar (ed. John Bryden & Robert Storey), *The political economy of rural development: modernisation without centralisation?* (Delft, Netherlands, 2006).
Bumsted, J.M., *The people's clearance: Highland emigration to British North America, 1770–1815* (Edinburgh, 1982).
Burnett, John A., 'Ethnic culture in transition? Gaelic Scotland, 1939–1965' (PhD, University of Sunderland, 2000).
—— 'The Highlands and Islands of Scotland as a "cultural museum": the domestic consequences of migration, 1945–2000', *Immigrants and Minorities*, 20:1 (2001), 35–70.
—— 'Into the whirling vortex of modernity': cultural developments in the Scottish *Gàidhealtachd*, 1939–1965' in Liam Kennedy & R.J. Morris (eds), *Ireland and Scotland: order and disorder, 1600–2000* (Edinburgh, 2005), pp 175–88.
Burnett, Kathryn A., 'Local heroics: reflecting on incomers and local rural development discourses in Scotland', *Sociologia Ruralis*, 38:2 (1998), 204–24.
Burnett, Ray, 'Highland land raids: their contemporary significance' in I. Adams & J. Law (eds), *Land for the people* (Blackford, Perthshire, 1985), pp 12–18.
—— *Benbecula* (Torlum, 1986).
—— 'The cheviot, the stag and the last munro': constructs of 'wilderness, the Highlands and subalternity', paper to *A' Chànain, Am Mac-Meanma agus Cruth na Tìre ann an Gàidhlig na h-Eireann is na h-Albann*, Sabhal Mòr Ostaig, An t-Eilean Sgitheanach 3–5 Sultain 1999.
—— '*Tir nam beann, nan glean 's nan gaisgeach*: colonialism, complicity and the Gael', paper to *Rannsachadh na Gàidhlig Scottish Gaelic studies 2000 conference*, University of Aberdeen, 2–4 Aug. 2000.
'Caird, J.B., 'The creation of crofts and new settlement patterns in the Highlands and Islands of Scotland', *SGM*, 103:2 (1987), 67–75.
Caird, J.B., & H.A. Moisley, 'Leadership and innovation in the crofting communities of the Outer Hebrides', *Sociological Review*, 9 (1961), 85–102.
Calder, Jenni, *The nine lives of Naomi Mitchison* (London, 1997).
Cameron, A.D., *Go listen to the crofters: the Napier Commission and crofting a century ago* (Stornoway, 1986).
Cameron, James, *The old and the new Highlands and Hebrides* (Kirkcaldy, 1912).
Cameron, Lord John, 'Ten years in the Highlands', *Scotland* (Jan. 1957).
Cameron, Revd Hector, *Handbook to the islands of Coll and Tiree* (Glasgow, 1937).
Cameron, Ewen A., *Land for the people? The British government and the Scottish Highlands, c.1880–1925* (East Linton, 1996).
—— 'The political influence of Highland landowners; a reassessment', *Northern Scotland*, 14 (1994), 27–46.
—— 'The Scottish Highlands as a special policy area, 1886 to 1965', *Rural History*, 8:2 (1997), 195–215.

—— 'The Scottish Highlands: from congested district to objective one' in T.M. Devine & R.J. Finlay (eds), *Scotland in the twentieth century* (Edinburgh, 1996), pp 153–69.

Campbell, J.F., *Popular tales of the west Highlands orally collected*, 2 vols (Edinburgh, 1862).

Campbell, J.L., *Gaelic in Scottish education and life: past, present and future* (Edinburgh, 1945).

—— 'Introduction' in J.L. Campbell (ed.), *Tales of Barra told by the Coddy* (Edinburgh, 1960), pp 15–40.

—— (ed. & trans.), *Stories from South Uist told by Angus MacLellan* (London, 1961).

Campbell, J.L., & T.H. Hall, *Strange things: the story of Fr Allan McDonald, Ada Goodrich Freer, and the Society for Psychical Research's enquiry into Highland second sight* (London, 1968).

Carmichael, Alexander, *Carmina Gadelica: charms of the Gaels, hymns and incantations*, 2 vols (Edinburgh, 1900).

Carter, Ian, 'Six years on: an evaluative study of the Highlands and Islands Development Board', *Aberdeen University Review*, 45:149 (1973), 55–78.

—— 'The Highlands of Scotland as an underdeveloped region' in E. De Kadt & G. Williams (eds), *Sociology and development* (London, 1974), pp 279–311

Chapman, Malcolm, *The Gaelic vision in Scottish culture* (London, 1978).

Cheape, Hugh, *Tartan: the Highland habit* (2nd ed., Edinburgh, 1995).

Clyde, Robert, *From rebel to hero: the image of the Highlander, 1745–1830* (East Linton, 1995).

Cockburn, Lord Henry, *Circuit journeys* (London, 1848).

Colley, Linda, *Britons: forging the nation, 1707–1837* (New Haven & London, 1992).

Collier, Adam, *The crofting problem* (Cambridge, 1953).

Conservative and Unionist party, *Tory challenge* (London, 1948).

—— *Scottish affairs* (London, 1954).

—— *Agriculture and the nation* (London, 1959).

Cooper, Derek, *Road to the Isles* (London, 1979).

Craig, David, *On the crofters' trail: in search of the clearance Highlanders* (London, 1990).

Cregeen, Eric, 'The changing role of the House of Argyll in the Scottish Highlands' in N.T. Phillipson & R. Mitchison (eds), *Scotland in the Age of Improvement* (Edinburgh, 1970), pp 5–23.

Crofters Commission, *Annual report for 1957* (Edinburgh, 1958).

D'Arcy, Julian, *Scottish skalds and sagamen: Old Norse influence on modern Scottish literature* (East Linton, 1996).

Darling, F. Fraser (ed.), *West Highland Survey: an essay in human ecology* (London, 1955).

Darling, F. Fraser, & R.S. Barclay, 'Recent changes in crofting populations', *Scottish Agriculture*, 28:3 (1948–9), 121–9.

Devereux, E., 'Saving rural Ireland: Muintir na Tire and its anti-urbanism, 1931–1958', *Canadian Journal of Irish Studies*, 17 (1991), 23–30.

Devine, T.M., *The Great Highland Famine* (Edinburgh, 1988).

—— 'The emergence of the new elite in the western Highlands and Islands,

1800–1860' in T.M. Devine (ed.), *Improvement and Enlightenment* (Edinburgh, 1989), pp 108–35.

—— *Clanship to crofters' war: the social transformation of the Scottish Highlands* (Manchester, 1994).

—— *Scotland's empire, 1600–1815* (2003).

Dewey, C., 'Celtic agrarian legislation and the Celtic revival: historicist implications of Gladstone's Irish and Scottish Land Acts, 1870–1886', *Past & Present*, 64 (1974), 30–70.

Dodgshon, R.A., *From chiefs to landlords: social and economic change in the western Highlands and Islands* (Edinburgh, 1998).

Donaldson, William, *The Highland pipe and Scottish society, 1750–1950: transmission, change and the concept of tradition* (East Linton, 2000).

Dorian, Nancy C., *Language death: the life cycle of a Scottish Gaelic dialect* (Philadelphia, PA, 1981).

Durkacz, V.E., *The decline of the Celtic languages* (Edinburgh, 1983).

MacInnes, Angus Edward, *Eriskay, where I was born* (Edinburgh, 1997).

Eldridge, J. & L., *Raymond Williams: making connections* (London, 1994).

Ellis, Peter Berresford, *The Celtic dawn: a history of pan celticism* (London, 1993).

Erskine, R., 'Celt, Slav, Hun and Teuton', *Scottish Review*, 37 (1914), 315–25.

Fenyo, Kristina, *Contempt, sympathy and romance: Lowland perceptions of the Highlands and the Clearances during the Famine years, 1845–1855* (East Linton, 2000).

Ferguson, Malcolm, *Rambles in Skye* (Glasgow, 1885).

Finlay, R.J., 'Pressure group or political party? The nationalist impact on Scottish politics, 1928–1945', *Twentieth-Century British History*, 3 (1993), 274–97.

—— Caledonia or north Britain? Scottish identity in the eighteenth century' in D. Broun, R.J. Finlay & M. Lynch (eds), *Image and identity: the making and remaking of Scotland through the ages* (1998), pp 143–56.

Frazer, James George, *The golden bough: a study in magic and religion*, 12 vols (London, 1911–15).

Freer, A.G., *Outer Isles* (Westminster, 1902).

Fry, Michael, *Patronage and principle: a political history of modern Scotland* (Aberdeen, 1991).

—— *The Scottish empire* (Edinburgh, 2002).

Fullerton, Allan, & Charles R. Baird, *Remarks on the evils at present affecting the Highlands and Islands of Scotland* (Glasgow, 1838).

Fulton, R. (ed.), *Iain Crichton Smith: selected poems, 1955–1980* (Loanhead, 1981).

Gaskill, H. (ed.), *Ossian revisited* (Edinburgh, 1991).

Gibbons, Luke, *Transformations in Irish culture* (Cork, 1996).

Gillanders, F., 'The economic life of Gaelic Scotland today' in Thomson & Grimble (eds), *The future of the Highlands* (1968), pp 93–150.

Gillies, W. (ed.), *Gaelic and Scotland: Alba agus a' Ghaidhlig* (Edinburgh, 1989).

—— 'A century of Gaelic scholarship' in Gillies (ed.), *Gaelic and Scotland* (1989), pp 3–21.

—— 'The future of Gaelic studies' in Gillies (ed.), *Gaelic and Scotland* (1989), pp 22–43.

Gold, John R., John Gold & Margaret M. Gold, *Imagining Scotland: tradition, representation and promotion in Scottish tourism since 1750* (Aldershot, 1995).
Gordon, Paul Seton, *The charm of the hills* (London, 1912).
—— *The immortal isles* (London, 1926).
—— *The charm of Skye* (London, 1929).
Graham, C., & R. Kirkland (eds), *Ireland and cultural theory* (Basingstoke, 1999).
Grant, James Shaw, *Highland villages* (Edinburgh, 1980).
—— *The hub of my universe* (Edinburgh, 1982).
Grant, Lachlan, *A new deal for the Highlands* (Oban, 1935)
Gray, M., *The Highland economy, 1750–1850* (Edinburgh, 1957).
Grigor, I.F., *Mightier than a lord* (Stornoway, 1979).
Grimble, I., *The trial of Patrick Sellar* (London, 1963).
—— 'Caithness and Sutherland' in D.E. Butler & A. King (eds), *The British general election of 1966* (London, 1966), pp 227–32.
—— 'Introduction' in Thomson & Grimble (eds), *The future of the Highlands* (1968), pp 1–25.
—— *The world of Rob Donn* (Edinburgh, 1979).
—— 'The poet and scholar as journalist', *SGS, special volume, feill-sgribhinn do Ruaraidh MacThomais*, 17 (1996), 159–71.
Grimond, Jo, *The new liberalism* (London, 1958).
Gunn, Neil M., 'And then rebuild it: an economists Scotland of tomorrow', *Scots Magazine* (Dec. 1939).
—— 'Drains for the Kraal', *Glasgow Herald* (1 Jan. 1941).
—— 'Awakening of a nation', *Daily Record* (27 Dec. 1944).
Hanham, H.J., *Scottish nationalism* (Cambridge, MA, 1969).
—— 'The development of the Scottish office' in J.J. Wolfe (ed.), *Government and nationalism in Scotland* (Edinburgh, 1969), pp 17–27.
—— 'The problems of Highland discontent, 1880–1885', *Transactions of the Royal Historical Society*, 14 (1969), 21–65.
—— 'Religion and nationality in the mid-Victorian army' in M.R.D. Foot (ed.), *War and society: historical essays in honour and memory of J.R. Western, 1928–1971* (London, 1973), pp 163–7.
Harper, M., *Adventurers & exiles: the great Scottish exodus* (London, 2003).
Hart, Francis R., 'The hunter and the circle: Neil Gunn's fiction of violence' in G. Ross Roy (ed.), *Studies in Scottish literature* (Columbia, SC, 1971), pp 65–82.
Hart, F.R., & J.B. Pick, *Neil M. Gunn: a Highland life* (London, 1981).
Harvie, C., 'Labour and Scottish government: the age of Tom Johnston', *Bulletin of Scottish Politics*, 1:2 (1981), 1–20.
—— *No gods and precious few heroes: twentieth-century Scotland* (Edinburgh, 2000).
—— *Scotland and nationalism: society and politics, 1707–1994* (4th ed., London, 2004).
Hunter, J. (ed.), 'Sheep and deer: Highland sheep farming, 1850–1900', *Northern Scotland*, 1 (1973), 199–222.
—— 'The politics of Highland land reform, 1873–1895', *SHR*, 53 (1974), 45–68.
—— 'The Gaelic connection: the Highlands, Ireland and nationalism, 1873–1922', *SHR*, 54 (1975), 178–204.
—— (ed.), *For the people's cause: from the writings of John Murdoch* (Edinburgh, 1986).

—— *The claim of crofting: the Scottish Highlands and Islands, 1930–1990* (Edinburgh, 1991).
—— *On the other side of sorrow: nature and people in the Scottish Highlands* (Edinburgh, 1995).
—— *The making of the crofting community* (2nd ed., Edinburgh, 2000).
—— 'The Scottish Highlands: a contested country' in *Fonn's duthchas: land and legacy* (Edinburgh, 2006), pp 1–59.
Hutchinson, George Hely ('Sixty-one'), *Twenty years' wild sport in the Hebrides* (London, 1873).
Hutchinson, John, *The dynamics of cultural nationalism* (London, 1987).
Hutchison, I.G.C., *Scottish politics in the twentieth century* (Basingstoke, 2001).
Inglis, John ('The Governor'), *A yachtsman's holidays or cruising in the west Highlands* (London, 1879).
Jackson, K.H., 'The situation of the Scottish Gaelic language and the work of the Linguistic Survey of Scotland', *Lochlann*, 1 (1958), 228–34.
Johnston, Russell, *Highland development* (Edinburgh, 1964).
Johnston, Thomas, *Memories* (London, 1952).
Kellas, J.G., *Modern Scotland: the nation since 1870* (London, 1968).
—— *The Scottish political system* (3rd ed., London, 1984).
—— 'Highland migration to Glasgow and the origin of the Scottish labour movement', *Bulletin of the Society for the Study of Labour History*, 12 (1966), 9–12.
Keltie, J.S. (ed.), *A history of the Scottish Highlands, Highland clans and Highland regiments* (Edinburgh & London, 1875).
Kennedy-Fraser, Marjory, & Kenneth MacLeod (eds), *Songs of the Hebrides volume I: collected and arranged for voice and pianoforte with Gaelic and English words by Marjory Kennedy-Fraser and Kenneth MacLeod* (London, 1909).
—— *Songs of the Hebrides volume II* (London, 1917).
Kiberd, Declan, *Inventing Ireland: the literature of the modern nation* (London, 1996).
Kidd, Colin, 'Race, empire and the limits of nineteenth-century Scottish nationhood', *The Historical Journal*, 46:4 (2003), 873–92.
—— *Subverting Scotland's past: Scottish Whig historians and the creation of an Anglo-British identity, 1689–c.1830* (Cambridge, 1993).
King, Georgiana Goddard, 'Fiona MacLeod', *Modern language notes*, 23 (June 1918), 352–6.
Knox, John, *A view of the British Empire*, 2 vols (3rd ed., London, 1785).
Labour Party Scottish Council, *Plan for post-war Scotland* (Glasgow, 1941).
Labour Party, *Campaign quotations: a political reference book telling who said what where and when* (London, 1951).
—— *Forward Scotland* (Glasgow, 1949).
—— *Go-ahead Scotland* (Glasgow, 1965).
—— *Labour Party Scottish council report* (Glasgow, 1952).
—— *Scottish local government, 1952* (Edinburgh, 1952).
—— *Signposts for the sixties* (London, 1961).
—— *Twelve wasted years* (London, n.d., but c.1963).
Leneman, L., *Fit for heroes? Land settlement in Scotland after World War One* (Aberdeen, 1989).

Levitt, I., 'The creation of the Highlands and Islands Development Board, 1935–65', *Northern Scotland*, 19 (1999), 85–105.
Liberal Party, *Partners in a new Britain* (London, 1963).
Lindsay, Maurice, *History of Scottish literature* (London, 1977).
Lockhart, J.G., *The life of Sir Walter Scott Bart., abridged from the larger work* (London, 1898).
Logan, James, *The Scottish Gael, or Celtic manners preserved among the highlanders; being an historical and descriptive account of the inhabitants, antiquities & national peculiarities of Scotland; more particularly of the northern or Gaëlic parts of the country, where the singular habits of the aboriginal Celts are most tenaciously retained* (London, 1831).
Lorimer, H., 'Guns, game and the grandee: the cultural politics of deer-stalking in the Scottish Highlands', *Ecumene*, 7:4 (2000), 431–59.
—— 'Ways of seeing the Scottish Highlands: authenticity, marginality and the curious case of the Hebridean blackhouse', *Journal of Historical Geography*, 25:4 (1999), 517–33.
Lynch, Michael, *Scotland: a new history* (London, 1991).
—— 'Scottish culture in its historical perspective' in P.H. Scott (ed.), *Scotland: a concise cultural history* (Edinburgh, 1993), pp 15–46.
Lynch, Peter, *The history of the Scottish National Party* (Cardiff, 2002).
MacAulay, Donald (ed.), *Nua-bhardachd Ghaidhlig: modern Scottish Gaelic poems* (Edinburgh, 1976).
—— 'Canons, myths and cannon fodder', *Scotlands*, 2 (1994), 35.
Mac'illedhuibh, Donnachadh, *Death to the Highland Scot? An exposure of British government policies in Scotland* (Glasgow, 1944).
MacBean, Lachlan, 'The Gael as seen in his language' in N. Munro (ed.), *The old Highlands: being papers read before the Gaelic society of Glasgow, 1895–1906* (Glasgow, 1908).
MacColl, Allan W., *Land, faith and the crofting community: Christianity and social criticism in the Highlands of Scotland, 1843–1893* (Edinburgh, 2006).
MacCombie Smith, W., *Men or deer in the Scottish glens* (Inverness, 1893).
McCrone, D., A. Morris & R. Kiely, *Scotland the brand: the making of Scottish heritage* (Edinburgh, 1995).
McCrone, D., *Understanding Scotland: the sociology of a nation* (2nd ed., London, 2001).
McCrorie, James N., *The Highland cause: life & times of Roderick MacFarquar* (Regina, 2001).
MacCuish, D.J., 'Reform of crofting tenure', *TGSI*, 48 (1974), 557–83.
MacCulloch, J.A., *The misty Isle of Skye: its scenery, its people, its story* (Edinburgh, 1905).
MacDhunleibhe, Uilleam, *Duain agus orain* (Glasgow, 1882).
MacDiarmid, J.M., *The deer forests and how they are bleeding Scotland white* (2nd ed., Glasgow, 1926).
MacDonald, Angus, 'Modern Scots novelists' in H.J.C. Grierson (ed.), *Edinburgh essays in Scots literature* (Edinburgh, 1933).
MacDonald, Colin, *Echoes of the glen* (Edinburgh, 1936).

MacDonald, D.J. (ed. B. Innes), *Chi mi: the poetry of Donald John Macdonald* (Edinburgh, 1998).
MacDonald, F. (ed.), 'Colloquium: Susan Parman's *Scottish crofters: a historical ethnography of a Celtic village*', *JSHS*, 24:2 (2005), 159–81.
MacDonald, F.J., 'Last days of Gaelic', *Saltire Review*, 5:14 (1958), 14–20.
MacDonald, Revd Fr J.A., 'The poetry of Donald Allan MacDonald', *TGSI*, 58 (1992–4), 32–50.
—— (ed.), *Orain Dhòmhnaill Ailean Dhòmnaill na Bainich: the songs of Donald MacDonald, 1906–92* (Benbecula, 1999).
MacDonald, Kenneth D., 'The Gaelic language, its study and development' in Thomson & Grimble (eds), *The future of the Highlands* (1968), pp 175–201.
MacDonald, Sharon, *Reimagining culture: histories, identities and the Gaelic renaissance* (Oxford, 1997).
MacDonnell, Margaret, *The emigrant experience: songs of Highland emigrants in North America* (Toronto, 1982).
MacEwen, Sir Alexander M., *The thistle and the rose: Scotland's problem today* (Edinburgh, 1932).
MacGillivray, Alan, 'Exile and empire' in D. Gifford (ed.), *The history of Scottish literature: vol. 3, the nineteenth century* (Aberdeen, 1988), pp 411–27.
MacGregor, Alasdair Alpin, *Behold the Hebrides!* (London, 1925).
—— *The haunted isles* (London, 1933).
MacInnes, A.E., *Eriskay, where I was born* (Edinburgh, 1997).
MacInnes, A.I., *Clanship, commerce and the House of Stuart, 1603–1788* (East Linton, 1996).
—— 'Scottish Gaeldom; the first phase of clearance' in T.M. Devine & R. Mitchison (eds), *People and society in Scotland, vol. 1, 1760–1830* (Edinburgh, 1988), pp 70–90.
—— 'The Crofters' Holdings Act: a hundred-year sentence', *Radical Scotland*, 25 (1987), 24–6.
MacInnes, J., 'A Gaelic song of the Sutherland Clearances', *Scottish Studies*, 8 (1964), 104–6.
MacIntyre, R.D., *State subsidies for private tyrannies* (Glasgow, 1949).
MacIver, Mary & Hector, *Pilgrim souls* (Aberdeen, 1990).
Mackay, I.R., *Who are the Highlanders?* (Inverness, 1966).
Mackenzie, Alexander, *The Highland Clearances: or, a strange return by the Highland chiefs for the fidelity of the clans: being an account of the Glengarry, Strathglass, Kintail, Glenelg, Skye, Uist, Barra, Coigeach, Sutherland and other evictions in the Highlands since the Battle of Culloden: with an appendix on the Highland crofters: reprinted, revised and extended from the Aberdeen 'Daily Free Press'* (Inverness, 1881).
Mackenzie, Alexander, *Voyages from Montreal, on the River St Lawrence, through the continent of North America, to the frozen and Pacific oceans* (London, 1801).
MacKenzie, John (ed.), *Sar-obair nam bard Gaelach, or the beauties of Gaelic poetry* (4th ed., Edinburgh, 1865).
MacKenzie, Osgood H., *A hundred years in the Highlands* (London, 1921).
MacKenzie, Sir George S., *A general survey of the counties of Ross and Cromarty* (London, 1810).

MacKenzie, W.M., *Hugh Miller: a critical study* (London, 1905).
Mackie, R.L. (ed.), *A book of Scottish verse* (London, 1967).
Mackillop, Andrew, *'More fruitful than the soil': army, empire and the Scottish Highlands, 1715–1815* (East Linton, 2000).
MacKinnon, K., *Gaelic? A past and future prospect* (Edinburgh, 1991).
Maclean, Calum, *The Highlands* (Inverness, 1975).
MacLean, Catherine, 'Getting out and getting on: Scottish Highland migration in the first half of the twentieth century', *Rural History*, 11 (2000), 231–48.
MacLean, Malcolm, & Christopher Carrell (eds), *As an fhearann: from the land* (Edinburgh, 1986).
MacLean, Sorley, 'The poetry of the Clearances', *TGSI*, 38 (1937–41), 293–324.
—— (ed. W. Gillies), *Ris a' bhruthaich: criticism and prose writings* (Stornoway, 1985).
—— 'Vale of tears: a view of Highland history to 1886' in Maclean and Carrell (eds), *As an fhearann* (1986), pp 9–18.
—— (ed. C. Whyte), *Dain do Eimhir agus dain eile: poems to Eimhir and other poems* (Glasgow, 2002).
MacLeod, D.J., 'Gaelic prose', *TGSI*, 49 (1974–6), 198–230.
—— 'Gaelic: The dynamics of a renaissance' in Gilles (ed.), *Gaelic and Scotland* (1989), pp 222–9.
MacLeod, Donald, *Gloomy memories in the Highlands of Scotland: versus Mrs Harriet Beecher Stowe's sunny memories in (England) a foreign land: or, a faithful picture of the extirpation of the Celtic race from the Highlands of Scotland* (Glasgow, 1857).
MacLeod, Fiona (William Sharp), *Pharais: a romance of the isles* (Derby, 1894).
—— 'A group of Celtic writers', *Fortnightly Review*, 71 (1899), 34–48.
—— *Iona by sundown shores* (London, 1900).
—— *The winged destiny: studies in the spiritual history of the Gael* (London, 1904).
MacLeod, Morag, 'Folk revival in Gaelic song' in Ailie Munro (ed.), *The democratic muse: folk music revival in Scotland* (2nd ed. Aberdeen, 1996), pp 124–37.
MacLeod, Revd Norman, *Reminscences of a Highland parish* (London, 1863).
McLeod, Wilson (ed.), *Revitalising Gaelic in Scotland: policy, planning and public discourse* (Edinburgh, 2006).
McNeil, Kenneth, *Scotland, Britain, empire: writing the Highlands, 1760–1860* (Columbus, OH, 2007).
MacPhail, I.M.M., *The crofters' war* (Stornoway, 1989).
Martech Consultants Limited, *Highland opportunity: a report for the Scottish vigilantes association* (Invergordon, 1964).
Massey, D., & P. Jess (eds), *A place in the world? Place, culture and globalisation* (Oxford, 1995).
Mather, Alexander S., 'Government agencies and land development in the Scottish Highlands: a centenary survey', *Northern Scotland*, 8 (1988), 39–50.
—— 'The congested districts board for Scotland' in W. Ritchie, J.C. Stone & A.S. Mather (eds), *Essays for Professor R.E.H. Mellor* (Aberdeen, 1986).
Matheson, W. (ed.), *The songs of John MacCodrum* (Edinburgh, 1938).
Meek, D.E., 'Gaelic poets of the land agitation', *TGSI*, 49 (1977), 309–76.
—— (ed.), *Tuath is tighearna: Tenants and landlords (an anthology of Gaelic poetry of*

social and political protest from the Clearances to the land agitation, 1800–1890) (Edinburgh, 1995).
—— 'The language of heaven? The Highland churches, culture shift and the erosion of Gaelic identity in the twentieth century' in R. Pope (ed.), *Religion and national identity: Wales and Scotland, c.1700–2000* (Cardiff, 2001), pp 307–37.
Melman, Billie, 'Claiming the nation's past: the invention of an Anglo-Saxon tradition' in J. Reinharz & A. Geilhardt (eds), *The impact of western nationalisms* (London, 1992), pp 221–41.
Miller, W.L., *The end of British politics?* (Oxford, 1981).
Mitchison, Naomi, 'Gaelic with an Oxford accent', *Scots Independent* (Mar. 1942).
—— *Lobsters on the agenda* (London, 1952).
—— *Highlands and Islands* (Glasgow, 1953).
—— 'Commission offers nothing to average Scot', *London Forward* (11 Aug. 1954).
—— 'For the Highlands with love and anger', *New Statesman and Nation* (30 Apr. 1955).
—— 'Living in Scotland to-day', *Scottish Field* (May 1955).
—— 'Is Carradale Highland?', *Scottish Field* (July 1955).
—— 'Action by the Highland Panel', *Guardian* (19 Oct. 1955).
—— 'Living in Scotland', *Scottish Field* (Feb. 1956), 51–3.
—— 'Murder in our Scottish schools', *Scotsman* (23 June 1956).
—— 'Home thoughts from Italy – II: culture ... for export', *Glasgow Herald* (18 Oct. 1958).
—— 'Oh, rowan tree', *Good Housekeeping* (July 1959).
—— 'In a far, rainbow country', *Scotland's Magazine* (Dec. 1959).
—— 'Debate on island's future', *Glasgow Herald* (6 Oct. 1961).
—— 'Other happiness, other risks', *Guardian* (18 May 1964).
—— 'Letters from a tribe', *New Statesman* (16 Oct. 1964).
—— 'Checking Highland "brain drain"', *Glasgow Herald* (9 Dec. 1964).
Mitchison, R., 'Book reviews', *SHR*, 51 (1972), 197–8.
—— 'The Highland Clearances', *SESH*, 1 (1981), 4–24.
Moffat, A., 'Beyond the Highland landscape' in Maclean and Carrell, *As an fhearann* (1986), pp 65–71.
Moisley, H.A., 'The Highlands and Islands: a crofting region?', *Transactions of the Institute of British Geographers*, 31 (1962), 83–95.
Morley, Averil, & F. Fraser Darling, 'The social situation' in Darling (ed.), *West Highland Survey* (1955), 281–405.
Morrison, Hew (ed.), *Songs and poems in the Gaelic language by Rob Donn* (Edinburgh, 1899).
Morton, H.V., *In search of Scotland* (1929).
Mulock, Thomas, *The western Highlands and Islands of Scotland socially considered, with reference to the proprietors* (Glasgow, 1850).
Munro, Neil, 'Introduction' in N. Munro (ed.), *The old Highlands: being papers read before the Gaelic society of Glasgow, 1895–1906* (Glasgow, 1908), pp 9–12.
Murchison, Revd T.M., 'Highland life as reflected in Gaelic literature', *TGSI*, 38 (1937–41), 217–42.

—— (ed.), *Sgriobhaidhean Choinnich MhicLeoid: the Gaelic prose of Kenneth MacLeod* (Edinburgh, 1988).
Murdoch, W. Blaikie, *The spirit of Jacobite loyalty* (Edinburgh, 1907).
Murray, Amy, *Father Allan's island* (Edinburgh, 1936).
Murray, I. (ed.), *Beyond the limit: selected shorter fiction of Naomi Mitchison* (Edinburgh, 1986).
Murray, W.H., *Highland landscape* (Aberdeen, 1962).
Necker, L.A., *Travels in Scotland* (London, 1821).
Newby, Andrew G., *Ireland, radicalism and the Scottish Highlands, c.1870–1912* (Edinburgh, 2007).
Newton, Michael, *A handbook of the Scottish Gaelic world* (Dublin, 2000).
—— *Warriors of the world: the world of the Scottish Highlanders* (Edinburgh, 2009).
Nic-a-Phearsain, Mairi, *Dain agus orain Ghaidhlig* (Inverness, 1891).
Nicolson, C. (ed.), *Iain Crichton Smith: critical essays* (Edinburgh, 1992).
O'Dell, A.C., & K. Walton, *The Highlands of Scotland* (London, 1962).
Oliver, James, 'Scottish Gaelic identities: contexts and contingencies', *Scottish Affairs*, 51 (2005), 1–24.
Orr, W., *Deer forests, landlords and crofters: the western Highlands in Victorian and Edwardian times* (Edinburgh, 1982).
Payne, Peter L., *The hydro: a study of the major hydroelectric schemes undertaken by the north of Scotland hydroelectricity board* (Aberdeen, 1988).
Peel, C.V.A., *Wild sport in the Outer Hebrides* (London, 1883).
Pennant, Thomas, *A tour in Scotland, 1769* (2nd ed., London, 1772).
Pennell, Joseph, & Elizabeth Robins, *Our journey to the Hebrides* (London, 1890).
Phillips, Morgen, *Labour in the sixties* (London, 1960).
Pittock, Murray H., *The myth of the Jacobite clans* (Edinburgh, 1995).
Pottinger, George, *The secretaries of state for Scotland, 1926–76* (Edinburgh, 1979).
Prebble, John, *The Highland Clearances* (London, 1963).
Price, R., 'Whose history, which novel? Neil M. Gunn and the Gaelic idea', *Scottish Literary Journal*, 24:2 (1997), 85–102.
Pringle, Trevor R., 'The privation of history: Landseer, Victorian and the Highland myth' in S. Daniels & D. Cosgrove (eds), *The iconography of landscape* (Cambridge, 1988), pp 142–61.
Quigley, Hugh, 'The Highlands of Scotland: proposals for development', *Agenda*, 3 (1944), 77–96.
Ray, Christopher, 'Towards a theory of the dialectic of local rural development within the European Union', *Sociologia Ruralis*, 37:3 (1997), 345–62.
Richards, Eric, *The leviathan of wealth: the Sutherland fortune in the industrial revolution* (London, 1973).
—— *A history of the Highland Clearances*, 2 vols (London, 1982; 1985).
Robertson, Iain, 'Governing the Highlands: the place of popular protest in the Highlands of Scotland after 1918', *Rural History*, 8:1 (1997), 109–24.
Ross, Donald, *Real Scottish grievances* (Glasgow, 1854).
—— *The Russians of Ross-shire, or massacre of the Rosses in Strathcarron* (Glasgow, 1854).

Sage, Revd Donald, *Memorabilia domestica* (London, 1889).
Scottish council of the Labour Party, *Go-ahead Scotland* (Glasgow, 1965).
Scottish Labour, *Let Scotland prosper* (Glasgow, 1958).
Scottish Labour Party, *Plan for post-war Scotland* (Glasgow, 1941).
Shand, Alexander I., *Letters from the Highlands* (Edinburgh, 1883).
Sharp, William, 'Introduction' and 'notes' in E.A. Sharp (ed.), *Lyra Celtica* (Edinburgh, 1896).
Shaw, Margaret Fay, *Folk songs & folklore of South Uist* (2nd ed., Oxford, 1977).
Skewis, W. Iain, 'Transport in the Highlands and Islands' (PhD, University of Glasgow, 1962).
Smith, Iain Crichton, 'The future of Gaelic literature', *TGSI*, 43 (1960–63), 172–80.
—— 'Gaelic master: Sorley Maclean', *Scottish Review*, 34 (1984), 4–10.
—— 'The poetry of Derick Thomson' in I.C. Smith, *Towards the human: selected essays* (Edinburgh, 1986), 136–43.
Smith, John S. (ed.), 'The position of Gaelic and Gaelic culture in Scottish education' in Grimble & Thomson (eds), *The future of the Highlands* (1968), pp 57–92.
—— *The third statistical account of Scotland: the County of Caithness* (Edinburgh, 1988).
—— 'Schools, Gaelic teaching in' in Thomson, *Companion to Gaelic Scotland*, pp 259–62.
Smout, T.C., *A history of the Scottish people, 1560–1830* (London, 1969).
—— 'Book reviews', *SHR*, 49 (1970), 112–13.
—— 'An ideological struggle: the Highland Clearances', *Scottish International*, 5 (Feb. 1972), 13–16.
—— 'Tours in the Scottish Highlands from the eighteenth to the twentieth centuries', *Northern Scotland*, 5 (1983), 99–121.
—— *A century of the Scottish people, 1830–1950* (London, 1986).
SNP, *Policy of the Scottish National Party* (1950).
—— *Scotland's present position* (Glasgow, 1952).
—— *Province or nation? A national party talk as broadcast by radio free Scotland* (Glasgow, n.d.).
—— *Scotland in 1957: a political and economic review* (Glasgow, 1957).
Stafford, Fiona, *Sublime savage: a study of Macpherson and the poems of Ossian* (Edinburgh, 1988).
Starmore, Graham, 'The Knoydart alternative', *North*, 7 (July/Aug. 1980).
Stewart of Garth, Col. David, *Sketches of the character, manners and present state of the Highlanders of Scotland*, 2 vols (Edinburgh, 1822).
Stiùbhart, D.U. (ed.), *The life & legacy of Alexander Carmichael* (Ness, Isle of Lewis, 2008).
Thayer, George, *The British political fringe* (London, 1965).
Thompson, F., *Highland way of life: today* (Inverness, 1966).
—— *The Highlands and Islands advisory panel a review of its activities and influence, 1946–1964* (Stornoway, 1978).
—— *History of An Comunn Gaidhealach: the first hundred (1891–1991)* (Inverness, 1992).
Thomson, Derick S., *The Gaelic sources of MacPherson's Ossian* (Edinburgh, 1952).

—— 'The Gaelic oral tradition', *Proceedings of the Scottish anthropological and folklore society*, 1 (1954), 1–17.
—— 'The role of the writer in a minority culture', *TGSI*, 44 (1964–6), 256–71.
—— (ed.), *An introduction to Gaelic poetry* (London, 1974).
—— 'Gaelic in Scotland: the background' in D.S. Thomson (ed.), *Gaelic in Scotland* (Glasgow, 1976), 1–10.
—— 'Gaelic literature' in P.H. Scott (ed.), *Scotland: a concise cultural history* (Edinburgh, 1993), pp 127–43.
—— *The companion to Gaelic Scotland* (London, 1994).
—— & Ian Grimble (eds), *The future of the Highlands* (London, 1968).
Trevor-Roper, Hugh, 'The invention of tradition: the Highland tradition of Scotland' in E. Hobsbawm & T. Ranger (eds), *The invention of tradition* (Cambridge, 1983), pp 15–41.
Urquhart, Sir Robert, 'Highland crofting, seen in its national and international contexts', *Advancement of Science*, 21 (1964), 48–50.
Vane, Col. W.M.F. MP, 'Free enterprise in forestry', *Tory challenge*, 2:5 (1947), 6.
Victoria, Queen, *Leaves from the journal of our life in the Highlands* (London, 1868).
—— *More leaves from the journal of a life in the Highlands* (London, 1884).
Walker, Graham, *Thomas Johnston* (Manchester, 1988).
Weir, Alastair MacNeill, *Highland plan* (Glasgow, 1945).
Welch, Robert (ed.), *W.B. Yeats: writings on Irish folklore, legend and myth* (London, 1993).
Whyte, C., 'Derick Thomson: reluctant symbolist', *Chapman*, 38 (spring 1984), 1–6.
—— 'George Campbell Hay: Nationalism with a difference' in D.S. Thomson (ed.), *Gaelic and Scots in harmony* (Glasgow, 1988), pp 116–35.
—— *An aghaidh na siorradheachd, In the face of eternity* (Edinburgh, 1991).
Whyte, Ian D., *Scotland before the Industrial Revolution: an economic and social history, c.1050–c.1750* (London, 1995).
Williams, Basil, *The life of William Pitt, earl of Chatham, vol. ii* (London, 1913).
Williams, Raymond, *Keywords* (London, 1976).
Wilson, James, *A voyage round Scotland* (Edinburgh, 1842).
Withers, C.W.J., 'The Scottish Highlands outlined: cartographic evidence for the position of the Highland-Lowland boundary', *SGM*, 98:3 (1982), 143–57.
—— *Gaelic in Scotland, 1698–1981: the geographical history of a language* (Edinburgh, 1984).
—— *Gaelic Scotland: the transformation of a culture region* (London, 1988).
—— 'The historical creation of the Scottish Highlands' in I.L. Donnachie & C.A. Whatley (eds), *The manufacture of Scottish history* (Edinburgh, 1992), pp 143–56.
—— 'Place, memory, monument: memorializing the past in contemporary Highland Scotland', *Ecumene*, 3:3 (1996), 325–43.
—— *Urban Highlanders: Highland-Lowland migration and urban Gaelic culture, 1700–1900* (East Linton, 1999).
Wittig, Kurt, *The Scottish tradition in literature* (Edinburgh, 1972).
Womack, Peter, *Improvement and romance: constructing the myth of the Highlands* (London, 1989).

Wood, Emma, *The hydro boys: pioneers of renewable energy* (Edinburgh, 2002).
Wordsworth, Dorothy, *Recollections of a tour made in Scotland, AD1803* (London, 1874).
Young, Douglas, *Fascism for the Highlands* (Glasgow, 1943).
—— 'A sketch history of Scottish nationalism' in Neil MacCormack (ed.), *The Scottish debate: essays on Scottish nationalism* (London, 1970), pp 5–20.
Young, K., *Sir Alec Douglas-Home* (London, 1970).
Youngson, A.J., *After the 'Forty-five': the economic impact on the Scottish Highlands* (Edinburgh, 1973).

Index

A' choille ghraumach, 45
absentee landlords 33, 168, 171, 172, 174–5, 203, *see also* Knoydart
administrative concept of Highlands and Islands, 17–18
Advisory Council on Education, 231, 232
Advisory Panel on the Highlands and Islands, *see* Highland Panel
afforestation schemes, 114, 226
agriculture
  government commitment to, 113, 226
  improvement ideas, 32, 118
  nationalization, 105
  see also crofting
Agriculture (Scotland) Act (1948), 111, 138, 165
air bases (military), 137
air services, 113
airports, 137
Albert, Prince Consort, in Scotland, 68–71
alienation, 49–50
aluminium factories, 116, 137
Am Bàrd Bochd 256, *see also* MacLeod, Norman
Am Fasgadh, 255
ambivalence to traditions, 192
Americanisms, 214
An Aimsir Cheilteach: the Celtic Time, 99
An Comunn Gàidhealach, 128, 192, 218–19, 220, 222, 223, 226, 227, 230, 231, 233, 234, 235, 238, 239, 240, 248–51, 252, 255, 257, 260, 261, 262, 263, 265
An Gaidheal, 21, 218, 219, 220, 221, 224, 226, 229, 230, 234, 239, 240, 241, 244, 245, 246, 249
An Gaidheal Og, 234
ancillary employment, 169–70, 200, 203
ancillary industries, 115–16
Anderson, I.F., 13
anglicization
  as Anghillicization, 108
  cult of, 22
  of the Highlands, 22, 32

Anglo–British nationalism, 66
Anglo–Quisling elements, 107
Anglo–Saxon identity, 80
anglophobia, 86
Annexing Act (1752), 60
anti-Celtic backlash, 80
anti-industrialism, 270
Applecross, 221
Ardnamurchan, 221
Argyll, 18
Argyll education committee, 211
Army School of Piping, 236
Arnold, Matthew, 79
arterial roads, 112

Balfour Commission, 120
Balmorality, 26, 59, 67–78, 85, 108, 246, 248
Bannerman, John M., 128, 219, 230–1, 235, 236–7, 247, 248, 262
Barra, 142, 218, 258
basic Highland question, 223
Battle of the Braes, 50, 55
Battle of Greenyards, 40–1
BBC Scottish Home Service, 253
Beeching rail cuts, 150, 155, 163
Beeching Report, 156, 157, 158, 160
Beeching, Richard (later Lord), 150, 155, 158–9
begging bowl dependancy culture, 247
Benbecula, 137, 228
Bernera Riot, 42–3
bilingual areas, 19
bilingualism 266, *see also* Gaelic
bilingualism committee of the Scottish Council for Research in Education, 238
black houses, 85, 111, 167
Blackie, John Stuart, 43, 50, 52–3
Blair, Hugh, 62
bliadhna nan caorach (year of the sheep), 34
bliadhna an losgaidh (year of the burnings), 36
boat slips, 113

299

Bonnie Prince Charlie, *see* Stuart, Charles Edward
Book of the Clearances, 53
Book of the Dean of Lismore, 63
Boreraig clearances, 46
Bowie, Dr, 197
Braemar Highland games, 70
breac-Gàidhealtachd (speckled Gaeldom), 18
Breadalbane, Lord, 69
Breton culture, 219
British European Airways, 113
British Transport Commission, 155, 156
Brocket, Lord 119, 120, 223, *see also* Knoydart
Brora industry, 202
Brown, John, 75
Brown, Oliver, 107, 108, 139–40
Bruce, R.H.W., 163
The bull calves, 186
Butcher's broom, 185

Caddell, Robert, 64
Cairncross, Alec, 166, 187
Caithness
  Dounreay nuclear site, 203, 213
  as part of Highlands, 18
Calvinism, 81
Cameron, Dr John, 224, 233–4, 238
Cameron, John Cameron, Lord, 119, 150, 151–3, 155, 158, 159, 161, 179
Cameron of Lochiel, Lieutenant-Colonel D.H., 156
Cameron Report, 119–20
Campbell, J.F., 82
Campbell, John Lorne, 216, 218, 219, 236, 241, 268–9, 275
Canadian Boat Song, 49, 78, 79
Canna, 275
Carmichael, Alexander, 82
Carmina Gadelica: hymns and incantations, 82
Carr, Sir John, 66
Carradale, 206
Catholicism, 81–2
CDB (Congested Districts Board), 56, 89
ceilidh culture, 44
ceilidh house decline, 254, 258
Celtic League, 100
Celtic nationalism, 81, 99–100
Celtic twilight movement, 58, 59, 78–85, 79, 87, 88, 90, 98, 271, 277
census (of 1951), 221, 235, 251

census (of 1961), 22, 221, 263
census (of 2001), 280
The charm of the hills, 83
The charm of Skye, 83
Churchill, Winston, 103
cinema and the Highlands, 59
clan chiefs, as landlords, 32, 33
Clann Albainn, 226, 227
Clansman ferry, 162
clash of social philosophies, 184, 268
Clearances
  and economic theories, 39
  in fiction, 185
  Glencalvie, 39
  Glengarry, 35
  ignored by tourists, 72
  Islay, 41
  Kildonan, 35, 37–8
  legacy of, 31–2
  Lewis, 40–4, 50, 51
  mass clearance in West, 40
  and pamphleteers, 29
  pauperization, 32, 37–8
  resistance to, 36
  Ross-shire, 40
  Skye, 46–7, 51
  Strathnaver, 35, 36
  Sutherland, 34, 35, 36
  written stories about, 269–70
Climbing up towards Ben Shiant, 41
Cnoc nan Ros, 235
Coll, 142
collective identity, 50
Collier, Adam, 183, 184, 187, 188, 189–90, 193, 197, 202–3, 268
Collinson, Francis, 241
colossus of advancing materialism, 219
Columba ferry, 162
Colville, Secretary of State Lord, 143
commando training, 137
Committee of Enquiry into Crofting Conditions, 152
Committee of Ferries in Great Britain, 113
communal centres, 106
communications network, 128
Comunn na h-Òigridh, 234, 235
Comunn nan Albannach, 80
Congested Districts Board (CDB), 56, 89
Conservative constituencies, 122
Conservative Party/Government, 97, 102, 103, 107, 108, 116, 117, 120, 122, 123, 124, 142, 143, 145, 171, 172, 178, 184

Index

Cooper Commission/Report, 138, 139, 140
Cooper, Lord, 140
cooperative movement, 127
corruption allegations, 140
Council of Industry, 136–7
Council of Ministers, 136
Crofter Counties Scheme, 112
crofter MPs, 55
crofterization, 32
The Crofters' Banner, 55
Crofters Commission, 121, 124, 125, 127, 130, 135, 136, 152, 164, 165–77, 184, 185, 186, 188, 190, 199, 261
   Annual report for 1960, 173, 176
Crofters' Grants Scheme, 127
Crofters' (Scotland) Act (1886), 51, 56, 88–9, 170, 271, 274
Crofters (Scotland) Act (1961), 175, 176
Crofters (Scotland) Bill (1955), 171–2
The crofters' struggle, 54
Crofters' War, 50, 55, 88
crofting, 18, 24–5, 32, 37, 38, 88, 111, 131–2, 135, 141, 150, 164, 165, 165–77, 190–1, 202, 264, 268, 271, 274, 275, 277
crofting counties, 18, 97, 112
The crofting problem, 183, 187
Croick Church, 39
Culloden, Battle of (1746), 58, 60, 66, 271
Culloden Gaelic visitor centre, 255
cult of anglicization, 22
cult of Ossian, *see* Ossian
cultural nationalism and SNP, 101
Cumberland, Duke of, 59

Dall, Ailean 35, *see also* MacDougall, Allan
daoine uasal (gentlemen of the clan), 33
Darling, F. Fraser, 184, 187, 188, 201–2, 223, 261
David MacBrayne's Ltd, *see* MacBrayne's
Death to the Highland Scot, 107
decline, 85–91
deer, 32, 42–4, 53, 108, 128, 138, 145, 270
Deer Park Raid, 44, 50
defence spending, 137
demoralization, 85–91
Department of Agriculture, 113, 165, 172, 225
depopulation, 124, 128, 131, 137, 210, 221, 222, 227, 258, 262, 273, 279, 281
depression, 85–91
Depression (1930s world), 88

destitution test, 40
Development areas 116, 199, *see also* Highland development
Dhòmhnaill Ailean Dhòmhnaill na Bainich, *see* MacDonald, Donald Allan
dhùthaich (homeland), 49
diaspora *see* emigration
dìleas, 247
Dillon, Professor Myles, 241
Direadh a-mach ri Beinn Shianta, 41
Disruption (of 1843), 39
Distribution of Industry Act (1945), 111, 116, 148
Distribution of Industry Act (1954), 199
Distribution of Industry Act (1960), 132
Donn, Rob 33, 45, *see also* Mackay, Rob Donn
Dounreay nuclear site, 203, 213
drainage supplies, 126
The drinking well, 185
Duncan, Joseph F., 268, 274
Dunkirk, 220
Dunmore, Earl of, 54
dùthchas, 32, 168
dying tongue, *see* Gaelic, decline of

economic development 15–16, 272–4, *see also* Highland problem
Edinburgh
   capital city status, 102
   visit of George IV, 65, 66, 68
Edinburgh University
   Celtic Department, 240
   School of Scottish Studies, 240, 242, 253
education, 112, 209–15, 230–9, 266, 279
Education (Scotland) Act (1918), 210
Education (Scotland) Act (1945), 238
Education (Scotland) Act (1946), 112
Education (Scotland) Fund, 112
educational experiments, 234–9
Eigg, 83
Eilean a' Cheo, 55
electricity
   connection costs, 142
   distribution, 106
   island budget, 142
   and social life, 258
   supply to remote communities, 141–3, 258
   see also hydro-electricity; NSHEB
Elliot, Secretary of State Walter, 102

emigration, 30, 38, 40, 44–50, 63, 89, 185, 198, 199, 227, 258, 269, 274
employment, 114, 115, 137, 144, 198, 200, 203, 222, 227
English influence on Scottish politics, 195–6
English language dominance, 245
entrepreneurial activity, 202, 247
equalization grants, 111, 112
Eriskay, 82
Erskine of Marr, Ruaraidh, 80, 86, 133
ethnic identity, 25, 35
evangelical Presbyterianism, growth of, 32
evictions, *see* Clearances
exile, 48–9

Faed, Tom, 48
famine, 38
Fascism for the Highlands, 104, 140
fatalism, feeling of, 32, 38–40
Father Allan's island, 82
Fearann Domhnaill, 261
Federal Union of European Nationalities (FUEN), 100
Ferguson, Malcolm, 73
Ferguson, Murdo, 254
ferry services, 113, 156, 159, 161–2, 205
51st Highland Division, 220
Fios thun a Bhaird, 41
First World War, 86
FIS (Folklore Institute of Scotland), 236, 241
fishing
  decline of, 128, 152
  government commitment to, 113
  industry, 114, 131–2, 150, 275
  nationalization of, 105
  as tourism, 74
fishing boat finance, 114, 127
folk revival, 253
Folklore Institute of Scotland (FIS), 236, 241
Folksongs and folklore of South Uist, 241
food subsidies, 137–8
Foot, Dingle, 103
forestry, 113, 153, 164
  jobs, 114, 144
Forestry Act (1945), 144
Forestry Commission, 114, 120, 122, 130, 136, 143–5, 197, 278
Fort William
  aluminium factory, 116, 137
  growth pole, 155
  pulp mill, 129, 156

Fort William–Mallaig railway, 112, 156
'45 Rising, *see* Jacobite Rising
Forward Scotland, 117–18, 151
Foulis, Hugh, *see* Munro, Neil
Foyers aluminium factory, 116
Frazer, James George, 79
Free Church of Scotland, 39
Freer, Ada Goodrich, 82
FUEN (Federal Union of European Nationalities), 100
further education colleges, 211
The future of the Highlands, 263–4, 281
The future of Scotland, 197

Gael
  identity of, 243–5
  image of, 245–52
Gaeldom
  loss of values, 33
  paradoxes of, 24–6
Gaelfonn, 254
Gaelic, 14, 17
  attempts to preserve, 191–3, 212–16, 237–8, 259–61, 265
  decline of, 13, 14, 17, 19, 21, 22, 24, 184, 191, 221–3, 226, 227, 228, 230–4, 251–2, 257–8, 280
  difficulties facing, 136, 203, 265–7
  in the forefront, 20
  and Highland Panel, 150
  influx of non-speakers, 203
  Parrot Gaelic, 249
  politicization of, 54
  positive discrimination, 203
  reading and writing in, 22
  in schools, 213–16, 230–9
  and Scottish identity, 17, 25
  and Scottish universities, 239–43
  spoken abroad, 245
Gaelic academia criticized, 239–40
Gaelic ambivalence to traditions, 192
Gaelic awareness, 195
Gaelic broadcasting, 253
Gaelic culture
  death of, 33
  and *Gàidhealtachd*'s problems, 188
  and modernization, 16
  rejuvenation, 53
Gaelic ethnic identity, 25, 262
Gaelic folk songs from the Isle of Barra, 241
Gaelic Golden Age, 25, 44, 79
Gaelic Highlands, 191, 244

Index

Gaelic informal committee, 236
Gaelic informal education scheme, 251
Gaelic learners' camps, 235, 237
Gaelic mind, 268
Gaelic movement augmented, 52
Gaelic pressure groups, 219
Gaelic prose, 19–20, 23
Gaelic publishing, 21
Gaelic radio, 253–5
Gaelic recordings, 254
Gaelic renaissance, 280
Gaelic Society of Glasgow, 87
Gaelic Society of Inverness, 23, 29, 52, 54, 90
Gaelic songs in schools, 235
Gaelic-speakers as proscribed race, 37
Gaelic-speaking
  by county, 19
  community, 17
Gàidhealtachd (land of the Gael) term, 14, 17–19, 25, 29, 31, 33, 45, 49, 58, 59, 66, 110, 134, 136, 172, 175, 187, 188, 194, 198, 205, 210, 219, 221–3, 225, 230–4, 236, 238, 239, 241, 243, 245, 252, 257, 261–3, 266, 269–73, 275, 280, 281
Gairm, 21–2, 256, 265
The Garb of Old Gaul, 68
George IV, King, royal visit (of 1822), 65, 66, 68
Gillanders, Farquhar, 264, 277, 278
Gillespie, 88
Glasgow
  accents, 260
  and Gaelic-speaking community, 17
  Glasgow fair excursionists, 83
  migration to, 45, 49
Glasgow Herald, 155, 158, 160, 162
Glen Affric, 139
Glencalvie clearances, 39
Glenelg, 137
The gloomy forest, 45
Gloomy memories, 107–8, 278
Go-ahead Scotland, 132
The golden bough: a study in magic and religion, 79
Gordon, Paul Seton, 83
government
  agencies, 197–204
  and the Highlands, 193–7
  prevarication, 230
  sympathetic consideration by, 223

Government of Scotland Bill (1924), 87
Gow, Alexander, 55
gramophone record industry, 254
Grant, Donald, 234
Grant, Isabel F., 255, 256
Grant, James Shaw, 176, 179, 184, 186–7, 202, 203, 206, 219, 226
Great Charter (England), 68
Great Glen, 137
Great Highland Famine, 38
Great improvers, 63
The grey coast, 185
Grimble, Ian, 30, 281
Grimond, Jo, 103, 172
grouse estates, 128
Gunn, Neil Miller, 166, 183, 184, 185, 187, 189, 190–1, 192, 193, 194, 195, 197–200, 201, 202, 203, 205, 206, 212, 216, 217, 219, 226, 227, 255, 274
Gur muladach a tha mi, 45

hand-knitting, 114
Harris
  Harris Tweed industry, 114, 200–201
  poverty in, 72
  transport, 161
Hay, George Campbell, 98–9
Hay, J. MacDougall, 88
HDA (Highland Development Association), 129
health provision, 111–12, 126
heart of Scotia, 272
Hebrides ferry, 162
hereditary succession in crofting, 170
herring fishing, 114
Herring Industry Act (1944), 114
HIDB (Highlands and Islands Development Board), 132, 136, 145, 177, 178, 179, 183, 199, 266, 273, 279
The Highland Association, 219
The Highland Clearances, 31, 278
Highland Clearances, *see* Clearances
Highland committee (of Highland Panel), 149–50
Highland culture, 183–217
Highland development, 129, 130–1, 197–204
Highland Development Agency, 230
Highland Development Area, 111, 116
Highland Development Association (HDA), 129
Highland Development Authority, 146

Highland Development Board, 106, 147, 154
Highland Development Group, 155
Highland Development League, 90, 229
Highland Folk Museum, 255
Highland games, 63, 70, 106
Highland and Islands Advisory Panel *see* Highland Panel
Highland and Islands Committee, 146
Highland Land Law Reform Association (HLLRA), 52, 53
Highland Land League, 86, 87
Highland League, 147
Highland Panel, 110, 113, 114, 119, 127, 129, 136, 143, 146–65, 178, 184, 186, 188, 190, 199, 224, 229, 230, 274
Highland plan, 106, 141
Highland problem, 15, 18, 24, 39, 52, 61, 86, 109, 117, 125, 133, 146, 150, 183, 187, 188, 194, 199, 200, 216, 223, 263, 272–4
  and government agencies, 135–79
Highland question, 24
Highland regiments, 58–9, 68, 69, 75, 76, 108, 137, 220
Highland Society of Edinburgh, 63
Highland Society of London, 63
Highland surnames, 276
Highland transport authority, 160
Highland Transport Board (HTB), 163
Highland Transport Inquiry, 159, 160
Highland way of life, 26, 169, 177, 184, 188, 217, 220, 252, 258, 273, 277
Highland year of culture, 279
The Highlander, 20, 51
Highlanders
  accents, 260
  appearance, 63, 66–7
  awareness of deprivation, 259
  common identity of, 52, 67
  dangerous behaviour of, 71–2, 74–5, 246
  as demeaned by tourism, 206–7
  and environment, 62
  fighting prowess, 76–8
  invented, 70
  involvement in politics, 196
  likened to Swiss, 43
  loyal image of 75, *see also* Balmoralism
  in merchant navy, 137, 220
  nostalgia, 191
  popular image/romantic view of, 24–5, 53, 58, 60, 62, 67, 69, 73, 75, 83, 84, 90–1, 188–9, 193, 208, 245–52, 271
  qualities of, 57
  quality of life, 115
  as redundant population, 46
  Scott's image of, 67
  seen as indolent, 73
  seen as primitive, 73
  in Seven Years War, 76
  special characteristics, 201
  standard of living improvement, 190
  valorization of image, 75–6
  as victims, 32, 34–6
  violent image of, 77
Highlands
  in cinema, 59
  compared to Ireland, 50, 51
  cultural perspective, 269–72
  definition of, 17–18
  and government, 193–7
  image of, 58, 60, 66, 72, 245–52
  imposition of English language, 61
  improvement strategies, 183–217
  invented tradition of, 58–78
  London's indifference to, 123
  and mainland standards, 200
  in permanent time warp, 16
  as playground, 128
  policy of improvement, 61
  as political problem, 25–6
  post-war visions, 104–9
  poverty and idealized image, 72–3, 75
  recreational needs, 203–4
  romantic view of, 53, 58, 60, 69, 83, 84, 90–1, 188–9, 193, 236
  seen as colonial outpost, 75
  special status, 160
  tourism, 43
  and Victoria, 68–71
  see also Highlanders
Highlands Committee, 147
Highlands Development Agency, 121
Highlands Development Authority, 121
The Highlands and Islands (Collier), 187
The Highlands and Islands (Mitchison), 186
Highlands and Islands Development Board (HIDB), 132, 136, 145, 177, 178, 179, 183, 199, 266, 273, 279
Highlands and Islands (Medical Services) Scheme (1913), 111
The Highlands of Scotland, 58
The Highlands today, 183
Hill Farming Act (1946), 138
Hilleary Committee/Report, 91, 184, 194

Index

The history of the feuds and conflicts among the clans, 77
History of the Highland Clearances, 29–30, 108
HLLRA (Highland Land Law Reform Association), 52, 53
holiday houses, 208
Home, Lord (Sir Alec Douglas-Home), 103
hospital building, 111–12
House of Argyll, 26
house modernization, 85, 111
house prices, 206
housing, 111, 126, 279
HTB (Highland Transport Board), 163
hunting, 74
Hutchinson, Revd George Hely, 74
hydro board *see* NSHEB
Hydro-Electric Development (Scotland) Act (1943), 138
hydro-electric power, 96, 107, 110, 118, 123, 137, 138–9, 140, 141–2, 167, 189, 198, 225, 226, 253, 281

I have been a fugitive since autumn, 45–6
identity of the Gael, 243–5
image of the Gael, 245–52
The immortal isles, 83
In search of Scotland, 57, 59
industry, 90–1, 116, 127, 131–2, 133, 156, 164, 199, 202, 222
informal home rule, 133
injustice, sense of, 32
The inquiry into the Scottish economy see Toothill Report
Inshore Fishing Industry Act (1945), 114
Institute for Highland Resource Development, 212
invented tradition of Highlands, 58–78
Invergordon, 137
Inverness Courier, 118
Inverness Experiment, 238–9
Inverness–Invergordon growth pole, 155
Inverness-shire, 18
Iona, 81
Island Problem, 130
Islay, 41
isolation of communities, 127

Jacobite defeat (of 1746), 57–8
Jacobite Rising (of 1745–6), 42, 57–8, 60, 65, 66, 75, 270, 271
Jacobites, support for, 66

Jacobitism, fascination for, 70
Johnson, Samuel, 60, 77
Johnston, Russell, 129–31
Johnston, Tom Secretary of State, 102, 104, 108, 109, 136–7, 138, 140, 141, 148, 272, 273

kelp industry, 46
Kennedy-Fraser, Marjory, 82
Kilbrandon, Lord, 159
Kildonan clearances, 35, 37–8
kilts, 192, 244
Kinlochleven aluminium factory, 116
Kintyre, 206, 213
Knoydart, 137
  land raid, 119–20, 219, 223–4, 229
Kyle ferry terminal, 113
Kyle of Lochalsh, 137

Labour Party Scottish Council, 105
Labour Party/Government, 86, 87, 95, 96, 97, 101–2, 102, 104, 105, 106, 107, 108, 109, 111, 112, 115, 117, 119, 125, 131, 132, 138, 141, 144, 145, 147, 151, 171, 172, 178, 184, 224, 229, 230, 247
Lallans dialect, 213–14
land bank, 164
land of the Gael, *see Gàidhealtachd*
land issues in history, 14
land and language, 50, 52–6
land reform, 165–6
land-use changes, 34
Land-use in the Highlands, 164, 165
landlords
  absentee 33, 168, 171, 172, 174–175, 203, *see also* Knoydart
  financial ruin of, 40
Landseer, Sir Edwin, 71
language education, 212–14
The last of the clan, 48
learners' camps, 235, 237
Let Scotland prosper, 124, 125, 131–2, 145
Lewis
  attitudes to non-Gael, 261
  Bernera Riot on, 42–3
  clearances on, 40–4, 50, 51
  Deer Park Raid, 44, 50
  Riot Act read, 44
  tweed industry, 114, 200–201
Liberal Party, 103–4, 129, 130, 131, 172, 178
Linguistic Survey of Scotland, 241
Lismore, 142

Livestock Rearing Act (1951), 138
living standards, 113
Livingstone, William 35, 41, *see also* MacDhunleibhe, Uilleam
lobster fishing, 114
Local Employment Act (1960), 125, 129
local government weakness, 196–7
Locker-Lampson, Commander, 107
Lonely am I, 45
Lordship of the Isles, 25
loss of place, 40–2
loss, sense of, 32–3
The lost glen, 185
Lovat, Lord, 157
Lowlanders, hatred of, 35

Mac a' Ghobhainn, Iain, *see* Smith, John
MacAlpine, John, 48
MacAulay, Fred, 253
MacBrayne's (ferries), 113, 156, 161, 162, 205
MacCallum, Major, 139–40
MacCodrum, John 33, 45, *see also* Mhic Fhearchair, Iain
MacColla, Fionn (Tom Macdonald), 209, 215
MacCormick, John, 101
MacDhunleibhe, Uilleam, *see* Livingstone, William
MacDiarmid, Hugh, 58, 86
MacDonald, Donald Allan 21, 257–8, *see also* Dhòmhnaill Ailean Dhòmnaill na Bainich
MacDonald, Donald John, 21
MacDonald, Finlay J., 222, 228, 233
MacDonald, Fr Allan, 82
MacDonald, Fr John A., 21
MacDonald, Kenneth D., 265
MacDonald, Lord, 45, 46
MacDougall, Allan, *see* Dall, Ailean
MacEwen, Sir Alexander, 87, 90–1, 281
McGhill–eain, Somhairle, 13, *see also* MacLean, Sorley
MacGregor, Alasdair Alpin, 83
Mac'illedhuibh, Donnachadh, 107, 108, 140, 144
MacIntyre, Dr Robert, 101, 119, 120
Mackay, Rob Donn, *see* Donn, Rob
MacKenzie, Alexander, 29, 41, 78, 108
MacKenzie Committee, 143
MacKenzie, Compton, 83, 246
MacKenzie, Osgood Hanbury, 73

MacKenzie, Sir George, 63–4
MacKinnon, Revd Kenneth, 243, 252, 255, 256
MacLachlainn, An Lighiche Iain, *see* MacLachlan, Dr John
MacLachlan, Dr John 41, 42, *see also* MacLachlainn, An Lighiche Iain
MacLean, John, 45
MacLean, Sorley, 13, 14, 20, 29, 44, 84, 98, *see also* MacGhill–eain, Somhairle
MacLennan, Iain, 244
MacLeod, Angus, 254
MacLeod, Donald, 29, 36, 37, 107–8, 278
MacLeod, Donald (Gaelic singer), 254
MacLeod, Donald John, 20
MacLeod, Fiona, 58, *see also* Sharp, William
MacLeod, Kenneth, 82–3
MacLeod, Morag, 252–3
MacLeod, Neil, 84
MacLeod, Norman 256, 257, *see also Am Bàrd Bochd*
Macmillan, Harold, 276
MacMillan, Malcolm, 149, 167, 172, 175
MacNeill, Secretary of State Hector, 166
MacPherson of Drumochter, Lord, 143
MacPherson, James, 59–60, 62, 63, 67
MacPherson, Margaret, 166, 171
MacPherson, Mary 55, 58, 84, *see also* Màiri mhòr nan Oran
MacQuisken, F.A., 107
MacRae, Farquar, 231–2
MacRae, John, 45
Macrihanish, 137
Màiri mhòr nan Oran, *see* MacPherson, Mary
Marxism and history, 29
Matheson, Sir James, 46
Meek, Donald, 44
Merchant Navy service, 137, 220
Mhic Fhearchair, Iain, *see* MacCodrum, John
Middleton, George, 142
military bases, 137
Miller, Hugh, 29, 40, 50
Mineral Resources Panel of the Scottish Council, 115
Ministry of Defence, 227
missile-testing, 227–8
Mitchison, Dick, 185
Mitchison, Naomi, 149, 153, 164, 184, 185–6, 187, 189, 190, 191, 192, 194, 195, 196, 197–201, 203, 205, 206–7,

Index 307

208, 210, 211, 212–15, 217, 219, 226, 274
modernization
  and cultural loss, 16
  and Gaelic culture, 13, 16, 141–3, 191, 253, 258, 265
  ways of seeing, 15–19
Moidart, 137
Monarch of the Glen, 71
Montgomery, Mary, 279, 280, *see also* NicGumaraid, Màiri
Morley, Averil, 275, 276, 278
Morrison, Ronald, 236
Morton, H.V., 57, 59, 60
Motherwell by-election (SNP), 101
Mull, 205–6, 211, 221
Mulock, Thomas, 29, 40
Munro, Neil, 88
Murchison, Revd Tom, 21, 223, 224, 229, 245, 249, 251–2
Murdoch, John, 20, 50, 51–2
Murdoch, W. Blaikie, 66
Murray, Amy, 82
Murray, W.H., 278

Napier Commission (1844), 55
National Forest Parks, 115
National Health Service (Scotland) Act (1947), 111–12
National Land Survey, 123
National mod, 248–51, 254
National Parks, 115, 211, 226
National parks and the conservation of nature in Scotland, 226
National Resources Council, 164
National Trust for Scotland, 278
nationalization of industries, 105
native view of Highlands, 14
Nature Conservancy, 123
naval bases, 137
negligent indifference, 223
Ness, James, 156
New Deal Liberalism, 101
The New Liberalism, 103–4
The new road, 88
news in 1930s, 13–14
NicGumaraid, Màiri 279, *see also* Montgomery, Mary
Noble, Secretary of State Michael, 142, 163
nodal growth points, 199
North Uist, 142, 161

Norway Highland Panel visit/report, 149, 153–5, 159, 161, 164
nostalgia, 45–6
notion of Highlands, 16
NSHEB (North of Scotland Hydro-Electric Board), 96, 122, 124, 136, 138, 141–2, 143, 163, 225, 274, 278
Nutt, Alfred, 250

O mo dhùthaich, 's tu th'air m'aire, 47–8
O my country, I think of thee, 47–8
Oban Times, 56
O'Dell, A.C., 281
one-nation rhetoric, 121
oral tradition, 215
Orkneys, 17, 18, 142
Ó Siochfhradha, Pádraig, 240–1
Ossian legend/phenomenon, 58, 59, 60–1, 62, 63, 66, 67, 79, 82, 246, 271
Our journey to the Hebrides, 72
outsider view of Highlands, 14
overseas settlements, 45

pan-Celticism, 99, 100–1
Para Handy, 88
paradoxes of Gaeldom, 24–6
Parrot Gaelic, 249
Partners in a new Britain, 128
pauperization, 32, 37–8
peat, 115, 225
Pennell, Elizabeth Robins, 72
Pennell, Joseph, 72
PEP (Political and Economic Planning) report, 151
per capita income, 126
Perth Gaelic Society, 53
Perthshire, as part of Highlands, 18
piers, 113
piping, 63, 64–5, 78, 236
Pitt, William the Younger, 76
Plan for post-war Scotland, 95, 96, 104, 105, 106, 119
planned regional development, 97
poetry, 132–3
The poetry of the Clearances, 29
Policy of the Scottish National Party, 123
Political and Economic Planning (PEP) report, 151
Polwarth, Lord, 156
Popular tales of the west Highlands orally collected, 82

population 37, 97, 120, 198, 205, 273, *see also* depopulation
potato failure, 38
Prebble, John, 30–1, 278
Presbyterianism, growth of, 32
private landlordism, 105, 119
professional Gaels, 239
A programme of Highland development, 109, 110, 112, 113, 116, 120, 146, 148, 178, 203, 229
psyche of Highlands, 16
pulp mill (Fort William), 129, 156

quality of life, 115
quarrying, 115
Queen Victoria meeting the Prince Consort, 71
Queen Victoria sketching at Loch Laggan, 71
Quigley, Hugh, 57, 58

radio, 13, 191, 253
railways, 85, 150, 155–8, 160, 163
reconstruction, 109–16, 222–30, 258, 263
Red Deer Commission, 145
regeneration period, 117–25
regional development, 125–32
relief for poverty, 40
religious instruction in Highlands, 61
Renan, Ernst, 79
resistance, 30, 50–2, 85
Review of Highland policy, 126
Road to the Isles, 112
roads, 112, 157–9, 207–8
Robertson, David, 98, 133
Rockets galore, 83
Ross & Cromarty, 18
Ross, Donald, 29, 40
Ross, Secretary of State Willie, 132, 178, 273
Ross-shire clearances, 40
Rothiemurchus estate, 137
Rough Bounds area, 137
Rousay, 142
Royal Commission on Scottish Affairs, 121–2, 149, 195
Rural Water Supplies and Sewerage Act (1944), 111
Russell, George, 79

'*S mi ar fògradh bho fhoghair*, 45–6
St Andrew's House, influence on Highlands, 104, 136, 189, 194, 233, 273

St Valery, 220
Saltire Review, 228
Saltire Society, 102
Scapa Flow, 137
scenery and tourism, 208
school language restrictions, 213–14
School of Scottish Studies, 240, 242, 253
Scotland in 1957, 123
Scotland
 confused national identity, 65
 in Enlightenment, 61
 as post-colonial, 123
 as serf of socialism, 103
 as two-party state, 133
Scotlandshire: England's worst-governed province, 107, 139
Scots National League, 80
The Scotsman, 147, 149
Scott, Sir Walter, 58, 60, 64, 65, 66, 67, 70, 193
Scottish Affairs, 122
Scottish Agricultural Organisation Society, 147
Scottish Board for Industry, 142
Scottish Committee of the Council of Industrial Design, 116
Scottish Convention, 101
Scottish Council, 147
Scottish Council for Development and Industry, 148, 156
Scottish Council for Research in Education, 238
Scottish Daily Express, 254
Scottish Education Department (SED), 209, 230, 231, 232
The Scottish Highlands: a contested country, 280
Scottish Home Service (BBC), 253
Scottish Labour Party conference (1958), 102
Scottish Land Court, 175, 224
Scottish national identity, 25, 65, 67
Scottish national image, 65, 66
Scottish National Parks Committee, 226
Scottish National Party (SNP), 97, 101, 103, 104, 105, 106, 107, 108, 122, 122–3, 123, 132, 139, 140, 144, 145
Scottish nationalism, 58, 65, 86, 87, 96, 97, 99–104
Scottish Office 136, *see also* St Andrew's House
Scottish Renaissance, 58

Index 309

Scottish Society for the Propagation of Christian Knowledge, 26
Scottish Tourist Board, 114, 204, 255
Scottish universities, 239–43
Scottish Vigilantes Association, 157
Scottish workforce size, 126
sea links, 159, 161
seaweed, 115
Second World War
  commando training, 137
  impact on Highlands, 137, 221, 245, 252, 272
  military service in, 220
Secretary of State for Scotland, 102–3
SED (Scottish Education Department), 209, 230, 231, 232
seeing the Highlands, 14
Sellar, Patrick, 30, 35, 36
The serpent, 185
service industry tourism, 207
seven men of Knoydart, 119–20
Shall Gaelic die?, 95, 96
Shapinsay, 142
Sharp, William, 79, 80, 81, 83, *see also* MacLeod, Fiona
Shaw, Margaret Fay, 236, 241–2
sheep, 32, 34–5, 38, 46, 270
Shetland
  electricity supply, 142
  knitwear industry, 114
  as part of Highlands, 17, 18
Signposts for the sixties, 128
The silver darlings, 185
Sinclair, Sir Archibald, 103
Sketches of the character, manners and present state of the Highlanders of Scotland, 68, 77
Skewis, Dr W. Iain, 159–60
Skye
  Battle of the Braes, 50, 55
  clearances, 46–7, 51
  and emigration, 45
  Gaelic speakers in, 221
  tourism, 205
  transport, 161
  and wireless, 14
The Skye Crofters, 84
Smith, Iain Crichton, 23, 95, 96, 98
Smith, John 42, *see also* Mac a' Ghobhainn, Iain
Smith, John A., 265–7
Smout, T.C., 30

Sobieski Stuarts, 67
social habits, 253
social philosophies, clash of, 184, 268
social structure, 202
Songs of the Hebrides, 82
South Uist, 21, 228, 257
souvenirs, 207
special reorganization committee (*An Comunn*), 231, 234
speckled Gaeldom *see breac-Gàidhealtachd*
speculative land purchase, 139–40
Spiorad a' charthannais, 42
The spirit of Jacobite loyalty, 66
The spirit of kindliness, 42
sporting estates, 42–4
squatters and crofting, 261
State subsidies for private tyrannies: the lessons of Knoydart, 119
steamer links, 85, 156
steamer subsidies, 113
Stewart, Colonel David of Garth, 65, 68, 77
Stornoway, 137
Stornoway Gazette, 176, 184, 186, 246, 261
Storport, 71–2
Strange things, 268
Strathclyde, Lord, 142, 143
Strathnaver clearances, 35, 36
Stuart, Prince Charles Edward (Bonnie Prince Charlie), 66, 67, 70
Stuart, Secretary of State James, 103, 122, 172
Suishnish clearances, 46
Sun circle, 185
Sutherland, 18
  clearances, 34, 35, 36
Swedish timber houses, 111
Swordale learner's school, 235

Tales of Barra told by the Coddy, 218
Tarbert, Harris, poverty in, 72
tariff barriers, 159
tartan mania, 66, 67, 68
taxation, 114
Taylor Commission/Report, 166–72, 269, 274
Taylor, Thomas, 166
textiles, 113, 114, 150
Thompson, Frank, 277
Thomson, Derick, 22, 98, 220, 265, 276
tir is teanga, 50, 52–6
To introduce the Hebrides, 13
Toothill Report, 125–6, 129, 155

Tory challenge, 122
tourism, 58, 62, 64–5, 68, 69, 72, 83, 105–6, 113, 114–15, 130, 153, 204, 205–8, 226, 245, 246, 255–6, 257, 264
tradition, invented, 58–78
transport, 85, 106, 112, 126–7, 130, 150, 225, 279
Treaty of Union (1707), 103
Trevelyan, Sir Charles, 39
The trial of Patrick Sellar, 30
Trunk Roads Act (1946), 112
tweed industry, 114, 200–201

Uist rocket range, 227–8
unified resource development, 229
union of Celtic peoples, 100
Unionist experiment, 133
universities in Scotland, 239–43
University of Highlands proposal, 130, 209–10, 212–13, 240
Urquhart, Sir Robert, 172–3

Vatersay, 142
vicious land system, 51
victims, Highlanders as, 32, 34–6
Victoria, Queen, in Scotland, 68–71, 108
voice of the Gael, 19, 20, 23, 24
voice of the Highlander, 219

Walton, K., 281
water supply, 126, 167
Waverley, 65
Weir, Alastair MacNeill, 106, 141, 147

welfare/welfarism, 167, 198, 258, 259, 260, 263
West Highland Survey, 187, 188, 202, 223, 226, 258, 275
West Highland Water Power Bill (1929), 89–90
West Stirling Gazette, 141
Western Isles Crofters' Union, 175
Westminster government, 195–6, 198
Westwood, Secretary of State Joseph, 148, 223–4
Whalsey, 142
Whiskers galore, 246
Whisky galore, 83, 246
white heat of technical revolution slogan, 131
Wilson, James, 73
Winans, William Louis, 44
The winged destiny: studies in the spiritual history of the Gael, 81
wireless, 13, 191, 253
Womack, Peter, 272
women's needs in post-war Highlands, 169–70
Wood, Wendy, 99
Woodburn, Secretary of State Arthur, 139
Wordsworth, Dorothy, 63

Yeats, W.B., 85
yell for light campaign, 142
Young, Douglas, 104, 108, 140

zones of growth, 155
Zuckerman Committee, 145